THE CAMBRIDGE COMPANION TO
TRANSNATIONAL AMERICAN LITERATURE

For two decades, the "transnational turn" in literary studies has generated enormous comment and controversy. This *Companion* provides a comprehensive account of the scope, impact, and critical possibilities of the transnational turn in American literary studies. It situates the study of American literature in relation to ethnic, postcolonial, and hemispheric studies. Leading scholars open up wide-ranging examinations of transnationalism in American literature – through form and aesthetics, theories of nation, gender, sexuality, religion, and race, as well as through conventional forms of historical periodization. Offering a new map of American literature in the global era, this volume provides a history of the field, key debates, and instances of literary readings that convey the way in which transnationalism may be seen as a method, not just a description of literary work that engages more than one nation. Contributors identify the key modes by which writers have responded to major historical, political, and ethical issues prompted by the globalization of literary studies.

YOGITA GOYAL is Associate Professor of English and African-American Studies at the University of California, Los Angeles. She is the author of *Romance, Diaspora, and Black Atlantic Literature* (Cambridge University Press, 2010) and editor of the journal *Contemporary Literature.*

A complete list of books in the series is at the back of this book.

D1484186

THE CAMBRIDGE
COMPANION TO
TRANSNATIONAL AMERICAN
LITERATURE

THE CAMBRIDGE
COMPANION TO
TRANSNATIONAL
AMERICAN
LITERATURE

EDITED BY
YOGITA GOYAL

CAMBRIDGE
UNIVERSITY PRESS

CAMBRIDGE
UNIVERSITY PRESS

University Printing House, Cambridge CB2 8BS, United Kingdom

One Liberty Plaza, 20th Floor, New York, NY 10006, USA

477 Williamstown Road, Port Melbourne, VIC 3207, Australia

4843/24, 2nd Floor, Ansari Road, Daryaganj, Delhi – 110002, India

79 Anson Road, #06-04/06, Singapore 079906

Cambridge University Press is part of the University of Cambridge.

It furthers the University's mission by disseminating knowledge in the pursuit of
education, learning, and research at the highest international levels of excellence.

www.cambridge.org
Information on this title: www.cambridge.org/9781107448384
DOI: 10.1017/9781316048146

© Yogita Goyal 2017

First published 2017

Printed in the United States of America by Sheridan Books, Inc.

A catalogue record for this publication is available from the British Library.

Library of Congress Cataloging-in-Publication Data
Names: Goyal, Yogita, editor.
Title: The Cambridge companion to transnational American
literature / edited by Yogita Goyal.
Description: Cambridge : Cambridge University Press, 2017. | Series: Cambridge
companion to literature | Includes bibliographical references and index.
Identifiers: LCCN 2016041859| ISBN 9781107085206 (hardback) |
ISBN 9781107448384 (paper back)
Subjects: LCSH: American literature – History and criticism. | Transnationalism
in literature. | Postcolonialism in literature. | Literature and transnationalism –
United States. | BISAC: LITERARY CRITICISM / American / General.
Classification: LCC PS169.T73 C36 2017 | DDC 810.9/355–dc23
LC record available at https://lccn.loc.gov/2016041859

ISBN 978-1-107-08520-6 Hardback
ISBN 978-1-107-44838-4 Paperback

CONTENTS

List of Contributors   *page* ix
Chronology   xiii

Introduction: The Transnational Turn   I
YOGITA GOYAL

PART I   SHAPE OF THE FIELD

I Unsettling American Literature, Rethinking Nation and Empire   19
SHELLEY FISHER FISHKIN

2 American Literature, World Literature   37
WAI CHEE DIMOCK

3 The Transnational Turn and Postcolonial Studies   53
YOGITA GOYAL

4 Transnational Aesthetics   72
RUSS CASTRONOVO

PART II   LITERARY HISTORIES

5 Transnationalism and Nineteenth-Century Literature   91
JOHANNES VOELZ

6 Transnational Modernisms   107
JESSICA BERMAN

7 Transnational Postmodern and Contemporary Literature   122
DAVID JAMES

CONTENTS

PART III   CRITICAL GEOGRAPHIES

8   Black Atlantic and Diaspora Literature   143
DESTINY O. BIRDSONG AND IFEOMA KIDDOE NWANKWO

9   Borders and Borderland Literature   157
JOHN ALBA CUTLER

10 American Indian Transnationalisms   174
JODI A. BYRD

11 Pacific Rim and Asian American Literature   190
VIET THANH NGUYEN

12 Hemispheric Literature   203
MARÍA JOSEFINA SALDAÑA-PORTILLO

PART IV   LITERATURE AND GEOPOLITICS

13 Transnational Feminism   221
CRYSTAL PARIKH

14 Queer Transnationalism   237
PETRUS LIU

15 Islam and Transnationalism   251
TIMOTHY MARR

Further Reading   269
Index   289

CONTRIBUTORS

JESSICA BERMAN is Professor of English and Director of the Dresher Center for the Humanities at the University of Maryland, Baltimore County (UMBC). She is the author of *Modernist Fiction, Cosmopolitanism and the Politics of Community* (2001) and *Modernist Commitments: Ethics, Politics and Transnational Modernism* (2011), and editor of *A Companion to Virginia Woolf* (2016). Berman is a coeditor of the American Comparative Literature Association's decennial Report on the State of the Discipline (2016) and also coedits, with Paul Saint-Amour, the Modernist Latitudes book series. She is the 2016–17 President of the Modernist Studies Association.

DESTINY O. BIRDSONG is a poet, essayist, and educator whose creative and critical work centers on the intersectionality of gender, socioeconomics, national/transnational identities, cultural trauma, and health in Afro-Diasporic women's literature. As a poet, her poems have either appeared or are forthcoming in *African American Review, At Length, Baltimore Review, Indiana Review*, and elsewhere. Her critical work includes "'Memories that are(n't) mine': Matrilineal Cultural Trauma, Inscription, and Defiant Reinscription in Natasha Trethewey's *Native Guard*," which recently appeared in *African American Review*. She is a recipient of the Academy of American Poets Prize, and has received fellowships from Cave Canem and BinderCon. She currently works as a research coordinator for a community-centered narrative project at Vanderbilt University.

JODI A. BYRD is a citizen of the Chickasaw Nation and Associate Professor of English and Gender and Women's Studies at the University of Illinois at Urbana-Champaign where she is also a faculty affiliate at the National Center for Supercomputing Applications. She is the author of *Transit of Empire: Indigenous Critiques of Colonialism* (2011), and her articles have appeared in *American Indian Quarterly, Cultural Studies Review, Interventions, J19, College Literatures, Settler Colonial Studies Studies*, and *American Quarterly*. Her teaching and research focuses on issues of indigeneity, gender, and sexuality at the intersections of political studies, postcolonial studies, queer studies, and comparative ethnic studies. Her current manuscript in process, entitled *Indigenomicon: American*

Indians, Videogames, and Structures of Genre, interrogates how the structures of digital code intersect with issues of sovereignty, militarism, and colonialism.

RUSS CASTRONOVO is Tom Paine Professor of English and Dorothy Draheim Professor of American Studies at the University of Wisconsin-Madison. He has written or edited eight books, including most recently, *Propaganda 1776: Secrets, Leaks, and Revolutionary Communications in Early America*. He is the winner of the 2016 Chancellor's Distinguished Teaching Award. His current research examines the intellectual and literary history of US conservatism.

JOHN ALBA CUTLER is an Associate Professor of English and Latina/o Studies at Northwestern University. He is the author of *Ends of Assimilation: The Formation of Chicano Literature* (2015), as well as articles in such journals as *American Literary History*, *American Literature*, *Aztlán: A Journal of Chicano Studies*, and *MELUS*. His current research focuses on Spanish-language periodicals published in the United States in the early twentieth century.

WAI CHEE DIMOCK is William Lampson Professor of English and American Studies at Yale University. She has published widely on American literature of every period, and is best known for *Through Other Continents: American Literature Across Deep Time* (2007). Editor of *PMLA* and film critic for the *Los Angeles Review of Books*, her essays have also appeared in *Critical Inquiry*, the *Chronicle of Higher Education*, the *New York Times*, and *The New Yorker*.

SHELLEY FISHER FISHKIN is the Joseph S. Atha Professor of Humanities, Professor of English, and Director of American Studies at Stanford University, and is the award-winning author, editor or coeditor of more than forty books and more than one hundred articles, essays, columns, and reviews. She holds a Ph.D. in American Studies from Yale, is a former President of the American Studies Association, and is a founding editor of the *Journal of Transnational American Studies*. She has lectured on American Studies in Beijing, Cambridge, Coimbra, Copenhagen, Dublin, Guangzhou, Hong Kong, Hyderabad, Kolkata, Kunming, Kyoto, La Coruña, Lisbon, Nanjing, Regensburg, Seoul, St. Petersburg, Taipei, Tokyo, and across the United States. Her most recent book is *Writing America: Literary Landmarks from Walden Pond to Wounded Knee* (2015).

YOGITA GOYAL is Associate Professor of English and African American Studies at the University of California, Los Angeles. She is the author of *Romance, Diaspora, and Black Atlantic Literature* (2010) and editor of the journal *Contemporary Literature*. She is a guest editor of a special issue of *Research in African Literatures* on "Africa and the Black Atlantic" (45.3 Fall 2014) and the recipient of fellowships from the ACLS, NEH, and University of California President's office. Her current book project, *Slavery and the Transnational Reinvention of Form*, traces contemporary ideas of the global to the Atlantic slave narrative, in order to rethink race and racial formation in a global frame.

DAVID JAMES is Reader in Modern and Contemporary Literature at Queen Mary, University of London. Among his recent books are *Modernist Futures* (2012) and edited volumes including *The Legacies of Modernism: Historicising Postwar and Contemporary Fiction* (2012), *The Cambridge Companion to British Fiction since 1945* (2015), and *Modernism and Close Reading* (2018). For Columbia University Press, he coedits the book series *Literature Now*. He is currently completing *Discrepant Solace: Contemporary Writing and the Work of Consolation* (forthcoming).

PETRUS LIU is Associate Professor of Humanities at Yale-NUS College and the author of *Stateless Subjects: Chinese Martial Arts Literature and Postcolonial History* (2011) and *Queer Marxism in Two Chinas* (2015), and a coeditor (with Lisa Rofel) of "Beyond the Strai(gh)ts: Transnationalism and Queer Chinese Politics," a special issue of *positions: east asia cultures critique*. Liu is currently working on a new book project titled *Cold War Aesthetics in East Asia*.

TIMOTHY MARR is Bowman and Gordon Gray Distinguished Term Associate Professor of American Studies at the University of North Carolina at Chapel Hill. He is the author of *The Cultural Roots of American Islamicism* (2006). He has written widely on Herman Melville and is coeditor of *Ungraspable Phantom: Essays on* Moby-Dick (2006). He is writing a book that examines the imperial interrelations between US Americans and the Muslim Moros of the southern Philippines from 1898 to 1946.

VIET THANH NGUYEN is the author of the novel *The Sympathizer* (2015) and two scholarly works, *Race and Resistance: Literature and Politics in Asian America* (2002) and *Nothing Ever Dies: Vietnam and the Memory of War* (2016). With Janet Hoskins, he coedited *Transpacific Studies: Framing an Emerging Field* (2014). He is an Associate Professor of English and American Studies and Ethnicity at the University of Southern California, and the recipient of fellowships from ACLS and the Radcliffe Institute for Advance Study.

IFEOMA KIDDOE NWANKNO is Director of the Program in American Studies, Associate Professor of English, and Chancellor's Higher Education Fellow at Vanderbilt University. Her work centers on intercultural and intergenerational relations, particularly as they surface in literary and digital texts, autobiographies, and popular music by Afro-descendants in the United States, Caribbean, and Latin America. Her publications include *Black Cosmopolitanism: Racial Consciousness and Transnational Identity in the Nineteenth Century Americas* (2005); "Bilingualism, Blackness, and Belonging"; "Race and Representation in the Digital Humanities;" "The Promises and Perils of U.S. African American

Hemispherism"; *Rhythms of the Afro-Atlantic World* (coedited with Mamadou Diouf); and *African Routes, Caribbean Roots, Latino Lives*. She is founding director of the Voices from Our America and Wisdom of the Elders digital humanities and public scholarship projects.

CRYSTAL PARIKH is Associate Professor at New York University in the Department of Social and Cultural Analysis and the Department of English, where she also currently serves as the Director of Graduate Studies. In addition to numerous articles, she is the author of *An Ethics of Betrayal: The Politics of Otherness in Emergent U.S. Literature and Culture* (2009), which won the Modern Language Association Prize in United States Latina and Latino and Chicana and Chicano Literary Studies. Parikh is currently completing her second monograph, *Writing Human Rights*, and has coedited *The Cambridge Companion to Asian American Literature* (2015) with Daniel Y. Kim.

MARÍA JOSEFINA SALDAÑA-PORTILLO is a Professor with the Department of Social and Cultural Analysis and the Center for Latin American and Caribbean Studies at NYU. She has published more than twenty articles in the United States and Latin America on revolutionary subjectivity and subaltern politics; development studies and U.S. imperialism; racial formation in the United States and Mexico; and Latino cultural studies. Her most recent book, *Indian Given: Racial Geographies Across Mexico and the United States*, compares racial formation in the two countries from the colonial period through the present (2016). In 2015 Saldaña-Portillo coedited *Des/posesión: Género, territorio, y luchas por la autodeterminación* with Marisa Belausteguigoitia Rius. Her first monograph is *The Revolutionary Imagination in the Americas and the Age of Development* (2003).

JOHANNES VOELZ is Heisenberg-Professor of American Studies, Democracy, and Aesthetics at Goethe-Universität Frankfurt, Germany. He is the author of *Transcendental Resistance: The New Americanists and Emerson's Challenge* (2010) and the forthcoming *The Poetics of Insecurity: American Fiction and the Uses of Threat* (Cambridge University Press). He has coedited several books, most recently *The Imaginary and Its Worlds: American Studies After the Transnational Turn* (with Laura Bieger and Ramón Saldívar, 2013), and he has edited two recent special issues: Security and Liberalism (*Telos* 170, 2015) and *Chance, Risk, Security: Approaches to Uncertainty in American Literature* (*Amerikastudien / American Studies* 60.4, 2016).

CHRONOLOGY

Estimated late 1400s to late 1500s	formation of the Iroquois Confederacy between Mohawk, Oneida, Onondaga, Cayuga, and Seneca nations around what was later named Lake Ontario
1492	Genoan Christopher Columbus sails from Spain across the Atlantic Ocean, landing in modern-day Bahamas, Cuba, and Haiti
1493	Columbus's second voyage; establishment of Spanish colony on Hispaniola (Haiti)
1494	Treaty of Tordesillas between Spain and Portugal, mediated by Pope Alexander VI's edict of *Inter Caetera*, divides territorial sovereignty of present and future New World discoveries
1497	Italian explorer Giovanni Caboto (John Cabot) lands on the North American mainland, claiming modern-day Newfoundland for King Henry VII of England
1500–02	Amerigo Vespucci sails down the eastern coast of South America
1502–04	Columbus's fourth voyage sails down the coast of Central America
1507	"America" first appears in print as a toponym on German cartographer Martin Waldseemüller's map titled *Universalis Cosmographia*
1511	foundation of Santa Maria del Darien, the first Spanish town on the American continents

1513	Spanish explorer Juan Ponce de León lands on the coast of Florida
1514	Bartolomé de las Casas writes to the Spanish Crown to petition for improved treatment of native peoples in the Americas
1519–21	Hernan Cortes leads a Spanish military campaign against the Aztecs, destroying Aztec populations and making the Aztec capital Tenochtitlan the new capital of his imperial government, now Mexico City
1526	Spanish explorers bring enslaved Africans to modern-day South Carolina
1534	French explorer Jacques Cartier lands on a peninsula at the mouth of the St. Lawrence River, claiming the land as French territory
1572	following the murders of two Spanish ambassadors, Inca royal Tupac Amaru is executed by Spanish soldiers
1608	Quebec City founded as the capital of New France
1619	English colonialists form the colony of Jamestown in modern-day Virginia, with twenty Africans as indentured servants
1620	separatist English Puritans led by William Bradford establish a colony at Plymouth Plantation, in Massachusetts Bay
1630–54	Dutch colonials occupy northeastern Brazil and develop sugar plantations, using African slave labor
1630–60	around 200,000 immigrants from the British Isles cross the Atlantic to the Americas
1634–38	Pequot War, a series of military conflicts between Pequots and New England colonists and their Narragansett and Mohegan allies, decimating the Pequot population
1664	English seize New Amsterdam from the Dutch and rename it New York
1675–78	King Philip's War, a series of military conflicts between Wampanoags led by Metacom and Puritan New Englanders

1701	Great Peace of Montreal, a peace treaty signed by the governor of New France and representatives from forty native nations
1713	Treaty of Utrecht ends War of Spanish Succession; France cedes territorial control of Acadia (modern-day Maine and Quebec) to Great Britain and renounces claims to British territories in Canada
1733	150 African slaves revolt in the Danish-controlled island of St. John, capturing a fort in Coral Bay, but are ultimately defeated by Swiss and French troops from Martinique
1740	British Parliament passes a law allowing Jews to becomes citizens in British American colonies
1756–63	Seven Years' War, concluded by the Treaties of Hubertusberg and Paris; Britain acquires modern-day Quebec and Nova Scotia (then New France) from France, and acquires Florida from Spain in exchange for returning Cuba to Spanish rule; in the Caribbean, Britain claims the Grenadines, Tobago, St. Vincent, Grenada, and Dominica
1770	Boston massacre, British troops fire into a crowd, prompting public outcry and protests
1773	Boston Tea Party, protest against taxation
1775–83	American Revolution, war of independence waged against Britain by American colonies
1776	creation of the Viceroyalty of the Rio de la Plata, with capital in Buenos Aires
1776	Anglo-Americans in the British colonies declare independence from England, founding the United States of America
1777	Continental Congress adopts the Articles of Confederation, the first US Constitution, and approves the first official flag of the United States
1780–81	Jose Gabriel Tupac Amaru II leads an indigenous uprising against the Spanish in Peru

1780s–1830s	Comanche empire in modern-day Texas maintains active commercial trade with both Mexico and the United States
1783	Treaty of Paris, Britain acknowledges American independence
1783	Black loyalists and former slaves emigrate from Virginia and South Carolina to British Nova Scotia on the (ultimately unfulfilled) promise of free land
1784	first ship of the US-China trade departs from New York City
1787	Articles of Confederation are replaced by the United States' modern Constitution
1787	Northwest Ordinance establishes a blueprint for populating US territory north of the Ohio River
1789	George Washington elected president of the United States
1790	the United States passes its first national copyright law
1791	the City of Washington in the District of Columbia is founded as the new US capital
1791	Bill of Rights is ratified, comprising first ten amendments to the constitution
1791–1804	Haitian Revolution, a successful slave revolt in the French Caribbean at Saint Domingue, establishes Haiti, the second independent republic in the Americas
1799–1804	Prussian naturalist Alexander von Humboldt tours South America, Cuba, and Mexico
1795	Naturalization Act establishes guidelines for US citizenship
1795	Treaty of San Lorenzo (Pickney Treaty) designates the boundaries between US territory and Spanish colonies in East and West Florida; the United States gains navigational rights on the Mississippi River
1800	Gabriel Prosser leads a slave revolt in Richmond, Virginia
1803	Louisiana Purchase, France sells more than 800,000 square miles of North American territory to the United States, more than doubling the latter's size

1804	Meriwether Lewis and William Clark depart from St. Louis with a young Shoshoni woman, Sacajawea, reaching the Pacific in 1805
1806	Louisiana legislation known as the "Black Codes" or *Codes Noirs* strengthens the power of creole slave-owners
1806–21	Neutral Ground Agreement maintains a no-man's land on a large strip of border territory between Spanish Texas and Louisiana
1807	Portuguese monarchy moves to Brazil due to the Franco-Spanish invasion of Portugal
1808	England and the United States legally ban the transatlantic slave trade; internal slave trade continues
1809	the United States annexes territories in western Florida from Spain
1810–21	Mexican War of Independence, initiated by Catholic priest Miguel Hidalgo y Castilla
1810–28	excepting Cuba and Puerto Rico, all previous Spanish American colonies gain independence from Spain
1812–15	the United States declares war on England, resulting in the War of 1812, ended by the Treaty of Ghent
1813	Gutierrez-Magee invasions; a small army of Mexicans and Anglo-Americans cross the Louisiana border into Texas, declaring independence of Texas before being defeated by Spanish royalists
1816	(US) American Colonization Society founded in Washington, DC, with the goal of repatriating Africans and African Americans to Africa
1817	the First Seminole War in Florida begins
1819	*americanos* led by Simon Bolivar defeat Spanish troops at the Battle of Boyaca and declare independence of the Republic of Colombia
1819	Transcontinental Treaty (Adam-Onis Treaty) makes Florida a US territory, establishes a new border between

the United States and New Spain (Mexico), and Spain recognizes US territorial claims west to the Pacific coast

1820	Missouri Compromise divides the United States into slaveholding and non-slaveholding sections
1821	Sequoyah invents the Cherokee syllabary, which will be used in printing *The Cherokee Phoenix*
1822	Denmark Vesey leads a slave revolt in Charleston, South Carolina
1822	Liberia is created as a US colonial state in Africa
1822	under Emperor Dom Pedro I Brazil declares independence from Portugal
1822–24	Haiti occupies Santo Domingo
1823	Alexander Lucius Twilight becomes the first African American to receive a bachelor's college degree, from Middlebury College in Vermont
1823	*Johnson v. McIntosh*, the US Supreme Court rules that Native Americans can occupy but never own US territory
1823	in a speech to Congress, US President James Monroe delivers what will become known as the "Monroe Doctrine," declaring the end of European imperialism throughout the Americas
1825	Erie Canal opens for traffic
1826	delegates from new Spanish American nations gather in Panama City at the Congress of Panama (or Panamerican Congress) to develop a unified American geopolitics; US delegates are invited but do not attend (one dies en route, the other arrives late)
1827	the Cherokee Nation establishes its constitution and founds the first Native American newspaper, *The Cherokee Phoenix*, in New Echota, Georgia.
1830	Gran Colombia fractures into the sovereign nations of Ecuador, Venezuela, and New Grenada; death of Simon Bolivar

1830	Indian Removal Act passed by US Congress forcibly relocates Native American tribes from their ancestral territories in the southeast to the east of the Mississippi River, anticipating the "Trail of Tears" to modern-day Oklahoma
1831	Nat Turner leads a slave revolt in Southampton County, Virginia
1831	*Cherokee Nation v. Georgia* establishes native territories as "domestic dependent nations" within the United States, despite the arguments of Cherokee Chief John Ross before the US Supreme Court
1831	William Lloyd Garrison creates the antislavery journal *The Liberator*
1833	abolition of slavery in the British West Indies
1834	US artist George Caitlin visits the Comanche center of *Comancheria* on a US peace mission
1836	US settlers in Texas successfully win independence from Mexico in a series of battles including the Battle of the Alamo
1838	approximate beginnings of the interstate Underground Railroad, a secret network to help enslaved people in the southern United States escape to the free states in the north or to Canada
1838	Trail of Tears – forced journey of about 15,000 Cherokee Indians from Georgia to present-day Oklahoma
1839	fifty-three enslaved Africans led by Joseph Cinque revolt aboard the Spanish slaver *Amistad*, which is ultimately captured off the coast of Long Island by the US Navy
1840	collapse of the Central American Federation creates nations of Nicaragua, Honduras, Costa Rica, El Salvador, and Guatemala
1840	Great Peace of 1840 creates a diplomatic alliance between Comanches, Kiowas, Naishans, Cheyennes, and Arapahoes, who often fought together against Euro-Americans in Texas

1844	Samuel Morse invents the telegraph
1845	US annexation of the previously independent territory of Texas
1845	John Sullivan uses the phrase "manifest destiny" to promote annexation of Texas and Oregon country
1846–48	the United States declares war on Mexico, ended by the Treaty of Guadalupe Hidalgo; the United States pays Mexico $15 million to cede territories comprising modern-day California, New Mexico, and portions of Arizona and Nevada
1847	Mormons led by Brigham Young settle in Salt Lake City, Utah
1848	the first women's rights convention is held in Seneca Falls, New York
1849	Harriet Tubman escapes from slavery and becomes a crusader for the Underground Railroad
1849	California Gold Rush greatly increases migration to the western coast of North America from Mexico, the United States, Hawaii, Peru, China, Ireland, and Germany
1849–86	Apache Wars; armed conflicts between US military and Apache nations in the wake of US annexation of earlier Mexican territory
1850	US Fugitive Slave Act legally requires US citizens in "free" states to aid in remanding escaped slaves to their owners
1850	Compromise of 1850, comprising five separate bills to resolve conflicts between slave and free states regarding territories acquired during the Mexican-American War
1850	Brazil officially ends its transatlantic slave trade, but slave trade continues until 1888
1854	*People v. Hall*, California Supreme Court declares that Chinese immigrants are classified as nonwhites and thus are ineligible to testify against a white person in US courts

1857	*Dred Scott v. Sandford*, US Supreme Court rules that African Americans are not citizens, and are not entitled to federal protection
1858	Series of debates between Abraham Lincoln and Senator Stephen A. Douglas
1859	Abolitionist John Brown captures a federal arsenal at Harpers Ferry, Virginia
1861–65	US Civil War between North and South, the Union and the Confederacy, over slavery results in more than 600,000 deaths
1862–67	unsuccessful French invasion of Mexico by Napoleon II
1863	Abraham Lincoln issues the Emancipation Proclamation
1865	Lincoln assassinated
1865	Thirteenth Amendment to the Constitution ratified, prohibiting slavery
1867	US purchases the territory of Alaska from Russia for $7.2 million
1866–71	War of the Triple Alliance between Paraguay and an allied Argentina, Brazil, and Uruguay results in Paraguay's defeat and the decimation of its population
1867	The British North America Act of 1867 creates the confederated state of the Dominion of Canada, dividing the preexisting Province of Canada into Ontario and Quebec and joining them geopolitically to Nova Scotia and New Brunswick
1868	native *cubanos* resist Spanish imperial rule in the Ten Years War
1868	Burlingame Treaty between the United States and China establishes formal relations and encourages emigration from China to the United States
1868	Fourteenth Amendment to the Constitution ratified, granting citizenship to all persons born or naturalized in the United States, included freed slaves

1869	the Union Pacific–Central Pacific is completed, the first transcontinental railroad in North America, with significant labor from Chinese immigrants
1870	Fifteenth Amendment to the Constitution ratified, granting African American men the right to vote
1871	Indian Appropriations Act denies independence of Native nations, establishing them as "wards" of the US federal government, later affirmed in *United States v. Kagama* (1886)
1876–1911	Mexican veteran Porfirio Diaz seizes power in a political coup, assuming the Mexican presidency for thirty-six years
1879–83	War of the Pacific between Chile and allied Bolivia and Peru arises over territorial mining rights; Chile's victory results in a large acquisition of coastal land from Peru and Bolivia, making Bolivia a landlocked country
1882	Chinese Exclusion Act stifles immigration to the United States from China
1883	the United States adopts standard time in time zones
1884	by appealing to the readership of his newspaper *The New York World*, Hungarian emigrant to the United States Joseph Pulitzer raises more than $100,000 to fund the construction of the pedestal for the Statue of Liberty
1885	transcontinental Canadian Pacific Railroad is completed
1886	the French government ships the would-be Statue of Liberty in pieces to the United States
1886	Abolition of slavery in Cuba
1886	American federation of labor established
1887	Dawes General Allotment Act promotes Native American assimilation by breaking up tribal ownership of common land
1888	Abolition of slavery in Brazil
1890	massacre at Wounded Knee Creek of 150 Sioux by US soldiers

1890	National American Woman Suffrage Association founded
1892–1954	16 million European immigrants to the United States pass through Ellis Island during its period as an immigration inspection station
1893	World's Columbian Exposition held in Chicago
1895–98	Cuban War of Independence successfully removes Spanish colonial rule in Cuba with US intervention (see Spanish-American War)
1896	*Plessy v. Ferguson*, US Supreme Court rules that segregation is legal when segregated services are "separate but equal," enabling repressive Jim Crow laws in the South
1898	Spanish-American War, the United States occupies Spanish territories of Cuba, Puerto Rico, and Guam, also acquiring the Philippines and annexing the Kingdom of Hawai'i as a protectorate
1900	First Pan-African Conference, London, organized by Henry Sylvester Williams
1901	US Supreme Court begins a series of "insular cases," which establish that inhabitants of US territories acquired in the Spanish-American War do not automatically possess constitutional rights; future "unincorporated territories" exist in the Philippines (1898–1946), American Samoa (1899), the Panama Canal Zone (1904–79), and the US Virgin Islands (1917)
1902	Cuba attains national independence; Platt Amendment imposes US protectorate status on Cuba
1903	Panama attains national independence from Colombia, with US naval assistance. The Hay-Bunau-Varilla Treaty establishes US control over the Panama Canal Zone and begins construction of the Panama Canal (completed in 1914)
1908	*Partido Independiente de Color* founded by Afro-Cuban veterans in Cuba to combat anti-black racism in newly independent Cuba
1908	Bureau of Investigation established, to become Federal Bureau of Investigation in 1935

1909	National Association for the Advancement of Colored People (NAACP) founded as an interracial pro–civil rights coalition, partially in response to the 1908 race riots in Springfield, Illinois
1910–20	following a series of military coups of revolutionary and counterrevolutionary leaders, Mexican Revolution results in a new constitution in 1917; around 200,000 Mexican refugees relocate to the United States and other nations in South and Central America
~1910–30	Great Migration: between 5 million and 6 million African Americans relocate from the rural southern United States to the urban North and Midwest, largely in response to continued social violence and inequality in the southern states
1911	Society of American Indians founded by self-identified "Red Progressives" to promote Pan-Indian political cooperation and mutual education
1912–33	the United States occupies Nicaragua to oversee the construction of the Nicaraguan Canal connecting Atlantic and Pacific oceans; the United States withdraws with the onset of the Great Depression
1914–18	World War I
1915–34	US invasion and occupation of Haiti
1917	the United States purchases Virgin Islands from Denmark
1917	Asiatic Barred Zone Act, supported by the 1924 Johnson-Reed Act, effectively ends all immigration to the United States from Asia and southern and eastern Europe; Asian exclusion would not be repealed until the 1952 Immigration and Nationality Act
1919	Paris Peace Conference and the Treaty of Versailles
1919	First Pan-African Congress organized by W.E.B. Du Bois and Ida Gibbs Hunt, assembling delegates from fifteen nations to advocate for national self-sovereignty and infrastructural development in occupied African nations

1919–22	The Black Star Line and Black Cross Navigation and Trading Company developed by native Jamaican Marcus Mosiah Garvey to transport goods and African American peoples throughout the Atlantic; in 1920, Garvey announces the "Declaration of Rights of the Negro People of the World" to a crowd of 25,000 in Madison Square Garden
1920	19th Amendment grants US women the right to vote
1920	League of Nations founded in Geneva with the goal of maintaining world peace through disarmament and arbitration
1920s–1930s	Harlem (New Negro) Renaissance; a flowering of new cultural and artistic expressions by African American artists and cultural critics in the urban northeastern United States
1924	National Origins Act bases immigration quotas on US racial demographic, effectively barring immigration from Asia and southeastern Europe
1924	Indian Citizenship Law grants formal US citizenship to Native Americans in the territorial United States
1926–27	Nicaraguan Civil War following a conservative coup of the democratically elected government, ended by the Peace of Tipitapa and US arbitration
1927	First solo nonstop transatlantic flight by Charles Lindbergh
1929	the beginning of the Great Depression
1929	constitution of the Universal Negro Improvement Association and African Communities League (UNIA-ACL) formally approved
1930	Nation of Islam founded in Detroit and Chicago by Wallace Fard Muhammad and Elijah Muhammad
1932	First solo transatlantic nonstop flight by Amelia Earhart
1932–35	Chaco War fought between Bolivia and Paraguay over the disputed territory of the Chacao Boreal, resulting

	in two-thirds of the disputed land being annexed by Paraguay
1933	New Deal recovery measures enacted by US Congress
1934–39	labor strikes and riots in British-occupied Honduras, Trinidad, Saint Kitts, Barbados, and Jamaica resisting economic exploitation form the foundation of labor unions and political organizations promoting national independence
1935	Works Progress Administration established and Social Security Act passed
1938	Fair Labor Standards Act passed, setting minimum wage at 25 cents per hour
1939	*El Congreso Nacional del Pueblo de Habla Hispana*, a convention of hispanophone peoples of the United States, is held in Los Angeles
1939–45	World War II
1942	representatives from twenty-six Allied nations meet in Washington, DC to sign the Declaration of the United Nations
1942–45	following Japan's bombing of Pearl Harbor in Hawai'i in 1941, around 120,000 Japanese Americans are transported to internment camps throughout the United States
1944	International Monetary Fund formed at the Bretton-Woods conference in New Hampshire
1944	National Congress of American Indians formed to combat US federal assimilationist policies and promote tribal sovereignty, anticipating the American Indian Movement formed in Minneapolis, Minnesota in 1968
1945	the United States drops atomic bombs on Hiroshima and Nagasaki
1945	United Nations is established

1945	Fifth Pan-African Congress held in Manchester, United Kingdom; passes antiracist, anti-imperialist, and anticapitalist resolutions
1945	Philippines liberated from Japanese occupation, declares national independence in 1946
1945	Aimé Césaire elected mayor of Fort-de-France and deputy to the French national Assembly for Martinique
1946	US Congress establishes the Indian Claims Commission to negotiate financial settlements to Native Americans for broken treaties and seized lands
1947	Central Intelligence Agency established
1947	the Inter-American Treaty of Reciprocal Assistance (Rio Treaty) is signed in Rio de Janeiro by American nations, establishing a doctrine of "hemispheric defense" against invasions of the Americas
1948	Organization of American States (OAS) founded as an intercontinental political body promoting hemispheric solidarity through economic and military cooperation
1948	Marshall Plan begins, providing aid for European postwar recovery
1948–58	Colombian Civil War; sporadic rural armed conflicts between paramilitary groups representing the nation's Conservative, Liberal, and Communist parties, resulting in the bipartisan National Front
1949	North Atlantic Treaty Organization (NATO) formed as a peacetime military alliance between Canada, the United States, and western European nations against the Soviet Union
1950–53	Korean War between Communist and non-Communist forces; US forces committed to battle without congressional approval by President Truman
1951	American Studies Association founded
1952	Puerto Rico becomes a US Commonwealth

1953–59	Cuban Revolution; socialist revolutionaries under Fidel Castro overthrow the US-backed dictatorship of Fulgencio Batista; the United States imposes an embargo against Cuba
1954	*Brown v. Board of Education* rules that racial segregation in schools is unconstitutional
1954	General Joseph McCarthy begins hearings investigating the US Army on charges of being sympathetic to communism
1954–75	Vietnam War: the United States joins forces of South Vietnam against the Viet Cong and the North Vietnamese Army
1959	Saint Lawrence Seaway is opened as a joint infrastructural project between the United States and Canada
1959	Alaska becomes the forty-ninth US state and Hawaii the fiftieth.
1960s	the *Movimiento Estudiantil Chican@ de Aztlán* (M.E.Ch.A), a student-led movement promoting civil rights, education, and organization of Chicano/a youth, spurs activism in US schools and universities
1960	US Congress passes the Guam Organic Act, establishing the government of Guam
1960	students from North Carolina Agricultural and Technical University in Greensboro, North Carolina, stage weeks of nonviolent sit-ins at the lunch counter of a Greensboro Woolworth department store; after five months of refusing service to black patrons, the business rescinds its "Whites Only" policy
1961	US-backed paramilitary group invades Cuba's Bay of Pigs, intending to overthrow the country's communist government; the failed invasion results in the Cuban Missile Crisis, in which the Soviet Union relocates nuclear missiles (withdrawn in 1962) to Cuba to prevent further harassment by US forces
1961	American Indian Chicago Conference gathers 700 delegates from 64 tribes to develop and discuss the "Declaration of Indian Purpose"

1961	assassination of Dominican Republic President Rafael Trujillo, ending his thirty-year dictatorship
1962	Cuban Missile Crisis
1963	Reverend Martin Luther King, Jr. (assassinated 1968) delivers his "I Have a Dream" sermon to an audience of more than 200,000 during the March on Washington for Jobs and Freedom, organized to protest the continued legal and social oppression of African Americans
1963	US President John Fitzgerald Kennedy is assassinated in Dallas, Texas, by Lee Harvey Oswald
1964	US Congress enacts the Civil Rights Act, outlawing segregation or discrimination based on an individual's race, color, religious creed, sex, or national origins
1965	Dolores Huerta and Cesar Chavez found the United Farm Workers (UFW) association in Delano, California, now the United States' largest farm worker union. The UFW allies with Filipino grape pickers in Delano to promote the Grape Boycott, a labor strike against California grape growers, which lasts from 1965 to 1970
1965	Malcolm X (El-Hajj Malik El-Shabazz) is assassinated by members of the Nation of Islam on February 21, prior to his scheduled speech before the Organization of Afro-American Unity, held in the Audubon Ballroom in Manhattan
1965	Dominican Civil War; overthrow of President Donald Reid Cabral by "Constitutionalist" rebels, resulting in the creation of the Inter-American Peace Force (disbanded in 1967)
1966	*Miranda v. Arizona* establishes Miranda rights
1967	*Loving v. Virginia*, US Supreme court strikes down ban on interracial marriage
1967	the Mexican American Youth Organization (MAYO) is established at St. Mary's College in San Antonio, Texas
1967	death of Che Guevara in Bolivia

1968	worldwide social protests, centering on liberation from repressive governments, feminism, and anticapitalist, antiwar, and antiracist struggles
1968	more than 10,000 Latino high school students in Los Angeles stage citywide walkouts to protest unequal treatment by the LA United School District, which punished Latino students for speaking Spanish on school property; thirteen students are arrested on charges of disorderly conduct and conspiracy
1968	Indian Civil Rights Act guarantees the application of certain constitutional civil rights within tribal governments
1969	astronauts land on the moon
1969	the First Chicano Liberation Youth Conference, convened in Denver, Colorado, issues the *Plan Espiritual de Aztlán*, a manifesto advocating for Chicano nationalism
1969–71	Native Americans occupy Alcatraz Island for nineteen months to protest US governmental injustice to native peoples, reaching more than 400 occupiers at the protest's height; ended when the US government cuts electricity, water, and phone communication to the island
1970	African American political activist Angela Davis is arrested in New York City by FBI agents for her alleged involvement in the attempted escape of a Marin County, CA prisoner, in which a judge was taken hostage; an all-white jury acquits Davis in 1972
1971	Alaska Native Claims Settlement Act grants territorial titles to Alaskan native corporations
1973	The Bahamas attains national independence from England; constitutional autonomy had already been granted in 1964
1973	Chilean President Salvador Allende is assassinated in a coup led by General Augusto Pinochet with the assistance of the CIA; Pinochet remains Chile's dictator until 1990

1974	*Lau v. Nichols*, US Supreme Court rules that school must provide special services for students unable to speak English
1974	Women of All Red Nations (WARN) formed, gathering more than 300 women from 30 native tribes in Rapid City, South Dakota, to advocate against forced sterilization and for improved health care in native communities and the acknowledgment of treaty rights
1975	Voting Rights Act of 1965 is extended to "Hispanic Americans"
1976	the second Group of Seven (G-7) Summit held in Dorado, Puerto Rico
1977	Black feminists of The Combahee River Collective in Boston issue "The Combahee River Collective Statement," critiquing white feminists for failing to address issues confronting women of color
1979	the United States establishes diplomatic relations with People's Republic of China
1979	Three Mile Island accident
1979–81	Iran hostage crisis
1980	first referendum on Quebec independence, resulting in a narrow majority vote for Quebec to remain in Canada; the vote is repeated in 1995, producing an even narrower majority
1983	the United States invades Grenada, toppling its Marxist government
1985	Iran-Contra Scandal; President Reagan administration authorizes sale of arms to Iran in exchange for release of US hostages and to fund the anticommunist Contra terrorist group in Nicaragua
1985–86	dissolution of military dictatorships in Brazil, Haiti, and the Philippines
1985–90	restoration of democratic governments in Argentina, Brazil, Uruguay, and Chile

1989	the United States invades Panama, deposing dictator Manuel Noriega and reinforcing military control over the Panama Canal
1989	fall of the Berlin Wall, radical political transformation of the Eastern Bloc
1990	German reunification
1991	North and South Korea admitted to the UN
1991	the Soviet Union dissolves, fifteen former Soviet states declare independence
1991	US-led coalition invades Iraq in response to Iraq's invasion of Kuwait in Operation Desert Storm
1992	Los Angeles uprising, following the jury acquittal of four police officers accused of beating Rodney King
1992–95	War in Bosnia, Yugoslavia disintegrates, genocides and war crimes
1992–95	Crisis in Somalia, the United States sends troops in 1992; two Black Hawk helicopters shot down and nineteen US Army Rangers die in a citywide firefight in Mogadishu in 1993; the UN withdraws in 1995
1993	US military raids the compound of the Branch Davidians, a religious sect led by David Koresh in Elk, Texas, resulting in a fifty-one-day armed standoff ending in a gun battle in which both US soldiers and Branch Davidians die; Koresh is also killed
1993	truck bomb detonated at the base of the World Trade Center in New York
1993	Oslo Accord, Israel accepts Palestine Liberation Organization as the representative of Palestinians, and PLO recognizes Israel's right to exist in peace
1994	on January 1, North American Free Trade Agreement (NAFTA) legislation takes effect, creating a trilateral trade bloc between Canada, Mexico, and the United States
1994	Chiapas Conflict (or Zapatista Uprising) in Mexican state of Chiapas between Mexican government and

paramilitary Zapatistas, demanding territorial and cultural sovereignty from Mexico

1994   the United States invades Haiti and reinstates the President Jean-Bertrand Aristide, who had been overthrown by a military coup in 1991

1994   in one of the most highly publicized trials in US history, former National Football League player Orenthal James (O.J.) Simpson is acquitted for the accused murders of his ex-wife Nicole Simpson and Ronald Goldman

1994   "Don't ask, don't tell" (DADT) instituted in the US military, forbidding homosexual and bisexual military personnel from speaking about their sexual orientation while in a professional capacity

1995   Oklahoma City bombing by domestic terrorists Timothy McVeigh and Terry Nichols

1995   formation of the World Trade Organization (WTO), an intergovernmental regulating body of international trade

1996   Welfare Reform Act signed by President Bill Clinton

1996   Proposition 209, or the California Civil Rights Initiative, passes by popular vote, prohibiting affirmative action policies in state institutions, including the University of California system; the constitutionality of Prop. 209 has been affirmed by the California Supreme Court in 2000 and 2010

1997   remains of Che Guevara repatriated from Bolivia to Cuba

1999   on April 20, Eric Harris and Dylan Klebold murder thirteen people and injure many others before committing suicide at Columbine High School in Columbine, Colorado, using guns purchased through friends and public gun shows

2001   Al Qaeda operatives hijack and crash two commercial airliners into the World Trade Center in New York and another one into the Pentagon in Virginia (the fourth hijacked plane does not make it to its presumed target thanks to the passengers' attempt to retake control on board); the United States declares war on and invades Afghanistan less than a month later

2001   U.S.A. P.A.T.R.I.O.T. Act (Uniting and Strengthening America by Providing Appropriate Tools Required to Intercept and Obstruct Terrorism) signed into law, granting unprecedented surveillance and detention capabilities to the US federal government

2001   the Development, Relief, and Education for Alien Minors (D.R.E.A.M.) Act bill, proposing a process for granting undocumented immigrants to the United States conditional and then permanent residency, is introduced to and rejected by the US Senate; reintroduced in 2009, the bill again fails to pass

2001   World Conference Against Racism, Durban, South Africa

2002   President George W. Bush labels Iran, Iraq, and Korea "an axis of evil" in his first State of the Union address

2003   US invasion of Iraq with military support from England, Australia, and Poland, deposing the Ba'athist government under Saddam Hussein

2003   1st Congress of the International American Studies Association held in Leiden, Netherlands

2005   Hurricane Katrina

2003   Latinos become the nation's largest minority group, at 37.1 million. The number is expected to triple by the year 2050.

2004   the Minuteman Project begins to organize anti-immigrant activists at the U.S./Mexico border

2001–06   creation of Wikipedia (2001), Facebook (2004), YouTube (2005), and Twitter (2006)

2007   1 billion global Internet users

2007   UN issues Declaration on the Rights of Indigenous Peoples, supporting the sovereignty and preservation of native cultures but not creating any international laws to that effect (the United States does not endorse the Declaration until 2010)

2008	election of Barack Hussein Obama, the United States' first African American president
2008	Lehman Brothers bankruptcy; global financial crisis and economic recession
2010	British Petroleum oil rig *Deepwater Horizon* explodes in the Gulf of Mexico, leading to the largest oil spill in US history
2010	Don't Ask, Don't Tell repealed
2011	Occupy Wall Street protests begin
2011	Arab Spring begins, a series of demonstrations and protests against repressive regimes in the Middle East and North Africa
2011	Al-Qaeda founder Osama bin Laden is killed in a raid on a compound in Pakistan conducted by the US Navy SEALs
2012	on December 14, Adam Lanza murders twenty children and six staff members in a mass shooting at Sandy Hook Elementary School in Newtown, Connecticut, before committing suicide
2013	revelation of widespread surveillance and spying by the National Security Agency; Edward Snowden reveals himself as the source of the NSA leaks
2014	new Iraqi government closes the Abu Ghraib prison complex, occupied by the US military from 2004 to 2006 as a detention zone for Iraqis
2014	Michael Brown shot and killed; beginning of the Black Lives Matter movement
2015	US embassy reopens in Havana, Cuba, for the first time since its closing in 1961 by President Dwight Eisenhower
2015	*Obergefell v. Hodges*, gay marriage legalized in all fifty states by the US Supreme Court

YOGITA GOYAL

Introduction: The Transnational Turn

America's history, her aspirations, her peculiar triumphs, her even more peculiar defeats, and her position in the world – yesterday and today – are all so profoundly and stubbornly unique that the very word "America" remains a new, almost completely undefined and extremely controversial proper noun. No one in the world seems to know exactly what it describes, not even we motley millions who call ourselves Americans.

James Baldwin[1]

Over the last three decades, it has become commonplace to declare a transnational turn in American literary studies. While the publication of a volume like this one may be seen as a sign that the often-declared turn has finally arrived at its destination, any survey of the state of the field of American literary studies would belie such an assumption. It may well be true that neither the analysis of US empire nor the study of American writers in the world would require special pleading today, and yet little seems settled about the scope, method, or value of transnationalism. Even the title "transnational American literature" raises more questions (and likely more hackles) than it resolves.[2] Does "American" include just the United States or does it refer to the vaster Americas as a hemispheric, regional formation, with complex links to Asia, Africa, and elsewhere? Similarly, does "transnational" refer to non-US writing, replacing the category of Third World literature, or does it function as a euphemism for minority, ethnic, or multicultural US literature? Moreover, if the key motivation behind transnational study is to decenter the nation, does not the very notion of transnational American emerge as an oxymoron? For many, such a title will inevitably signal the exact intellectual provincialism it is designed to displace, reverting to a familiar exceptionalism. For others, the term usefully contains the history of that very violence,

Acknowledgments: I would like to thank Ray Ryan for suggesting I edit this volume, and all the contributors for their hard work. I would also like to thank Jordan Wingate for research assistance and for helping compile the chronology and further reading.

and stages the many contradictions and productive ambiguities limned by James Baldwin in the epigraph that opened this chapter.

Similarly, it is not immediately clear where a genealogy of transnationalism should begin. One possible beginning would be the founding of the nation in 1776, but that date would immediately need to yield to earlier moments – to 1492, for instance, which itself must necessarily be displaced as origin. Another would take us to the Cold War origins of Area Studies, while yet another might focus on the social movements of the 1960s that led to widespread transformation of society, not least the demands and agitation of students that led to the founding of black studies and ethnic studies departments. Moreover, some academic fields have always been transnational, and recent work might simply be seen as offering new wine in old bottles. While Paul Jay is right in noting that "since the rise of critical theory in the 1970s, nothing has reshaped literary and cultural studies more than its embrace of transnationalism," a fair amount of confusion persists regarding what going beyond the borders of the nation-state as an object of analysis does to the study of American literature.[3] Clearly, it is difficult to assign a beginning or end to transnationalism, a factor evident in the lengthy yet incomplete chronology that opens this volume. While it matters where we begin or which genealogy we trace – Cold War, slavery, left internationalism, empire, genocide, settler colonialism – little consensus may be said to exist on the subject.

Why then a volume on transnational American literature, when skeptics and dissenters would question both title and genealogy, and perhaps even more significantly when there already exist numerous manifestos for and against transnationalism?[4] For me, the urgency comes from the fact that critics of the transnational turn have not succeeded in outlining a satisfactory alternative. While few would deny the phenomenal impact of the transnational turn on every aspect of American literary criticism, it is equally true that few other things have been more debated or seen as suspect. This combination results in polemical disavowals of the transnational on the one hand and ongoing manifestos for the need for the transnational on the other. Implicit in all such dialogues is the notion that a better transnationalism is possible, and I confess that I too am guilty of this charge. For those who complain that transnational American studies reinforces American exceptionalism, surely a return to national canons or isolationist doctrines is not feasible or desirable. Similarly, it seems difficult to argue for ignoring the ways in which the globe has always been connected, and perhaps even more so today, through networks of power, commerce, culture, and resistance. Critics of the transnational thus rarely champion the nation, arguing instead for various ways of making transnational analysis better. Even if transnational American seems redundant or an oxymoron, alternately too celebratory of a crossroads of cultures or too dystopian in its attack on US empire, surely the need for ongoing analyses of the histories that have brought us here and paths to a better future lie in engaging with what Baldwin terms the meaning of America itself, to understand which he had to leave the United States but also to return to it.

In *Nobody Knows My Name*, Baldwin describes his realization that his time in Europe was ending and that he needed to return to the very home he fled from because even though "the world was enormous and [he] could go anywhere in it [he] chose," to truly understand himself, he had to return to "the fury of the color problem."[5] In France, he realized that he was "as American as any Texas G.I.," finding a kinship with white Americans that he would never have been able to achieve in the United States, not least in their common distance from Europe.[6] At the same time, Baldwin's discovery of what being American means also comes via an encounter with Africans whose migrations signal another history – that of France's colonies. In "Encounter on the Seine" Baldwin explains the alienation of the African American in Paris by way of contrasting his relation to Europe to that of the "African Negro" from one of France's colonies: "They face each other, the Negro and the African, over a gulf of three hundred years – an alienation too vast to be conquered in an evening's good will, too heavy and too double-edged to be ever to be trapped in speech. This alienation causes the Negro to recognize that he is a hybrid," leading to a further realization of his connection to his homeland – which turns out to be America, not Africa. Baldwin concludes, "[I]n this need to establish himself in relation to his past he is most American, this depthless alienation from oneself and one's people is, in sum, the American experience."[7]

The complexity of Baldwin's internationalism is beyond the scope of this introduction, and has already been probed in scholarly accounts of his relation to Turkey, Africa, France, the Caribbean, and Britain.[8] The diverse geographies of black internationalism and the integral role of travel and migration in the constitution of the self are now familiar and uncontroversial concepts for students of American literature. In other words, few would dispute the relevance of Turkey as a haven, to take one example, to Baldwin's thinking. What raises concern, I think, is the seeming prescriptiveness that often accompanies transnationalist manifestos. That is to say, such approaches do not just emphasize the unexpected troubling of any familiar model of self and other through a mapping of transnational routes; they insist that we cannot understand a figure like Baldwin – his search for freedom, his theory of love, his experience of race, his exploration of sexuality, his encounter with whiteness – without engaging with what his various global encounters meant to him.

If many accounts of the transnational turn are guilty of such prescription, it is worth recalling that it is likely a sense of political urgency that frames such language. Amy Kaplan and Donald Pease's landmark volume, *Cultures of United States Imperialism*, turns to 1950s American Studies and 1980s diplomatic history to clarify its intent to combat Cold War understandings of US imperialism and its ongoing disavowal in Iraq.[9] Many accounts of the transnational also derive their sense of urgency from the "War on Terror" declared by the United States in 2001 in response to the 9/11 attacks and ongoing military incursions in Afghanistan and Iraq. The work of the New Americanists that has been central to studies of nation and empire since the 1990s was also deeply invested in connecting the study of race, ethnicity, class, and nation to social movements involved in struggles for enfranchisement and social justice.[10] Much of this work was new historicist in method, and intent on rebutting a national identity rooted in exceptionalist notions and racist, militarist, and imperialist habits. As Winfried Fluck put it, "[T]ransnationalism promises a regeneration of the field and its long overdue liberation from what Amy Kaplan has called the tenacious grasp of American exceptionalism."[11] More recently, in *Formations of United States Colonialism*, Ayosha Goldstein explains how the United States "do not comprehensively delineate an inside and outside of the nation-state," but rather a "volatile assemblage" of unincorporated territories, state governments, indigenous nations, military bases, and export-processing zones. To attend to these shifting configurations of power is to fully understand what Goldstein terms "the colonial present."[12]

Still, given the fact that we now have more than two decades of scholarship to build on, perhaps a homogenizing approach to such political exigencies is no longer necessary. This volume, accordingly, does not promote a single approach to the transnational. Some contributors are skeptical of its value, others assume its relevance, while still others create new itineraries in relation to period or theme without making a case for or against transnationalism. In the midst of the robust debates around the subject in the last few years, what has often been missing is an account of literary method, in part because the political concerns outlined earlier have been so pressing. But precisely because recent years have seen increasing calls for closing the book on the task of ideological demystification or symptomatic reading, more complex and textured accounts of the relation between what Fluck has called aesthetic versus political transnationalism have become necessary.[13] Rather than viewing the charge of the field as either resisting or celebrating globalization, unveiling latent truths about militarism and empire or simply describing their historical formation, or moving away from such concerns toward surface or data, it is more helpful to reach for a suppler analysis of history and literature, to map itineraries that neither follow the reach of capital or the military nor ignore it. Similarly, rather than lumping together all transnational approaches as variations on the theme of American exceptionalism (including those who say it is never possible to do so, those who do not even wish to try, and those who view it as a self-congratulatory gesture alone), my hope is that the variety of methods outlined in the essays here will help stretch the boundaries of existing approaches and make visible new forms of connection and difference. While this may seem like a plea for a middle ground – between aesthetic and political transnationalism, or the study of the world versus that of the home – I'm actually suggesting something else: not quite Hawthorne's neutral territory, but perhaps another ground or another world, maybe an ocean or two, and spaces in between.

It is further conceivable to look back at the last three decades and claim that transnational frames have now become normative rather than insurgent in American literary studies, and yet the task of explaining "where we stand" today remains vital.[14] Ongoing efforts to relate the study of debt and neoliberalism to empire and militarism, the housing crisis to terror, reparations to the refugee crisis all offer possible openings. Recent developments in the analysis of settler colonialism, indigeneity, and sovereignty, cross-racial and cross-ethnic comparative work looking for the "intimacies of four continents" and the solidarities developed among African American and Palestinian activists, all suggest new ways of mapping the globe.[15] Even as the charge of understanding US empire continues to require vigilance, this volume also tracks other kinds of possibilities opened up by the transnational turn – cosmopolitan travels, linguistic encounters, oceanic adventures, freedom dreams, and paranoid linkages.

Accordingly, the chapters that follow offer a comprehensive account of the scope, impact, and critical possibilities of the transnational turn, situating the study of American literature in relation to ethnic, postcolonial, hemispheric, and global studies. Drawing on a wide array of interpretive methods, this volume's essays index the dynamism of the field, offering conceptual tools for understanding the current state of scholarship, but also suggesting new directions of growth. Rather than promoting a single transnational method, the various chapters provide state-of-the-field analyses contextualizing and demonstrating the implications of their topics for scholars of US literary and cultural studies at large. Each chapter includes close readings and textual case studies of the particular phenomena on which it centers, offering refreshing new analyses of such authors as Gloria Anzaldúa, Bartolomé de Las Casas, W.E.B. Du Bois, C.L.R. James, William Faulkner, Sesshu Foster, Margaret Fuller, Amitav Ghosh, Jessica Hagedorn,

Laila Halaby, Mohsin Hamid, Joy Harjo, Henry James, Gayl Jones, Mohja Kahf, Rachel Kushner, Ben Lerner, Paule Marshall, José Martí, Claude McKay, Herman Melville, Pedro Mir, Frank Norris, Ruth Ozeki, Mark Twain, Karen Russell, Luis Alberto Urrea, Walt Whitman, Malcolm X, and Karen Tei Yamashita. Contributors also reckon with important critiques and engage the potentially transformative impact of transnationalism in American literary studies.

Since the 1960s, social movements such as civil rights, feminism, the antiwar movement, and other social justice crusades have transformed literary canons, placing gender and sexuality as well as race and ethnicity at the center of the study of culture and replacing exceptionalist visions of American innocence with an analysis of imperial actions that link the United States with other European powers. More recently, hemispheric, transatlantic, and postcolonial frames have reshaped literary studies, bridging boundaries that have long confined cultural inquiry within narrow frameworks of nation, ethnicity, or language. Highlighting American literature's encounter with (as well as integration into and circulation through) the rest of the world and exploring the construction of the foreign and the domestic; global and local identities; and questions of translation, multilingualism, and worldliness, the essays in this volume probe the ramifications of the transnational turn in all its complexity. How does one distinguish transnationalism from past and present discourses of internationalism, cosmopolitanism, and globalization? How does transnationalism intersect with global capitalism and neoliberalism? What kinds of innovations in form and poetics does a transnational frame enable? How does a focus on empire and migration reframe the study of ethnicity, race, gender, sexuality, region, and class? What are the reading practices of a research methodology for transnational American literary studies?

It is sometimes said that transnationalism can mean all things to all people. At its worst, a transnational frame elides historical differences and local specificity in the name of easy comparisons and a promotion of hybridity. Some forms of transnational study may reiterate exceptionalist legacies that link Americanization to progress and modernity and suggest the inevitability of US domination of the world, keeping the canonical text at the center with a few ethnic exceptions that prove the rule. At its best, however, a transnational approach can unsettle nationalist myths of cultural purity, reveal through comparison the interconnectedness of various parts of the world and peoples, and offer an analysis of past and present imperialisms. It can help map the increasing awareness and cross-cultural dialogue of the Information Age, where the diffusion of cultural forms through immigration and the spread of capital and commodities is ubiquitous and dazzling in both speed and reach. No longer viewing literature as the expression of a national essence, transnational approaches radically reformulate the basic object and scope of literary analysis in and about the United States. Moving beyond the usual impasse of America as empire or colony, exception or exemplar, the transnational turn offers a valuable occasion for examination and critique. Because transnational frames do not argue for the demise of nations, but for a rethinking of them, they can help counteract triumphalist discourses of globalization. Rather than simply resorting to a premature celebration of a postnational or globalized world, transnationalism becomes the occasion for the questioning of nation and alternative formations to the nation – like world systems and world literature – by emphasizing flows and migration but also revealing the synergy of cultural and economic aspects of such histories.

Reading for transnationalism in American literature often denotes interpretations of canonical texts through new frameworks of migration, empire, and globalization. It also offers a useful rubric for comparative ethnic studies, enabling reading across varieties of ethnic literature in a cross-cultural fashion rather than pairing ethnic texts with Anglo-American ones in a binary of majority/minority. Recent shifts in geographical scale offer new frameworks of Black Atlantic, Hemispheric, Asian-Pacific, and Transnational Indigenous Studies. Perhaps most clearly, transnationalism serves as a replacement for the outdated category of multicultural literature, and as an acknowledgment of the interconnectedness of the United States with the rest of the world through circuits of capital and culture.

Recent reformulations of American Studies have argued that the goal of such work is not to export and champion an arrogant nationalism but to understand the meanings of "America" and American culture in all their complexity. To do so, it is crucial to interrogate borders within and outside the nation, rather than reinforce them as naturalized or inviolate. Such moves are part of the transnationalist emphasis on seeing the United States as part of a world system in which multidirectional flows of capital, commodities, people, and ideas restructure national traditions, throwing into question political, geographical, and epistemological boundaries and bringing into view crossroads and contact zones. Comparative studies of race, slavery, terrorism, indigeneity, and citizenship reveal phenomena thought of as natural to be constructed and contingent, themselves shaped through intertwined histories that can no longer be read in insular fashion. Instead of seeing transnationalism as something wholly new, the chapters in this volume draw from fields like ethnic studies and black studies, which were transnational from their very inception. Rather than assigning an automatic politics, the essays show that there is nothing intrinsically radical or complicit about a transnational turn and instead present it as an occasion for examination and critique.

Shape of the Field

Part I of this volume takes up the conceptual meaning of key terms such as nation, empire, travel, translation, and aesthetics. This part also explicates the historical and institutional contexts of transnationalism, delving into its relation to Postcolonial Studies and World Literature, both of which have been areas of lively debate.

Shelley Fisher Fishkin ruminates on her groundbreaking 2004 presidential address to the American Studies Association that declared the transnational turn in American literature to reflect on how the paradigm shift since then has reshaped our thinking of nation and empire. She argues that examining the cultural work of American texts that travel across the world and are translated, adapted, and otherwise appropriated makes us rethink any automatic understanding of hegemony or counter-hegemony. Similarly, authors who travel find themselves transformed by the cultures they encounter. Fishkin offers a comprehensive survey of the rich literature on transnational American scholarship generated over the last decade, ranging widely over such canonical US writers as Walt Whitman and Mark Twain, as well as global ones like the Dominican poet Pedro Mir and the Iraqi poet Saadi Youseff.

In recent years, Goethe's term *Weltliteratur* has undergone a revival, and the category of World Literature has come to assume a prominent role in discussion about comparative work. Chapter 2 examines American literature in relation to frames of World Literature, in dialogue with such models of critical regionalism as nation, globe, and planet. Wai Chee Dimock has emphasized a planetary perspective and interdependencies between the local and the distant, linking Asian, Caribbean, and American texts through "deep time." Here, she expands on this notion to ponder the possibilities of a networked world literature and a crowd-sourced literary field, tracing a low-level affect and a watered-down tragedy in C.L.R. James's reinvention of Herman Melville's *Moby Dick* from the perspective of mariners, renegades, and castaways. In Amitav Ghosh's hands in the Ibis trilogy, a true lingua franca emerges in his Indian Ocean English, neither simply pidgin nor a debased language, but a joyful mixture that relies on improvisation rather than purity.

My consideration of the vexed relation between postcolonial and American literary studies explores the internal colony thesis popular in the 1960s, tracing it to the efforts of W.E.B. Du Bois to imagine the struggles of African Americans for racial justice with larger global struggles for decolonization and labor rights. Considering the difficulties inherent in theorizing such antiracist and anti-imperial solidarities, I offer a genealogy of postcolonial studies by tracing the variable vectors signified by the term – a body of literature, a set of theories, and a critical method of inquiry. Exploring the distances traveled in Teju Cole's 2011 novel, *Open City*, I analyze the weight of historical trauma alongside the lure of cosmopolitanism in contemporary postcolonial literature, as well as the instability inherent in the very rubric of the postcolonial.

It is often assumed that attention to the seemingly political topic of transnationalism must mean disregarding formal and aesthetic questions in literary analysis. However, questions of form are central to the study of American literature and transnationalism, opening up new avenues for exploring the migration and reinvention of genres, revealing previously thought national forms to be more contaminated or plural in origin. Russ Castronovo approaches these concerns by tracing the often fraught and contingent relation between transnational commerce and transnational aesthetics, between a world market and world literature. While notions of transnational aesthetics can provide a check on the presumed singularity of national culture, they also navigate the prospect of the universal within and against the realities of commodity culture, leading to a blurring of the lines of a global economy and a global aesthetic. Frank Norris, for example, imagines an American literature pushing so far westward that it arrives in the East, thus completing a circle free of any conflicts or rough edges.

Literary Histories

Part II offers new interpretations of canonical American literature in three distinct historical periods through new frameworks of migration, empire, and globalization. For many scholars, transnationalism is useful as a rubric, since it is not limited to a particular time period (in contrast to globalization, for instance, which usually refers to the last few decades) and enables a considerable historical span from early American writing to modern and contemporary literature.

Although transnationalism may be new to academic currency, it nevertheless names a deeply rooted historical phenomenon, one multiply represented in American literature, especially in the nineteenth century, as debates over expansionism, immigration, citizenship, and imperialism shaped literary landscapes. In reading nineteenth-century American literature, Johannes Voelz cautions scholars about current critical investments that cannot help structure our relation to the past. Considering the Transcendentalist interest in cosmopolitanism and romantic conceptions of world literature, Voelz shows how literary fields develop in relation to social and political movements but are not reducible to them. What emerges in this map of the nineteenth-century literary landscape is the paradox of searching for transnational public spheres or a politics of resistance while grappling with the ambiguous relation between imperialism and transnationalism, as well as a worry that the two cannot always be separated.

Themes of exile and expatriation have always been central to the study of modernism. Transnational approaches expand on these themes to explore how modernist writers imagine and represent other worlds in relation to their own, thus broadening the modernist archive in temporal and spatial terms. Jessica Berman finds transnationalism useful for understanding the complex social and textual interconnections of modernisms across the world as well as for offering an optic through which we understand modernism's reckoning with the frame of the nation. Refusing to prioritize actual travel alone, Berman shows how even a figure like William Faulkner, famous for his regional focus, benefits from being resituated alongside black US writers like Toni Morrison and Latin American writers like Mario Vargas Llosa. Emphasizing the cosmopolitan travels of Henry James and Gertrude Stein beside the more oppositional vagabondage of Claude McKay, Berman applauds the ability of transnational frames to displace the nationalist binaries that have constituted the study of modernism, dividing international and vernacular modernisms or cosmopolitan and fugitive forms of travel.

For David James, new fictions of transnationalism help rethink received notions of postmodernism as well as its still-evolving relation to notions of the contemporary. Focusing on formal techniques often associated with postmodernism – including self-reflexivity, metafiction, collage, and multi-perspectivalism – James shows how such writers as Karen Tei Yamashita, Ruth Ozeki, and Jessica Hagedorn are able to navigate the competing pulls of local particularity and global encounters. Refusing to equate transnationalism with cosmopolitanism alone, James finds critiques of neo-imperialism and commercialism in an array of recent fiction, not least in their formal innovations. Learning to represent worldliness in all its complexity remains both an object and a challenge for contemporary writing and criticism.

Critical Geographies

Part III considers recent shifts in geographical scale and the corresponding new frames of Black Atlantic, Borderlands, Hemispheric, Asian-Pacific, and Transnational Indigenous Studies. As Paul Gilroy urges in *The Black Atlantic*, a national frame must be replaced by a transnational one to understand the flow of black culture, people, and commodities across and between national boundaries, in oceanic spaces, and beyond fixed notions of cultural or ethnic purity.[16] The long history of Pan-Africanism and black internationalism further requires a diasporic and comparative frame of analysis for understanding key literary moments such as the Harlem Renaissance or the Black Arts Movement, anchored not by fixed locations within the United States alone, but hailing the horizons of Europe and Africa, the Caribbean and Latin America. Reading African American texts from the nineteenth century to the present, which focus on a range of transnational sites, Destiny Birdsong and Ifeoma Nwankwo emphasize the cultural work performed by women writers mapping migration and diaspora. *The History of Mary Prince*, for example, testifies at once to the cause of abolition and to the rights of colonial inhabitants of the British Empire, revealing an identity that is simultaneously West Indian and transatlantic. Birdsong and Nwankwo argue for the importance of gender, particularly the relation between mother and daughter, in their analysis of diaspora by way of a reading of Paule Marshall's *Brown Girl, Brownstones*.

Chicana and Chicano studies take the border of the United States and Mexico as the principal object of analysis, drawing on a spatial lexicon to understand questions of identity, homeland, migration, and displacement. Raising important questions about translation and the limits of monolingual approaches, border and borderland studies emphasizes the rise of American imperialism and westward expansionism in the aftermath of the Monroe Doctrine (1823), the annexation of Texas (1845), the Mexican-American War (1846–48), the Spanish-American War (1898), and into the twentieth century. Gloria Anzaldúa's influential concept of borderlands in *Borderlands/La Frontera: The New Mestiza* (1997) draws attention to contact zones and in-between spaces, stressing the mobility and hybridity of cultural identities and moving away from nationalist frameworks in favor of such concepts as *mestizaje*. John Alba Cutler traces some of the tensions between the borderlands paradigm and the transnational turn, explaining why the two methods have sometimes been at cross-purposes and outlining a way forward that combines the two. Reading recent fiction by Sesshu Foster, Rosario Sanmiguel, and Luis Alberto Urrea that demonstrates the urgency of the borderlands framework, Cutler shows how a focus on the border makes visible the most damaging effects of global capital.

At the center of any transnational frame of analysis are questions of roots and routes, indigeneity and place, mobility and migration. American Indian literature grapples with precisely these questions, offering important correctives to existing theories of nationalism and transnationalism by highlighting issues of sovereign Native nations and the analytical framework of the United States as a settler colony. Jodi Byrd shows that even as the transnational turn in American literary studies did the necessary work of expanding critical horizons and highlighting colonial and postcolonial dispossessions, it often collapsed Indigenous Peoples into nationally organized racial formations. Tracing the ways in which Indigenous literary studies has resisted the notion of transnationalism, Byrd weighs the valence of concepts of sovereignty, settler colonialism, and canon formations in recent debates on the subject. Advocating decolonial research methods and an orientation toward the communities one serves, Byrd shows how American Indian authors offer the best vocabularies for fathoming such charged issues.

The specific site of the nation and its processes of racialization were the first concern of Asian Americanist literary scholars. However, since Asian American as a term was invented by the Pan-Asian movements of the 1970s, it was always imagined as an aggregate identity rather than one that prioritized national origins. More recently, thinking outside, beyond, and across national boundaries, especially toward Asia, the field has shifted from the focus of immigrant writers of the pre–World War II era on assimilation, stereotypes, cultural nationalism, and gender toward diaspora and globalization. Older distinctions between immigrant and native give way to an increasing and all-pervasive mobility, as Asian America is rethought through hemispheric, archipelagic, and oceanic frames, most often summed up by the term Pacific Rim. Viet Nguyen skillfully traces the shifting relation between the two terms, reminding us that the idea of the Pacific Rim since the 1960s was an economic one, in service of global capital, just as the act of claiming America by Asian American writers often also meant embracing US empire. Karen Tei Yamashita's writing offers a perfect example of the overflowing of racial and geographic boundaries as well as the navigation of disjunctive economic and cultural agendas. For Nguyen, while it may seem that Asian American better retains a sense of the political history of resistance that called it into being, and Pacific Rim seems more fully ensnared in capitalist or imperialist desires, the larger horizon the Pacific offers still remains ethically urgent for the field of Asian American studies.

The hemispheric concept is not new in literary discourse but has recently emerged as a vital reframing of American literary production through explorations of connections between hemisphere and nation, networks of race, ethnicity, and class that pre-date nation formation, and analysis of imperialism in the Americas. To avoid intellectual provincialism, it is important to recognize that "American" must be resisted as a default term for the United States, as Latin Americanists have long argued. Instead, it is necessary to think of the Americas as a hemispheric, regional formation, emerging out of a series of colonial conflicts and engagements. Hemispheric frames call into play a north-south rather than an east-west axis, reorienting, for instance, Southern US studies toward Central America and the Gulf of Mexico, or an American Mediterranean, or toward Latin America and Africa. A comparative approach to the study of race, ethnicity, diaspora, and migration illuminates the complexity of the nation-state as the agent of hegemony or (in many Latin American countries) the form through which US imperialism may be resisted. Maria Josefina Saldaña-Portillo calls attention to these overlapping and sedimented histories, providing a rich account of the political desires animating a hemispheric turn, which can often recenter the United States in the name of decentering it. Calling for a hemispheric literature from below, she reads Bartolomé de Las Casas's *apologia* as a defense of indigenous reason and a challenge to enlightenment philosophies of origin and ownership. Ending with an analysis of contemporary fascination with narco-culture, Saldaña-Portillo underscores the ongoing political urgency of hemispheric work.

Literature and Geopolitics

Finally, Part IV relates the study of gendered forms to colonialism, modernity, terror, and globalization. How does the experience of travel shape constructions of gender and sexuality? How did 9/11 and representations of a Muslim other impact and reshape American literature? How are conceptions of the homeland raced and gendered, and how do concepts of sexuality travel or translate?

For Crystal Parikh, the benefits of transnational analysis for feminism are clear. In contrast to older concepts of a global sisterhood, transnational feminism analyzes the historical and continuing impact of imperialism, showing how there is no feminism free of asymmetrical power relations or structural inequality. Feminist critiques of nationalism, as well as gendered constructions of the foreign, emphasize the intersectionality of race and nation, gender and sexuality, region and class. Drawing on the insights of women-of-color feminists, Parikh argues that transnational feminism helps expand and revise notions of what constitutes American literature and authorship, bringing into view alternate imaginaries based on women's daily lives and identities. Reading Karen Russell and Ruth Ozeki's recent novels as instances of transnational feminist practice, Parikh uncovers an ethics of place in their environmentalist explorations of family history and geological time of the planet. Tracing what Rob Nixon terms "slow violence" in these works, Parikh shows how feminist affiliations materialize only when the specificity of place and experience is taken into account fully.[17]

Scholars have recently emphasized a transnational turn in lesbian and gay studies and queer theory. The goal of such work is to study the effect of the increasingly transnational mobility of people, media, commodities, discourses, and capital on local, regional, and national modes of sexual desire, embodiment, and subjectivity. How do theories of sexuality complicate the task of transnational studies, including analysis of nation, migration, and the global? Moreover, what difference does a transnational frame make to the study of sexuality, corporeality, and intimacy? Petrus Liu explains how transnational analysis since the 1990s has complicated the familiar blueprint of Stonewall-based queer American history, making visible other modernities and sexual histories. But the difficulties of such work recall for Liu earlier debates about social constructionism and essentialism, questioning the meaning of sexuality as essence or discursive effect. Theorizing queer transnationalism thus involves managing the conflicting claims of queer critiques of heteronormativity with postcolonial critiques of allochronism – the tendency to deny coevalness to the other. Showing that transnationalism is not a recent import to the field of queer studies, Liu finds in formative works of queer theory by Judith Butler and Eve Sedgwick lingering anthropological assumptions about abstractions like the West and the non-West.

Taking up the relation between Islam and transnational studies, Timothy Marr shows how Islamic transnationalism precedes the modern nation-state. Forms of African American Islam – ranging from slavery to the Nation of Islam – illustrate not only the resonant questions of citizenship and nativism within the United States but also the effort to navigate capitalism in a global frame. Recent literary works by Laila Halaby, Mohsin Hamid, and Mohja Kahf reveal how Islam is situated within discourses of multicultural diversity on the one hand and excluded as an alien threat on the other, as Muslim American immigrant writers construct a transnational Muslim public sphere as a possible counter. In this discussion, transnational approaches help counter the nativist imaginaries that demonize Islam, offering longer histories of cultural encounter beyond and before the nation-state, as well as exploring an alternative ethics of contact.

NOTES

1 James Baldwin, "The Discovery of What It Means To Be an American," in *Nobody Knows My Name* (1954). *Collected Essays* (New York: Library of America, 1998), 137–143; quotation on 137.
2 Janice Radway in "What's in a Name?" questions the use of "American" to define an area of study, considering the merits of such alternatives as "United States Studies," "Inter-American Studies," and "Intercultural Studies" (*American Quarterly* 51.1 [1999]: 1–32).
3 Paul Jay, *Global Matters: The Transnational Turn in Literary Studies* (Ithaca: Cornell University Press, 2010), 1.
4 Among many others, see *Post Nationalist American Studies*, John Carlos Rowe, ed. (Berkeley: University of California Press, 2000); *Futures of American Studies*, Donald Pease and Robyn Weigman, eds. (Durham: Duke University Press, 2002);

Hemispheric American Studies, Caroline Levander and Robert Levine, eds. (New Brunswick: Rutgers University Press, 2008); *Globalizing American Studies*, Brian T. Edwards and Dilip P. Gaonkar, eds. (Chicago: University of Chicago Press, 2010); and *Re-Framing the Transnational Turn in American Studies*, Winfried Fluck, Donald Pease, and John Carlos Rowe, eds. (Hanover: Dartmouth College Press, 2011).

5   Baldwin, "American," 136–37.

6   Ibid. 137.

7   James Baldwin, "Encounter on the Seine: Black Meets Brown," in *Notes of a Native Son* (1955). *Collected Essays* (New York: Library of America, 1998), 85–90; quotation on 89.

8   See for instance *James Baldwin: America and Beyond*, Cora Kaplan and Bill Schwarz, eds. (Ann Arbor: University of Michigan Press, 2012) and *James Baldwin's Turkish Decade: Erotics of Exile*, Magdalena Zaborowska (Durham: Duke University Press, 2009).

9   Amy Kaplan and Donald Pease eds., *Cultures of United States Imperialism* (Durham: Duke University Press, 1993).

10 Donald Pease, "National Identities, Postmodern Artifacts, and Postnational Narratives." *boundary* 2 19.1 (1992): 1–13; quotation on 3.

11 Winfried Fluck, "A New Beginning? Transnationalisms," *New Literary History* 42.3 (2011): 365–84; quotation on 365.

12 Alyosha Goldstein, ed., *Formations of United States Colonialism* (Durham and London: Duke University Press, 2014), 1, 2, 6.

13 See Fluck, "A New Beginning?" To take one example of recent calls to rethink our reading practices, Stephen Best and Sharon Marcus in "Surface Reading: An Introduction" (*Representations* 108 [Fall 2009]) point to the images of torture at Abu Ghraib that circulated freely on the Internet and seemed to require little exegesis of power and humiliation, asking scholars to withdraw from the assumption that the work of literary criticism and that of political activism are one and the same.

14 Matthew Frye Jacobson, "Where We Stand: US Empire at Street Level and in the Archive," *American Quarterly* 65.2 (2013): 265–90.

15 Lisa Lowe, *The Intimacies of Four Continents* (Durham: Duke University Press, 2015); Patrick Wolfe, *Settler Colonialism and the Transformation of Anthropology* (New York: Cassell, 1998); Jon Soske and Sean Jacobs, eds. *Apartheid Israel: The Politics of an Analogy* (Chicago: Haymarket Books, 2015); and Robin Kelley, *Freedom Dreams: The Black Radical Imagination* (Boston: Beacon, 2002).

16 Paul Gilroy, *The Black Atlantic: Modernity and Double Consciousness* (Cambridge, MA: Harvard University Press, 1995).

17 Rob Nixon, *Slow Violence and the Environmentalism of the Poor* (Cambridge, MA: Harvard University Press, 2013).

PART I

Shape of the Field

I

SHELLEY FISHER FISHKIN

Unsettling American Literature, Rethinking Nation and Empire

In 2004, in my presidential address to the American Studies Association, "Crossroads of Cultures: The Transnational Turn in American Studies," I asked what the field of American Studies would look like "if the transnational rather than the national were at its center." I applauded the fact that transnational topics and approaches were indeed already proliferating in our field, as scholars increasingly paid attention to "the ways in which ideas, people, culture, and capital have circulated and continue to circulate physically, and virtually, throughout the world."[1] Over the last decade, the paradigm shift that I welcomed has increased, and many of the changes I called for in the culture of our profession have come to pass as well – such as more multilingual research and greater engagement with scholarship produced around the world. All of this work has helped unsettle some of our assumptions about our object of study.

Discussions of canonical American literature in the past focused mainly on texts written in English and published and read in the United States. But how does our understanding of American literature and our thinking about nation and empire change when we look at texts that travel and the cultural work they do around the world? When and how do we explore issues of translation, adaptation, and appropriation? How can reading American literature in global perspective expose US-based Americanists to conversations about nation and empire that are inflected by national histories other than our own? How can doing so remind us that what is hegemonic in one context may be counter-hegemonic in another? As we will see, probing a great Dominican poet's "countersong" to Walt Whitman can give us new insight into the complexities of Whitman's voice and vision as well as contradictions that America, as well as its greatest poet, embody. And seeing Mark Twain as Chinese writers saw him during much of the twentieth century can restore to us a Twain that his countrymen had little use for at the time – a Twain who believed that criticizing his nation's imperial adventures abroad was his duty as a citizen – and was as American as apple pie. As we reappraise critiques of imperialism from writers like Twain and Melville, the roots of their iconoclasm remain a puzzle. What role might travel have played in prompting them to ask questions about nation, empire and American identity that few of their peers were asking? These are some of the questions that this essay explores. Given the limitations of space, this essay focuses on two important threads running through work on transnational American literature produced between 2005 and 2015: (1) examinations of *texts that travel* and the cultural work they do around the world; and (2) examinations of *authors who travel* and how travel and migration have shaped the texts they produce. I consider how this scholarship – on both canonical figures in American literature and new voices – complicates our thinking about nation and empire in generative ways.

Traveling Texts

A rich vein of scholarship in transnational American literary studies mined during the last decade has involved examinations of how American literary texts travel and the cultural work they do around the world, often bringing into focus new perspectives on nation and empire in the process. Texts by Walt Whitman, Edgar Allan Poe, Harriet Beecher Stowe, Langston Hughes, Helen Hunt Jackson, Gloria Anzaldúa, Younghill Kang, and Mark Twain have figured centrally in these discussions.

Walt Whitman emerges from these recent studies as a poet who is both an emblem of his nation and a betrayer of his nation; a champion of capitalist individualism and a socialist revolutionary; the embodiment of patriotic American nationalism and a prophet of transnationalism; a humble egalitarian and a brash imperialist. The contradictions of this complex and multivalent writer are limned brilliantly by the great Dominican poet Pedro Mir, whose "Contracanto a Walt Whitman" is increasingly getting the attention it has long deserved as one of the most intriguing Latin American critiques of US imperialism. Mir's "Contracanto a Walt Whitman" celebrates Whitman's appealing egalitarian validation of common people while blasting the outrageous arrogance and imperiousness of his country's ideology of manifest destiny. In section 12 of the poem, in a sly satiric act of ventriloquism, Mir has Sinclair Lewis's eponymous character Babbitt sing his own version of "Song of Myself." Speaking in the voice of "I, Babbitt, a cosmos, child of Manhattan," Mir demands that the countries of Central and South America be brought to him on the caterpillar treads of tanks, and, amid awful smells, they are delivered. Mir writes,

> – Yo, Babbitt, un cosmos,
> un hijo de Manhattan.

Él os lo dirá
– Traedme las Antillas
... sobre los caterpillares de los tanques
traedme las Antillas.
    Y en medio de un aroma silencioso
allá viene la isla de Santo Domingo.
– Traedme la América Central.
    Y en medio de un aroma pavoroso
allá viene callada Nicaragua.
Traedme la América del Sur....[2]

The poet returns to addressing Walt Whitman in section 13, but refers to him as "tattered Walt Whitman," saying, one cannot recognize him today – "because your sign is guarded in the vaults of Banks, because your voice is in islands guarded by reefs of bayonets and daggers...."[3] As I noted in 2005, Mir's "Countersong" asks us to examine how democratic openness and imperious arrogance can coexist as they do in both Whitman's text, and America itself.[4] Víctor Figueroa suggests in "Colonial Grammar" (2007) that "the semantic ambiguity of Whitman's pronouns *I* and *mine*" might "imply that they were already invested in imperial designs that Babbitt's appropriation only makes explicit."[5] In the final portion of the poem, he notes that Mir "announces the advent of a new pronoun, 'nosotros,' a 'we' that will collectively rescue the Whitmanian vision betrayed by the U.S."[6] Miguel Alejandro Valerio expands on this theme in "Nosotros para nosotros" (2014), writing that "*Mir, como muchos de sus contemporáneos, ve los ideales whitmanianos sequestrados por el sistema capitalist.imperialista. Mir quiere rescatar y redefinir esos ideales*," a perspective voiced as well by Rivera (2006) and Batista (2009).[7] Ultimately, in Figueroa's view, both "fictional characters (Mir's Babbitt and Whitman's poetic persona) anchor their pronouns (*I* and *mine*) in imperial logic that not surprisingly makes them part of the same grammar of colonial domination." Figueroa reads Mir's poem as "an extremely accurate and powerful portrayal ... of the colonial condition," a condition "sustained by the myth of a 'lack' in the colonized that does not exist in the colonizer," who "can always claim to be 'a cosmos.'" In Figueroa's view, Mir's efforts to both celebrate and transcend Whitman's rhetoric with his own "countersong" may be seen, in part, as an effort to "re-imagine aspects of the Dominican Republic's convoluted historical relations with the 'colossus of the north'" – including "the U.S. occupation from 1916 to 1925, an uneasy cold war/good neighbor alliance during much of Trujillo's regime, another occupation in 1965, and armed and political resistance." Figueroa views Mir's poem as a "masterful presentation of colonial tensions experienced from the inside."[8] Other recent work such as Laura Lomas's *Translating Empire: José Martí, Migrant Latino Subjects, and American Modernities* (2009) amplifies our understanding of the key role Whitman has played in helping other writers from Latin America, such as Martí, refine their ideas of regional and national identity.[9]

Beyond Latin America, as well, Whitman's texts have helped writers think through ideas of national and regional identity in the contexts of their own national histories. For example, Jeffrey Einboden's impressive *Nineteenth-Century U.S. Literature in Middle Eastern Languages* (2013) examines choices that Israeli writer Simon Halkin made in his 1952 Hebrew translation of *Leaves of Grass* "during a crucial period of Israeli self-definition" – particularly Halkin's melding of Biblical language and contemporary Israeli idioms in an effort to replicate Whitman's own fusion of the form and language of the psalms with modernist content, and also as a way of exploring issues of national identity.[10] And in a chapter titled "American 'Song' of Iraqi Exile: Whitman and Saadi Youssef," Einboden analyzes how Iraqi poet Saadi Youssef's 1976 Arabic translation of *Leaves of Grass* charts "alternative geopolitical contexts for Leaves," allowing it to explore challenges facing Iraq as a nation (extending "an Arab dialogue on Whitman reaching back to the very first years of the twentieth century.") He tell us that Youssef translates the title of Whitman's "To a Stranger" as "*Ilā Gharīb*," a title "that does indeed signify 'To a Stranger,'" but "could also imply 'To an Exile,' the Arabic replacement for 'stranger'" that carries with it the connotation, as well, of "alien" or "émigré," in the process "reflecting obliquely a 'trail of exile'" that Youssef himself will pursue.[11] Two years after he translated the poem, Youssef himself became an exile from Saddam Hussein's Iraq.

During the last decade, there has been worthwhile research on translations and adaptations of texts by other canonical writers in addition to Whitman, and on what we can learn about nation and empire by examining the cultural work of these texts. While translating American literature can help a nation distance itself from US hegemonic power in one context, in another it can play a role in a nation's efforts to extricate itself from its past and take its place in modernity. For example, in *Translated Poe* (2014), edited by Emron Esplin and Margarida Vale de Gato, Christopher Rollason suggests that in Mexico "translations of Poe tales and poems followed an imperative of reclaiming from US colonizing power certain cultural-linguistic markers ingrained in the native traditions," while in Turkey, by way of contrast, Hivren Demir-Atay shows that after the collapse of the Ottoman Empire, translations of Poe into Turkish played a role in "the cultural affirmation of the Turkish republic," which depended on "linguistic modernization, separation from Arabic and Persian, and the introduction of more westernized narrative forms."[12]

Sarah Meer's wide-ranging and erudite *Uncle Tom Mania* (2005) includes fascinating discussions of nationalistic uses to which Harriet Beecher Stowe's *Uncle Tom's Cabin* was put in England soon after it appeared. She notes that a tone of nationalistic self-congratulation pervaded many of the twenty-some stage productions based on the novel mounted in London between 1852 and 1855, reminding audiences that Britain had ended slavery in its colonies nearly two decades earlier. At a City of London Theatre, George flees "'[t]o the British land ... to the shore that with one touch can break thro' the bond of slavery as a thread, and shake defiance with her flag to all nations that encouraged it!' ... In the operatic version he apostrophized the country" as a land where "all are free" and "where British justice regulated the law." In another production, "the governor of Canada declares the runaways free under a Union Jack to the music of 'Rule Britannia.'"[13]

Vera M. Kutzinski's "'Yo también soy América': Langston Hughes Translated" (2006) and *The Worlds of Langston Hughes* (2012) examine translations of Hughes's most popular poems in Latin America (such as "I, Too" and "Negro") to probe the ways in which translators "more often than not, appropriated Hughes's poems for their own nationalist agendas."[14] Noting that "Many Latin Americans blithely regarded racial prejudice entirely as a US import," Kutzinski observes that

> The discourse of anti-US imperialism so pervasive in Latin America during the aftermath of the Spanish-Cuban-American War (1895–98), and quite insepa-rable from nationalist ideologies, provided translators and commentators alike with fertile ground for analogizing external and internal colonization: that is, they likened Latin American reactions to US neocolonial expansionism to the predicament of anti-black racism which Hughes scorned in so many of his poems. Such analogies also facilitated the absorption of Hughes's poems about racial oppression into the discourse of revolutionary class struggle radi-ating outward from the Soviet Union, especially during the 1930s.[15]

Kutzinski's meticulous analysis demonstrates the ways in which Latin American translators' "selection of poems and their actual translations con-structed Hughes's verse in Spanish as a vehicle for nationalist and shared anti-imperialist identification."[16] In a related vein, Susan Gillman's "*Otra Vez Caliban*/Encore Caliban: Adaptation, Translation, Americas Studies" (2008) and Raúl Coronado's "The Aesthetics of Our America" (2008) explore in pro-ductive ways how the "translation," "adaptation," and "transculturation" of Helen Hunt Jackson's *Ramona* provided a vehicle for Latin American writ-ers to explore (among other topics) "the visible presence of North American imperialism in Latin America."[17]

The multilingual complexity of works by late twentieth-century writer Gloria Anzaldúa may well defy translation, but these works have nonetheless traveled widely and had a major impact around the world on thinking about national borders that are the legacies of imperial conquest in a range of contexts: a special issue of *Signs* in 2011, for example, included essays by European scholars who use concepts drawn from Anzaldúa's work as a vehicle for reflecting on nation, citizenship, anti-immigrant violence in Europe.[18] Grażyna Zygadło, for example, discusses the reasons why Anzaldúa's work speaks as deeply as it does to Zygadło's students at the University of Lodz, where Polish social, religious, and political history as well as contemporary conditions allow her students to identify profoundly with Anzaldúa's engagement with struggles over ethnic and national identity and language, and with her focus on ethnicity- and gender-related exploitation and violence; on the persecution of minorities; on capitalism and migrant workers; and on the artificial nature of national borders.[19]

During the last ten years, the travels of American literary texts in Korea, Japan, and China have received increasing attention from scholars based in Asia. Their articles and books on Asian responses to both twentieth-century Asian American texts and nineteenth-century canonical American texts have enhanced our insight into the role these texts have played in shaping Asian attitudes toward national identity in a range of imperial encounters.

As Kun Jong Lee notes, Younghill Kang's *The Grass Roof* (1931), the first Korean American novel, was not translated into Korean until 1977, and did not attract the attention of literary scholars in based in Korea until the 1990s.[20] But despite being a book that only a relatively small number of Koreans could even read in the 1930s, *The Grass Roof* was loudly acclaimed in Korea soon after it came out. As Chris Suh notes in a 2014 paper, Koreans in Korea applauded the novel out of gratitude that it "had drawn the attention of Anglophone readers to Korea's colonial situation," and out of a sense of national pride sparked by "the accolades it got in the American press.[21] (These factors overshadowed flaws they saw in its depiction of their country.) In 1946, the Military Government the United States established in the southern half of the country liked the book so much that they brought Kang, now an American, back to Korea to run their public information office and even "'made *The Grass Roof* required reading for every G.I. in Korea.'"[22] (Suh notes that the same military officials who brought Kang back to Korea "became furious when Kang, after returning to the United States a year and a half later," published an essay "in which he argued that the country recently 'liberated' by the United States was now filled with corruption, hunger, poverty, and political chaos. The US Military Government, Kang explained, had the 'agency' to 'correct the evils of the provisional regime' yet it refused do anything."[23] Suh observes that most of the Koreans who had taken issue with Kang's portrayal of Korea in *The*

Grass Roof now "celebrated his depiction of the country under American rule."[24])

Although for some sixty years after Kang's first book appeared, the only Korean scholars who paid attention to Korean American literature were Koreanists teaching in Korean departments, Kun Jong Lee notes in a 2012 article that early in the 1990s, Americanist scholars in Korea "started to study Korean American literature as a part of American literature," producing in the process "some significant scholarship with uniquely Korean perspectives" that examined Asian American literature in "a comparative, transnational, and translingual context."[25] He cites, for example, a 2008 article by So-Hee Lee that reads Nora Okja Keller's novel "*Fox Girl* in juxtaposition with Jung-Mo Yoon's *Goppi* (*The Bridle*), a Korean camptown narrative."[26] Kun Jong Lee notes the aptness of discussing these two novels focused on camptown sex workers (written by authors who had previously published full-length novels about comfort women – Yoon's *Mommy's Name Was a Chosenpee*, in Korean and Keller's *Comfort Woman*, in English); So-Hee Lee's article, he tells us, highlights how "the neo-colonial relationship between Korea and the US and domestic political atmosphere (from the Cold War ideology to the anti-Americanism) affected the private lives of sex workers in camptowns around US military installations in Korea from the 1960s to the 1980s," while also showing "how the novelists' ideologies inform their protagonists' struggle between gender identity and nationalist consciousness."[27]

Bookended by Tsuyoshi Ishihara's *Mark Twain in Japan: The Cultural Reception of an American Icon* (2005) and Selina Lai-Henderson's *Mark Twain in China* (2015), the last decade has seen the global travels of texts by Mark Twain get more sustained attention than they have during the entire century since Twain's death.[28] One of the many strengths of Ishihara's book is his description of the nation-building role Twain's books played in Imperial Japan (where a translation of the *Prince and the Pauper* was thought to help reinforce lines of authority sanctioned by a society ruled by an Emperor), as well as the role they played during the Allied Occupation (where a translation of *Huck Finn* was taught in schools to help reinforce democratic ideas). Also interesting is Ishihara's ability to situate Japanese translators' misreading of the racial politics of *Huck Finn* (and their decision to simply cut key scenes involving Jim) in the context of the difficulty Japan has when it comes to acknowledging Japanese racism toward colonized minorities within its own culture. Lai-Henderson's fascinating book ventures into both of these areas, as well: she explores the nation-building, political uses to which China put texts by Mark Twain (for example, a sketch almost unknown in the

United States called "Running for Governor" is known by nearly every Chinese schoolchild, celebrated – somewhat justly – as a biting critique of the flaws of a two-party system); and she puts problems Chinese translators have with the word "nigger" in the context of the history of racism and discrimination in China. Lai-Henderson's detailed examination of China's appreciation of Twain's anti-imperialism fleshes out in constructive ways my own discussion in *The Mark Twain Anthology* (2010) and in "Transnational American Literary Studies: The Case of Mark Twain" (2011) of the widespread recognition of Mark Twain's anti-imperialism in China during a period when this aspect of his work was largely ignored in the United States. I argued that while Twain was valued as an important anti-imperialist writer in China from 1960 on, in the United States he was viewed primarily as a humorist until the 1990s.[29]

Scholars have increasingly shown over the last decade that engaging well-traveled texts by American authors has helped writers in Latin America, Europe, and Asia forge national and regional identities of their own, while also probing the impact of US, Soviet, and Japanese imperialism on their nations and their region. Analyzing translations and adaptations of these traveling texts has been an important dimension of this research. Although the study of translations and adaptations of American literature around the world has played a relatively minor role in American studies in the past, the kinds of research noted here may well serve as an impetus for change.[30]

Traveling Writers

Scholars have been devoting attention during the last ten years not only to the travels of texts but also to the travels of authors and to the perspectives on nation and empire that a study of this dimension of these authors' work can yield. In addition to coming up with fresh perspectives on how travel shaped the writing of canonical figures like Herman Melville, Mark Twain, and James Baldwin, scholars have been exploring this topic in the context of work by writers who have not previously been the subject of much scholarly attention. Publication during the last decade of new work by writers for whom travel and migration was a formative experience is likely to enrich the study of this topic in the future.

New perspectives on what Herman Melville's travels taught him about American empire emerge from recent work by Lawrence Buell, Rüdiger Kunow, and Greg Grandin. In "Ecoglobalist Affects: The Emergence of U.S. Environmental Imagination on a Planetary Scale" in the collection *Shades of the Planet* (2007), Buell calls Melville "the first canonical U.S. author to have sojourned in the developing world, and to perceive the effects of gunboat diplomacy there from the standpoint of its indigenous victims."[31] Painting Melville as a writer with deep interest in "the rise of U.S. industrial might on a global scale," Buell discusses *Moby-Dick* as the "first canonical novel about an extractive industry of global" dimensions.[32] In "Melville, Religious Cosmopolitanism and the New American Studies" (2011), Rüdiger Kunow recuperates Melville's critique of missionaries and his respect for the native cultures he encountered during his travels, suggesting ways in which Melville's travels may have helped him raise questions about the extension of Western influence in the developing world that few of his peers were raising at the time.[33] In "The Two Faces of Empire" (2014), Greg Grandin writes that "the main characters in Melville's *Moby-Dick* and *Benito Cereno* represent the dark corrupting branches of American imperialism."[34] Although "whaling took place in a watery commons open to all," Grandin reminds us that sealing, the brutal land-based industry at the center of *Benito Cereno*, "predicted today's postindustrial extracted, hunted, drilled, fracked, hot and strip-mined world."[35] Grandin expands on this analysis in his brilliant 2014 book *Empire of Necessity: Slavery, Freedom, and Deception in the New World*, which sets Melville's fiction in the broader context of both the centrality of slavery to empire in the nineteenth century and the imperial reach of extractive industries in the modern world.[36]

The ways in which Mark Twain's travels shaped his thinking about nation and empire has been the subject of a number of studies during the last ten years, including work by Hua Hsu, John Carlos Rowe, Tsuyoshi Ishihara, Selina Lai-Henderson, Hsuan Hsu, and myself – works that analyze the impact of Twain's travels in India, Africa, and Australasia on his growing opposition to American imperialism in the Philippines and his support of the Boxer rebellion in China.[37] In an astute reading of *Following the Equator*, John Carlos Rowe demonstrates that

> there is political purpose to the digressive style of *Following the Equator* and a more coherent criticism of European imperialism – modern globalization – in the entire work, especially when we understand how Twain is trying to work within what he understands as very deep-seated assumptions about the superiority of Anglo-American 'civilization' among his readers.

Rowe believes "there is considerable evidence in *Following the Equator* that Twain's own attitudes were transformed by what he witnessed, read, and gathered in conversations during his round-the-world tour."[38] Ishihara, Harris, and Messent similarly find Twain's travels to be a pivotal factor that drives his evolving hostility to imperialism. Messent observes that Twain's "transnational positioning – crossing between countries and retaining a certain objectivity and independence as a result – allowed him to hold political views that cut against hegemonic national interests (in this case both British and American)."[39] In a similar vein, Hua Hsu calls for "a reappraisal of Twain as a trans-Pacific traveler, an American with a consciously *global* viewpoint."[40] "Roughing it on the road," Hua Hsu writes "Twain achieved insights into the human condition and the tenuousness of national affiliations that were unavailable to his more provincial peers."[41]

While the second half of Lai-Henderson's *Mark Twain in China* focuses on the travels of Twain's works, the first half addresses Twain's own travels, finding in the lessons he learned as he came face to face with some of the abominations of European imperialism in India, South Africa, Ceylon, Australia, and New Zealand, the seeds of his sympathy for the Boxers who wanted to rid China of foreigners, and his antipathy toward missionaries and others who were smug in their conviction of the superiority of their religion, language, culture, and way of life. Both Lai-Henderson and Hsuan L. Hsu suggest that Twain's travels helped him recognize – and be repulsed by – the ways in which the lives of imperialism's victims around the globe were "wasted," and by the ways in which his own and other nations were whitewashing the devastation for which they were responsible. In an inspired chapter titled "Body Counts and Comparative Anti-Imperialism," Hsuan Hsu demonstrates how in *Following the Equator* "Twain uses numbers to convey the deadly and unsustainable nature of colonialism and racialized labor."[42]

Scholars during the last few years have also been probing the impact that travel had on twentieth-century minority US writers' understanding of nation and empire. The travels of black and Jewish American writers to Moscow during the interwar years – what Claude McKay described in 1922 as the "magic pilgrimage" – are at the center of Steven S. Lee's *The Ethnic Avant-Garde* (2015). Lee's efforts to recapture the "magic behind the 'magic pilgrimage'" helps illuminate how their encounter with "visions of world revolution in which the ethnic Other took the lead" (as well as exposure to Moscow's brand of multiculturalism and Leninist critiques of imperialism) shaped their ideas about what their own nation was and what their place in it might be.[43] In *The Borderlands of Culture*, Ramón Saldívar explores the ways in which Américo Paredes's travels to Japan, China, and Korea after World War II "exposed him in a crucially formative way to the differing ethno-cultural complexities that imperialism and modernization in their multiple varieties had bequeathed to both the Americas and the Far East."[44] Those complexities, he argues, shaped Paredes' future writing about the US-Mexico borderlands.

In *James Baldwin's Turkish Decade: Erotics of Exile* (2008), Magdalena Zaborowska explores how Baldwin's extended stays in Turkey between

1961 and 1971 shaped his thinking about nation and empire. She observes that Baldwin believed that "what Turkey could teach America" was "'a kind of sense of other people and how to deal with other people' that it learned after having ceased to be an empire, a sense that the United States could not yet attain, bent as it was on building its own."[45] Zaborowska notes that Baldwin's sojourn in Turkey shaped his thinking about the very category of "nation": "In a 1970 interview Baldwin proclaimed, 'I don't believe in nations any more. Those passports, those borders, are as outworn and useless as war.'"[46]

Ideas of nation and nationality are interrogated in similarly radical ways by Jahan Ramazani in *A Transnational Poetics* (2009) and by Paul Giles in *The Global Mapping of American Literature*, (2011), who discuss the folly of trying to squeeze writers such as T.S. Eliot, W.H. Auden, Denise Levertov, Sylvia Plath, Gertrude Stein, and Elizabeth Bishop into doggedly "nation-centric" categories that reduce the significance of the time they spent traveling and living outside of the United States.[47] Their suggestion that we highlight writers' transnational affinities, allegiances, influences, and identifications rather than solely national ones opens up fruitful approaches to a growing body of writers whose travels make these issues particularly salient but who may have been neglected precisely because of that reason. For example, in *Transpacific Migrations: Student Migration and the Remaking of Asian America* (2013), Chih-Ming Wang recovers and analyzes a body of work that has received almost no attention by scholars: writing in both English and Chinese by Chinese students who came to America for their studies from the middle of the nineteenth century through the 1970s, writers who "develop a double identification with Asia and America, holding fast to both national identity and politics and a transnational vision of modernity." Wang's virtuoso examination of these neglected memoirs, novels, and poems in Chinese and English illuminates the complexities of how these students make their way through competing ideas of nation and empire, and how they made a space for themselves in a "transnational cultural political space" that Wang calls "Asia/America."[48]

Although Wang mentions Shirley Geok-lin Lim briefly in another context, Lim – a writer of Chinese descent who grew up in Malaysia, came to Brandeis for graduate study as a Fulbright scholar in 1969, and has been producing celebrated poetry, fiction, and criticism since 1980 – might well be "Exhibit A" for both Wang and Ramazani when it comes to the perils of following "nation-centric" models of literature and thereby redlining writers who are transnational at their core and cannot be easily assimilated into one national tradition. As I noted in 2013 in "Mapping American Studies in the Twenty-First Century," when Lim's first book of poems, *Crossing the Peninsula*, which focused on her memories of Malaysia, won the Commonwealth Writers' Prize in 1980, she was the first Asian and the first woman to be honored with that award. But the book was not recognized in Malaysia because it was written in English. Lim learned, to her surprise, that only poems written in Bahasa Malaysia counted as national literature there. Lim's own work might best be understood as belonging to a category of "literature of the transnational" (to borrow a term Lim herself used in her essay "Immigration and Diaspora.")[49]

"Literature of the transnational" is the only category in which it makes sense to put a trilingual collection edited by Jill Anderson with photos by Nin Solis entitled *Los Otros Dreamers*, published in Mexico in 2014.[50] The highly original book is a collective *testimonio* by young people who have been deported to Mexico by the US government, or who made the difficult decision to return on their own after facing obstacles in the United States. These twenty-six undocumented youth wrote their autobiographical narratives in English, Spanish, or Spanglish or told them to Anderson and edited them in collaboration with her. The voices with which they communicate the experience of being victimized by the bureaucracies of two nations, yet not being fully anchored in or welcomed by either – of riding a see-saw of hope and disappointment on both sides of the border – are poignant and candid meditations that show them experiencing, questioning, doubting, and affirming the idea and reality of what it means to be "in" and "of" a "nation."[51]

Questions about what it means to be in "in" and "of" a "nation" figure prominently in *Pachinko,* the novel that American writer Min Jin Lee has just completed. Born in Seoul, Lee moved to the United States when she was seven; her first novel, the acclaimed *Free Food for Millionaires*, was about Korean immigrants and their children in New York. But *Pachinko* is about Koreans in Japan, a country in which she lived from 2007 to 2011. The discrimination and uncertainty that her characters suffer resemble the precarity and lack of belonging experienced by *Los Otros Dreamers* – for Koreans in Japan, even if they were born there, live under constant threat of deportation. Her characters' lives are indelibly marked by the anti-Korean prejudice they encounter in Japan, an ugly by-product of the history of Japanese imperialism. *Pachinko* promises to be a valuable addition to the "literature of the transnational."[52]

Coda: Whitman in Iraq and His Iraqi Poet-Translator in Whitman's New York

In 2007, Saadi Youssef, one of Iraq's greatest modern poets, visited New York, the hometown of Walt Whitman, whose work he had translated into Arabic three decades earlier. He chronicled his residence there in *New York Qaṣīdas*, initiating what Jeffrey Einboden calls "a dizzying act of circular translation":

> Self-consciously situated in the wake of 9/11 and the ensuing 'war on terror,' Youssef's exilic sojourn performs a stunning and sophisticated return, no longer translating an Arabic Whitman in Baghdad, but composing a new Arabic Whitman in Brooklyn. Comprising more than 200 lines, and more than twenty subtitled sections, the *New York Qaṣīdas* unfold a wandering narrative, suffused throughout by Whitmanian echoes; it is, however, only near the end of this sequence that Whitman explicitly emerges invoked and invited to accompany Youssef as he navigates urban streets and sites. Traversing Manhattan landmarks...Youssef's circuitous route leads him finally to the Brooklyn Bridge, a locale where Whitman's precedent is irrepressible, erupting onto the surface of Youssef's poetry.[53]

Einboden then quotes an excerpt from "Youssef's drifting dialogue with Whitman":

> [The Civil war ended, O Walt Whitman. But the black soldiers who
> Fought in the way of freedom, and the out-of-work cotton plantation
>   slaves, these are they
> That live in Harlem, and Brooklyn, and the Bronx, and Manhattan ...
> These are they whom you loved, and for whom you sung, and who
>   sung for you, they still
> Sleep in the public parks and eat from the garbage][54]

Youssef's translation thirty years earlier of "To a Stranger" as "*Ilā Gharīb*" takes on new meaning here. Einboden writes, "Seeming now to reflect the social injustices highlighted in [the section quoted above], Youssef's translation, with its ambiguous title, signifying both 'Stranger' and 'Exile' (*Gharīb*) – continues a narrative of vagrancy, recalling the estrangement and dispossession witnessed by Youssef in Brooklyn's 'public parks.'"[55] In the next two sections of the poem, Youssef reprints his translation of "To a Stranger" with the original English, as well, and then resumes his "direct dialogue with Whitman." "Briefer than his imagined tour" in the earlier part of the poem, "this new appeal to Whitman nevertheless seems more potent, Youssef interrogating his American icon on contemporary geopolitics":

> [The *gharīb* (i.e. 'stranger') which you sang
> And the *gharīb* (or *Ghraib*) which you didn't sing ...
> and the *gharīb* (or *Ghraib*) which lies yet closer than me ...
> Has there reached you, here, news of it, O my comrade, Walt Whitman?
> Has there reached you the soldiers of "*Abū Ghraib*"?
> Have they informed you?][56]

Youssef returns to his translation of Whitman from thirty years earlier and finds implied in the title he chose (*Ilā Gharīb*) haunting resonance with the name of notorious Iraqi prison, Abu Ghraib. Einboden suggests that "Youssef recognizes new possibilities in his old translation of 'To a Stranger,'" this poem no longer situated in New York 'public parks' but also in a jail on the outskirts of Baghdad, reflecting not only on US dispossession but also on Iraqi captivity ..."[57]

What are we to do with this border-crossing, time-traveling, language-melding, intertextual, online virtual conversation between a traveling text and a traveling writer who translated it? This *sui generis* poem is both more and less than an "adaptation." Is it American literature? Iraqi literature? Literature of the transnational? None of the above? All of the above? As texts and writers travel more easily both physically and virtually in a twenty-first-century world of digital replication and instant communication, conundrums like these are likely to continue to unsettle us for years to come.

NOTES

1 Shelley Fisher Fishkin, "Crossroads of Cultures: The Transnational Turn in American Studies. Presidential Address to the American Studies Association, November 12, 2004." *American Quarterly* 57.1 (2005): 17–57.

2 Pedro Mir, "Contracanto a Walt Whitman," in *Contracanto a Walt Whitman; canto a nosotros mismos* (Guatemala: Ediciones Saker-Ti, 1952), 68. The paraphrasing that precedes this quotation is my own.

3 Mir, "Contracanto," 72. The translation is my own.

4 Shelley Fisher Fishkin, "Whitman's 1855 *Leaves of Grass*: Borders and Boundaries," presented at the 2005 meeting of the American Studies Association in Washington, DC.

5 Víctor Figueroa, "Colonial Grammar: Ambivalent Imperial Pronouns in Pedro Mir's 'Contracanto a Walt Whitman,'" *Caribe: revista de cultura y literatura* 10.2 (2007–2008): 53.

6 Figueroa, "Colonial Grammar," 50.

7 Miguel Alejandro Valerio, "Nosotros para nosotros," *Revista Cronopio*, Edición 38 (February 21, 2014). Web, <www.revistacronopio.com/?p=9851>; Jacqueline Rivera Rivera, "De cantos y contracantos: Divergecias y convergencias en la textualización del yo/nosotros en Walt Whitman y Pedro Mir," *Horizontes* 48.95 (October 2006): 77–116; José Manuel Batista, "Ni cósmico, ni democrático: El *Contracanto a Walt Whitman* de Pedro Mir," *Symposium* 62.4 (Winter 2009): 235–57.

8 Figueroa, "Colonial Grammar," 55–56, 59.

9 Laura Lomas, *Translating Empire: José Martí, Migrant Latino Subjects, and American Modernities*. Durham, NC: Duke University Press, 2009.

10 Jeffrey Einboden, *Nineteenth-Century U.S. Literature in Middle Eastern Languages* (Edinburgh: Edinburgh University Press, 2013), 8, and chapter 5, "The *New Bible* in Hebrew: Whitman and Simon Halkin," 125–55.

11 Einboden, *Nineteenth-Century U.S. Literature in Middle Eastern Languages*, 157, 165, and chapter 6, "American 'Song' of Iraqi Exile: Whitman and Saadi Youssef," 156–86.

12 Emron Esplin and Margarida Vale de Gato, "Introduction: Poe in/and Translation" in *Translated Poe*, Emron Esplin and Margarida Vale de Gato, eds. (Bethlehem, PA: Lehigh University Press, 2014), xix. Excerpted in *Journal of Transnational American Studies* 6:1 (2014). Web, <http://escholarship.org/uc/item/1c13k85x>.

13 Sarah Meer, *Uncle Tom Mania; Slavery, Minstrelsy, and Translantic Culture in the 1850s*. Athens: University of Georgia Press, 2005, 142.

14 Vera M. Kutzinski, "Yo también soy América: Langston Hughes Translated." *American Literary History*, 18.3 (Fall 2006): 551; Kutzinski, *The Worlds of Langston Hughes: Modernism and Translation in the Americas* (Ithaca, NY: Cornell University Press, 2012).

15 Vera M. Kutzinski, "Yo también," 551–52.

16 Ibid. 554.

17 Susan Gillman, "Otra Vez Caliban/Encore Caliban: Adaptation, Translation, American studies. *American Literary History*, 20.1–2 (Spring–Summer 2008): 187–209, 188; Raúl Coronado, "The Aesthetics of Our America: A Response to Susan Gillman," *American Literary History*, 20.1–2 (Spring–Summer 2008): 210–16.

18 See a special issue of *Signs* (37.1 [2011]) edited by Norma Cantú, "Comparative Perspectives Symposium: Gloria E. Anzaldúa, an International Perspective." In this issue, see Norma Cantú, "Doing Work that Matters: Gloria Anzaldúain the International Arena" (1–5), 2; Romana Radlwimmer,"Searching for Gloria Anzaldúa: A Fictional Dialogue on Realities Somewhere Between Austria and Spain" (18–23); Maria Antònia Oliver-Rotger, "Gloria Anzaldúa's Borderless Theory in Spain" (5–10); María Henríquez-Betancor, "Gloria Anzaldúa in the Canary Islands" (41–46); Paola Zaccaria, "Mediterranean Borderization" (10–18).

19 In the same collection, Grażyna Zygadło, "'Where the Third World Grates Against the First': Teaching Gloria Anzaldúa from a Polish Perspective" (29–34), 30.

20 Kun Jong Lee, "An overview of Korean/Asian American literary studies in Korea, 1964–2009," *Inter-Asia Cultural Studies*, 13:2 (2012): 275–85, 276.

21 Chris Suh, "East Goes West, and Back to East: Koreans, Korean Americans, and Transnational Receptions of Younghill Kang's *The Grass Roof*." Unpublished award-winning paper presented at the Association for Asian American Studies Conference San Francisco 2014.

22 Chris Suh, "East Goes West," citing Kang to Perkins, May 3, 1947, Series 3, Subseries 3A, Box 86, Folder: "Younghill Kang (2)," Archives of Charles Scribner's Sons.

23 Chris Suh, "East Goes West," citing Kang, "How It Feels to Be a Korean … in Korea," *United Nations World* 2.4 (May 1948): 18–19.

24 Chris Suh, "East Goes West."

25 Lee, "Korean/Asian American literary studies in Korea," 276, 280.

26 Ibid. 280.

27 Ibid. 280.

28 Tsuyoshi Ishihara, *Mark Twain in Japan: The Cultural Reception of an American Icon* (Columbia: University of Missouri Press, 2005); Selina Lai-Henderson, *Mark Twain in China* (Stanford, CA: Stanford University Press, 2015).

29 Jim Zwick's crucial recovery of the anti-imperialist Twain in *Mark Twain's Weapons of Satire: Anti-Imperialist Writings on the Philippine-American War* (Syracuse, NY: Syracuse University Press, 1992) was the beginning of this reevaluation. For an overview of Zwick's impact, see Shelley Fisher Fishkin, "Reflections," *The Mark Twain Annual* 8 (2010), 22–28. I made a point of including in the *Mark Twain Anthology* a piece that was well known in China and virtually unknown in the United States, which has since become a key text cited by other scholars writing about Mark Twain and imperialism: Lao She (Yuan Kejia). "Mark Twain: Exposer of the 'Dollar Empire.' A Speech by Lao She Commemorating the Fiftieth Anniversary of the Death of Mark Twain," *US-China Review* 19 (Summer 1995): 11–15. Reprinted in Shelley Fisher Fishkin, ed., *The Mark Twain Anthology: Great Writers on His Life and Works*, 283–88. Translated by Zhao Yuming, Sui Gand, and J.R. LeMaster. New York: Library of America, 2010.

30 Stanford's American Studies Program, for example, now allows majors to fulfill one of three courses required in "Literature, Culture and the Arts" with a course in Translation Studies.

31 Lawrence Buell, "Ecoglobalist Affects: The Emergence of U.S. Environmental Imagination on a Planetary Scale." In *Shades of the Planet: American Literature as World Literature*, Wai Chee Dimock and Lawrence Buell, eds. (Princeton, NJ: Princeton University Press, 2007), 239.

32 Lawrence Buell, "Ecoglobalist Affects," 239.

33 Rüdiger Kunow, "Melville, Religious Cosmopolitanism and the New American Studies" *Journal of Transnational American Studies* 3.1 (2015). Web, <http://escholarship.org/uc/search?entity=acgcc_jtas;volume=3;issue=1>

34 Greg Grandin, "The Two Faces of Empire." *The Nation*. 27 January, 2014. Web, <www.thenation.com/article/two-faces-empire/>.

35 Ibid.

36 Greg Grandin, *Empire of Necessity: Slavery, Freedom, and Deception in the New World*. (New York: Metropolitan Books/Henry Holt and Company, 2014).

37 Hua Hsu, "The Trans-Pacific Lessons of Mark Twain's 'War-Prayer,'" in "*New Perspectives on 'The War-Prayer': An International Forum*," edited by Shelley Fisher Fishkin and Takayuki Tatsumi. *Mark Twain Studies* 2 [Japan], 2006. Hsu's article was republished in a "Reprise" section of *Journal of Transnational American Studies* 1.1 (2009). Web, <http://escholarship.org/uc/item/666369jq#page-1>; John Carlos Rowe, "Mark Twain's Critique of Globalization (Old and New) in *Following the Equator, A Journey Around the World* (1897)," *The Arizona Quarterly* 61.1 (Spring 2005): 109–35; Tsuyoshi Ishihara, "Mark Twain's Travel Books and Empire: The Transformation of Twain's Views on Non-Western Others and the Western Self." *Waseda University Faculty of Education Academic Research* 54:19 (February 2006). Web, <https://dspace.wul.waseda.ac.jp/dspace/bitstream/2065/5484/1/eigoeibunp19-34ishihara.pdf>; Selina Lai-Henderson, *Mark Twain in China* (Stanford, CA: Stanford University Press, 2015); Hsuan L. Hsu, *Sitting in Darkness: Mark Twain's Asia and Comparative Racialization* (New York: New York University

Press, 2015); Shelley Fisher Fishkin, "Transnational Twain" in *American Studies as Transnational Practice: Turning Toward the Transpacific*, Yuan Shu and Donald Pease, eds. (Hanover, NH: Dartmouth College Press, 2016), 109–38; Susan K. Harris, *God's Arbiters: Americans and the Philippines, 1898–1902* (New York: Oxford University Press, 2011); Peter Messent, "'Not an Alien but at Home': Mark Twain and London" in *Cosmopolitan Twain*, Ann M. Ryan and Joseph B. McCullough, eds. (Columbia: University of Missouri Press, 2008), 187–210.

38 Rowe, "Mark Twain's Critique of Globalization," 111–12, 116.

39 Messent, "'Not and Alien but at Home,'" 209.

40 Hua Hsu, "The Trans-Pacific Lessons of Mark Twain's 'War-Prayer.'"

41 Ibid.

42 Hsuan L. Hsu, *Sitting in Darkness*, 150. For a related discussion of Twain's experimental strategies for dramatizing the toll imperialism takes on its victims, see the discussion of "The Stupendous Procession" on pp. 153–58 in Shelley Fisher Fishkin, "Mark Twain and the Jews," *Arizona Quarterly* 61.1 (Spring 2005): 137–66.

43 Steven S. Lee, *The Ethnic Avant-Garde: Minority Cultures and World Revolution* (New York: Columbia University Press, 2015), 1–2.

44 Ramón Saldívar, *The Borderlands of Culture: Américo Paredes and the Transnational Imaginary* (Durham, NC: Duke University Press, 2010), 10.

45 Magdalena J. Zaborowska, *James Baldwin's Turkish Decade: Erotics of Exile* (Durham, NC: Duke University Press, 2008), 204.

46 Ibid. xviii.

47 Jahan Ramazani, *A Transnational Poetics* (Chicago: University of Chicago Press, 2009); Paul Giles, *The Global Mapping of American Literature* (Princeton, NJ: Princeton University Press, 2011).

48 Chih-ming Wang, *Transpacific Articulations: Student Migration and the Remaking of Asian America* (Honolulu: University of Hawai'i Press, 2013), 1, 135.

49 Shelley Fisher Fishkin, "Mapping American Studies in the Twenty-First Century," *The Transnationalism of American Culture*, Rocio Davis, ed. (New York: Routledge, 2013), 21; Shirley Geok-lin Lim, "Immigration and Diaspora," in *An Interethnic Companion to Asian American Literature*, King-Kok Cheung, ed. (Cambridge: Cambridge University Press, 1996), 299.

50 Jill Anderson and Nin Solis, eds. *Los Otros Dreamers* (Mexico City: Dream in Mexico/Ciudad de México/U.S. Mexico Foundation, 2014).

51 Ibid.

52 Min Jin Lee generously shared unpublished chapters of her forthcoming novel, *Pachinko*, with me, on which these comments are based. An early version of a portion of the book, the prize-winning story titled "Motherland" appeared in the *Missouri Review* in 2002 (*Missouri Review* 25.1 [2002]: 9–26). See Min Jin Lee, *Pachinko* (New York: Grand Central Publishing, 2017).

53 Einboden, *Nineteenth-Century U.S. Literature in Middle Eastern Languages*, 173. "For Youssef's [*New York Qaṣīdas*], which he dates to 2008, and notes its authorship between 2006 and 2007 in London and New York, see his website: www.saadiyousif.com/home/index.php?option=com_content&task-view&id=682&Itemid=44. All subsequent quotations from Youssef's

sequence will be derived from this online source" (212). The website is almost entirely in Arabic. Exceptions are Youssef's decision to provide "his Arabic translation of 'To a Stranger' followed by this poem's English original" (177). The English translations of other parts of *New York Qaṣīdas* in this essay are Einboden's.

54 Einboden, *Nineteenth-Century U.S. Literature in Middle Eastern Languages*, 177.

55 *Ibid.* 178.

56 Ibid. 178.

57 Ibid. 178.

2

WAI CHEE DIMOCK

American Literature, World Literature

In thinking about American literature as world literature, I would like to begin with a theory that has dominated our thinking for some time: Pascale Casanova's account of the "world republic of letters," in her influential book of that title.[1] For Casanova, world literature comes into being when a handful of texts are lifted from their local contexts and circulated across national borders, when they are "consecrated" at the literary Greenwich meridian – Paris – and admitted into a rarefied pantheon. World literature would not have been possible, in short, without a global gate-keeping process, one the subjects a text to

> transmutation in the alchemical sense. The consecration of a text is the almost magical metamorphosis of an ordinary material into "gold," into absolute literary value ... Paris is not only the capital of the literary world. It is also, as a result, the gateway to the "world market of intellectual goods," as Goethe put it; the chief place of consecration in the world of literature. (125–26)

Casanova cites William Faulkner as an exemplary case. She points to the translations of Faulkner into French by Maurice-Edgar Coindreau, which, she claims, sealed his worldwide reputation, culminating in the Nobel Prize in 1949. Starting out in Mississippi, Faulkner ends up in the most cosmopolitan, and most exclusive, of clubs, with members such as Samuel Beckett, Octavio Paz, Gabriel Garcia Marquez, and Gao Xingjian – all Nobel laureates, all of whom had been consecrated in Paris before ascending to the very top in Stockholm.

Casanova might have a point. Still, her world republic of letters, in being so relentlessly centralized and hierarchical, might strike some of us as less a "republic" than a panopticon. Not only is there a strong presumption here in favor of literature as an institutional artifact; this strong presumption also carries with it a predictable outcome, giving us an operating system in which a single, unchanging metropolitan center dominates a globalized field, dominates even those texts that have no chance of ever being consecrated.

Casanova's paradigm seems to need qualification, then, both on factual grounds – did those French translations alone catapult Faulkner to fame, and is the Greenwich meridian always Paris? – and as a conceptual template for theorizing "world" literature. In light of what we have learned about non-centralized, non-hierarchical online networks, it is worth thinking of a "world" antithetical to the one she describes: at some distance from seats of power, without institutional prestige, but also without the high mainten-ance cost of prestige, an alternative to the high-power and highly restrictive centralized model.

Gilles Deleuze, Felix Guattari, and Bruno Latour are helpful in reorient-ing us in this general direction; for this essay, though, I would especially like to draw on a book focusing on the Internet: *Networked*: *The New Social Operating System*, by Lee Rainie and Barry Wellman.[2] Rainie and Wellman call attention to "partial membership" as an online form of collectivity with as yet unknown potential. By this they have in mind filiations that are inter-mittent rather than full-time, voluntary and context-based rather than insti-tutionally certified, replacing vertical edicts with horizontal exchanges. The ties that result – say, on Twitter or Facebook – are weak ties. But because their membership threshold is low, they also tend to multiply fairly easily, a side development that can be counted on to recur, interfering with any strong claim about the airtight closure of a centralized regime.

A "networked" world literature, then, rather than giving the last word either to hierarchical institutions or to individual texts as sovereign products of single authors, calls attention to the continual emergence of contributing players, tangential to but not without bearing on the existing corpus. It is a poetics of second chance and second look. What results is a "crowdsourced" literary field, input-accepting and variant-rich, still being tinkered with – remixed, repurposed, replotted – the collective (and by no means unified) effort of many. Networks of this sort are impossible to supervise and impos-sible to put a stop to. They suggest that any individual text is bound to fall short – in the sense that it cannot be its own sequel, its own endpoint – precisely because it is singular, the work of one pair of hands, and arrested at one particular moment in time. Falling short is both an individual limit and a necessary spur to the inventiveness of others; the codependency that results binds any given author to any number of would-be authors. Untried options subsequently explored, roads not taken subsequently visited: these time-delayed feedback loops make up the improvised structures of these peripheral networks. Through these long-distance, not necessarily recupera-tive, though sometimes surprisingly illuminating turns, happening as much by chance as by design, traces of the unactualized past can be carried into the future, and ill-defined shadows can be given alternate outlines.

Crowdsourcing Melville

Without further ado, then, let me turn to three figures – Herman Melville, C. L. R. James, and Amitav Ghosh – to give a practical demonstration of one such peripheral network. I begin with James. No matter how we look at it, *Mariners, Renegades, Castaways* is a strange book, a reading of Melville, but not one Melville scholars would approve. James began writing this book on June 10, 1952, when he was arrested by the US Immigration and Naturalization Services, sent to Ellis Island and detained for the next six months, before being deported later that year for passport violations. It was on Ellis Island, surrounded by the world's immigrant population, that a prophetic vision came to him, a "natural and necessary conclusion," he said, to "the miracle of Herman Melville."[3] James writes:

> A great deal of this book was written on Ellis Island while I was being detained by the Department of Immigration. The Island, like Melville's *Pequod*, is a miniature of all the nations of the world and all sections of society. My experience of it and the circumstances attending my stay there have so deepened my understanding of Melville and so profoundly influenced the form the book has taken, that an account of this had seemed to me not only a natural but necessary conclusion. This is to be found in Chapter VII. (3)

This was the plan. What actually happened was a little different. The first edition, privately published in 1953, did not sell well; of the 20,000 copies printed, all but 2,000 were returned to the author. That same year, negotiating with his British publisher, Frederick Warburg, James seemed already reconciled to the excision of Chapter VII, the very chapter he had previously taken pride in. Writing to a friend, "S," on August 12, 1953, he said he was hoping to "publish in England an edition of MRC, cutting out VII and rewriting VI to make it an embodiment of the ideas in the Leyda letter."[4] Chapter VII was indeed left out of the 1978 Bewick edition and the 1985 Allison and Busby edition. It was not until 2001, when Donald Pease brought out a new edition from the University Press of New England, that the chapter was restored, and the book finally took the form that James had first envisioned.

What to make of this less-than-reassuring publication history? As a thought experiment, I would like to side momentarily with skeptical editors and readers, seeing Chapter VII as they did: as extraneous, unwarranted, and unduly biased by the actions of the US Immigration and Naturalization Services. In what sense is James's six-month sojourn on Ellis Island a sequel to Melville's novel? Is it up to him to decide this is a "natural and necessary conclusion" for a work imagined by its nineteenth-century author to be already complete? How much after-the-fact input can a text accept, and how far can it be bent to accommodate new circumstances of reading? Can we go so far as to say that it is *shareable*, a form of work divided between authors and readers, a form of work done at multiple sites and at multiple points in time, with Ellis Island joining Pittsfield, Massachusetts, as scenes of production?

Interminable Work

I put the question this way – in terms of work, and a sense of it as ongoing and unending – because this is what James himself seems to have in mind. The title of his book, "Mariners, renegades, & castaways," is taken from *Moby-Dick* in the context of work, the habitual state of "the arm that wields a pick or drives a spike":

> If then, to meanest mariners, and renegades and castaways, I shall hereafter ascribe high qualities, though dark; weave among them tragic graces; if even the most mournful, perchance the most abased, among them all, shall at times lift himself to the exalted mounts; if I shall touch that workman's arm with some ethereal light; if I shall spread a rainbow over his disastrous set of sun; then against all mortal critics bear me out in it, thou just spirit of Equality, which has spread one royal mantle of humanity over all my kind.[5]

In one sense, these are stirring words, a stirring tribute to the lowly worker, lifting him up, claiming for him the "high qualities" traditionally reserved for the well-born. In Melville's formulation, though, these high qualities also happen to be dark, woven with tragic graces. The ethereal light shining upon the workman's arm also happens to be coming from a disastrous set of sun.

The workingman in Melville is deliberately elevated only to be brought low, hit by a catastrophe guaranteed to happen. James not only calls attention to this (one of his chapters is titled "Catastrophe"); he insists on coming back to it, giving it renewed attention, the benefit of a second look. It is important to do this, since *Moby-Dick* is not the same book the second time around. What we see "at first sight," he says, is indeed tragedy on a grand scale: "an industrial civilization on fire and plunging blindly into darkness … the world of massed bombers, of cities in flames, of Hiroshima and Nagasaki" (45). But this is not the only the novel *Moby-Dick* could be, not the only future it has to offer. It is worth taking another look, because "when you look again, you see that the crew is indestructible. There they are, laughing at the terrible things that have happened to them. The three harpooners are doing their work" (45).

Doing their work. For James, there is a world of significance in that phrase, in the form of the present participle, an action begun in the present and carried on into the future. It is this verb tense and its work-based form of continuity that give him the idea that the apparently finished *Moby-Dick* is actually less finished than we think. Far from being a closed chapter, it is still a work-in-progress. It can be reassembled, recombined, taken in entirely new directions. Melville's novel can be any number of things, many of these not emerging for many years to come. It not only accepts input from readers; it needs that input, readers who will revisit it, retrofitting it for contexts it could not have known about. *Moby-Dick*, according to James, is entirely *updatable*. It never stops changing along with the changing world; the feedback loop into it is never closed. It is this in-progress ontology of the text that gives his theory of work the centrality that it enjoys, the sense of primacy, efficacy, and necessity. If texts are always left in a state of incompletion, there is always more work, a lot more work, for everyone to do.

Work, in short, is both the baseline condition of the crew on the *Pequod* and the baseline condition that allows a succession of readers to have continued input into it, a text that is, mistakenly, imagined to be authored by just one person. For James, these two baseline conditions are one and the same: one implies the other and necessitates the other. The cross-mapping between these two suggests that there is no end to work, there being always a need for it. It suggests as well that what there is a need for is in fact its lowest common denominator, the least specialized, least glamorous part of it, what can be crowdsourced without difficulty and over and over again. Low-grade repeatability is its lifeline to the future, what guarantees its usefulness across time. And so, when it comes to work on the *Pequod,* we should not be surprised that there is no attempt on his part to play up the nobility of the crew, to turn them into superworkers, superheroes. On the contrary, what is key here is just how ordinary these people are, lacking in distinction, lacking even anything that might make them noteworthy victims: "[T]hey are not suffering workers, not revolutionary workers, nor people who must be organized ... What matters to them primarily, as it does to all workers, and in fact to all people, is the work they do everyday, so many hours a day, nearly every day in the year" (22).

This description of work might seem less than thrilling, a regimen mindlessly routine. But for James the routineness is the point. Dwelling on it, he also registers a significant departure from Melville, an implied critique, as well as an alternative ending to *Moby-Dick* itself. In Melville, work is simply the background, the preexisting condition of those to whom something very bad eventually happens. As the background, it is not the main event, not a force actively shaping the ensuing drama. It has no power to determine the outcome, to avert disasters, to go forward into the future. It is static and non-evolving: the background, and never more than the background. Work, in James's updated version of the novel, has an entirely different status. Not just a given, it is a future-producing agency. The persistence of work, the continued need for it, suggests that workers have a durable place in the world, so interminable as to be seemingly "indestructible."

Switching Genres

But is it indeed true that interminable work can give workers a claim to the future? Can this background condition become the main show? And can it function as the equivalent of a present participle, which, even if it does not absolutely shield the workers from harm, can nonetheless give them an in-progress robustness conjecturally but not implausibly suggested by the verb form itself?

What James has done, it seems, is to have turned *Moby-Dick* around, undoing its severity, undoing its closure, and, in doing so, also switching the novel from its more obvious genre to one less obvious, one that takes a second look to detect. From being tragedy on a grand scale, it has been revealed to be something less grand, but perhaps also less tragic. It does not quite become comedy, even though James seems to want to give it a push in that direction, going so far as to say that "almost every sentence" of the novel "can be the subject of a comic strip" (21). He points to this passage from Chapter 60 about the all-ensnaring coils of the whale-line, and the habit of mind that sailors develop as a result: "Yet habit – strange thing! What cannot habit accomplish? – Gayer sallies, more merry mirth, better jokes, and brighter repartees, you never heard over your mahogany, than you will hear over the half-inch white cedar of the whale-boat, when thus hung in hangman's nooses."[6] For most readers, this might not seem a pivotal moment. For James, it is absolutely crucial, so crucial that it needs to be read more than once:

> Melville is so gay that at a first reading you can easily miss the significance of those last sentences for the world we live in. But re-read them. The humor and the wit of the mariners, renegades and castaways are beyond the cultivated inter-changes of those who sit around mahogany tables. They have to be. Hangman's nooses hang loose around the necks of countless millions today, and for them their unfailing humor is an assertion of life and sanity against the ever present threat of destruction and a world in chaos. (25)

In James's "second look" version – no longer pure tragedy – the humor and the wit count as much as the nooses around the necks. The former does not completely negate the latter; what it does, though, is make the ending less certain, turning it from being the last word to something considerably less, and, in being less, in not quite achieving the finality that tragedy calls for, also getting out from under it, taking tentative steps toward its antithesis.

This genre switching, this weakening dependency on one and half-accomplished migration into another, seems to rest on three things: first, the below-the-threshold potentiality of a text; second, the presence of readers also with this below-the-threshold potentiality; and finally, the crowdsourcing they participate in. This is the spin that James puts on what Ahab calls the "little lower layer." For him, the little lower layer has to do, above all, with those mariners, renegades, and castaways who make up the background of the novel; it has to do with their work routine; and, when it does manifest itself, it takes the form of a humor that cuts across and cuts into the generic conventions of tragedy. But James is not entirely clear – at least not yet – about why that might be the case. All he says is this:

> They are a world-federation of modern industrial workers. They owe allegiance to no nationality. There are Americans among them, but it is the officers who are American. Among the crew nobody is anything. They owe no allegiance to anybody or anything except the work they have to do and the relations with one another on which that work depends. (20)

James's "world-federation" seems to exist so far only as negatives: the workers are non-Americans; they are nobodies; they owe no allegiance to any nation. Together, however, they do add up to something, though what that is remains wishful, ill-defined. It is only from hindsight, with additional input from historians themselves inspired by James, that we can begin to see what this term might entail.

Peter Linebaugh and Marcus Rediker, in their classic study, *The Many-Headed Hydra: Sailors, Slaves, Commoners, and the Hidden History of the Revolutionary Atlantic* (2000), have raised the possibility of just such a seaborne "world-federation," made up of "variously designated dispossessed commoners, transported felons, indentured servants, religious radicals, pirates, urban laborers, soldiers, sailors, and African slaves," united by their low opinion of high authorities, and, when they saw fit, breaking out into strikes and mutinies that often took their superiors by surprise. Linebaugh and Rediker compare these insurrections to the "long waves" of the Atlantic, which, finally hitting the shore as breakers, might seem to be from nowhere, when in fact they have been a long time coming. The strength of these waves depend on "the length of its fetch, or the distance from its point of origin. The longer the fetch, the greater the wave."[7] The hard-to-detect currents of the Atlantic need significant distances to make themselves felt. Likewise, their human equivalents, what Linebaugh and Rediker call the "planetary currents" of the world's migrant labor, also needed significant distances to do the same. Ocean voyages lasting for years gave their dormant capabilities a chance to form "new and unexpected connections," so unexpected that, to the casual observer, they must seem "accidental, contingent, transient, even miraculous."

This is the second time we are hearing that word and its cognate: "miracle," "miraculous." Tracing a developmental arc from James to Linebaugh and Rediker, it speaks to a felt need on the part of all three to name a phenomenon not yet fully understood, but empirically observable, when hitherto unpromising players suddenly prove themselves capable of feats no one would have suspected. "Miracle" is a shorthand for this, for all those moments when a marginal group suddenly exposes a gap in the dominant explanatory theory, turning its hitherto dismissible marginality into a force to reckon with. James has always been interested in minor miracles of this sort, carrying no divine sanction, but the stuff history is made of.

The Black Jacobins

His earlier book, the by-now classic *The Black Jacobins* (1938), has been about just such an unlikely switch. The slave population of San Domingo, hitherto "trembling in hundreds before a single white man," suddenly and inexplicably turned into fierce fighters, successfully waging a twelve-year guerrilla war, defeating "the local whites and the soldiers of the French monarchy, a Spanish invasion, a British expedition of some 60,000 men, and a French expedition of similar size under Bonaparte's brother-in-law."[8] This was the only slave revolt that led to the founding of a state, the Republic of Haiti. And strangest of all was the transatlantic network this marginal group was able to forge, winning the support of the Jacobins in the midst of the French Revolution. James's chapter titles speak for themselves: Chapter 4, "The San Domingo Masses Begin," followed by Chapter 5, "And the Paris Masses Complete." He writes: "from indifference in 1789," the French insurgents had by 1792 come to "detest no section of the aristocracy so much as those whom they called 'the aristocrats of the skin' ... Henceforth the Paris masses were for abolition, and their black brothers in San Domingo, for the first time, had passionate allies in France."[9] All in all, "revolution moves in a mysterious way its wonders to perform."[10]

James himself is no stranger to such wonders; indeed, the very existence of *The Black Jacobins* is a testimony of sorts. The book was published in London in 1938, but the idea had been germinating in his head even before

he left Trinidad in 1932. Long impatient with books detailing only the subjugation of slaves, he looked to books from France with a different perspective as soon as he arrived in London, discussing these every day with his
friend, Harry Spencer, at the teashop. Spencer urged him to write a book of
his own:

> I told him that I had to go to France to the archives, I didn't have the money
> as yet but I was saving. He asked me how much money I would need and
> I told him about a hundred pounds to start with. He left it there but a few
> days afterwards put ninety pounds in my hands and said, "Onto France, and if
> you need more, let me know." As soon as the summer season was over (I was
> a cricket reporter), off I went and spent six months in France covering ground
> at a tremendous rate.[11]

Who would have thought that a colonial from Trinidad, born to a lower-
middle-class family, going to England only because of his friendship with
a cricket player, the future Lord Constantine, would be capable of a book
like this? And who would have thought that the research would be financed
by an English shopkeeper? In its provenance no less than its argument, *The
Black Jacobins* points to private affect as miracle-working, a key ingredi-
ent in James's social and political life, and a much-needed ally in his life-
long battle with Stalinism ("Night after night he would address meetings
in London and the provinces, denouncing the crimes of the blood-thirsty
Stalin, until he was hoarse," Frederick Warburg reported[12]). Against the
iron-fisted apparatus of the Communist Party and its claim to being the
"vanguard" of the revolution,[13] private affect is an admittedly low-level, but
all the same undeniable reality for many, to be honored precisely because
it is pre-institutional, not rising to articulate thought, not in line with the
party apparatus, and an alternative template for participatory democracy
for just that reason.

Low-Level Affect

Raymond Williams would later refer to this low-level affect as a "structure
of feeling," not quite a philosophy or worldview, but simply a "practical
consciousness of a present kind, in a living and interrelating continuity."
Practical consciousness of this sort, Williams goes on to say, "cannot without loss be reduced to belief-systems, institutions, or explicit general relationships, though it may include all these as lived and experienced, with or
without tension."[14] It is this practical consciousness that James associates
with the resilience of those who work every day, not so much as organized
labor, as he is careful to emphasize, but simply as people thrown together

by economic necessity, and dependent on one other out of that necessity. Just that, he says, is enough to create a bond, a pool of knowledge and a principle of connectivity, giving everyone a modest but functional purchase on the world.

In *Beyond a Boundary* (1963), James famously begins with the question: "What does he know of cricket who only cricket knows?"[15] A parallel question could be asked in *Mariners, Renegades & Castaways*: "What does he know of work who only work knows?" The answer, in both cases, is "enough." Cricket, James says in *Beyond a Boundary*, has taught him to "fight the good fight with all my might. I was in the toils of greater forces than I knew. Cricket had plunged me into politics long before I was aware of it. When I did turn to politics I did not have too much to learn."[16] His epistemology is not one positing a sharp break between experience and knowledge, with the former inadequate and inferior to the latter. On the contrary, it is experience, especially when it resides in the work routine, that instils in each worker an intuition and a competence that allow them to navigate the world. In an essay entitled "Every Cook Can Govern," James notes that in ancient Greece, the work of government was rotated among all its citizens, randomly picked each time by sortition, or lottery. Greek democracy was founded on an "extraordinary confidence" in the "ability of the ordinary person, the grocer, the candlestick-maker, the carpenter, the sailor, the tailor," trusting that each, when "chosen by lot" to govern collaboratively, would be able to do so.[17] The same confidence should be placed on sailors who know their ships, the oceans, and seaborne planet. These people are "federated by nothing. But they are looking for federation."[18] They will always be here, with a work-based claim to the future.

This is what Melville has overlooked. In taking work to be an inert background, he has granted it no dynamic relation to time. That dynamic relation creates consequential actors out of those we would otherwise imagine to be without agency. Melville is wrong then, not to take these people more seriously and not to give serious consideration to the question: "Why doesn't the crew revolt?" Clearly, there is another story to be told. And here is where Ellis Island comes in, for James's own experience here, mingling with those who come through it – the twentieth-century descendants of Melville's mariners, renegades, castaways – has given him just what he needs to add another chapter to *Moby-Dick*, bringing its background population into relief, giving them an evolving script not possible within the existing narrative. Not everyone could agree, of course.[19] But at least one reader of Melville would.

Indian Ocean English

Amitav Ghosh's connection to Melville, like James's, is very much a side development, and, in his case, with a switchability still more pronounced, a degree of equivocation or even downright self-contradiction intriguing to behold. On the one hand he is on record as saying that, of all nineteenth-century authors he is indebted to "Melville most of all," that *Moby-Dick* is "inexhaustible in its inspiration." In a November 19, 2008 interview with Christopher Lydon on Radio Open Source, a WBUR talk show, Ghosh said he would "love to recapture the cosmopolitan vision" of "Obama's true precursor." He went on:

> One of the most wonderful things about Melville is that he was just about the only one of the nineteenth century nautical writers who paid enough attention to the world of the sea to write about Indian sailors ... It is so rare actually to find a believable representation of an Asian ... You remember, in *Moby Dick*, the 40th chapter, all of the sailors sing in different languages, and then suddenly you discover that this ship, which is a Nantucket whaling ship, actually has forty different nationalities on board, including Indians.[20]

A very different picture emerged, however, in an essay published just a few months earlier, in the Mumbai-based *Economic and Political Weekly*. That essay, entitled "Of Fanas and Forecastles: The Indian Ocean and some Lost Languages of the Age of Sail," looks at nineteenth-century literature only in passing, its overwhelming focus being on the "indigenous sailors from the Indian Ocean areas – Arabs, Chinese, East Africans, Filipinos, Malays, and South Asians," collectively known as the "lascars." "This truly diverse group gave the world, in the eighteenth and nineteenth centuries, the Laskari language," drawn from "the English, Malay, Hindustani, Chinese, Malayalam and the entire Babel of languages spoken on board."[21] How this mongrel tongue fares in Melville's hands is indicative of the *failure* of western authors to come to grips with this astonishing linguistic form. Turning to the very same *Moby-Dick* chapter, Chapter 40, he would later single out for praise on the WBUR show, Ghosh here observes that, among the polyglot crew on the *Pequod*, "There is of course a token lascar, whose contribution to the merriment consists of: 'By Brahma! Boys, it will be douse sail soon. The sky-born, high-tide Ganges turned to wind! Thou showest thy black brow Seeva!' "[22]

Melville is not even trying and failing here; there is simply no attempt on his part to sound the least bit like actual Laskari. This less-than-inspiring performance makes *Moby-Dick* not so much a precedent-setting forerunner as an especially dismal example of inadequate writing. Ghosh's commitment to Indian Ocean languages, like C. L. R. James's commitment to work, thrives on its weak connection to this novel, though, in his case, also dependent on the latter as a negatively inspiring template. The *Ibis* trilogy that results, beginning with *Sea of Poppies* (2008), followed by *River of Smoke* (2011), and ending with *Flood of Fire* (2015), retraces *Moby-Dick*'s voyage, crossing the same three oceans – the Atlantic, the Indian Ocean, the South China Sea – but offering passage to a very different kind of linguistic freight, and stopping at places the *Pequod* never visited.

Ghosh gives us, in fact, not a single Laskari language, spoken by the entire floating population from one end of the Indian Ocean to the other, but at least four variants, showcased at different stages in the trilogy. *Sea of Poppies* gives us Laskari perhaps in its purest form (if this is not a contradiction in terms), spoken by the crew's leader, Serang Ali. Here, under the guise of translating for Jodu, another Lascar sailor, Ali freely offers marital advice of his own about Paulette Lambert, daughter of a deceased botanist now eating "big-big rice" in the household of Benjamin Burnham, shipowner and opium trader:

> "Launder say father-blongi-she go hebbin. That bugger do too muchi tree-pijjin. Allo time pickin plant. Inside pocket hab no cash. After he go hebbin cow-chilo catchi number-two-father, Mr. Burnham. Now she too much muchi happy inside. Eat big-big rice. Better Malum Zikri forgetting she. How can learn sailor-pijjin, allo time thinking ladies-ladies? More better keep busy with laund'ry till marriage time."
>
> The malum took unexpected umbrage at this. "Hell and scissors, Serang Ali!" he cried, springing to his feet, "Don you never think of nothin but knob-knockin and gamahoochie?"[23]

While one would expect Ali to talk the way he does, Zachary, the second mate (known to the sailors as "Malum Zikri"), born and raised in Maryland, seems to be learning fast as well, developing a version of Indian Ocean English all his own – oddly, with African American syntax and phonetics mixed in. Ghosh is not primarily interested in native tongues, what people start out with. It is the subsequent switches, the imperfect crossovers into new languages, that preoccupy him, a spectrum of variation changing with the scenes of action successively encountered. *River of Smoke*, the second in the trilogy, opens with a "mixture of Bhojpuri and Kreol" (as we are told upfront) spoken by Deeti, Ghazipur native now living on the island of Mauritius: "Revey-te! È Banwari, è Mukhpyari! Revey-té na! Haglé ba?" But this creolized form quickly gives way to yet another, this time the pidgin English spoken around Canton, especially in Fanqui-town, the foreign enclave with the thirteen factories. Bahram Modi, leader of the Parsi merchants from Bombay, and Chi-mei, the Chinese woman he would end up having an extended liaison with, seem to be having fun conversing in this language:

> When she tried to pull off his sacred waist-strings he whispered: "This piece thread blongi joss-pidgin thing. No can take off."
>   She uttered a yelp of a laugh. "What Joss-pidgin thread also have got?"
>   "Have. Have."
>   "White Hat Devil have too muchi big cloth."
>   "White Hat Devil have nother-piece thingi too muchi big."[24]

Pidgin English is not a debased form of English in the *Ibis* trilogy. It is a language unto itself, with a working grammar and a colorfully improvised vocabulary used to good effect by the two speakers. It is a lingua franca as no pure language can be.

In fact, it is the disappearance of this shared tongue, in *Flood of Fire*, that signals the end of an era. This last volume of the trilogy, featuring the run-up to the First Opium War followed by the outbreak of hostilities, and dominated throughout by the rigid hierarchy among the sepoy ranks making up the bulk of the British forces, seems a backlash against the two precursors. Kesri Singh, a sepoy in the Bengal Native Infantry, defends his sister Deeti in Hindustani, in complete sentences, strictly unadulterated: "*Aur ham tohra se achha se jaana taani!* And I know her better than you!" And his superior, Subedar NirdhaySingh, responds in kind: "*Abh hamra aankhi se dur ho ja!* Now get out of my sight, Kesri Singh! I never want to set eyes on you again."[25] The required translation speaks for itself. Pure Hindustani is purely incomprehensible to anyone not knowing the language. Mongrel English, on the other hand, though initially a challenge, is accessible by all and hospitable to all, a means of communication crucial to the health and vitality of this polyglot world. There is no better accompaniment to the First Opium War than the silencing of this tongue.

Watered-Down Tragedy

The stage is set for a purely tragic ending, and yet this is just what Ghosh seems to have avoided. In an inspired resequencing of the tragic form, the catastrophe in *Flood of Fire* is not bunched together at the end, but spread out across almost the entire second half of the book, with mass casualties among Chinese civilians, of course, and two discreetly reported though no less hallowing deaths among its main characters. But when the novel actually comes to an end, it is on a very different note. This mindboggling switch would probably not please everyone, but before it closes, *Flood of*

Fire circles all the way back to the opening pages of *River of Smoke*, to the gathering of La Fami Colver, picking up on Deeti's point-by-point explication of the painting in her shrine, known as "The Escape," and delivered as usual in her signature mixture of Bhojpuri and Kreol:

> "Ekut. Ekut!" Deeti would cry, and that great horde of bonoys, belsers, bowjis, salas, sakubays and other relatives would follow her finger as she traced the path of Jodu's sampan as it edged across the bay, from the Kowloon side, to draw up beside the *Ibis*, which was all but empty …
>
> There vwala!
>
> Her finger would come to rest on Serang Ali: You see him, this gran-koko with a head teeming with mulugandes? This is the great burrhuriya who had once again thought up the plan for their escape.[26]

The *Ibis* is the means of escape for Jodu, and for Maddow Colver, formerly Kalua, driver of an oxcart in Ghazipur, now a gun-lascar for the East India Company, but destined to become patriarch of the very La Fami Colver now assembled. This ship is not sucked into a vortex, like the *Pequod*. Ghosh's only concession to Melville is by way of another ship, the *Anahita,* which, thanks to the 3,000 chests of opium it is carrying, has been much more in the spotlight. A little before the end of *Flood of Fire* this ship meets its end in a manner distinctly reminiscent of *Moby-Dick*. The *Pequod* has gone under spinning in an ever-contracting orbit: "And now, concentric circles seized the lone boat itself, and all its crew, and each floating oar, and every lance-pole, and spinning, animate and inanimate, all round and round in one vortex, carried the smallest chip of the *Pequod* out of sight."[27] The *Anahita* also spins around and around in that way, but with a crucial difference: "Then with gathering speed, the *Anahita* began to spin as the water dragged her under. A whirlpool took shape around the stricken ship, and as she was vanishing into it, the spinning whorls seemed to race towards the longboat. But then a wave took hold of the boat and carried it away, pushing it towards East Point."[28] Unlike the all-engulfing vortex in *Moby-Dick*, this one destroys the ship but not the crew. The destructive agent here, after all, is not a super-intelligent sperm whale but a regular typhoon. This is not a tale of vengeance in which all perish, but one in which a wave happens to come along to give everyone a lucky break.

The *Ibis,* meanwhile, is undamaged. As it is spirited away from Hong Kong, it is manned by a crew of six, representing both sides of the Opium War, including Serang Ali and Jodu fighting on the Chinese side and Kesri and Maddow Colver on the side of the British. The pivotal role of Serang Ali is telling, though probably to no one's surprise. For though he has appeared savage-looking at first glance, with a "mouth that was constantly in motion, its edges stained a bright, livid red: it was as if he were forever smacking his lips after drinking from the open veins of a mare, like some bloodthirsty Tartar of the steppes,"[29] a second look reveals that the mouth in question is stained with no more than betel juice. Looking initially like one of Fedallah's "tiger-yellow" crew in *Moby-Dick*, Ali proves to be the comic heart of the *Ibis* trilogy, afloat in an ocean utterly beyond his control, but surviving, at least for the time being, with skill, effort, and luck. Gone now are the high drama and concentrated furor of Ahab's monomania. What Ghosh offers instead is watered-down tragedy, as broad-based and mixed-up as the Indian Ocean English that inhabits it. C. L. R. James would have been elated.

NOTES

1 Pascale Casanova, *The World Republic of Letters* (Cambridge, MA: Harvard University Press, 2007).
2 Gilles Deleuze and Felix Guattari, *A Thousand Plateaus*, trans. Brian Massumi (Minneapolis: University of Minnesota Press, 1987); Bruno Latour, *Reassembling the Social: An Introduction to Actor-Network Theory* (New York: Oxford University Press, 2005); Lee Rainie and Barry Wellman, *Networked: The New Social Operating System* (Cambridge, MA: MIT Press, 2012).
3 C. L. R. James, *Mariners, Renegades & Castaways: The Story of Herman Melville and the World We Live In*, ed. Donald E. Pease (Dartmouth, NH: University Press of New England, 2001), 3. All other page citations to this edition appear in parenthesis in the text.
4 Frank Rosengarten, *Urbane Revolutionary: C. L. R. James and the Struggle for a New Society* (Jackson: University of Mississippi Press, 2008), 193. The "Leyda" in the "Leyda letter" was Jay Leyda, author of the *Melville Log*, with whom James was corresponding.
5 Herman Melville, *Moby-Dick*, Hershel Parker and Harrison Hayford, eds. (New York: Norton, 1967), 104.
6 Ibid. 240.
7 Peter Linebaugh and Marcus Rediker, *The Many-Headed Hydra: Sailors, Slaves, Commoners, and the Hidden History of the Revolutionary Atlantic* (Boston: Beacon Press, 2000), 1.
8 C. L. R. James, *The Black Jacobins: Troussaint L'Overture and the San Domingo Revolution* (Harmondsworth: Penguin, 2001 [1938]), xviii. For a helpful historical overview, see Robin Blackburn, "*The Black Jacobins* and New World Slavery," in *C. L. R. James: His Intellectual Legacies*, Selwyn Cudjoe and William Cain, eds. (Amherst: University of Massachusetts Press, 1995), 81–97.
9 James, *The Black Jacobins*, 98.
10 Ibid., xvi–xvii.
11 Ibid., xv.
12 Kent Worcester, *C. L. R. James: A Political Biography* (Albany: State University of New York Press, 1996), 48.
13 These arguments were developed in detail in two books James coauthored with Grace Lee and Raya Dunayeskaya: *Notes on Dialectics,* privately circulated in

1948, published in 1980; and *State Capitalism and World Revolution*, prepared for the World Congress of the Fourth International in 1951.

14 Raymond Williams, *The Country and the City* (London: Chatto and Windus, 1973), 132.

15 C. L. R. James, *Beyond a Boundary* (London: Hutchinson, 1963), 50.

16 Ibid., 71. For the centrality of cricket to James's thinking, see Sylvia Winter, "Beyond the Categories of the Master Conception: the Counterdoctrine of the Jamesian poiesis," and Neil Lazarus, "Cricket and National Culture in the Writings of C. L. R. James," both in *C. L. R. James's Caribbean*, Paget Henry and Paul Buhle, eds. (Durham, NC: Duke University Press, 1992), 63–91, 92–110; Sylvia Winter, "In Search of Matthew Bondman: Some Cultural Notes on the Jamesian Journey," in *C. L. R. James: His Life and Work*, ed. Paul Buhle (London: Allison and Busby, 1986), 131–45; Grant Farred, "The Maple Man: How Cricket Made a Postcolonial Intellectual," in *Rethinking C. L. R. James*, ed. Grant Farred (Cambridge: Blackwell, 1996), 165–86; Christopher Gair, "Beyond Boundaries: Cricket, Herman Melville, and C. L. R. James's Cold War," in *Beyond Boundaries: C. L. R. James and Postnational Studies*, ed. Christopher Gair (Ann Arbor, MI: Pluto Press, 2006), 89–107.

17 C. L. R. James, "Every Cook Can Govern: A Study of Democracy in Ancient Greece," in *The Future in the Present* (London: Allison & Busby, 1977), 160–74, quotation from 163.

18 C. L. R. James, *Mariners, Renegades, & Castaways,* 154.

19 For three critical accounts of *Mariners, Renegades & Castaways* from three different perspectives – focusing on Ahab, Ishmael, and the crew respectively – see Cedric Robinson, "C. L. R. James and the World-System," and William Cain, "The Triumph of the Will and the Failure of Resistance: C. L. R. James's reading of *Moby-Dick* and *Othello*," both in *C. L. R. James: His Intellectual Legacies*, 244–59, 260–76; and Donald Pease, "Doing Justice to C. L. R. James's *Mariners, Renegades & Castaways*," *boundary 2* (2000): 1–19.

20 In an interview with Christopher Lydon, Ghosh says that he would "love to capture the cosmopolitan spirit" of Melville, the "true percursor to Barack Obama." Interview available at <http://radioopensource.org/amitav-ghosh-and-his-sea-of-poppies/>.

21 Amitav Ghosh, "Of Fanas and Forecastles: The Indian Ocean and Some Lost Languages of the Age of Sail," *Economic and Political Weekly* (June 21–27, 2008), 56–62, quotation from 56.

22 Ibid.

23 Amitav Ghosh, *Sea of Poppies* (New York: Farrar, Straus and Giroux, 2008), 186–87.

24 Amitav Ghosh, *River of Smoke* (New York: Farrar, Straus and Giroux, 2011), 67–68.

25 Amitav Ghosh, *Flood of Fire* (London: John Murray, 2015), 173, 174.

26 Ibid., 607.

27 Melville, *Moby-Dick*, 469.

28 Ghosh, *Flood of Fire*, 586.

29 Ghosh, *Sea of Poppies*, 14.

3

YOGITA GOYAL

The Transnational Turn and Postcolonial Studies

"We are not the villains of our own stories."
Teju Cole, *Open City*

"The field of American studies was conceived on the banks of the Congo" –
so begins Amy Kaplan in her foundational essay on the cultures of US
imperialism, tracking Perry Miller's epiphany in "the jungle of central
Africa" about his discovery of America.[1] For Miller, seeking the "adventure" that World War I had offered his predecessors, "the adventures that
Africa afforded were tawdry enough, but it became the setting for a sudden epiphany of the pressing necessity for expounding [his] America to
the twentieth century."[2] As Chinua Achebe has shown, Africa as the setting for the exploration of the Western mind has a long colonial history,
and Miller seems to be checking off every box in the colonial rulebook as
he supervises the unloading of drums of oil in "that barbaric tropic" and
becomes aware not just of his own "republic's appalling power" but its
"uniqueness" as the "future of the world."[3] Miller in the Congo has generated numerous interpretive scenes of distance and intimacy, of American
innocence and empire, and of the uses of Africa as the ground for white
male redemption. At its most elemental, as a founding scene of imperial longings (where an "errand into the wilderness" produces American
identity), such a tableau should point the way toward a clear intersection
of the study of transnational American literature and the field of postcolonial studies. For Matthew Frye Jacobson, for instance, the connection is so obvious that he quips that he "once thought to write a history
of US empire, but soon discovered that empire *is* US history."[4] Certainly,
both historical explorations (manifest destiny and the frontier, territorial
expansion and genocide, slavery, segregation, and Jim Crow) and analyses
of contemporary formations (settler colonialism, new regimes of security
and surveillance, war and incarceration) should all offer promising points
of entry into such a discussion.

And yet, connecting the United States to the postcolony has been a fraught enterprise, at best. Although Kaplan's observation in 1993 about the mutual invisibility of the two fields – "the absence of empire from the study of American culture, and the absence of the United States from the postcolonial study of imperialism" – no longer holds true, there continues to be resistance to this intersection, as well as confusion about what it might entail.[5] To be sure, over the last three decades, the study of such unincorporated territories as Hawaii, Puerto Rico, and Guam has flourished, as have new explorations of militarism and surveillance, war and occupation, and slavery and genocide. But a dialogue with postcolonial critique, a clear articulation of the relation of the United States to European empires of the past, or a public accounting of the neocolonial power of the United States, has remained elusive. In part this might be a result of the nature of American empire: its very condition of existence is to insist that "there is no American Empire."[6] Even Michael Hardt and Antonio Negri seem to participate in this disavowal when they claim that what distinguishes empire in the current moment is that "our postmodern Empire has no Rome" – in other words, there is no center to the new empire, as "imperial power is distributed in networks, through mobile and articulated mechanisms of control."[7] But surely the conjunction of expansion, imperialism, intervention, counterrevolution, and aerial bombing with the suffusion of neoliberal policies makes the United States not just the new Rome – a hegemon and superpower for the post–Cold War era – but an empire par excellence that must be seen as part of the same story of industrial revolution, mercantile capital, slavery, colonialism, and neocolonialism. If the transnational turn is to prove to be something other than another variant on US exceptionalism, not only must the intersection of the United States and the postcolonial be more thoughtfully examined, but the question of what distinguishes the US empire from other imperial regimes must also be answered.

In part, the challenge here is to define the scope of postcolonial inquiry. On the one hand, by definition, postcolonialism offers an expansive frame and seems to allow for, even to invite comparisons, suggesting that something still links the places that were once colonized. On the other, many have sought to thwart such comparisons in recent years in favor of the singularity of a local, national, or regional space of cultural production. While it was once common to find references to "the postcolonial condition," "the postcolonial woman," or "the postcolonial other," such ahistorical abstractions have become rarer. The tendency in the field is toward the local, toward historical specificity, and in favor of particular instantiations that may stand as a rebuke to a generalized worldliness or globalism. We may point to Fredric Jameson as the best example of the tendency to generalize, when he claimed that all Third World literature should be read as a national allegory, and consider Dipesh Chakrabarty's advocacy of "provincializing" as a critical goal as the marker of withdrawal from universalizing claims about a singular postcolonial paradigm.[8] Given this shift, assimilating US literature into the ambit of the postcolonial continues to seem suspect, and if Americanists have resisted postcolonial work, postcolonial critics have also questioned the inclusion of the United States within their purview, fearing absorption into a more hegemonic framework.

Moreover, any academic field requires parameters of some sort. To say, for instance, that postcolonialism encompasses "all the culture affected by the imperial process from the moment of colonization to the present day" is to presumably exclude nothing since (at least) 1492.[9] Similarly, to view the United States as the original postcolony, and early American writers as postcolonial, risks erasing necessary distinctions of hierarchy and hegemony.[10] The differential status of the nation in the two spaces makes comparison difficult, as fulfilling the nationalist project of decolonization continues to hold meaning in many former colonies. This is why, most often, the analogy is not between the United States and the postcolony as a whole, but rather between minority or ethnic US writers and postcolonial writers. That is to say, rather than comparing Herman Melville, Ernest Hemingway, or Cormac McCarthy to postcolonial writers, it is far more common to see connections drawn to Zora Neale Hurston, Maxine Hong Kingston, or Toni Morrison. Reading Morrison alongside Salman Rushdie or J.M. Coetzee in fact requires little preface, and it is routine to see such connections.[11] Homi Bhabha aligns *Beloved* with the "transnational histories of migrants, the colonized, or political refugees," and Wai Chee Dimock draws maps of comparison across the United States, the Caribbean, and further afield via deep time and creole English.[12] Similarly, such influential analytics as minor transnationalisms or the Global South or Afro-Asia enable a variety of connections and comparisons.[13]

The Internal Colony Analogy

It is worth recalling though that such seemingly new efforts to theorize the Global South have a prehistory. During the era of decolonization and the ferment of the new social movements of the 1960s, it was common to invoke the framework of internal colonialism to situate the position of minorities within the United States. Any question of the relation between the transnational turn in American literary studies and postcolonial studies must therefore reckon with the question of analogy and its history. How is the United States – a former colony that became an empire of its own – to be thought of next to the former colonies of European empires? Or, as many have argued, should the question take a different form: How might the experiences of racialized minorities in the United States be akin to (though not reducible to) those of colonized populations in Africa, Asia, and the Caribbean?

For W.E.B. Du Bois – perhaps the premier theorist of modern transnationalism – to define "the problem of the twentieth century" as "the problem of the color-line" meant connecting his conception of African American identity, culture, and politics to those of "men in Asia and Africa, in America and the islands of the sea."[14] Constructing a systematic interpretive framework for understanding African American history as a part of a larger worldwide negotiation of race, labor, capitalism, war, and imperialism, Du Bois insisted that African Americans constituted a "nation within a nation" that was connected, though not reducible, to a world proletariat. He also sought to exchange the "spiritual provincialism" of American race politics with the "wider understanding with the brown and yellow peoples of the world."[15] For Du Bois, "the strange meaning of being black" would emerge only when understood as a phase of a larger problem – "the relation of the darker to the lighter races of men" worldwide.[16] This meant understanding that "we American Negroes are the bound colony of the United States just as India is of England."[17] In *Dusk of Dawn*, pondering the resonant question, "What is Africa to me," Du Bois explains that though his answer would once have been "fatherland" or "motherland," over time he came to understand a more complex relation, not quite captured by notions of diasporic racial heritage or ancestral connection. He learned that "the physical bond is least and the badge of color relatively unimportant save as a badge; the real essence of this kinship is its social heritage of slavery; the discrimination and insult; and this heritage binds together not simply the children of Africa, but extends through yellow Asia and into the South Seas."[18]

Such connections are, of course, not unique to Du Bois, and analogies between race and coloniality have been at the center of such key moments of Afro-Asian and black internationalism as the historic Bandung Conference (1955). Robert Blauner's 1969 thesis of African Americans as an internal colony in the United States, Kenneth Clark's notion of Harlem as an internal colony, or Harold Cruse's conception of domestic colonialism all attest to the extent of disaffection from the nation as well as the search for genuine alternatives to political options that seemed to be dead ends at best.[19] The era of Black Power in the 1960s consistently promoted the notion that the struggle for racial justice within the United States was parallel to decolonization in Africa, Asia, and the Caribbean.[20] But while such an analogy may be politically appealing enough to appear as an imperative, historically it has proven impossible to instantiate, as the work of decolonization and that of dismantling Jim Crow does not – could not – follow parallel routes.

In thinking of the relation between American literature and postcolonial studies, how might we recover the political potential of such imagined solidarities without resorting to a discourse of sameness, or reifying the very real differences between them? One possible path is by creating fuller genealogies of decolonization and anticolonial thought as co-emergent, and in contrapuntal dialogue, with antiracist efforts in the United States, though not fungible with them. Such efforts should also prompt new readings of nations and nationalisms, distinguishing among reactive, utopian, and regressive forms rather than presuming an automatic occlusion of feminist and subaltern collectivities in any turn to the nation. A fresh way to approach the twice-told tale of the schism between postcolonial and American studies then is through the global visions offered by the black radical tradition, inspired by figures like Du Bois, relentlessly internationalist, and always looking for solidarities and harmonies across divides of nation, race, and class to prefigure currently influential notions of a Global South.[21]

But often, scholars of ethnic studies worry that, as an academic field, postcolonialism becomes a way to study problems from places far away, relocating the site of struggle between a European colonizing power and the native resistance elsewhere, in another time, thus taking away from the exploration of inequality at home.[22] At the same time, postcolonial scholars worry about the risk of absorbing the postcolonial in the hegemony of the United States, and search for alternative approaches to the intersection.[23] As is well known, even as Edward Said claimed that Western knowledge could not be separated from the colonial project, *Orientalism* (which set the stage for many decades of postcolonial inquiry) omits any discussion of the United States.[24] For Donald Pease, such a refusal to include the United States replicates long-standing notions of US exceptionalism, reaffirming rather than challenging the contradictory notion of "global dominance without colonies."[25]

The sheer number of programmatic essays that seek to explain whether the United States is postcolonial or not is symptomatic of the anxiety around this intersection (and it is important to call it an intersection rather equate the two), particularly of the relation between the ethnic, minority, or racialized populations within and those without. Clearly, there are real difficulties in comparing and reading together cultures that are neither the same nor incommensurably different, neither substitutable nor hermetically sealed off. The persistent instability and proliferation of terms – decolonial, post-national, neoliberal, imperial, global, planetary – is another symptom of such anxiety. All these terms are necessarily ideological – common terms like "Third World," "developing nations," and "Commonwealth" were discontinued for political reasons – and their suggested replacements have at most times seemed to satisfy no one. If, as Kaplan suggests, "American and European imperialism" may be seen as having "divergent yet intertwined histories," it should surely be possible to create better narratives that explain analogy and difference, conquest and resistance, continuity with the past and divergence from it.[26] The growing study of transnationalism and empire in relation to American literature requires comparisons of older and newer forms of empire, a theorization of the relation between racialized minorities in the core and majorities in the periphery, as well as an expansion of postcolonial conceptions of race.

Doing so does not mean renewing analogy as a keyword for the field, or even as a political aspiration. Rather, it means being attentive to the difficulty of internationalism as well as to its texture – aesthetic and political – and to taking on the critical task of patiently narrating a fuller, richer account of the histories that have led us to the present historical conjuncture. In this task, the "freedom dreams" and truly global imagination of a figure like Du Bois articulate the shifting relations among and across Americans and people in Africa, India, Japan, Russia, and China.[27] But it also means paying heed to those voices that questioned the premise of the utopian notion of the coalition of the darker peoples of the world and advocated national or local anchors instead.

For Frantz Fanon, the leading theorist of decolonization, "the problems which kept Richard Wright or Langston Hughes on the alert were fundamentally different from those which might confront Leopold Senghor or Jomo Kenyatta."[28] While Fanon conceded that similar issues of cultural erasure, accusations of inferiority or barbarism, and assaults on the sense of self characterize both sets of experiences, he emphasizes the schisms that became visible in the movement between the first congress of the African Cultural Society held in Paris in 1956 and the second one, where "American Negroes realized that the essential problems confronting them were not the same as those that confronted the African Negroes" and formed a separate American society (216). While race – or blackness – created the conditions of possibility for a shared experience, for Fanon, the "historical character of men" is formed in specific circumstances and cannot be extended across heterogeneous locales. Indeed Fanon ends *The Wretched of the Earth* by differentiating the fate of Europe, the United States, and the post-colony. Fanon urges the decolonized to leave behind the lessons of Europe and to forge a new path, since Europe is characterized by "a succession of negations of man, and an avalanche of murders" (312). Rather, the task for the new nations of the Third World is to bring to fruition the failed Enlightenment project, to start "a new history of Man" (315). What Fanon says about the United States is also instructive. "Two centuries ago," he notes, "a former European colony decided to catch up with Europe. It succeeded so well that the United States of America became a monster, in which the taints, the sickness, and the inhumanity of Europe have grown to appalling dimensions" (313). That Fanon envisages the destiny of the Third World as a refusal to imitate Europe in the manner of the United States suggests that he clearly distinguishes between the United States and the post-colony as possible sites of revolution – the former already a failure and now the oppressor itself, and the latter a potentiality.

In contrast to Du Bois, who establishes the basis for a comparison, Fanon seems to reject it. It is thus difficult to know what his prophecies entail for the African American, and whether he would see the aforementioned Wright or Hughes as a part of the American failure or of postcolonial promise. But perhaps the real story here is the way in which Fanon would become an iconic symbol for Black Power struggles, and how many of the African American thinkers he seems to distance (including Wright, but also Angela Davis and Stokely Carmichael) were profoundly inspired by his thinking on race and revolution, and continued to formulate a notion of a nation within a nation that needs a revolution to be free. Angela Davis, to take one powerful example, draws on Fanon's writings about the Manichean state of the colony and his account of the Algerian war against the French to formulate a radical vision of prison abolition. She insists that Fanon's analysis of the role of the colonial police is an appropriate description of the function of the police in America's ghettos."[29] Accordingly, the "ghetto" in the United States was an "internal colony, a miniature manifestation of colonial dynamics," and the value of the internal colony analogy is not about the accuracy of sociological taxonomies, but about potential paths of resistance. More recently, she continues such efforts, finding "transnational solidarities" by connecting the militarization of the police in places like Ferguson, Missouri, to the "continuous assault on people in occupied Palestine," reminding us that the St. Louis County police chief received "counterterrorism" training in Israel, and calling for an "intersectionality of struggles."[30]

Indeed, one could turn to any number of moments of Black Atlantic history and find it difficult to either erase the distinctions between Africa and the Americas or to reify them. Doing so also requires a careful sifting through of the different meanings of race and nation in the two contexts, as Fanon urges, since even when intellectuals across the Atlantic speak a common language of racial nationalism, it often indicates differential purchase. The variant of prophetic black nationalism known as Ethiopianism, for example, propagated by such diasporic thinkers as Alexander Crummell and Edward Wilmot Blyden, acquired a significantly different political form in the hands of such anticolonial leaders as Kwame Nkrumah and Jomo Kenyatta. Both of these figures once studied in the United States, and were deeply influenced by back-to-Africa notions that fused diaspora and race in a powerful brew, but went on to shape the histories of decolonization by transplanting nationalism into a local context, even as they remained engaged with Pan-African possibilities. Reading such diasporic intellectual traffic through the insights of both African American studies and postcolonial African studies allows us to link race and coloniality together, neither as proxies nor as antagonists, but as twinned, mutually constitutive, overlapping, and contrapuntal histories.[31]

In recent years, the heated language around President Barack Obama's mirroring of American blackness in a global circuit, or the novelist Chimamanda Ngozi Adichie's playful treatment of the split between American and non-American blacks in *Americanah*, testifies to the complex set of identifications and routes of race, nation, and diaspora, suggesting the need for greater suppleness in our critical paradigms.[32] Imagining a transnational American literary studies that neither absorbs the postcolonial nor sidelines it requires asking for more ways to connect and to differentiate, without a contraction of one into the other. To understand this more fully, it is necessary to briefly revisit the twice-told tale of the genealogy of postcolonial studies, and to clarify some necessary distinctions among literature, theory, and method.

The Three Objects of Postcolonial Studies: Literature, Theory, Method

The genealogy of the academic field of postcolonial studies and its relation to such allied terms as global, transnational, hemispheric, or planetary has been described so many times that it would be redundant to do so here. However the story is told – whether as an account of such prominent intellectuals as Edward Said, Gayatri Spivak, and Homi Bhabha, an ideological clash between Marxists and poststructuralists in the 1990s, or a tussle between mid-century anticolonial humanists and late twentieth-century cosmopolitan exiles – the field's intersection with the United States has always proved thorny.[33] I want to suggest that this is because the rubric of postcolonial names at least three different objects at once in the US academy: a body of literature, a set of theories, and a method of inquiry. Each of these offers variable possibilities for the study of transnational American literature at this particular historical conjuncture. I remain committed to delimiting the body of literature claimed by the rubric "postcolonial" rather than absorbing it in such categories as global Anglophone or world literature. Postcolonial theory, I suggest, no longer operates as a clear referent for innovative work in the field. And finally, it is as method that postcolonial studies appears in clearest relation to US literary studies, as predecessor, guide, and companion.

As a body of Anglophone literature, postcolonial most often names the literature of the worlds colonized by the British. In other words, what was formerly known as Commonwealth literature or more broadly Third World literature became postcolonial literature since the 1980s. In its purview, most often, we find a limning of the colonial encounter, the revelation of the invention of tradition, and the elaboration of the confusion of categories produced by that violence. Yet another way of saying this is that the study of such writers as Raja Rao, Premchand, Thomas Mofolo, Sol Plaatje, Aimé Césaire, Pramoedya Ananta Toer, Naguib Mahfouz, Bessie Head, Jamaica Kincaid, Rokaya Hossein, Maryse Conde, Chinua Achebe, Salman Rushdie, Tayeb Salih, and Tsitsi Dangarembga most often uses the term "postcolonial." Clearly, such a diversity of authors (chosen more or less at random) names no coherent canon, and for perhaps practical or logistical reasons, much scholarship and pedagogy over the last four decades chose to proceed along broadly thematic, comparative lines, showing how writers from across the globe respond to a shared experience of colonial rule, but also emphasizing irreducible specificity of place.

No wonder a contemporary writer like Teju Cole dismisses the ubiquitous question of the label of the African writer as a limiting one:

> Not caring too much how I'm labeled has gotten me into a bit of trouble at times. Some Nigerians object to me being called an American writer, for example, as though I were shirking some invisible responsibility to be allied to one place and one place only. But, really, I don't care what I'm called: African, African-American, American-African, black American, Nigerian American, Nigerian, American, Yoruba. My writing has European antecedents, Indian influences, Icelandic fantasies, Brazilian aspirations.[34]

And yet Cole terms his novel, *Open City*, an "African book," haunted from beginning to end by the question of its protagonist's origin in Nigeria. Moving away from older notions of diaspora offered by thinkers like Du Bois or Fanon, and from the frame of racial solidarity or the internal colony analogy toward an exploration of more ambiguous and contradictory forms of contact, *Open City* helps change the conversation around what constitutes an "African book." Its catholicity of influences and inspirations and unexpected itineraries in New York, Brussels, and Lagos testify to the openness of the category of postcolonial literature. While postcolonial literature may well be defined as a body of work with the core mission of representing the experience of colonialism and its aftermath, it has never been content with writing back to the center, revising the colonial canon, or acceding to the ideological project of nation-building even though its rise may have accompanied the moment of nation-building.

Despite such openness, the term "postcolonial" has always carried a great deal of baggage, and for some critics "is haunted by the very figure of linear development that it sets out to dismantle."[35] It also suggests a premature celebration of the end of something that is still ongoing, or a tendency to organize everything along the axis of colonialism rather than invoking a longer *dureé* or a more complex set of interlocking historical forces. Moreover, its referent is often unclear – as Graham Pechey notes, "postcolonial has a banal sense which might apply equally to South Africa after 1910 and India after 1947: the sense of formal political independence, of having gone through a transfer of power." But, he continues, a stronger meaning emerges only when the paradox "that it takes anticolonial struggles to produce neocolonial conditions" is taken into account, and postcoloniality becomes the attempt to reckon with this paradox and the "irony of history" it represents.[36] Stuart Hall explains this best, calling for thinking "at the limit" rather than within familiar binaries of colonizer and colonized. Drawing on Derrida, Hall argues that all the key concepts in postcolonial studies should be understood as operating under erasure, a concept similar to Gayatri Spivak's claim that "the best of postcolonialism is autocritical."[37]

Part of the confusion arises from the fact that the referent "postcolonial" is both a geopolitical category and a conceptual one – the former standing in for real politics, the latter for catachresis. Aijaz Ahmad locates the origin of the term in debates in political science in the 1970s over state formation.[38] This means that, as Neil Lazarus notes, postcolonial in the early 1970s "was a periodizing term, a historical and not an ideological concept."[39] But as it took shape as an academic field, even though scholars defined it in subtle ways, it came to acquire ideological content associating it with a critique of nationalism, and an emphasis on migrancy, cosmopolitanism, and hybridity.[40] This constellation is what most people associate with postcolonial theory.

The interrogation of the national frame is thus almost synonymous with the academic discipline of postcolonial studies. Most of the foundational work in the 1980s and 1990s highlighted the exclusions of women, religious minorities, and the working class in elite constructions of the nation, and saw the project of decolonization as only ushering in, at best, an arrested form of development, still subject to economic control, bound to the colonial state by such institutions as prisons, the army, the census, and the survey, and lacking a cultural revolution that could successfully move beyond colonialism. All of this provided the political conditions for a necessary critique of the nation, but in some ways, this critique became axiomatic via the convergence of various forces, including the migration of intellectuals to the metropole and their subsequent championing of exile, their confluence with the ascendance of post-structuralist theory, and the synergy with linguistic postmodernism. At the same time, the end of the twentieth century saw a broader shift away from the nationalist emphasis of new social movements of the 1960s as well as the establishment of liberal multiculturalism in the United States. Along similar lines, the black British cultural studies project of dismantling Englishness and promoting diaspora dovetailed with the unpacking of national frames. Such an emphasis led to the prominence of a writer like Salman Rushdie, whose exuberant postmodern style, allegorical tendency, and interest in hybridity, migrancy, and imaginary homelands made him a poster child for postcolonial literature. But such concerns with magic realism are not shared across the varied landscape of the field, and recent years have brought much greater appreciation for local contexts of writing, with a renewed interest in realist and writing, market literature, and non-metropolitan print culture. For instance, writers with a strong local appreciation, such as Amit Chaudhury and Amitav Ghosh, have gained the prominence once reserved for a Rushdie, and magazines like *Chimurenga* and *Onitsha* market literature from Nigeria have called attention to regional networks of circulation that do not need to adhere to a Greenwich mean of a world republic of letters.[41] Notions of peripheral modernisms and realisms, a renewed focus on resistance literature, and the uneven and combined development of a literature of the world system help bridge earlier schisms between postcolonial literature and theory, illustrating some of the most refreshing engagements with form and history outside of reified notions of cosmopolitanism, subalternity, or hybridity.[42]

In contrast to such salutary efforts, recently, several critics have suggested that postcolonial critique has lost its urgency or at least its currency, and advocated even more capacious terms – ranging from global Anglophone to world literature to the planetary.[43] Theories debating whether the subaltern can speak outside the script of empire, tracking mimicry, hybridity, or sly civility, or even those advocating a return to humanism seem insufficiently supple enough to navigate contemporary forms of domination and resistance. It is fair to ask, however, if such a shift offers more than simply paralleling "the ascendancy of neo-liberal capitalism and its attendant discourses."[44] The frame of the global or the world certainly decenters the question of power inherent in the lexicon of postcolonial critique, and does not evoke the era of Bandung, the promise of national liberation, the possibility of revolution, or the ongoing need for resistance to global capital. A figure like Ngũgĩ wa Thiong'o, for instance, a monumental figure in postcolonial literature, cannot be assimilated into such expansive frames in any easy way since he continues to stress the significance of place, language, and culture that are rooted in Kenya, as well as insisting on the continuing need to decolonize the mind. Such expansive frames would in fact take us further away from the concerns of writers in postcolonial locations, and impose even more hierarchical and inaccurate abstractions and generalizations.

A notion of the waning of an undifferentiated postcolonial also seems wrong, since it fails to track the varied fortunes of the three aspects I have isolated: literature, theory, and method. It seems to me that what may indeed have waned is postcolonial theory (or at least a consensus around a particular set of theories along with notions of *the* postcolonial condition), and perhaps that waning need not be a cause for concern, since arguably many of the core tenets have simply passed into the mainstream of critical thinking. It is possible to locate postcolonial theory as the progenitor of a number of contemporary theoretical trends – including the critique of humanism and the exploration of post-humanism, eco-criticism and environmental studies, world literature, studies of the global South, hemispheric studies – and to track its diffusion into new forms, rather than proclaiming its ending. This transmission may even offer greater critical flexibility, as long as it is not used to declare endlessly the death of something that is the only rubric under which much of the world's population and its literature comes into view. While new ways of reading have been regularly proposed in recent years – ranging from surface reading to distant reading to reparative reading – they have all been more engaged with expounding on their dissatisfactions with ideology critique than offering new ways to think about race, nation, gender, and empire.

This is where it is worth recalling the third use of "postcolonial" – as method. As a lens through which to read literary texts, postcolonialism began as colonial discourse studies but was adopted in fields and historical periods far removed from its original location, from medieval to early modern, and helped reshape and transform almost every historical period and available critical method. It is here that the clearest conjuncture of American and postcolonial becomes visible as the task of the critic to learn to read US empire remains pressing and unavoidable. New frames of inquiry such as settler colonialism studies or comparative ethnic studies make possible ever more useful analyses of power and resistance. US empire today must remain one of the objects of the field – as part of its continuing, morphing existence as colonial discourse studies – as must the charge of analyzing how the United States relates to previous empires, especially its European predecessors from whom it split and reconstituted itself as a new empire. A second clear and urgent task involves the exploration of the relationship between US minorities and what Du Bois called the "darker world." In this effort, while Black Atlantic, hemispheric, and transnational Asian American approaches have already yielded thoughtful commentary, a greater effort to learn from the theorization of indigeneity remains urgent. As Jodi Byrd and Michael Rothberg argue, highlighting the genocide of indigenous peoples, their claims of sovereignty, and new frames of settler colonialism involves rethinking existing understandings of colonialism, internal colonialism, and nationalism.[45] Such projects may also bring new insights gleaned from reading the United States alongside such settler colonies as South Africa or Zimbabwe, helping dismantle the abstraction of "the West and the rest" that continues to shape geopolitics in an unequal world.[46]

To sum up, both postcolonial literature and postcolonialism as a method continue to thrive, and remain key resources and interlocutors for the study of transnational American literature. Indeed, the unwieldiness of the title phrase of this volume only makes sense because of the insights of postcolonial studies. For the rest of this essay, I want to focus on Teju Cole's *Open City*, not only because it instantiates the categorical confusion of the postcolonial in relation to the United States, and offers new ways of reading, but also for its suggestion of the urgency of a dialogue between the two spaces in order to understand better the global world order and the place of the United States within it.

Diaspora as Digression: Teju Cole's *Open City*

Apart from the fact that few will dispute the various locations of *Open City* – Lagos, Brussels, New York – or the clear cosmopolitan credentials of its author and protagonist, the novel resists any formulaic reading of a transnational imaginary. It is quite resistant, for instance, to a predictable account of diaspora, as its ornery Nigerian-German protagonist, Julius, feels impatient with "people who tried to lay claims" on him, be it an African cab-driver who expects a greeting from an African "brother" or a postal worker who wants to share his poetry about the "Motherland."[47] He even doubts the story of a Liberian refugee, whom he visits at a detention facility not out of empathy but simply to please a girlfriend, noting that "I had fallen in love with the idea" that "I was the listener, the compassionate African who paid attention to the details of someone else's life and struggle" (70). A similar

ironic distancing from familiar narratives about postcolonialism may be dis-
cerned in the novel, much of which could easily figure as a sly allegory about
critical practices of reading. More than anything else, Julius is a reader – of
landscape, other people, moments of time – and an aesthete, taking pleasure
in music, theory, fiction, and art, but seemingly able to wax philosophical
about anything under the sun, from 9/11 to bedbugs. Cole has suggested
that a "plausible framing device for *Open City* is a series of visits by Julius
to his psychiatrist." Like Julius, the psychiatry resident who walks the length
of the city mulling over life, the novel is also "interested in the kinship of
aboutness and avoidance" and the odd dynamics of "oversharing and evasion."[48] This makes the novel's ruminations applicable not only to the realm
of psychotherapy but also of literary interpretation, since the most crucial
lessons lie in the evocation of the "art of listening," or the "ability to trace
out a story from what was omitted" (9). Another way to say this might be
that *Open City* is not a primer on how to write about Africa, but perhaps is
one for how to read about Africa.

   That this is a startling contrast to Cole's social media presence, particularly his innovative work on Twitter, seems immediately clear. In such
efforts as the "Small Fates" project, "A Piece of the Wall," and "Seven Short
Stories about Drones," Cole emerges not only as a keen observer of urban
life but also as a trenchant critic of contemporary forms of inequality
and exploitation, whether of undocumented migrants along the Arizona-
Mexico border, those killed by drone strikes in Yemen or Pakistan, or
the "white savior industrial complex" evinced by Kony 2012, Nicholas
Kristof, or Oprah Winfrey.[49] The clean and precise anger of Cole the critic
of US empire is nowhere to be found in *Open City*, and the novel challenges rather than assumes the efficacy of any partisan positions. In other
words, on the one hand, the novel regularly ponders political atrocities –
from slavery to the Holocaust to 9/11 to Ellis Island to rape to indigenous
genocide to Japanese internment. On the other, its first-person narrator
recoils from commitment of any sort and is suspicious of ideology, attachment, and belief. In fact, *Open City* may easily be read as writing in the
wake of the desire to connect or to believe, a work in synchrony with
our post-critical times. It is in this sense – the refusal to reflexively associate a politics of resistance with the work of literature – that the novel
is instructive for the range of issues broached earlier in this chapter –
including the solidarities and fractures of black transnationalism and
the schism between postcolonial theory advocating hybridity or opacity and postcolonial literature gleaning ordinary life, both quotidian and
violent. The novel also insinuates the confluence of the postcolonial and
the American, figured here not least in the unremarkably interconnected

itineraries of Julius in New York, Brussels, and Lagos – unremarkable because he moves with ease rather than angst.

Isolated and prickly, but also meditative and intelligent, Julius seems consumed with self-reflection and yet appears elusive. His wandering does not imply the critique of the modernist flâneur (despite much critical celebration of the return of cosmopolitan flânerie), even if Julius admits to a suspicion of causes, since his "instinct was for doubts and questions" (206). It is more helpful to recall the practice of what Edouard Glissant termed *errance*, where the errant may rehearse the routes of travel as conquest, mastery, or discovery, and may seek an understanding of connection – of totality even (*totalité-monde*) – but always knows that this is an impossible quest.[50] Similarly, Glissant's notion of relation – not just looking back to one's own origin for understanding but rhizomatically, outward, elsewhere, for subterranean connections, transverse, and oblique, describes both Julius's thought processes and the narrative choices of this seemingly plotless novel, which could easily be read as one long digression. Cole had memorably joked that "had John Updike been African, he would have won the Nobel prize 20 years ago," pitying all "those writers who have to ply their trade from sleepy American suburbs, writing divorce scenes symbolized by the very slow washing of dishes."[51] Of course when he follows this up with a novel about New York in which almost nothing happens, it is difficult not to be amused. And yet, taking seriously his claim that *Open City* "is a narrative troubled from beginning to end by Julius's origin in Africa," it is worth pausing to reflect what a novel that seems to jettison most of the norms of contemporary writing (as James Wood notes, it is, above all, "original") offers for discussions of the state of the field of postcolonial literature.[52]

The most direct confrontation of the novel with these questions is when Julius encounters a young Moroccan named Farouq in Brussels, with whom he debates weighty political topics like Israel and Palestine, 9/11 and Islamophobia, but also the theories of Walter Benjamin and Paul de Man, and the meaning of postcolonial literature – the stakes of realism, authenticity, and audience. In his Internet shop, as people make calls to "Colombia, Egypt, Senegal, Brazil, France, Germany," Farouq seeks a way to understand "how people can live together but still keep their own values intact," evoking familiar notions of the crossroads and contact zones of culture in the face of difference (112). But Julius, though charmed by Farouq, is also repelled by his passion for politics and mocks his immersion in academic language. Seeing himself as far too urbane to use such language, Julius muses, "the victimized Other: how strange, I thought, that he used an expression like that in a casual conversation" (105). Always wanting to correct Farouq's slight slips in quoting intellectuals, Julius may well present a rare instance of a novel not mocking academic jargon (as Wood notes approvingly), but does seem to render a critique, and perhaps a caricature, of postcolonial notions of difference. Farouq, tellingly, admits that he "wanted to be the next Edward Said" (128). But with his academic career cut off as his thesis was rejected and charged with plagiarism a few days after 9/11, running the Internet shop and training to become a translator, Farouq does not seem like an adequate match for Julius's suave distinctions. But he does show Julius his own limits as well. Differing in their assessment of Tahar Ben Jalloun, Julius recognizes the available options to young intelligent men of color as either "to be enraged" like Farouq or to have "no causes" and become "magnificently isolated from all loyalties" like himself (107). He wonders if his apathy may not prove "an ethical lapse graver than rage itself" (107).

When we learn toward the end of the novel that Julius is confronted by Moji about his rape of her as a teenager, and realize that he does not remember or otherwise respond to the charge, it becomes clear that the novel is questioning rather than upholding a modernist male solipsistic wandering. Julius cannot be a custodian of cultural memory when his own is so partial. The solipsism of a figure like Julius and the passion of one like Farouq become reflections of each other, neither complete without the other. As readers, we are frustrated by Cole's refusal to have Julius respond to the revelation in any satisfying way. But this refusal suggests that we have to learn to read beyond conventional frames, beyond notions of diasporic solidarity, modernist flânerie, cosmopolitan travel (as Cole is not just Sebald meets Naipaul meets Coetzee), and begin to read less allegorically and more sensitively, recognizing the unreliability of narration and its refusal to offer "clear policy recommendations." When Julius says at the end of *Open City* that "we are not the villains of our own stories" (243), perhaps he offers an ongoing challenge for Americanist and postcolonial scholars as well. Maybe, like Julius, we are all unreliable narrators and imperfect historians. But, as Glissant reminds us, "the tale of errantry is the tale of Relation," and the path forward is only through dialogue.[53]

NOTES

1 Amy Kaplan, "'Left Alone with America': The Absence of Empire in the Study of American Culture," in Amy Kaplan and Donald Pease, eds., *Cultures of United States Imperialism* (Durham, NC: Duke University Press, 1993), 3.

2 Perry Miller, *Errand into the Wilderness* (Cambridge, MA: Harvard University Press, 1956), vii.

3 Chinua Achebe, "An Image of Africa: Racism in Conrad's *Heart of Darkness*." *The Massachusetts Review* 18.4 (1977): 782–94. Miller, "Errand," ix.

4 Matthew Frye Jacobson, "Where We Stand: US Empire at Street Level and in the Archive," *American Quarterly* 65.2 (2013): 265–90; quotation on 265.

5 Kaplan, "Left Alone with America," 11.

6 Ibid., 11.

7 Michael Hardt and Antonio Negri, *Empire* (Cambridge, MA: Harvard University Press, 2000), 317, 384.

8 Fredric Jameson, "Third-World Literature in the Era of Multinational Capitalism" *Social Text* 15 (1986): 65–88. Dipesh Chakrabarty, *Provincializing Europe: Postcolonial Thought and Historical Difference* (Princeton, NJ: Princeton University Press, 2000).

9 Bill Ashcroft, Gareth Griffiths, and Helen Tiffin, *The Empire Writes Back: Theory and Practice in Postcolonial Literatures* (London and New York: Routledge, 1989), 2.

10 Lawrence Buell "American Literary Emergence as a Postcolonial Phenomenon," *American Literary History* 4.3 (Fall 1992): 411–42.

11 See for instance, Sam Durrant, *Postcolonial Narrative and the Work of Mourning: J.M. Coetzee, Wilson Harris, Toni Morrison* (Albany: State University of New York Press, 2004).

12 Homi Bhabha, *The Location of Culture* (London and New York: Routledge, 1994); Wai Chee Dimock, "African, Caribbean, American: Black English as Creole Tongue" in *Shades of the Planet: American Literature as World Literature*, Wai Chee Dimock and Lawrence Buell, eds. (Princeton, NJ: Princeton University Press, 2007): 274–300.

13 See Francoise Lionnet and Shu-mei Shih, eds. *Minor Transnationalism* (Durham, NC: Duke University Press, 2005); the journal *The Global South*, and *Afro Asia: Revolutionary Political and Cultural Connections between African Americans and Asian Americans*, Fred Ho and Bill Mullen, eds. (Durham, NC: Duke University Press, 2008).

14 W.E.B. Du Bois, *The Souls of Black Folk* (New York: Oxford World's Classics, [1903] 2007), 15.

15 W.E.B. Du Bois, "The New Crisis," *The Crisis*, May 1925, 7–9.

16 Du Bois, *Souls*, 15.

17 W.E.B. Du Bois, "As the Crow Flies," *New York Amsterdam News* (April 10, 1943), 10.

18 W.E.B. Du Bois, *Dusk of Dawn: An Essay Toward an Autobiography of a Race Concept* (New Brunswick, NJ: Transaction Publishers, [1940] 1997),116–17.

19 Robert Blauner, "Internal Colonialism and Ghetto Revolt," *Social Problems*, 16.4 (Spring 1969), 393–408; Kenneth Clark, *Dark Ghetto: Dilemmas of Social Power* (New York: Harper and Row, 1965); Harold Cruse, *Rebellion or Revolution?* (New York: William Morrow, 1968).

20 Stokely Carmichael and Charles V. Hamilton, *Black Power: The Politics of Liberation in America* (New York: Random House, 1967).

21 Cedric Robinson, *Black Marxism: The Making of the Black Radical Tradition* (Chapel Hill and London: University of North Carolina Press, 1983), Robin Kelley, *Freedom Dreams: The Black Radical Imagination* (Boston: Beacon Press, 2002).

22 See Ann DuCille, "Postcolonialism and Afrocentricity: Discourse and Dat Course" in *The Black Columbiad*, eds. Werner Sollors and Maria Dietrich (Cambridge, MA: Harvard University Press, 1994): 28–41.

23 For Ruth Frankenberg and Lata Mani, post-civil rights is the proper analog to the postcolonial ("Crosscurrents, Crosstalk: Race, 'Postcoloniality' and the Politics of Location," *Cultural Studies* 7.2 [1993]: 292–310; while Jenny Sharpe reminds us that the history of postcolonialism must be situated within the story of liberal multiculturalism ("Is the United States Postcolonial?: Transnationalism, Immigration, and Race," *Diaspora: A Journal of Transnational Studies* 4.2 [1995]: 181–99), both pointing to the necessary differences between the two but also indicating the critical desire to connect.

24 Edward Said, *Orientalism* (London: Penguin Books, [1978] 1995). Said's later work in *Culture and Imperialism* (London: Vintage, 1993) rectifies that omission.

25 Donald Pease, "US Imperialism: Global Dominance without Colonies" in *A Companion to Postcolonial Studies*, Henry Schwarz and Sangeeta Ray, eds. (Malden, MA: Blackwell Publishing, 2005), 203.

26 Kaplan, "Left Alone with America," 18.

27 Kelley, *Freedom Dreams*.

28 Frantz Fanon, *The Wretched of the Earth*, trans. Constance Farrington (New York: Grove Press, 1963), 216, hereafter cited parenthetically

29 Cynthia Young, *Soul Power: Culture, Radicalism, and the Making of a U.S. Third World Left* (Durham, NC and London: Duke University Press, 2006), 206.

30 Angela Davis, *Freedom Is a Constant Struggle: Ferguson, Palestine, and the Foundations of a Movement* (Chicago: Haymarket Books, 2016), 139–40, 144.

31 See Yogita Goyal, *Romance, Diaspora, and Black Atlantic Literature* (Cambridge: Cambridge University Press, 2010).

32 Chimamanda Ngozi Adichie, *Americanah* (New York: Alfred A. Knopf, 2013).

33 For excellent histories in this vein, see Neil Lazarus, *The Cambridge Companion to Postcolonial Literary Studies* (Cambridge: Cambridge University Press, 2004); Ato Quayson, "Introduction: Postcolonial literature in a Changing Historical Frame" in *The Cambridge History of Postcolonial Literature* (Cambridge: Cambridge University Press, 2012); and Sangeeta Ray and Henry Schwarz, *Encyclopedia of Postcolonial Studies* (New York: Wiley Blackwell, 2016).

34 Teju Cole, interview with Aaron Bady, *Post45*, 19 January 2015. Accessed 12 February 2016, http://post45.research.yale.edu/2015/01/interview-teju-cole/.

35 Anne McClintock, "The Angel of Progress: Pitfalls of the Term 'Postcolonialism' " in *Colonial Discourse/Postcolonial Theory*, Francis Barker, Peter Hulme, and Margaret Iversen, eds. (Manchester: Manchester University Press, 1994), 253–66, quotation on 254.

36 Graham Pechey, "Post-Apartheid Narratives" in Barker et al., *Colonial Discourse*, 151–71, quotation on 152.

37 Stuart Hall, "When Was the 'Post-Colonial'? Thinking at the Limit," in *The Post-Colonial Question: Common Skies, Divided Horizons*, Iain Chambers and Lydia Curti, eds. (New York: Routledge, 1996): 242–60; Gayatri Chakravorty Spivak, "Foreword," Schwarz and Ray, *Companion to Postcolonial Studies*, xv. Although it is common to see postcolonial critique characterized as an antagonistic genre, writing back to the empire, much of the field has highlighted the insufficiency of binaries, whether from a poststructuralist perspective or a Marxist one. Even the most famous literary readings – Chinua Achebe on

Joseph Conrad, Edward Said on Jane Austen, or Gayatri Spivak on Charlotte Bronte – ask for nuance and complication, for complicity even, challenging cultural or civilizational notions of an immutable difference between East and West.

38 Aijaz Ahmad, *In Theory: Classes, Nations, Literatures* (Delhi: Oxford University Press, 1992).

39 Neil Lazarus, "Introducing Postcolonial Studies," *The Cambridge Companion to Postcolonial Literary Studies* (Cambridge: Cambridge University Press, 2004): 1–16, quotation on 2.

40 While Homi Bhabha and Gayatri Spivak are most often associated with such ideas, it is worth noting that Spivak has repeatedly cautioned against the "neo-colonial traffic in cultural identity and the slow and agonizing triumph of the migrant voice" ("How to Read a Culturally Different Book" in Barker et al., *Colonial Discourse*, 126–50, quotation on 127).

41 Access articles and information concerning print subscriptions at www .chimurenga.co.za.

42 See Benita Parry, "Aspects of Peripheral Modernisms," *Ariel* 401.1 (2009): 27–55; Colleen Lye and Jed Esty's special issue on peripheral realisms, *Modern Language Quarterly* 73.3 (2012); and the Warwick Research Collective's *Combined and Uneven Development: Towards a New Theory of World-Literature* (Liverpool: Liverpool University Press, 2015).

43 See Sunil Agnani et al., "Editor's Column: The End of Postcolonial Theory? A Roundtable with Sunil Agnani, Fernando Coronil, Gaurav Desai, Mamadou Diouf, Simon Gikandi, Susie Tharu, and Jennifer Wenzel," *PMLA* 122.3 (2007): 633–51. Also see Dipesh Chakrabarty, "Postcolonial Studies and the Challenge of Climate Change," *New Literary History* 43.1 (2012): 1–18.

44 James Graham, Michael Niblett and Sharae Deckard, "Postcolonial Studies and World Literature," *Journal of Postcolonial Writing* 48.5 (2012): 465–71, quotation on 465.

45 Jodi Byrd and Michael Rothberg, "Between Subalternity and Indigeneity," *Interventions* 13.1 (2011): 1–12.

46 That African American student protestors in 2015 across the United States drew inspiration from the "Rhodes Must Fall" campaign in South Africa is a sign of such alliances.

47 Teju Cole, *Open City* (New York: Random House, 2011), 40, 186, hereafter cited parenthetically.

48 Cole, interview with Aaron Bady, 2015.

49 Teju Cole, "The White-Savior Industrial Complex," *The Atlantic*, 21 March 2012. Accessed 10 February 2016, www.theatlantic.com/international/archive/2012/03/the-white-savior-industrial-complex/254843/.

50 Édouard Glissant, *Poetics of Relation*, trans. Betsy Wing (Ann Arbor: University of Michigan Press, 1997).

51 Teju Cole, *Everyday Is for the Thief* (New York: Random House [2007] 2014), 65–66.

52 Cole, interview with Aaron Bady, 2015; James Wood, "The Arrival of Enigmas," *The New Yorker* 28 February 2011.

53 Glissant, *Poetics of Relation*, 18.

4

RUSS CASTRONOVO

Transnational Aesthetics

The cultivation of aesthetic taste is most bountiful when art grows in a "national garden."[1] So averred the Victorian art critic and sometimes painter John Ruskin when he plotted art along the orderly rows of nationalism. The assumptions behind this layout of nationalist aesthetics had gained considerable currency ever since Johann Gottfried Herder in the eighteenth century had proposed that "a single nation speaks a single language."[2] Whereas every nation, if it were lucky enough not be divided by multilingualism, had at least one language, it seemed to Ruskin that whole swaths of the globe were devoid of any artistic development whatsoever. Listeners to Ruskin's lectures were to apply his remarks only to Western Europe, which boasted a lineage of art and literature that dated back to the classical era. But when it comes to ancient art, "there is none in America, none in Asia, none in Africa."[3] Contemporary literary criticism supported Ruskin's intuition that the expanse of a cultural desert lay beyond Europe, as Sydney Smith had asked in the *Edinburgh Review* only a generation before, "In the four quarters of the globe, who reads an American book? Or goes to an American play? Or looks at an American picture or statue?"[4] Such rough treatment creates the impression not only that aesthetics are purely a domestic matter but also that few nations have the wherewithal to make their art matter in the first place.

While critics such as Ruskin and Smith are not alone in seeing a huge cultural imbalance between European fine arts and crude American efforts, there is no denying that all sorts of traffic has circulated across the transatlantic routes of trade, intellectual exchange, and migration. Among the New World commodities like corn and slaves that found their way into gardens and plantations that were far more prosaic and brutal than what Ruskin had in mind for his "national garden," something more ineffable and potentially transformative also was diffused in this globalized economy. Tom Paine identified this furtive material as a gut instinct or affective sensibility, which, although it could not be empirically verified, could surely be felt. He called this quality "common sense," blending a number of different influences from novelistic sentimentality to a loose understanding of Enlightenment philosophy to argue for the profound significance of aesthetics to politics. Yet the knock against such anti-colonial critique is that aesthetic independence often lags behind political independence. The critiques of the art and literature of early America as imitative and jejune, an assessment that was often made by Britons as well as Americans themselves, would seem to confirm the improbability of a colonial backwater achieving the universalism implied by common sense.

Instead of aligning aesthetics with the rarefied world of masterpieces found in cathedrals or palaces, the notion of common sense plays on a much older understanding of aesthetics as an intensely human zone of emotion, sensation, and affect, what Susan Buck-Morss denotes as the entire "corporeal sensorium."[5] Strongly identified with the creole nationalism challenging the sway of the British Empire, the broadly shared feelings of political outrage that Paine sought to tap into and mobilize had nothing less than the entire globe as its horizon. The subject of *Common Sense* (1776) was "not local, but universal," he insisted, since it concerned the "power of feeling" and "affections" of all humanity.[6] Months before the inhabitants of British North America declared independence, Paine proclaimed that his countrymen's and countrywomen's true métier was not simply national but also transnational: their common feelings promoted a broad sense of identification that seemed "too limited for continental minds."[7] Of course, the historical irony is that the thirteen colonies that sought to leverage common sense against empire have now become a global hegemon in their own right. The universal language of aesthetics, as some critics charge, has been simultaneously expanded and narrowed to an American idiom to the point where it seems like "the writer is writing for a global West Village."[8] The universal, as we will see, is frequently intoned with a more parochial lilt that harnesses human sympathy, cosmopolitanism, and other transnational feelings for rather specific purposes.

Common Sense is recognized as a partisan propaganda tract, not an aesthetic treatise. Nonetheless, the global accents heard in this stirring critique of empire emerge from an aesthetic sensibility that is shared, theoretically speaking, by all human beings. Insofar as the word "aesthetic" recalls its ancient Greek meaning of "sense perception," the concept also includes a sociopolitical dimension in the proposition that every member of the human community can access this capability at a baseline level. Across the transatlantic enlightenment, the idea of common sense promoted the "fantasy that all men share a common set of convictions about material and moral reality."[9] Thus when Paine declares, "The birth-day of a new world is at hand," he is doing something more than offering a vision that is wider than a partitioning of the globe into quarters or fenced-in national gardens; he is also fusing aesthetics to politics in ways that expand the import of his anticolonial critique.[10]

This refusal to occupy any particular ground is what invests aesthetics with transnational potential. Notions of the common, whether as a shared set of feelings, general agreement about taste, or widely distributed political sensibility, suggest the potential for locating aesthetics on collective ground. Transnational aesthetics push readers and viewers out of the comfort zones associated with the presumed singularity of national culture. The paradox, however, is that this widened perspective threatens to condense into a global vision that is in many ways as singular as the national frame it has supposedly surpassed. The next section thus examines oscillating tensions, as the possibilities of transnational aesthetics swing between the prospect of human commonalty and the realities of commodity culture. These tensions are heightened, as the final sections of this essay set out to prove, when the lines between a global economy and a universal aesthetic become blurred.

From Common Sense to *Sensus Communis*

Although Immanuel Kant had his doubts about revolutionary activity, expressing the view that events in America fell short of "a true reform in one's way of thinking," he did take up – and transform – the idea of "common sense" in ways that imbued aesthetics with transnational potential.[11] Even more anxious about the momentous upheavals in eighteenth-century France than he was about the American Revolution, Kant "turns to aesthetics (*not* revolution)" as a means of "creating new political identities and regimes."[12] Far from a dismissal of art and beauty as apolitical, Kant's emphasis on the global geography of taste ensures that aesthetics are always shot through with an implicit and often utopian politics. His *Critique of Judgment* (1790) repeatedly finds itself mired in specific terrains of cultural difference, as Kant's references to East Asian jungles, Maori warriors, Iroquois chiefs, and other non-Europeans indicate. Each of these examples would seem to mark the limit of "common sense," since it is hard to imagine that Paine's incipient transnationalism of shared sentiments could adjust itself to such extreme differences. Then again, Kant translates – and transforms – "common sense" as *sensus communis* in order to redefine aesthetics as "*communal* sense," that is, an evaluative capacity in which individual judgment smoothly adjusts and peacefully aligns itself to collective thinking.[13] The Latin phrasing is not mere erudition; *sensus communis* implies "an extra sense – like an extra mental capacity – that fits us into a community," according to Hannah Arendt.[14] The question remains, however, whether this community can assume transnational, even global dimensions.

In simplest terms, *sensus communis* enables us to expand our likes and dislikes beyond narrow frameworks of individual taste or identity. Instead of proclaiming that "McDonalds serves the most tasty hamburger" or that "American football is the most pleasing sport to watch on television," we strive for a sense of taste whose ground is nothing short of human solidarity. Before accepting conventional wisdom based on local loyalties or making snap judgments rooted in provincial affiliations, we reflect and take into account how other members of a broadly construed "common" might also judge. We should not participate in aesthetics as we would in team sports, nor should we judge on the basis of brand loyalty to one franchise over another. As Terry Eagleton explains, "*sensus communis* is ideology purified, universalized and rendered reflective, ideology raised to the second power, idealized beyond all mere sectarian prejudice or customary reflex."[15] Freed of the cheerleading as well as the accusations that are endemic to any ideological terrain, aesthetics concern a species-wide sensibility that is as common as the basic outlines of humanity. It is for this reason that Kant distinguishes between "a culture of taste" and "a faculty of taste"[16]: whereas the former demands a consideration of history, cultural difference, and tradition, the latter opens out onto a purely theoretical landscape in which all such particulars are bracketed. Although rather abstract and airy, these contours also suggest the transnational flows that propel people and objects across oceans, mountain ranges, and state borders. The particulars of historical consciousness, on the other hand, would suggest that people and goods are set in motion by war, scarcity, and other phenomena that force inhabitants to become migrants and refugees. Only by jettisoning any concrete idea of culture or human geography can aesthetics offer perspective on a horizon that is hypothetically as large as the world itself. As we will see, this capability is what allows the Kantian promise of universal aesthetics to be absorbed into the wonders of global commodity culture.

For the moment, though, it is important to understand how transnational forces including travel, slavery, the extraction of natural resources, and natural history help imbue aesthetics with an atmosphere of worldwide consensus. This cosmopolitan significance becomes evident when Kant defines "the *beautiful*" as that "which pleases universally, without a concept." To illustrate this idea, Kant invokes a garden. But this garden is not any garden, least of all the "national garden" that Ruskin would later describe in his Manchester lectures. Instead, his subject is a pepper garden described by William Marsden in *The History of Sumatra* (1783). Traveling through the rainforest, this English traveler finds the sudden appearance of the orderly rows and symmetry of a pepper garden "beautiful" because it exhibits a "striking ... contrast ... to the wild scenes of nature which surround them."[17] The problem with this judgment, however, is that it does not spring from a sympathy for the common, which might cause a person, say Marsden, to effectively bracket his own subjective tastes so that along with everyone else he can apprehend the beautiful as an objective property of the pepper garden. Not *sensus communis*, but a more local feeling – call it *sensus europeanus* – is the source of Marsden's judgment: his aesthetic preference never frees itself from prior – and ultimately parochial – concepts about wilderness and civilization. Instead of exercising the widely shared "faculty of taste," Marsden is mired in a more particular "culture of taste" that is guided by differentiation. Kant's rejoinder to Marsden is instructive: let the Western explorer spend an entire day in a pepper garden and soon enough he will become fatigued by the "burdensome constraint upon the imagination" produced by the unending horticultural order.[18] Any aesthetic that surpasses the limits of a national horizon requires a counterpoint to disrupt the humdrum insularity of a homogeneous culture. For Kant, a little comparison goes a long way; that is, by treating aesthetics as contingent, we come to realize that beauty is itself a comparative zone. What, after all, could be more contingent than a Sumatran pepper garden, which is conditioned by geography, climate, culture, and the history of colonialism?

In short, the very ground of aesthetic universalism is contingent and particular. The world includes Königsberg as well as Sumatra, but it would be a mistake to confuse either locale with the world at large. The idea of the universal, like the global itself, is uneven terrain marked by constant variation, otherwise we would be stuck in dull, unchanging pepper gardens. This tension is intrinsic to the geography of aesthetics, since the beautiful is "at once subjective and universal ... at once individual and collective, island and bridge."[19] Like an island, the Sumatran counterpoint to European assumptions about the beautiful remains forever distinct; but like the imaginative bridge that by way of contrast connects an unfamiliar pepper garden to an English landscape garden, aesthetics provide points of contact and connection. Quite literally, transnational aesthetics inject a bit of spice into the bland taste of a national monoculture. Yet this dash of difference is predicated on the idea of exoticism, which suggests that any traffic crossing this bridge between cultures too often flows in only one direction. Kant's move in correcting Marsden is to show how rather smug metropolitan presuppositions can be offset by more cosmopolitan sensibilities.

Transnational aesthetics can encourage the widespread dispersion of new and, from one perspective, exotic ideas and feelings as part of an implicit politics. Anticipating the horticultural thematic that would draw Kant to the writings of English traveler to an island in the Indian Ocean, Paine described how political freedom had been transplanted in America. Liberty is a "celestial exotic stuck deep in the ground" of America, he penned in a poem published the year before *Common Sense*.[20] In "The Liberty Tree" (1775), freedom is a classical inheritance that overleaps centuries and oceans to flower in the New World. Once taking root, the liberty tree thrives and becomes a "native" species. But "native" is hardly the source for nativism. Instead, Paine imagines the liberty tree as a sort of transnational beacon – "The fame of its fruit drew the nations around" – that overrides the petty distinctions emanating from strict ideas about social hierarchy and national belonging. The aesthetic counterpoint that Kant locates in his awareness that Sumatra and a European garden are each exotic to one another is consistent with the "exotic" political ideas that have migrated to America across time and space. Despite the tendency to locate literature solely within the frame of national histories, Paine's poem offers a glimpse of the broader "transnational forces at work in [the] production" of national literary traditions.[21]

Yet any claims about the role of transnational aesthetics in communicating expansive ideas about art and politics are tempered by the sobering reminder that transnational currents are frequently driven by less lofty aims. Amid the pepper plants and liberty trees of a comparative aesthetics, the prosaic usefulness of corn discloses the ease with which the commodity, not the beautiful or liberty, supplies the truest approximation of the universal. Not long after stating that the petty affiliations associated with nationalism break down "when compared with the whole," Paine supplants this budding cosmopolitanism with the assertion, "Our corn will fetch its price in any market in Europe."[22] At first glance, this proposition follows the script of aesthetic judgment, since it is the object, not the subject, that has a universal value on which everyone can agree. It would seem that corn, unlike the dried leaves of tea that Paine's compatriots had thrown into Boston harbor a few years before, was an ideologically different species of transnational commodity than the goods that the British Empire was shipping from one set of colonies in Asia to another set in America. By imagining an alimentary object (instead of an aesthetic one) as the point of universal taste construed in the most literal terms, Paine seeks to establish the indispensability of America to transnational circuits of exchange.

In arguing this point, *Common Sense* only confirms Kant's suspicion that American aesthetics are too raw and underdeveloped to partake of *sensus communis*. The first book of the *Critique of Judgment* opens with an anecdote that comes at the expense of what for Kant must have been the prototypical New World inhabitant, an "Iroquois *sachem* who was pleased in Paris by nothing more than by the cook-shops."[23] Seemingly incapable of adopting the disinterested attitude necessary for aesthetic judgment, the Iroquois thinks only about his gut. There is nothing wrong with taste, but the problem here is that Kant takes this statement of satisfaction as a response, a particularly insufficient one, to the question of whether a thing is beautiful. The scenario initially seems promising for the transnational aesthetic sensibility that stands behind the political unity implied by *sensus communis*. What could be more transnational than an American subject taking in the beauties of a magnificent European capital? But the depressing reality for Kant is that cosmopolitan feeling cannot emerge when it is trapped in private instinct. Common sense is hardly *sensus communis*: whether it is Paine's business instincts about corn or the Iroquois's liking for an early version of fast-food takeout, American tastes remain too 'primitive' to enter the currents of the transnational.

The situation would hardly seem to have improved a hundred years later when an American finally enters the Louvre. As prototypical as Kant's Iroquois, Christopher Newman in Henry James's *The American* (1876–77) journeys to Paris in hopes of cultivating aesthetic taste and finding a European wife – at some level the two are identical pursuits for him – who will do justice to his inexhaustible supply of cash. From this vantage, it is hard to see what might be innovative about Newman, who never really makes good on the implications of his surname. His first name, he tells people, he shares with Christopher Columbus, and by reversing the direction of Columbus's voyage he discovers that any universal sensibility that men and women may share is undoubtedly founded on bad taste. Suffering from "an aesthetic headache" brought on by overindulging in the treasures of the Louvre, Newman finds his wandering attention seized by a pretty and flirtatious copyist, Mademoiselle Noémie Nioche.[24] In multiple senses, Mlle. Nioche converts art and beauty into commodities, and Newman, as "the American" of James's title, eagerly responds, buying one of her knockoffs for a tidy sum. Newman is satisfied with the transaction, since "if the truth must be told, he had often admired the copy much more than the original."[25] As the logic of the commodity privileges reproduction over authenticity, the point of universal accord is revealed to be not aesthetic sensibility but commercial availability. Transnational commerce is not the same as transnational aesthetics – until, of course, it is. Which is to say that before too long the lofty ideals about instinctive feelings and worldwide sensibilities become conducive to shipping corn abroad, eating foreign food, and buying tourist trash.

From Sympathy to Profit

The Americans of Kant's and James's respective imaginations exemplify the contradictions that accompany the "transnational turn" in American literary and cultural studies. From a distance, it may appear that the Iroquois sachem and Christopher Newman are living the cosmopolitan dream, employing their aesthetic tastes, no matter whether it is for cooked meat or inferior artistic imitations, to move beyond the narrow confines of Americanism. The Iroquois enjoys French food and Newman likes Spanish paintings hanging in a metropolitan art museum that are being copied by a French coquette. What could be more transnational than this series of associations and relays? Of course, the nagging problem is that these Americans' capacity for nonnational feelings never seems to advance beyond the primitive instincts that are the basis of aesthetics. The implicit criticism that Kant levels against the Iroquois and the irony with which James's narrator treats Newman is based on the suspicion that Americans remain too "indigenous," too confined by the idiosyncrasy of private tastes to step outside of their strictly local subjectivity. Although they might be found strolling about Paris like any flâneur, these subjects are so aesthetically deficient that they never approach a transnational consciousness.

Yet might something beautiful be created or recognized out of this experience of taste? The potential for something more – for example, a subjectivity that expands beyond an island-like autonomy, a sense of identification that is not wrapped up in national belonging, an appreciation of a wider social whole – remains part of the promise of aesthetics. The impact of cultural and geographic mobility encountered by these eighteenth- and nineteenth-century travelers to Paris should not be discounted. Laura Doyle has suggested that transnational forces and experiences can produce profound ontological dislocations that move national subjects to "a horizontal collective world in which bodily actions are multiply felt, witnessed, and internalized, and so have contagious effects."[26] In making this argument Doyle highlights the political effects of such interconnectedness by showing how British authorities in the slave societies of the Caribbean were forced to reckon with insurrectionary assertions of humanness erupting from Haiti and elsewhere. In this instance, transnational aesthetics expand access to the category of human – even if it is later severely retracted. "In the nation, territory and people are fused; in transnational formations, they are disarticulated," writes Donald E. Pease.[27] Once freed of the burden of sustaining narrow, monocultural thinking, identity becomes disaggregated and plural, open to the richness and diversity fueled by multiple encounters with the beautiful, the sublime, or other aesthetic experience. Whether it is the shared agreement that informs the beautiful or the temporary terror brought on by the sublime, aesthetics never wholly lose their antagonism to the singleness implied by national identity.

Aesthetic judgment overrides parochial affiliations because it necessarily requires people to evaluate a work of art or literature not as Americans who think according to national precepts, but as transnational subjects who, in the words of Jahan Ramazani, "imagine a world in which cultural boundaries are fluid, transient, and permeable."[28] This indifference to feelings of either national or aesthetic sovereignty suggests an antiracist orientation. As he entertains the cross-cultural possibilities of human beauty, Kant is forced to acknowledge that Asians, Europeans, and Africans will not see eye to eye when judging the beauty of the human form. "A Negro must have a different normal idea of the beauty of the [human figure] from a white man," he writes, but the catch is that he first stipulates that this difference occurs only under "empirical conditions."[29] Kant wants to bracket nationality, geography, and other "empirical conditions" in order to leave open the possibility of entering another zone of judgment, a non-verifiable reality, in which no differences in the perception of beauty would be upheld by racial distinctions. The goal is to push the assumptions and prejudices associated with the "culture of taste" to the sidelines and instead for subjects to be governed by the "faculty of taste" that is as elemental as human biology. Although Paine does not draw such fine-grained philosophical distinctions, across the body of his pamphlets and newspaper articles he consistently found Atlantic slavery to be against all the precepts of common sense.

The utopian promise – as well as the intractable historical problem – implicit in the broad faculty of taste and aesthetic judgment is that this generalized terrain prepares the ground for universalist claims. Detractors have pointed out, however, that the universal requires the exclusion of particulars, exposing aesthetic consensus as a "specious form of universalism" that never lives up to its heady idealism.[30] But the equally pressing worry is not that the universal is in actuality too limited, but that it is too aggrandizing in the manner that capitalism converts all spaces into marketplaces. World literature becomes a function of the world market, according to the brief remarks on literary history that one finds in the *Communist Manifesto* (1848). A residual Kantianism informs Marx and Engel's comments, as they observe that the bourgeois appreciation of property has become the new common sense. Trade, colonialism, and market expansion have given rise to "a cosmopolitan character" that infuses aesthetic as well as economic sensibilities.[31] A transnational and incipient global economy makes national aesthetics obsolescent: "national one-sidedness and narrow-mindedness become more and more impossible, and from the numerous national and local literatures, there arises a world literature."[32] To the extent that national and other local literatures have been displaced by world literature, as Marx and Engels assert, transnational aesthetic production and consumption harmonizes with the economic principles of capitalism. Colum McCann's novel *TransAtlantic* captures this confusion of transnational aesthetics and transnational commerce. Amid the historic sympathies that brought Frederick Douglass to Ireland on a lecture tour in 1845–46, US Senator George Mitchell to Belfast on a peace mission in 1998, and the aviators John Alcock and Arthur Brown to Galway in making the first nonstop transatlantic flight in 1919, McCann imagines an elderly woman who hopes to reap a windfall by selling a one-of-a-kind letter delivered in that historic flight from North America to Europe. What sort of profit can be realized from the artifacts of transnational sympathy? As it turns out, not much. Because the letter was never postmarked, its resale value is minimal.

The alignment of aesthetics and economics occurs not so much under the dreamy, utopian sign of the universal as within the commonsensical practices of the global. While the two terms may seem approximate synonyms for one another, the global bears the specific imprint of a world market. "The globalization of economies brings with it the globalization of cultures," as Paul Jay argues, making it at times difficult to distinguish economic production from aesthetic creation.[33] If, as the *Communist Manifesto* would have it, world literature has a tendency to piggyback on the advances of a world market, the lines between a global economy and aesthetic universalism become blurred. But unlike the irony in *TransAtlantic* that the first letter ever sent by airmail winds up being worth very little, the hopes for capitalizing on transnational visions are as wide as the globe itself.

From the Universal to the Global

No novel better clarifies the misrecognition of a transnational economy and transnational aesthetics for one another than Frank Norris's *The Octopus*. This monument of American naturalism anticipates the thorny questions that literary and cultural critics have been debating since the advent of the transnational turn: Is American literary transnationalism simply the new face of American exceptionalism?[34] Does the aspiration toward aesthetic unity foreshadow the political hegemony exercised by the forces of globalization?[35] Do aesthetics make empire seem beautiful? In staging these questions *The Octopus* makes a critical intervention into the conceptual tug-of-war between commodities and commonsense that, as we have seen, has been playing itself out in a long arc from Paine to Kant to James. At one level, the emphasis on transnationalism as an economic configuration had been part of the story since the Monroe Doctrine (1823), which, as Anna Brickhouse writes, pointed up "the disjunction between the hard-nosed economic policy engineered by the nation's political class and the hemispheric idealism" that potentially connected the United States to sister republics in Latin America.[36] The innovative transformation that Norris's novel registers is the aesthetic process whereby a global economy takes shape as a work of art. Up close, this global vision may feature all sorts of imperfections, but at a distance where only abstract forms can be glimpsed *The Octopus* presents the world as a cohesive, unified entity.

Where Paine pinned his hopes for cosmopolitanism on that particularly American commodity, corn, Norris sees the ubiquity of American wheat in the world market as a total work of art. Wheat is a lot like corn, but the important difference is that this commodity represents the complete conversion of beauty's theoretically limitless appeal into a numinous product that everyone across the globe can consume. Conceived as the first installment in a never-completed trilogy to be called "the Epic of the Wheat," *The Octopus* depicts art and economics on a global scale. Norris's title refers to the corporate tentacles of the California railroad that have corrupted electoral politics and squeezed out competitors, but the novel presents the organic beauty of wheat as something of a mystical counterforce that expands across the landscape as well. Economics have not totally supplanted aesthetics: as a commodity that is in universal demand, wheat paves the way for the American poet in the character of Presley, here presented as a poor imitation of Walt Whitman, to make his way to Asia. Although Presley's poetic vision never results in a work as stirring as Whitman's "Passage to India," the novel's concluding scene finds him on the deck of a clipper ship, its hold stuffed with grain, bound for the starving populations of Asia. He exemplifies the connection between world markets and world literature forecast by the *Communist Manifesto* a half-century before. Norris's novel reveals how at the start of the twentieth century transnational commerce converts artistic visions into the realities of trade. Yes, the expansion of global markets may bring about a situation in which "all that is solid melts into air," as Marx and Engels famously put it, but it is also the case that globalization makes real the shipping lanes and other infrastructures that enable the business practicality of common sense and the political idea of *sensus communis* to flow together.

No sooner is the confluence of transnational commerce and art established than *The Octopus* opens out onto a global vista so beautiful and complete that it overcomes any unresolved contradictions. After all the bomb throwing, bribery, and corporate scheming of the preceding six hundred pages, the novel ends with Presley projecting a worldwide feeling of *sensus communis* in "the great harvest" of American wheat that "rolled like a flood from the Sierras to the Himalayas to feed thousands of starving scarecrows on the barren plains of India."[37] His cosmopolitan vision of the globe as a single unit smoothes out the tensions that are created by a simultaneous reliance on patronizing assumptions about Third World helplessness and American resourcefulness. If "the 'transnational' bears a family resemblance to 'globalization," as Donald Pease asserts, then the predominant features it shares often seem to be American.[38] Paul Jay's worry about whether "the field of transnational literary studies is coming to be dominated by a single superpower" was anticipated more than a century ago when Norris in a series of aesthetic manifestoes lobbied for the practice of literary transnationalism that would be indistinguishable from American cultural imperialism.[39] Keenly aware that the Western frontier had closed, Norris advocated for the expansion of the American novel into the Far East. Since "the Anglo-Saxon in his course of empire had circled the globe and had brought the new civilization to the old civilization," it was now time to bring the novel back to the ancient steppes where sagas where first sung and epics set in hexameter.[40] American literature, according to Norris, pushes so far westward that it eventually arrives back in the East where storytelling originated.

This circle is a spatiotemporal feat that obliterates difference so that East and West become one. The vision of world literature as an effect of transnational exchange is highly aestheticized, taking formal shape as a circle so complete that, like the globe, it has no outside. Ever the poet, Presley subsumes any odd angles created by violence or inequality in his contemplation of "the full round of the circle whose segment only he beheld."[41] He participates in the bracketing of historical conflict and other contingencies that would otherwise disrupt his comprehension of the globe as a total work of art. From one perspective, this aesthetic sensibility opens out onto a single vision of humanity, but from a different vantage it offers a view whose wholeness in fact requires the incommensurability of Western civilization and the putative backwardness of "the East." In short, *The Octopus* lays out in painstaking detail how transnational literature authorizes a global sensibility that begins with "orientalism" and aspires to what Michael Hardt and Antonio Negri have described as empire. "The concept of Empire united juridical categories and universal ethical values," Hardt and Negri contend, "making them work together as an organic whole."[42] What Norris adds to this recognition is the insight that while empire may be fundamentally an unequal relation of power, it cannot be conceived or imagined without aesthetics.

More than a purely historical undertaking, empire emerges in a formal dimension that is emblematized by Norris's invocation of the circle, a perfect and total form, as the shape of early twentieth-century globalization. The opening of Asia-Pacific markets represents an aesthetic vista in addition to an encompassing commercial project. The "big picture" behind turn-of-the-century globalization is aesthetic: commonsense business plans about oceanic commerce match up with the formally abstract nature of *sensus communis* in a poetic circle and organic whole. Norris's idea of a transnational literary frontier, carried forth by the figure of an American poet headed so far westward that he will arrive in the East, aligns with the economic vision of a thoroughly integrated global market. The poet Presley takes with him the parting advice of the shipping magnate who underwrites this venture across the Pacific: "Tell the men of the East to look out for the men of the West. The irrepressible Yank is knocking at the doors of their temples and he will want to sell 'em carpet-sweepers for their harems and electric light plants for their temple shrines."[43] Unabashedly orientalist, this prediction looks to substitute wheat and other commodities to which everyone is forced to have access for an aesthetic culture where shared feelings for the beautiful create social cohesion.

Even though the Whitmanesque poet in *The Octopus* thinks that he is sounding "the world-wide keynote," his vision more readily is a global one that is literally financed by transnational capitalism. That is, he consistently mistakes the global expanse of world markets for aesthetic universalism. His confusion is not unlike the replacement of the idea of World Literature by Global Literature that critics have recently described. As opposed to "aspirations to true universality" implied by world literature, the global suggests the deep divisions and inequalities created by the such interlinked phenomena as global capitalism and global warming.[44] The globe may be coextensive with the world, but it is devoid of the wider "community sense" of the aesthetic. If the global "implies worldwide processes that polarize the conditions of the world's people," its standard-bearers have proved adept at using aesthetics to gloss over such tensions.[45] Norris understood this trade-off early on: his essay on the global frontier of fin-de-siècle American literature begins by invoking the recent landing of US marines in China, but the empirical reality of military aggression is soon subsumed under the idea – and idealism – of a world market so complete that it appears as an uninterrupted whole. And even though the narrator of *The Octopus* takes care to remember the lives shattered by the corporate power of the railroad, these discordant details ultimately find no place in the perfect form of the circle, itself an analogue for the globe.

What happens to the inassimilable remainders that fail to match up with this otherwise encompassing sensibility of a transnational whole? As Hardt and Negri write, "The space of imperial sovereignty ... is smooth." Divisions and fractures may be everywhere, but they are so abundant that "it only appears as a continuous, uniform space."[46] No gaps, no angles, no misalignments of art and commerce: this shape is the result of the encroachment of globalization on transnational aesthetics. The question that lingers is whether this arrangement is so completely a matter of rational commonsense that the aesthetic and political feelings associated with *sensus communis* are forever eclipsed.

NOTES

1 John Ruskin, *The Political Economy of Art: Being the Substance (with Additions) of Two Lectures Delivered at Manchester, July 10th and 13th, 1857* (London: Smith, Elder, 1857), 13.

2 Colleen Glenney Boggs, *Transnationalism and American Literature: Literary Translation, 1773–1892* (New York: Routledge, 2007), 1.

3 Ruskin, *Political Economy*, 122.

4 Sydney Smith, review of *Statistical Annals of the United States* by Adam Seybert in *Edinburgh Review* 33 (1820). Web, Google Books, accessed 12 May 2015.

5 Susan Buck-Morss, "Aesthetics and Anaesthetics: Walter Benjamin's Artwork Essay Recosidered," *October* 62 (Fall 1992): 5. See also Raymond Williams's entry on "Aesthetic" in his *Keywords: A Vocabulary of Culture and Society* (New York: Oxford University Press, 1983).

6 Thomas Paine, *Common Sense* in *The Thomas Paine Reader* (New York: Penguin, 1987), 66.

7 Paine, *Common Sense*, 82.

8 The Editors, "World Lite: What Is Global Literature," *N+1 Magazine* (Fall 2013). Web, <https://nplusonemag.com/issue-17/the-intellectual-situation/world-lite/>, accessed 24 July 2015.

9 Siân Silyn Roberts, *Gothic Subjects: The Transformation of Individualism in American Fiction* (Philadelphia: University of Pennsylvania Press, 2014), 26. In terming common sense a "nationalizing fantasy" Roberts overlooks wider, global impulses behind Paine's pamphlet.

10 Paine *Common Sense*, 109.

11 Immanuel Kant, "What Is Enlightenment?" in *Practical Philosophy*, trans. Mary J. Gregor (Cambridge: Cambridge University Press, 1999), 18.

12 Elizabeth Maddock Dillon, "Fear of Formalism: Kant, Twain, and Cultural Studies in American Literature," *Diacritics* 27.4 (1998): 54.

13 Immanuel Kant, *Critique of Judgment*, trans. J. H. Bernard (New York: Hafner, 1951).

14 Hannah Arendt, *Lectures on Kant's Political Philosophy* (Chicago: University of Chicago Press, 1982), 70. For a different valuing of aesthetics, one that

privileges brokenness over unity, see F. R. Ankersmit, *Aesthetic Politics: Political Philosophy Beyond Fact and Value* (Standford, CA: Stanford University Press, 1996), 17–18.

15 Terry Eagleton, *The Ideology of the Aesthetic* (Oxford: Blackwell, 1990), 96.

16 Kant, *Critique of Judgment*, 6.

17 William Marsden, *A History of Sumatra, Containing an Account of the Government, Laws, Customs and Manners of the Native Inhabitants, with a Description of the Natural Productions, and a Relation of the Ancient Political state of That Island* (London, 1784), 113. Web, Google Books, accessed 6 May 2015.

18 Kant, *Critique of Judgment*, 80.

19 Sean McCann, "The Ambiguous Politics of Politicizing, or De-Politicizing the Aesthetic" in *Poetics/Politics: Radical Aesthetics for the Classroom*, ed. Amitava Kumar (New York: St. Martin's, 1999), 49–50. For similar language, see Emory Elliot, who asks whether aesthetics constitute a "positive bridge" or "a tool of divisiveness, enmity, and oppression" ("Introduction: Cultural Diversity and the Problem of Aesthetics" in *Aesthetics in a Multicultural Age* [New York: Oxford University Press, 2002], 3).

20 Thomas Paine, "The Liberty Tree" in *Thomas Paine Reader*, 63.

21 Paul Jay, *Global Matters: The Transnational Turn in Literary Studies* (Ithaca, NY: Cornell University Press, 2010), 5.

22 Paine, *Common Sense*, 83.

23 Kant, *Critique of Judgment*.

24 Henry James, *The American* (New York: Penguin, 1986), 33.

25 James, *The American*, 34.

26 Laura Doyle, "Toward a Philosophy of Transnationalism," *Journal of Transnational American Studies* 1.1 (2009): 12.

27 Donald E. Pease, "Introduction: Re-Mapping the Transnational Turn" in *Re-Framing the Transnational Turn in American Studies*, Winifred Fluck, Donald E. Pease, and John Carlos Rowe eds. (Hanover, NH: Dartmouth College Press, 2011), 5.

28 Jahan Ramazani, "A Transnational Poetics," *American Literary History* 18.2 (Summer 2006): 355.

29 Kant, *Critique of Judgment*, 71.

30 Eagleton, *Ideology of the Aesthetic*, 9. See also Gayatri Chakravorty Spivak's comment that "top-down policy breaches of Enlightenment principles are more rule than exception" (*An Aesthetic Education in the Era of Globalization* [Cambridge, MA: Harvard University Press, 2012], 4).

31 Karl Marx and Friedrich Engels, *Manifesto of the Communist Party*. Web, www.marxists.org/archive/marx/works/download/pdf/Manifesto.pdf, accessed 13 May 2015.

32 Marx and Engels, *Manifesto*.

33 Jay, *Global Matters*, 23.

34 In addition to Pease, see Bryce Traister, "The Object of Study, or, Are We Being Transnational Yet?" *Journal of Transnational American Studies* 2.1 (July 2010): 1–28.

35 See Russ Castronovo, *Beautiful Democracy: Aesthetics and Anarchy in a Global Era* (Chicago: University of Chicago Press, 2007): 180–211.

36   Anna Brickhouse, *Transamerican Literary Relations and the Nineteenth-Century Public Sphere* (Cambridge: Cambridge University Press, 2004), 3.

37   Frank Norris, *The Octopus: A Story of California* (New York: Penguin, 1994), 651.

38   Pease, "Introduction," 3.

39   Jay, *Global Matters*, 27.

40   Frank Norris, "The Frontier Gone at Last" in *The Responsibilities of the Novelist and Other Literary Essays* (London: Grant Richards, 1903), 72. Similar notes are sounded in elsewhere in this volume of essays; see especially "The Great American Novelist" and "The Novel with a 'Purpose.'"

41   Norris, *The Octopus*, 651.

42   Michael Hardt and Antonio Negri, *Empire* (Cambridge, MA: Harvard University Press, 2000), 10.

43   Norris, *The Octopus*, 648.

44   The Editors, "World Lite" 11.

45   Ibid. 11.

46   Hardt and Negri, *Empire*, 190.

PART II

Literary Histories

5

JOHANNES VOELZ

Transnationalism and Nineteenth-Century Literature

Reading nineteenth-century American literature transnationally is a project that unmistakably bears the stamp of current-day critical investments. Whatever we impute to nineteenth-century authors – be it that they have always been transnational, that they resisted the transnational, or that they aimed to write the transnational into being – springs from early twenty-first-century concerns about the promises and challenges of overcoming the political, cultural, spatial, and temporal limits of the nation. In order not to let this hermeneutical premise lead to an all-out presentism, we can try and approach the transnational in nineteenth-century literature through a reconstruction of the historical conditions of our topic's second term: literature. As Richard Brodhead once put it, "[T]he most significant lines of division within the literary field are produced not by differences between authors or styles or periods or movements but by literature's responsiveness to the different *places* built for literature in American cultural life."[1] By taking into consideration some of the places literature inhabited in the social landscape, we come to see that the transnational in nineteenth-century literature had widely divergent meanings and uses. In this article I therefore aim to shed light on five different dimensions of reading the transnational. While the first three dimensions are derived from literary field constellations of the period under consideration, the final two will pay attention to critical paradigms that have become of great urgency in our own time. The first three paradigms discuss the transnational in the context of (I) world literature, (II) political and social movements on both sides of the Atlantic, and (III) the international novel; the concluding paradigms consider how American literature was geographically reimagined in (sometimes competing) hemispheric frameworks (IV) and read American literature in relation to its ideological implicatedness in American imperialism (V). Futile though the attempt would be to write a comprehensive history of nineteenth-century transnational American literature, I hope that the examples I have chosen from these five paradigms convey an impression of the scope of the transnational in this period. Its variegated uses may demonstrate that the transnational has not always fulfilled the critical needs of those currently espousing a "transnational turn" in American studies, but I hope that this will be taken as an invitation to reflexive literary study.[2]

I

When romanticism arrived in the United States during the 1830s, roughly four decades after its flourishing in Europe, its proponents – most of all the Transcendentalists – popularized an American version of the idea of world literature. They thus coupled the promotion of a national literary tradition with an outlook we now call transnational. To trace the contours of this understanding of world literature, we briefly need to recall some of the innovations of romanticism and their interdependence with the literary field.

The romantics established a new ideal of authorship, which emphasized the creative poet's sensitivity of perception and his power of expression. The apotheosis of the creative imagination, spelled out perhaps most influentially (at least for the reception of romanticism in the United States) by Coleridge in his *Aids to Reflection*, "suggested an aesthetic solution to the problems of faith in a rationalist age"[3] and at the same time dignified "the creative imagination as a source of quasi-divine authority."[4] Once the creative imagination became sacralized in this manner, aesthetics was no longer subservient to the doctrines of institutionalized religion. It is in this sense that the romantics effectively promoted an autonomous aesthetics.

In the United States, the romantic model of authorship emerged alongside the professional writer. Well into the 1830s, literary writers were expected to be amateurs who made their living in respectable professions. This situation began to change with the increasing commercialization of literature, which allowed Emerson, to take a famous example, to trade in his career as a minister against the career of a professional literary lecturer. But the specialization of the literary writer, enabled as it was by the emergence of the literary marketplace, did not provide any guarantee for cultural prestige. Romanticism supplied cultural legitimacy for the newly professional writer wedded to the ideal of aesthetic autonomy: surely a creative genius was ill-suited for the practice of a regular profession like the law.

The romantics' take on literary specialization also provided a particular interpretation of the new professional class of writers: if the poet was characterized by his creative imagination, then he belonged to a select group of kindred spirits defined solely by their shared access to a higher realm of ideas. This defining characteristic presupposed that true poets were not subject to social conventions and geographical boundaries. As Margaret Fuller phrased it, "I say, that what is limitless is alone divine."[5] Almost by definition, then, the romantic conception of literature had a cosmopolitan dimension, and the idea of "world literature," popularized by Johann Wolfgang von Goethe in a range of miscellanies starting in 1827 (among them his essay on the German translation of Thomas Carlyle's *Life of Schiller* – itself an instance of transnational crisscrossing), consequently fell on fertile ground in the United States.[6] This is true not only for the Transcendentalists but also for romantics like Melville, Hawthorne, and Poe.

Goethe never articulated a unified theory of world literature, but in most of his remarks on the topic, he emphasized the power of literature to bring different nations closer to each other; to focus, rather than on immitigable differences, on what was common to all men, and thereby to contribute to the "mutual recognition" among nations.[7] At least implicitly, such calls were seconded by the leading Transcendentalists. In *Walden* (1854), Henry David Thoreau incorporated a chapter on "Reading" in which he described books, in a riposte to Adam Smith's *The Wealth of Nations*, as "the treasured wealth of the world and the fit inheritance of generations and nations."[8] "Generations and nations" suggests that world literature not only contracted space but also time. Indeed, for Thoreau, the canon of great books (or "world-books," as Emerson called them[9]) pointed to a future in which not just different nations, but different ages would "successively deposit their trophies" in the "forum of the world."[10] Significantly, this future world republic of letters would not do away with nations but, as in Goethe's vision, would allow nations to flourish in mutual toleration. For Goethe, as for Emerson and Thoreau, the transnationalism furthered by world literature did not stand in opposition to the nation per se but only to the nation in its most restrictive dimension. Romantics on both sides of the Atlantic tended to follow the Hegelian idea that "a people can be considered as truly such only on condition of expressing an idea," as Victor Cousin, the French Hegelian popular among the Transcendentalists, put it.[11] It was in "the forum of the world" that a nation's "idea" could find full expression.[12]

Thoreau also exemplifies the ambiguous stance between elitism and democratic commitment from which American romantics approached world literature. On the one hand, "the works of the great poets have never yet been read by mankind, for only great poets can read them."[13] This idea is familiar also from Emerson[14] and, prior to that, from German romantics like Novalis, Schleiermacher, and the Schlegels.[15] Reading, understood as a noble exercise of the spirit, requires the same creative work of the imagination that goes into writing, and is thus reserved to the creative geniuses that make up the exclusive cosmopolitan group of newly professionalized, serious authors. On the other hand, Thoreau entertained the expressly democratic hope that in the United States "the village should [...] take the place of the nobleman of Europe. It should be the patron of the fine arts."[16] To achieve this, America stood in need of institutions of learning that would instill intellectual independence required for creative reading. In order to become a cosmopolitan poet, the common man needed, as Thoreau put it in a characteristic pun, "uncommon schools."[17]

Transcendentalists aimed to set an example in the uncommon schooling in world literature. They continuously referenced the scriptures of Asian religions, ranging from Hindu and Buddhist to Confucian and Zoroastrian texts – again, not because these texts provided glimpses into other cultures, but because they were pervaded, as Emerson contended, by a spirit that turned them into "living characters translatable into every tongue and form of life."[18] In 1858, Emerson moreover introduced the readership of the *Atlantic Monthly* to fourteenth-century Persian poet Hāfez (who had inspired Goethe's *West-Östlicher Divan*, from 1819) by translating into English chunks of his verses from the German translations of Joseph Freiherr von Hammer-Purgstall and adorning them with his own brand of commentary. Emerson made Hāfez (or Hafiz, as he spelled it) speak to his own time by presenting him as a fellow nonconformist, who fought the pervasive "air of sterility" with "large utterance": "What is pent and smouldered in the dumb actor, is not pent in the poet, but passes over into new form, at once relief and creation."[19] That Emerson made Hāfez sound like a version of himself underlines the point that world literature had the capacity to provide the romantic poet with cultural legitimacy because it allowed the American poet, culturally marginalized in his own land, to claim the authority of ancient cultural traditions. This, however, is not to suggest that cosmopolitanism was a ruse for the acquisition of distinction, but merely that the world literature-variant of transnationalism played an important role in the emerging field of professional letters.

II

For American romantics, art's disposition to transgress all boundaries ultimately reflected back on art itself. To be true to itself, art had to break open its own confines and transform life in its social and political dimensions. This idea, initially articulated by early romantics like Friedrich Schiller,[20] fit surprisingly well with the decidedly non-romantic doctrines of moral utilitarianism dominant in the United States of the late eighteenth and early nineteenth centuries. According to this position, "moral principle," in John Quincy Adams's words, "should be the alpha and omega of all human composition, poetry or prose, scientific or literary, written or spoken."[21] In one variant, then, the romantic embrace of world literature combined with the idea of the moral duty of the arts and ended up producing a strong commitment to political reform. As we will see, such reform agendas were by no means limited to matters concerning the United States; their framing tended to be transnational.

Margaret Fuller may be the best exemplar of the artist who subscribed to a romantic conception of world literature and translated it into transnational political action. As the editor of the Transcendentalist journal *Dial*, she articulated what historian Charles Capper has described as "a new *transnational* protodemocratic conception of the 'office' of the critic," which she later also applied to her work as literary editor of Horace Greeley's *New-York Tribune*.[22] Following that, she reported for the *Tribune* from her travels to Europe, where she became a witness to the democratic revolutions of 1848–49. As Larry J. Reynolds has described it, the revolutions "evoked an unprecedented outpouring of support from Americans, who attributed them to America's example. Sympathy meetings, banquets, toasts, poems, songs, marches, speeches, and resolutions in favor of the revolutions became a sign of the times."[23]

The majority of Fuller's dispatches were written from Rome, where she experienced the outbreak of the revolution and its eventual blood-stained failure. In Fuller's eyes, the cause fought for in Europe was the cause of universal liberty. But for her, the universal played out in material ways, and this meant that Europe and the United States needed to help each other mutually. While European revolutionaries needed the moral and material support from Americans, providing that support represented, in the words of critic Francesco Guida, "a golden opportunity for America to pursue a course that would be faithful to its origins."[24]

On her trip to Italy Fuller first stopped in England where she met exiled revolutionaries such as Giuseppe Mazzini and Adam Mickiewicz. That she met them here was no coincidence: a large number of European democrats and radicals made London their home, among them Lajos Kossuth, Giuseppe Garibaldi, and Karl Marx. "By 1840," writes historian R. J. M. Blackett, "Britain's support of these exiles had so enhanced her image that she was viewed as 'the moral arbiter of the western world'."[25] For the same reason, London also attracted African American and white American abolitionists. As David Brion Davis notes, "Beginning in the early 1830s, virtually every important African American leader" traveled to England, "hoping to gain British support for specific causes and to build what ... Frederick Douglass [called] a 'moral cordon' around the United States, so that slaveholders would be overwhelmed wherever they went by denunciations of their so-called peculiar institution."[26]

Abolitionism and the democratic revolutions of 1848, like other reform movements ranging from women's rights to temperance, were interlinked both institutionally and ideologically as subsets of what Fuller called "the cause of human freedom."[27] Moreover, abolitionism was a genuinely transnational movement, even after the emancipation of slavery in the British West Indies in 1834. But transnationalism in this case did not mean harmony or taken-for-granted solidarity: having traveled through Britain, such African American slave narrators as Harriet Jacobs and Frederick Douglass related to their American readers that "even the meanest and most ignorant among [the European poor] was vastly superior to the condition of the most favored slaves in America," as Jacobs wrote.[28] With such statements they aimed to disarm such pro-slavery ideologues as George Fitzhugh, who claimed that the southern slave was better off than the northern worker laboring under industrial "wage slavery."[29] Yet in England, that very argument was hurled at abolitionists by Chartists, whose democratic working-class movement coincided with the revolutions on the European continent. On the stage of transnational abolitionism, American activists visiting England unexpectedly found themselves, as Davis puts it, in a "contest between the two systems of oppression."[30] This required from American abolitionists delicate balancing acts of insisting on the difference between wage slavery and chattel slavery, while on the other hand trying to find common ground between both movements.

Abolitionism was transnational not only insofar as it played out in a transatlantic public sphere but also in the sense that one of its chief points of debate concerned the question whether the future of African Americans was to be seen outside the United States, be it in Africa or the southern Americas. While most abolitionists rejected the American Colonization Society's scheme of relocating blacks to Liberia as a flagrantly racist project, Robert S. Levine has shown that the *Dred Scott* decision of 1857, which denied citizenship to blacks in the United States, gave momentum to alternative emigration plans devised by black leaders. While Martin Delany explored possibilities of African American emigration to the Niger region of Africa, William Wells Brown and others preferred Haiti as "a site for a regenerative black nationalism in the Americas."[31] Even Frederick Douglass, who is usually seen as having been firmly committed to the United States, wrote in an editorial that "we can raise no objection to the present movement towards Hayti."[32] For Martin Delany, on the other hand, transnational abolition was tied to the possibility of hemispheric revolutionary violence, a vision he fleshed out in his novel *Blake; or, The Huts of America* (1859–62). White writers, too, imagined black revolutionary transnationalism. In *Dred* (1856), Harriet Beecher Stowe's figured the transnational as the Great

Dismal Swamp, while Melville, in *Benito Cereno* (1855), created geographical layers of revolution out of the unbounded sea and Haiti, the historical site of the first successful black revolution, which he evoked by naming the ship at the center of his narrative *San Dominick*.

III

From within the romantic literary field, the writings coming out of the activist strand of transnationalism generally appeared as belonging to the domain of literature, if only uneasily. Shortly after its publication, Margaret Fuller reviewed *The Narrative of the Life of Frederick Douglass* in the *New-York Tribune*, and though she could not bring herself to admit Douglass and black authors the likes of Alexandre Dumas and Frédéric Souliè to the elite circle of serious poets, she did place them in a second tier of what could be called "world literature light."[33] For Fuller, serious and light literature still inhabited the same cultural cosmos (which is why she reviewed Douglass in her position as *literary* critic), but over the ensuing decades the stratification of literature became increasingly pronounced, both regarding artistic norms and the social strata that made up the audiences of the various segments. As a result, the final decades of the century brought forth a literary field constellation in which the transnational played a very different role than it had for the romantics and their promotion of world literature.

At midcentury, roughly simultaneously with the emergence of a middlebrow sphere of domestic fiction and a lowbrow sphere of cheap fiction (like the dime novel and story-paper fiction), a "well-marked and well-supported zone of serious artistic authorship" took shape.[34] Magazines like *The Atlantic Monthly*, *Harper's New Monthly Magazine*, and *Scribner's Monthly*, all of which were founded in the 1850s, created a dense network of writers who belonged to what William Dean Howells called "the fine air of high literature."[35] This "fine air" undoubtedly smacked of class distinction, but it also carries echoes of romantic notions of autonomous aesthetics housed in a higher realm. For these writers committed to the art of the novel, achieving the "height" of their art became possible by turning cosmopolitan – a turn that at once signaled economic privilege and cultural sophistication. The literary magazines mentioned above featured writing that was nearly obsessed with Americans traveling abroad, and writers like Henry James, William Dean Howells, and Edith Wharton devised the corresponding genre of the "international novel" – often serialized in these very publications. Howells's *A Foregone Conclusion* (1875), James's *The American* (1877), and Wharton's novella *Madame de Treymes* (1907) all portrayed the failed social involvements of innocent Americans with European society. The latter they rendered as sophisticated in its cultural achievement (and thus as a necessary resource for the maturation of American civilization) but also as more rigidly structured and deeply marred by historically accrued guilt than the new world.[36]

For American realists, the concern with the transnational was by no means limited to the thematic level. As Winfried Fluck has shown, for these writers taking the novel seriously as an art form, and accumulating cultural capital from it, entailed working through and adapting the aesthetic practices of European realists, particularly of the French and Russian school (British fiction, by contrast, seemed outdated).[37] It is precisely by refraining from imitating European realism and instead using it for their own (national) purposes that American realists achieved an aesthetic transnationalism of their own.

IV

While I have so far reconstructed the transnational as a function internal to the nineteenth-century literary field, recent scholarship has added to this perspective by reconstructing alternative literary scenes that reached across (the partially still emergent) national borders of the Americas and that were marginalized in, if not outright excluded from, the mainstream literary field of the United States. Having up to now explored the uses of the transnational from within the national literary field, I will now turn to transamerican literary scenes that were exterior to that field (while often intersecting with it) and that can be described as having arisen from "the exterior borders of the modern/colonial world system," to use a phrase of Walter Mignolo's.[38]

Critic Anna Brickhouse conveys an impression of such hemispheric formations, which range, in her exemplifying catalog, "from the hispanophone-exile literary communities of 1820s Philadelphia and New York, to the 'golden age' of reformist literature in Cuba during the 1830s and 1840s, to the *Le Républicain* and *L'Union* writers of the Ignace Nau *cénacle* in 1830s Haiti, to the *L'Album littéraire* and *Les Cenelles* circle of Creole writers of color in New Orleans in the 1840s, to the landmark publication at mid-century of the monthly literary and historical periodical *El Museo Yucateco* in Campeche, Mexico."[39] Brickhouse describes such hemispheric literary scenes as "competing public spheres,"[40] a conceptual approach that highlights the political function of literature to constitute social constellations incongruous with national borders. Whereas the "literary field"–model I have employed so far highlights the ways in which particular forms of transnational aesthetics allowed writers to mark out distinct positions among their peers in the increasingly professionalized world of letters, critics working with the model of "competing public spheres" tend to emphasize how transnational cultural networks enabled the ideological contestation of US national narratives. This approach has thus been particularly useful for the now dominant version of transnational American studies, which is invested in the recovery work of writings (and their hemispheric spaces of circulation) that have been marginalized or repressed, and which thus practices a model of literary scholarship committed to a transnational politics of resistance.

Kirsten Silva Gruesz has perhaps gone furthest in bringing to light some of the print culture circuits in which such alternative public spheres materialized.[41] She reconstructs the literary aims and translation practices of nineteenth-century Spanish-language periodicals such as *El Clamor Público* of Los Angeles, *El Bejareño* and *El Ranchero* of San Antonio, *El Nuevo Mundo* of San Francisco, and *El Mundo Nuevo/La América Ilustrada* of New York, and she points out that their editors habitually juxtaposed texts (her study focuses on poetry) from the entire Spanish-speaking world, written, among others, by Mexican, Spanish, Cuban, New Granadan/ Colombian, and Venezuelan authors. "This is in addition," she explains, "to the occasional poem or dramatic excerpt from the Siglo de Oro (Cervantes, Rioja, Calderón), the Latin American colonial period (Sor Juana, Alonso de Ercilla), or the translations from Lamartine, Hugo, Béranger, Byron, Longfellow, Moore, Heine," and others.[42]

A particularly revealing case in point is *El Mundo Nuevo/La América Ilustrada*, published in New York between 1871 and 1875 by the Leslie publishing house, which ran several successful newspapers in German and Spanish. The biweekly *El Mundo Nuevo/La América Ilustrada* was modeled after *Harper's*, the *Atlantic*, or the *Century*, and it encouraged its readers, writes Gruesz, "to align themselves along multiple lines of affiliation: as residents or citizens of the United States who took pride in their cultural Hispanism, or as members of a far-flung transnational community of progressive, elite Spanish Americans."[43] The magazine's identification with New York and the United States signaled an uneasy proximity to northern ideas of modernization (even in the exigencies of relying on advertisers), but it also allowed for an inclusive hemispheric appeal: instead of having to point back to a particular homeland, the affiliation with New York allowed for the constitution of an inclusive Latin American cosmopolitanism organized around the Spanish language. As Gruesz remarks, editor and poet Enrique Piñeyro, one of many Cuban intellectuals who fled to the United States at the outset of the Ten Years' War in 1868, stressed "the power of print to keep the [Hispanophone] family together under the pressures of modernity"[44] and thus anticipated the editorial activism of poet-politician José Martí, who would arrive in New York from Cuba some ten years later, in 1880, and put into practice his vision of *Nuestra América* "as a linguistically based print community."[45]

In his famous essay "Nuestra América," published in 1891 in New York and Mexico City, the Cuban national hero called on tropes of republicanism ("good government") and literary and nationalist romanticism to redraw "America" along hemispheric lines. Against Spanish colonialism and US imperialism, he mounted the notion of *mestizo* – a racial and cultural impurity grown naturally. Rejecting narratives of progress and modernization, he held up organic hybridity against civilizational artificiality: "the autochthonous mestizo has vanquished the exotic Creole. There is no battle between civilization and barbarism, but between false erudition and nature."[46] From Emerson (Martí read him "feverishly"[47]), who some fifty years earlier had complained that "instead of Man Thinking, we have the Bookworm,"[48] Martí drew support for his cultural program of *mestizo*. In his view, "our America" had heeded Emerson's call: "[T]he imported book [has] been vanquished by natural man in America."[49]

Martí's writing style, steeped in the tradition of the literary essay, positions the literary as a critique of modern rationality and thus turns poetic language, as Julio Ramos writes, into "the form to be learned by good statespeople, 'creators,' in order to govern the *originary* world of America, centered in 'the soul of the land'."[50] In order to imagine a hemispheric mestizo America, Martí thus draws on romanticism for at least two purposes: not only does this tradition help conceptualizing the dynamic cultural transmutations of mestizo as natural, but it also provides the resource for authorizing mestizo *letrados* like Martí himself as the "unacknowledged legislators of the world," to speak with Shelley.[51]

V

As reconstructions of transamericanity stand in the service of an anti-imperialist politics, transnational critics have had to remain alert to the ways in which nineteenth-century hemispheric counter-publics could "reproduce the unevenness that has plagued the development of the Americas," as Jesse Alemán phrases it.[52] Transnational remappings of America thus remain indebted to empire criticism, a critical approach that gained prominence in the field of American studies roughly a decade prior to the so-called "transnational turn."[53] Indeed, in the age of transnationalism, the paradigm of empire criticism has remained particularly fruitful when it explores the ambiguities of texts and authors that waver between anti-imperialism and imperialism, or, put differently, between oppositional and hegemonic forms of transnationalism.

A good entry point into such ambivalent forms of imperialism is the work of Mark Twain, who was championed by none other than José Martí. Above all, it was Twain's *A Connecticut Yankee in King Arthur's Court* that found Martí's admiration. As Shelley Fisher Fishkin reports, "Martí wrote in *La Nación* in 1890, just a little over a month after *Yankee* was published, that the book was 'fueled by indignation' at 'the privileged classes who are beginning to rise on the backs of the poor,' that its author was 'exasperated' by 'injustice,' and that reading the book made Martí want to meet its author and congratulate him."[54] His praise went so far as to refer to Twain as "Nuestro Mark Twain"[55] – a badge of honor that at once made clear on which side of the hemispheric struggle between "false erudition and nature" Twain was to be found.

Yet, on the other hand, Twain's outspoken anti-imperialism has not stopped critics like Amy Kaplan from detecting deeply imperialist strands in his writing and thinking. Kaplan has proposed that "the national identity of Mark Twain, his 'Americanness,' was forged in an international context of imperial expansion" – a context that in her reading could be pinned down biographically: "[I]n his imperial encounter with Hawaii [during his first trip there in 1866], Twain honed the lenses – and blind spots – that he later turned on the legacy of slavery and race relations within the United States."[56] I have elsewhere argued against the premises of ideological subject formation that underlie accounts such as Kaplan's,[57] but if *Yankee*'s protagonist Hank Morgan ends up brutally destroying the medieval civilization he initially aimed to reform, the question indeed arises whether the novel construes the causes for this catastrophe as residing in Hank Morgan's modernizing reforms *gone wrong* or in the violence that inheres in the quasi-imperialist reform mission itself.

A similar tension is at play in Walt Whitman's paeans to cosmopolitan comradeship, "Salut Au Monde!" and "Passage to India." Whitman's earnest internationalism is as impressive as it is touching: verse after verse, page after page of "Salut" are spent directly addressing his readers in specific locales, creating a world map that defies the hierarchical gradations of the political maps that Whitman seems to have worked off of. Yet, while he claims to "mix indiscriminately," and thus "salute[s] all the inhabitants of the earth,"[58] and while he even thinks of "you each and everywhere whom I specify not, but include just the same!,"[59] he nonetheless repeatedly claims the exceptionalist position of speaking not quite on the same level as the countless specimen he greets, but "in America's name."[60]

It is by no means implausible to argue, following the lead of Betsy Erkkila, that Whitman's internationalist poems put forth a vision, as she says of "Passage to India," "of a world united in a common democratic culture by means of modern advances in communication and transportation."[61] But it is likewise the case that Whitman's passages about the effects of communication and transportation have the effect of uniting the world on most uneven terms. In "Salut," we read, "I see the tracks of the railroads of the earth/ ... I see them in Asia and Africa,"[62] and as Walter Grünzweig rightly notes, "these are colonial, and indeed imperial, achievements and technologies which are introduced at the expense of the global community."[63] But even if we concede that Whitman's poetry is in no way free from imperialist ideology, this does not reduce its transnational dimension to imperialism. After all, throughout the twentieth century Whitman has been of use for international leftist movements, including the communist "Third International,"[64] precisely because his poetry facilitates the kind of readings Erkkila proposes.

A final example of reading transnational American literature from within the paradigm of empire criticism takes us back to the early republic and the literary responses to the young nation's first national security crisis. No longer protected by the British (and French), US ships became subject to capture by pirates from the Barbary Coast. The literary result was a body of fictional and nonfictional captivity narratives that related cases of "white slavery" in the hands of Muslim captors (which was more or less implicitly compared to, and conflated with, chattel slavery in the United States). These texts provided a stage for imaginary encounters with Islam and thus gave rise to an Orientalist imagination that would resonate in later works such as Washington Irving's *The Alhambra: A Series of Tales and Sketches* (1832) and Edgar Allan Poe's *Tales of the Grotesque and Arabesque* (1840).

Next to Peter Markoe's novel *The Algerine Spy in Pennsylvania* (1787) and Susanna Rowson's drama *Slaves in Algiers* (1794), the most famous of these treatments of Barbary captivity is Royall Tyler's *The Algerine Captive* (1797). In the book's humorous first part, the protagonist Updike Underhill is a fool in the *picaro* tradition, but in the second part, the novel turns into the sentimental depiction of his abduction and enslavement. After his release, Underhill looks back on what he went through: "I suffered hunger, sickness, fatigue, insult, stripes, wounds, and every other cruel injury. ... I had been degraded to a slave, and was now advanced to a citizen of the freest country in the universe."[65] At this late stage, the novel insists on drawing sharp lines between the West and the rest, between the United States as the world's beacon of liberty and the despotic and cruel world of the Muslim Barbary pirates.

But this conclusion to the narrative belies Underhill's actual experiences during his captivity. His Muslim captors, he finds out little by little, equal him in their capacity for reason, generosity, and sentiment, so much so that he almost converts to their religion. It is "a rare cultural moment," writes Timothy Marr, "when the possibility of rational dialogue existed within American involvement with Mediterranean Muslims."[66] In light of the newly recognized rationality of the Muslims, "American involvement with Mediterranean Muslims" appears as the collusion of American sea trade and its derivative, the state-sponsored Barbary piracy, a most lucrative business in the mercantilist vein. For a little while, the Barbary pirates become imaginable as parasitical business partners, which differs from the liberal idea of a world society pacified by commerce insofar as parasites, no matter how enlightened, violently feed off their hosts. The novel suggests that the transnational ties of commerce and its attending civilized rationality may be possible, but can be realized only on the basis of violence – an insight that Tyler could only fathom by redrawing the boundary between democratic west and despotic east. Not only is this novel ambiguously situated between imperialism and transnationalism; it calls into question the very distinction between these two terms. Herein lies the truly troubling provocation empire criticism continues to offer to transnational American literary studies.

NOTES

1 Richard H. Brodhead, "The American Literary Field," in Sacvan Bercovitch ed., *The Cambridge History of American Literature, vol. 3: Prose Writing 1860–1920* (New York: Cambridge University Press, 2005), 13.

2 I borrow this phrase from Pierre Bourdieu and Loïc Wacquant. See their *Invitation to Reflexive Sociology* (Chicago: University of Chicago Press, 1992).

3 E. S. Shaffer, "Religion and Literature," in Marshall Brown, ed., *The Cambridge History of Literary Criticism, vol. 5: Romanticism* (Cambridge: Cambridge University Press, 2005), 143.

4 Lawrence Buell, *New England Literary Culture* (New York: Cambridge University Press, 1986), 69.

5 Margaret Fuller, *Summer on the Lakes, in 1843* (Boston: Little and Brown, 1844), 65.

6 Prior to Goethe, the term *Weltliteratur* had been used by Christoph Martin Wieland and Wilhelm August Schlegel (as early as 1802). See *Metzler Literaturlexikon*, ed. Günther and Irmgard Schweikle (Stuttgart: Metzler, 1984), 299.

7 Johann Wolfgang von Goethe, "German Romance," in *Werke (Hamburger Ausgabe), vol. 12: Schriften zur Kunst und Literatur, Maximen und Reflexionen* (München: Deutscher Taschenbuch Verlag, 1998), 362. Translation mine.

8 Henry David Thoreau, *Walden*, J. Lyndon Shanley, ed., in *The Writings of Henry David Thoreau* (Princeton, NJ: Princeton University Press, 1971), 102.

9   Ralph Waldo Emerson, "Shakespeare," in Alfred Ferguson et al., eds., *The Collected Works of Ralph Waldo Emerson, vol. 4: Representative Men* (Cambridge, MA: Belknap, 1987), 115.
10 Thoreau, *Walden*, 104.
11 Victor Cousin, *Introduction to the Philosophy of History* (Boston: Hilliard, Gray, Little, and Wilkins, 1832), 294.
12 For a fuller version of this argument, see my *Transcendental Resistance: The New Americanists and Emerson's Challenge* (Hanover, NH: University Press of New England, 2010), 205–43.
13 Thoreau, *Walden*, 104.
14 In "The American Scholar," Emerson famously contends that "there is then creative reading as well as creative writing" (Ralph Waldo Emerson, "The American Scholar," in Alfred Ferguson et al., eds., *The Collected Works of Ralph Waldo Emerson, vol. 1: Nature, Addresses, and Lectures* [Cambridge, MA: Belknap, 1971], 58).
15 See for instance, Novalis's dictum that "the true reader must be the extended author. He is the higher instance, who receives his subject-matter after it has already been prepared by a lower instance" (Novalis, *Werke*, ed. Gerhard Schulz [Munchen: Beck, 2001], 352, translation mine).
16 Thoreau, *Walden*, 109.
17 Ibid., 108.
18 Emerson, "Books," in Alfred Ferguson et al., eds., *The Collected Works of Ralph Waldo Emerson, vol. 7: Society and Solitude* (Cambridge, MA: Belknap, 2007), 111.
19 Emerson, "Persian Poetry," in Alfred Ferguson et al., eds., *The Collected Works of Ralph Waldo Emerson, vol. 8: Letters and Social Aims* (Cambridge, MA: Belknap, 2010), 131–32.
20 In his *Aesthetic Letters*, Schiller argued that "the attempt of a people that has reached maturity to transform its natural State into a moral one" could succeed only with the help of aesthetics: "it is through Beauty that we arrive at Freedom" (*On the Aesthetic Education of Man: In a Series of Letters*, trans. Reginald Snell [New Haven, CT: Yale University Press, 1954], 27, 29).
21 Adams as quoted in Buell, *New England Literary Culture*, 65.
22 Charles Capper, "Getting from Here to There: Margaret Fuller's American Transnational Odyssey," in Charles Capper and Cristina Giorcelli, eds., *Margaret Fuller: Transatlantic Crossings in a Revolutionary Age* (Madison: University of Wisconsin Press, 2007), 9.
23 Reynolds, "Introduction," in Margaret Fuller, *"These Sad But Glorious Days": Dispatches from Europe, 1846–1850*, eds. Larry J. Reynolds and Susan Belasco Smith (New Haven, CT: Yale University Press, 1991), 1.
24 Francesco Guida, "Realism, Idealism, and Passion in Margaret Fuller's Response to Italy," in Capper and Giocelli, *Margaret Fuller*, 160.
25 R. J. M. Blackett, *Building an Antislavery Wall: Black Americans in the Atlantic Abolitionist Movement, 1830–1860* (Baton Rouge: Louisiana State University Press, 1983), 4.
26 David Brion Davis, *The Problem of Slavery in the Age of Emancipation* (New York: Alfred Knopf, 2014), 297.
27 Fuller, *"These Sad But Glorious Days"*, 98.

28 Jacobs, *Incidents in the Life of a Slave Girl*, in William L. Andrews and Henry Louis Gates Jr., eds., *American Slave Narratives* (New York: Library of America, 2000), 927.

29 See George Fitzhugh, *A Sociology for the South: Or, the Failure of Free Society* (Richmond, VA: A. Morris, 1854).

30 Davis, *The Problem of Slavery*, 307.

31 Robert S. Levine, *Dislocating Race and Nation Episodes in Nineteenth-Century American Literary Nationalism* (Chapel Hill: University of North Carolina Press, 2008), 189.

32 Frederick Douglass, "Emigration to Hayti," *Douglass' Monthly* 3 (January 1861), 387, quoted. in Levine, *Dislocating Race and Nation*, 194.

33 See Margaret Fuller, Review of *Narrative of the Life of Frederick Douglass*, *New-York Daily Tribune*, 10 June 1845, in Judith Mattson Bean and Joel Myerson, eds., *Margaret Fuller, Critic: Writings from the New-York Tribune, 1844–1846* (New York: Columbia University Press, 2000), 131.

34 Brodhead, "The American Literary Field," 34.

35 Quoted in ibid.

36 Cf. Winfried Fluck, "Realismus, Naturalismus, Vormoderne," in Hubert Zapf, ed., *Amerikanische Literaturgeschichte* (Stuttgart: Metzler, 2004), 180.

37 Winfried Fluck, "Morality, Modernity, and 'Malarial Restlessness': American Realism in Its Anglo-European Contexts," in Robert Paul Land and G. R. Thompson, eds., *A Companion to American Fiction 1865–1914* (Malden, MA: Blackwell, 2005), 77–95.

38 Walter Mignolo, *Local Histories/Global Designs: Coloniality, Subaltern Knowledges, and Border Thinking* (Princeton, NJ: Princeton University Press, 2000), 11.

39 Anna Brickhouse, *Transamerican Literary Relations and the Nineteenth-Century Public Sphere* (New York: Cambridge University Press, 2004), 32.

40 Ibid. 26.

41 Kirsten Silva Gruesz, *Ambassadors of Culture: The Transamerican Origins of Latino Writing* (Princeton, NJ: Princeton University Press, 2002).

42 Ibid. 106.

43 Ibid. 187.

44 Ibid. 189.

45 Ibid. 192.

46 José Martí, "Our America," Appendix 1 in Julio Ramos, *Divergent Modernities: Culture and Politics in Nineteenth-Century Latin America*, trans. John D. Blanco, foreword by José David Saldívar (Durham, NC: Duke University Press, 2001), 296–97.

47 Julio Ramos, *Divergent Modernities: Culture and Politics in Nineteenth-Century Latin America*. trans. John D. Blanco. Foreword by José David Saldívar (Durham, NC: Duke University Press, 2001), 168.

48 Emerson, "The American Scholar," 56.

49 Martí, "Our America," 296.

50 Ramos, *Divergent Modernities*, 262.

51 Percy Bysshe Shelley, "A Defence of Poetry" [1821], in Mary Shelley, ed., *Essays, Letters from Abroad, Translations and Fragments* (London: Edward Moxon, 1840).

52 Jesse Alemán, "The Invention of Mexican America," in Russ Castronovo, ed., *The Oxford Handbook of Nineteenth-Century American Literature* (New York: Oxford University Press, 2012), 95.

53 The span of roughly ten years I derive from two landmark events: the publication of Amy Kaplan and Donald E. Pease, eds., *Cultures of United States Imperialism* (Durham, NC: Duke University Press, 1993), and Shelley Fisher Fishkin's Presidential Address at the 2004 annual meeting of the American Studies Association (published as "Crossroads of Cultures: The Transnational Turn in American Studies – Presidential Address to the American Studies Association, November 12, 2004," *American Quarterly* 57.1 [March 2005], 17–55).

54 Shelley Fisher Fishkin, "American Literature in Transnational Perspective: The Case of Mark Twain," in Caroline F. Levander and Robert S. Levine, eds., *A Companion to American Literary Studies* (Malden, MA: Blackwell, 2011), 281–82.

55 See ibid. 283.

56 Amy Kaplan, *The Anarchy of Empire in the Making of U.S. Culture* (Cambridge, MA: Harvard University Press, 2002), 52.

57 Johannes Voelz, *Transcendental Resistance: The New Americanists and Emerson's Challenge* (Hanover: University Press of New England, 2010).

58 Walt Whitman, *Leaves of Grass* (New York: Vintage/Library of America, 1992), 294.

59 Ibid. 295.

60 Ibid. 297.

61 Betsy Erkilla, *Whitman: The Political Poet* (New York: Oxford University Press, 1989), 266.

62 Whitman, *Leaves of Grass*, 290.

63 Walter Grünzweig, "Imperialism," in Donald D. Kummings, ed., *A Companion to Walt Whitman* (Malden, MA: Blackwell, 2006), 157.

64 Ibid. 152–56.

65 Royall Tyler, *The Algerine Captive* (New York: Modern Library, 2002), 225.

66 Timothy Marr, *The Cultural Roots of American Islamicism* (New York: Cambridge, 2006), 58.

6

JESSICA BERMAN

Transnational Modernisms

US modernism has always been transnational. That is to say, its texts, attitudes, audiences, and practitioners have always crossed national borders and challenged national literary pieties. Its iconic figures – think Henry James, Ezra Pound, T. S. Eliot, Gertrude Stein – are founding members of the expatriate club. Its archives or approaches – think Pound and Eliot, again, or more broadly, Claude McKay or Nella Larsen – come from many corners of the world. Even while the transnational dimensions of US modernism have sometimes appeared to be its limitations – or its liabilities – the imposition of firm national borders around modernist literary production and circulation remains impossible. Even modernists formerly identified with specific US locations, such as William Faulkner or William Carlos Williams, have more recently been understood to write within a broader context of transnational engagement.

In this sense, modernism is not different from other modes of US literature, which at least a generation of scholarship has taught us to understand as deeply entangled with global crosscurrents. Wai Chee Dimock teases out the "crisscrossing set of pathways, open-ended and ever multiplying" that constitute what we call American literature over the *longue durée*, and the "complex tangle of relations" that they create.[1] Those practicing hemispheric American studies or "border thinking" such as Gloria Anzaldúa, Ramon Saldívar, or Walter Mignolo point out the artificiality of assuming that US national borders coincide with the terrain of literary production and circulation, and posit instead a literary "trans-Americanity" open to contexts well beyond the United States.[2] Ifeoma Kiddoe Nwankwo and others have illuminated the transnational or cosmopolitan sensibilities motivating writers of African descent in the nineteenth century, arguing that they "reveal the struggle to define self and community between multiple local and global affinities" much as later Black diasporic writers do.[3] Scholars behind the "transnational turn" in American Studies have articulated the notion of America as a concept "always in process"[4] and part of "a world system, in which the exchange of commodities, the flow of capital, and the iterations of cultures know no borders."⁵ Within the world system, we might say, "American" or, perhaps more precisely, "US" literature signals a location or orientation, not an origin or endpoint.

But sliding all US literature into the rubric of a (contemporary version of) transnationalism risks eliding distinctions that matter. While the US self-concept can be seen as long constituted within a global or world system, this self-constitution follows a variety of processes over time and grows out of a range of motivations. And, as Arjun Appadurai long ago made clear, contemporary global flows of people, commodities, and culture follow new, often deterritorialized routes of travel and require different theoretical tools from those that fit the earlier nation-state/empire model.⁶ Jenny Sharpe has also pointed out that in the contemporary period multicultural, diasporic US citizens live a complex transnational existence that is neither easily swept into older models of immigration and assimilation nor subsumed within the existing categories of postcolonial theory.⁷ Certainly the flows of capital, commodities, and cultural objects under twenty-first-century conditions of globalization differ from those of the late nineteenth century, when Henry James was writing, despite the parallels between his struggles with literary piracy and contemporary clashes over intellectual production and property rights. And the Euro-focused cosmopolitanism of Gertrude Stein's writing or even the Asia-focused work of Pound should not be seen as exactly the same project as that of contemporary US writing with global sensibilities, such as fiction by Teju Cole, Junot Diaz, Dinaw Mengestu, or many others. In other words, recognizing transnationalism as a long-term, multifaceted project does not mean considering it as the same project, iterated over and over again, time without end.

Further, I want to suggest that the term "transnational" harbors a range of uses that also bear distinguishing. As applied to modernism, I use the term "transnational" to describe a web of social and textual interrelationships linking modernisms worldwide as well as a critical optic through which to see modernist attitudes and impulses that transcend and contend with the nation. While, as I will discuss, the celebrated cosmopolitanism of modernist writers such as Henry James and Gertrude Stein qualifies as transnational, as does work by the famous "lost" generation of expatriate writers including Harlem Renaissance figures such as Claude McKay, we can also understand such writers as Faulkner who remain in the United States or whose work focuses on US locations as transnational in significant ways.

I want to claim that we might best deploy transnationalism as a critical optic, practice, or critique of the discursive categories of nationalism as well as an attitude germane to a specific set of authors or a shorthand way to describe traveling texts.[8] My use of the term "transnational" in this way bears affinities with Jahan Ramazani's "transnational poetics" even as it also hopes to extend the term beyond the specific travels, influences, or allegiances of writers and their texts. Ramazani argues convincingly that "modernists translated their frequent geographic displacement and transcultural alienation into a poetics of bricolage and translocation, dissonance and defamiliarization."[9] Yet I would argue that the text need not be explicitly preoccupied with themes of dislocation, hybridity, or transculturation, nor the author an exile or itinerant, for a narrative to be called transnational. Even when resolutely local in its concerns or national in its literary ambitions, a narrative may also illuminate and engage the many nodes of interconnection, both literary and political, that interlink modernisms and modernities worldwide or draw on global contexts and categories (such as "negritude") that immediately insert it within a transnational frame.

In this sense, we might begin to allow "transnational" to function through the power of its prefix, indicating a position, action, or attitude toward the nation and its cultural apparatuses through what I have been calling an optic, rather than as an adjective describing a given set of texts or a new canon of writers. In this way the "trans" in transnational operates as a critical, space-clearing gesture[10] that opens out toward many possible responses to the nation rather than the sign of a specific temporal-historical location or disposition. The prefix "trans" shares the oppositional valence of such words as "transgress" and "transform." When we use the prefix "trans" to mean not just "across, on the far side of, … or over," but also "beyond, surpassing, transcending," it represents a challenge to the normative dimension of the original entity or space, a crossing over that looks back critically from its space beyond.[11] My way of understanding this use of "trans"[12] draws on its use in contemporary transgender and transsexual theory where the prefix has come to stand not just for gender or sexual identities that have moved from one side of a binary field to the other, but rather for "anything that disrupts, denaturalizes, rearticulates and makes visible" the links we assume to exist between a sexual body and the social roles it is expected to play. As Susan Stryker, Paisley Currah, and Lisa Jean Moore put it, considering the "relationality of [the hyphenated prefix] 'trans-'" rather than its attachment to substantive terms like gender or nation helps us see "the categorical crossings, leakages and slippages" in and around the term and to recognize its capacity to "disrupt or unsettle conventional boundaries," disciplines, and ideas.[13]

Like the critique of the sex/gender system instigated by transgender theory, but different from the current critical categories describing "world," "global," or even "planetary" literature, the "trans-national" as I conceive it serves to decenter the "national tradition" as an object of inquiry, exploring texts in relation to other, transnational horizons of expectations, even while recognizing the importance of their local aspirations. In this guise it functions as catachresis, much as post-coloniality does for Spivak, "reversing, displacing and seizing the apparatus of value-coding" rather than attempting to argue as though from entirely new ground.[14] In other words, it marks the struggle with the ongoing problematics of nation, empire, and globe while striving to open up a space of resistance to their hegemony.

Modernist Cosmopolitanism

US modernism arises in the late nineteenth and early twentieth centuries along with the development of new models of cosmopolitanism. For many of its practitioners, cosmopolitanism and modernism emerge in tandem as joint responses to the social, economic, technological, and aesthetic conditions of modernity. As I have argued elsewhere, one of the key concerns for many modernists was the pressure that modern forms of social organization and affiliation placed on models of identity and community.[15] Especially problematic was the seemingly inviolate link forged between local forms of community and the nation-state at the center of an imperial system, which seemed to call for new attitudes and ways of writing. As Edward Said suggests, "the formal dislocations and displacements of modernist culture" as well as its encyclopedic forms, its juxtapositions, and its ironic modes, emerge in part as a consequence of empire and thus from the pressure of the world on previously self-enclosed communities.[16] However, I claim that modernists respond to this pressure in complex ways, often using their writing to reimagine the relationship between community and world. For many writers, community becomes linked to a cosmopolitan perspective in a manner that revises and enriches both terms and that puts in question the nation-state as the primary locus of community belonging. In this guise, the often-remarked cosmopolitanism of US expatriate modernists appears less idiosyncratic – the result of a privileged international upbringing or disaffection from their birthplace – and more and more like creative opposition that leaves an instructive social and aesthetic legacy in its wake.

Early in his career, having recently decided to live in Europe, Henry James wrote of the "baleful spirit of the cosmopolite" and commented that "to be a cosmopolite is not, I think, an ideal; the ideal should be to be a concentrated patriot. Being a cosmopolite is an accident, but one must make the best of it." These remarks in the 1877 essay "Occasional Paris" express the same negative attitude toward what he called "living about" that he would place in the mouth of Mme. Merle in the later *The Portrait of a Lady*, who famously derided herself and the other expatriates around her as "mere parasites, crawling over the surface [of the earth]; we haven't our feet in the soil."[17] Despite his misgivings, James had concrete reasons for being unable to act as a concentrated patriot during the Russo-Turkish war, which involved much of Europe in a scramble to control the disintegrating Ottoman Empire. In England, where James had been living, the war prompted heightened rhetoric in the press and a pronounced expression of patriotism, which inspired the term *jingo*.[18] Despite his affinity for England, James despised the easy patriotism *cum* imperialism behind the British position. He chose "baleful" cosmopolitanism as an uneasy escape.

In the 1890s and into the twentieth century, James reengages with the problem of cosmopolitanism through texts that revolve around the tension between the local and the global, especially in terms of politics and commerce. In the 1890s the word "cosmopolitan" crops up more often in James's writing than at any other time in his career. He shapes cosmopolitanism into a motive at least equal to "concentrated patriotism" and juxtaposes it to national codes of behavior, the market-driven forces of immoderate or trumped-up speech, and ultimately the bellicose posturing of the United States around the time of the Spanish-American war. At the same time, the cosmopolitan is often a pawn in the commercial game of the international press, or a naïf who does not recognize the determining power of local authorities. Story after story from the period between 1892 and 1898, such as "Collaboration" and "Greville Fane," focus on artistic production and its conflict with the marketplace, or on the reemergence of national differences and patriotism even among those with cosmopolitan sympathies.

In James's major modernist work of the early twentieth century, the word "cosmopolitan" drops away, though it remains a singular preoccupation. Cosmopolitan characters proliferate in *The Wings of the Dove*, *The Ambassadors* and *The Golden Bowl* but the effort at reconciling local and global loyalties becomes more fraught and the struggle over US loyalties and commercial interests becomes more clear. As John Carlos Rowe puts it, characters like Maria Gostry, Lambert Strether, Maggie Verver, and Milly Theale "fail to reconnect their American identities with their international destinies" and often appear diminished by the struggle.[19] For Strether in *The Ambassadors*, cosmopolitanism can neither be reconciled with the demands of the US manufacturing town of Woolett nor acceded to as a permanent condition. In *The Golden Bowl*, Maggie Verver may play the role of the cosmopolitan woman applauded by the magazines for using her fortune to marry a prince, but she must ultimately maneuver between the expectations of American City and the exigencies of Prince Amerigo, a process that brands her as inescapably American. For all of these women in James's late novels, the price of playing on the cosmopolitan field is high, as is the danger of becoming reduced to a commodity in trade on the global market.

For Gertrude Stein, mapping functions as the key link between local belonging and transnational or cosmopolitan sentiments.[20] When she claims that "America is my country; Paris is my hometown," she insists that national identity and community feeling are distinct though paired terms, and that community may ultimately develop in conjunction with, rather than in opposition to, the cosmopolitan condition. For Stein, "geographical history" may bring both individual and national identities into being, but movement in space changes their relation, forcing us to seek community in the network of lines on a map, or in the juxtapositions inherent in landscape, or in the narrative extension of a shifting plural subject. From the linear, conventionally organic construction of identity that informs the opening pages of her early novel *The Making of Americans*[21] to the map-based model of experience that will predominate in the late *Ida: A Novel*, Stein's narratives develop a topographical notion of identity, which insists that a nomadic and polyvocal subjectivity leads toward a cosmopolitan model of belonging. In *The Geographical History of America* Stein creates landscape as the space of both literary and geographical wandering. As she writes, "wandering has something to do with the human mind."[22] America is important to Stein, not because of its specific history or its claim on her loyalty, but because it forces the issue of the relation of human mind to human nature and the relation of landscape to wandering, out of which comes modernist writing.

This connection from mapping to narration becomes more transnational in the geographical texts of the late 1920s and 1930s and in such late work as *Ida: A Novel* and the children's book *The World is Round*. In *Ida* Stein creates a subject who is protean, plural, and on the move from place to place – in many ways a cosmopolitan Everywoman. Ida emerges through her traveling. "Was she on a train or an automobile, an airplane or just walking ... She was saying, yes yes I like to be sitting. Yes I like to be moving...."[23] She is marked by the intersection of wandering and belonging; her location makes very little difference. "Ida did not go directly anywhere. She went all around the world. It did not take her long and everything she saw interested her."[24] Each new cycle of travel occasions a new set of relationships, often a new husband, and a new question, whether it be about herself or about the nature of the place in which she finds herself. Importantly, Ida wanders in and out of Washington, the only place where she settles for a time. But her wanderings abroad make clear that she is a global nomad whose travels connect her to many locations.

In *The World Is Round* (1938), the hero, Rose, wanders up a French mountain in order to sit down on the chair she has carried and contemplate a different perspective. The point is not, as has often been claimed, that Stein is here memorializing the French countryside, but rather that the roundness of the world, like the lines on the map of America, make wandering a mission. Travel in both *Ida* and *The World is Round* helps produce an iterative "I" who is constantly recreated by seeing from a new perspective or a new location. These texts, as indeed much of Stein's writing, represent the narrative inscription of a profoundly subtle form of cosmopolitanism, built on geographical principles of wandering and a challenge to conventional ways of construing identity and national belonging. She asks us to understand the full implication of the phrase, "America is my country but Paris is my home town," as the creation of an iterative model of affiliation that gives social and political dimension to the mission of wandering.

Vagabondage

For many writers of the Harlem Renaissance, such as Langston Hughes, Nella Larsen, and Claude McKay, the trope of transnational wandering or vagabondage emerges out of the conflictual history of black diasporic experience and is infused with a more oppositional social and political attitude than the cosmopolitanism of James or Stein. As Paul Gilroy claims, much Black Atlantic writing displays a seemingly paradoxical search for roots along with a celebration of travel as "a response to the successive displacements, migrations, and journeys (forced and otherwise) which have come to constitute these black cultures' special conditions of existence."[25] Many African American writers insist on their national belonging even while embracing the transnational, transcultural, and often global attitudes of *Négritude*, Garveyism, or pan-Africanism that are often in conflict with it and they create a version of modernism that places this conflict at its center. Brent Hayes Edwards calls this impulse "the practice of diaspora," which demonstrates the tension between structures of national organization and travel across languages and cultures, and which is always characterized by gaps, "unavoidable misapprehensions and misreadings" and the inevitable "trace or the residue of what escapes translation."[26] The gaps and translational residues that emerge through the diasporic practices of Black Atlantic writers also clearly illuminate the uneven development and relations of power within Atlantic modernity. In highlighting the experience of black people under these conditions of uneven development, the modernist work of writers like Hughes, Larsen, and McKay calls into question the discursive categories supporting the power of the nation-state and its structures of social relations, along with the version of modernity tied to it.

Claude McKay's life and work showcases the powerful, oppositional practice of diaspora – or what McKay will call vagabondage – within black transnational modernism. Born in Jamaica, McKay published two collections of dialect verse, *Songs of Jamaica* and *Constab Ballads*, before moving to the United States and writing the poetry that made him famous. His life travels mark him immediately as a transnational subject; his American-ness rests as much on his choice of the United States as his home (despite being denied entrance as a communist in the 1920s) as it does on his cross-border affiliations.

McKay's early dialect poetry displays his deep connection to the people and concerns of the place of his birth, while also demonstrating the translational quality of his poetic voice, which takes on multiple personae and voices both in this period and throughout his career. Poems such as "A Midnight Woman to the Bobby," as Jahan Ramazani points out, pivot between a folkloric impulse and metropolitan expectations, displaying "transnational dynamics of ambivalent resistance and adhesion."[27] The speaker, a prostitute, argues with a constable, challenging his status and accusing him of being a pawn of the colonial government.

> No palm me up, you dutty brute,
> You' jam mount' mash like ripe bread-fruit;
> You fas'n now, but wait lee ya,
> I'll see you grunt under de law.[28]

Ramazani makes clear that the poem "dramatizes McKay's self-division," since he was himself serving as a constable at the time of writing.[29] Again and again, the dialect poems show a complex and often double-voiced subject position, from which the constable is mocked by a poor local. The speaker often points out the irony of the constable's exercise of power in such a way as to use the very process of uttering the verse as a means to undermine his power, as, for example, in "The Apple-Woman's Complaint" in which the apple-seller tells the constable that if he prevents her from selling her apples, she is bound to become a thief: "Ef me no wuk, me boun' fe tief/S'pose dat will please de police chief!"[30] This multivalent, translational poetic voice is less visible in *Harlem Shadows*, which showcases a personal voice in often painful contact with the actualities of black US life in the 1920s. But it reemerges in the novels that follow.

Written in France after McKay's long period abroad, including time spent in the Soviet Union, *Home to Harlem* delves into "what [McKay] described as the 'semi-underworld' of single, black, working-class men."[31] It takes on the perspective of Jake, a longshoreman just returned from a tour of duty abroad as a sailor during World War I, but also creates a compendium of voices and perspectives from this "semi-underworld" of black US life. The novel opens with Jake musing on the use of the word "darkie" in England, continues in dialogue-driven form with quoted material in a variety of slangs, and encompasses overheard song lyrics and the literary musings of its writer-figure, Ray. While *Home to Harlem* stays close to Jake as we watch him attempt to make a home for himself in the African American community, it does so in a way that shows that community as multi-voiced, complex, and cross-connected to the world beyond the United States. For example, in the middle of the novel Jake gets instruction on "the beautiful ideas of Liberté, Egalité, Fraternité" as well as the meanings of the word "Sapphic and Lesbian" ("what is that there Leshbian?" Jake asks) from a poetry-loving, Haitian railway-car waiter named Ray.[32] Famous in the period for its clear-eyed look at the sometimes sordid details of black everyday life, *Home to Harlem* also innovates in what we might call its wandering voice and its frequent out-reference to the world beyond the constraints of black America.

Ray turns back up in *Banjo*, McKay's 1929 novel, which takes place among the black vagabonds from all parts of the world on the beach in Marseilles, bringing with him not only his poetic sensibility, and his Haitian roots, but his connection to vernacular variety. Having been rescued by Ray from overcharge in a French café, the hero, Banjo, exclaims, "Dawgs mah tail! ... I be fiddled if you don't handle this lingo same as I does American," making Ray think, "Banjo's rich Dixie accent went to his head ... and reminded him happily of Jake."[33] Thus the second novel circles back to the first, closing the loop of transnational migrancy and ensuring that we understand the interrelationship between vagabond Marseilles and down-at-heels Harlem. Musing on the appeal of the overwhelming variety of goods and people assembled on the docks of Marseilles, Ray ends by appreciating the "picturesque variety of Negroes. Negroes speaking the civilized tongues, Negroes speaking all the African dialects, black Negroes, brown Negroes, yellow Negroes. It was as if every country of the world where Negroes lived has sent representatives drifting in to Marseilles. A great vagabond host."[34] Clearly dialectal variety here represents a broad translational and transnational version of black common life.

Edwards calls McKay's political vision in this novel "vagabond internationalism" and recognizes it as a turn away from the communist ideal of a unified, universal proletariat that McKay had embraced in the mid-1920s. The black drifters on the beach in Marseilles disparage wage labor; Banjo plays as much for pleasure as for money. All, including Ray, resist any activity that seems to bring them into the realm of respectability or "civiliza-tion," even among workers. In *Banjo* McKay develops what Edwards calls an "extreme antinationalism" in which the principle of vagabondage – a footloose way of living disconnected from structures of community or mod-els of behavior – becomes the ideal. We learn that "the sentiment of patri-otism was not one of Ray's possessions, perhaps because he was a child of deracinated ancestry … It seemed a most unnatural thing to him for a man to love a nation." Instead of a nation, "the vagabond lover of life finds indi-viduals and things to love in many places." McKay's vagabondage thus takes Stein's wandering cosmopolitanism one step further, generating an oppos-itional perspective that endorses this kind of wandering "love" – small scale and temporary allegiances among footloose individuals, whether in Harlem or abroad – as an antidote to the "spiritual meanness" of nationalism (137). The source and importance of transnational black modernism, here, then, becomes the disruptive power implied by the prefix "trans," to "unsettle conventional boundaries," disciplines, and ideas while challenging "the operations of systems and institutions that simultaneously produce various possibilities of viable personhood, and eliminate others."[35]

A Transnational Optic

William Faulkner's life and work is so famously bound to Mississippi that it seems the antithesis of this kind of vagabondage. Yet if we look at his career with a transnational optic, exploring the ways that the interconnections, both literary and political, between modernisms and modernities worldwide emerge in Faulkner's work, we begin to see the global crosscurrents that lie beneath his life and work. Faulkner's early years displayed a desire to wander and the need to invent a variety of personae for himself, such as the dandyish "Count No-Count" from his college days or the rakish avia-tor post–World War I, that gesture toward the same footloose attitude as McKay's Marseilles vagabonds. Although his life and career have long stood as testaments to the importance of local color, local vernaculars, and the power of place in twentieth-century US literature, it thus bears remembering that the master of Oxford, Mississippi was not always "sole proprietor" of Yawknapatawpha county.

Looking at Faulkner's work and the Southern culture he describes through a transnational lens as deeply enmeshed within a hemispheric, transnational US history also alters our perspective on the aims and scope of his writing especially in the context of race. Not only does it push us to read Faulkner intertextually in connection with writers of the black US experience, such as Toni Morrison, or those in Latin America who were deeply influenced by his work, such as Gabriel García Márquez and Mario Vargas Llosa; it also asks us to explore the translocal, diasporic currents within the history of Faulkner's South, and the often centripetal energy lurking within his texts. In other words, a transnational optic on this most American of US modernists shatters the illusion that his Southern vernacular only pertains to the US South, and dismantles the assumption that the nation is the primary horizon of expectations for his writing.

Since Eric Sundquist's groundbreaking 1987 essay "Faulkner, Race and the Forms of U.S. Fiction,"[36] and Eduoard Glissant's important 1999 book *Faulkner, Mississippi,* an explosion of critical commentary has attempted this task of renewed vision.[37] If, for Glissant, the parallels between Oxford, Mississippi and his home island of Martinique, show a shared past enmeshed within the histories of the slave trade and plantation economies, the result is a poetics of indeterminacy, delay, and relation that brings the Martinican and Mississippian writers together in an almost shared style. Long, circuitous sentences, gaps in narrative logic, or a pieced-together perspective show the importance of "the hidden, ... the inexpressible,"[38] and the translational to the kind of writing that Glissant calls "creole." Creole or Creolization for Glissant marks a "limitless *métissage* [mix, cross-fertilization], its elements diffracted and its consequences unforeseeable ... into the explosion of cultures." But it is also the process by which a language makes contact and is shared and transformed over various routes of travel and linguistic itineraries, including "the structuring of supposed periphery as the Center, from the particular to a non-generalizing universal, with William Faulkner ... whose work practically never went beyond the limits of that 'postage stamp' of Yoknapatawpha County."[39] The translational discourses of the black diaspora, with the "misapprehensions and misreadings" that Edwards points out, lay out both the proving ground and the ultimate field of play for the Southern vernaculars of Faulkner's world.

Of all of Faulkner's texts, *Absalom! Absalom!* offers itself up to this transnational reading with the greatest alacrity. The epic tale of a poor white boy named Sutpen whose quest to avenge his affront at the plantation door of his father's employer leads to a life-long obsession with recreating that plantation for himself leans heavily on Sutpen's six-year sojourn in the Caribbean and his insertion into Haitian hierarchies of race and class. The phrase "so I went to the West Indies" repeats like a litany throughout this section of the novel, when Quentin Compson and his roommate Shreve are attempting to complete Sutpen's life story. But the description of the events in the West Indies take up only 5 pages (199–205) in this over-300-page book and it produces almost as many gaps or questions about events as revealing details.[40] Scholars have pointed to the fact that, though the text suggests that Sutpen was on the island during the Haitian Revolution helping a planter and his daughter survive and thus earning her hand in marriage, the timing for this event is far off. The Haitian Revolution occurred in 1791; by 1804, the Republic of Haiti became the first black state in the Americas. But Sutpen leaves Virginia in 1823, helps defend the French plantation in 1827, marries and has a son in 1829. Thus the violent conflagration Sutpen describes to Quentin's grandfather could not have been the famous Haitian revolution. The slaves Sutpen imports to Virginia, referenced throughout the novel as "wild negroes" who speak a tongue so strange it sounds to many unlike a language, must have once been free. As Richard Godden points out, "There were neither slaves nor French plantations on Haiti in 1827. Faulkner's chronology creates an anachronism that rewrites the one of the key facts of nineteenth-century black U.S. history."[41] For Godden that mistaken chronology underscores Sutpen's counterrevolutionary nature, the white who puts down the black Jacobean revolutionary. For Barbara Ladd, the references to Haiti and New Orleans serve to contrast the French-assimilated attitudes toward the creole versus US nationalist insistence on a strict black/white divide and the rule of one drop.[42] In a more recent, bold reading, John Matthews explains the text's silence about Sutpen's years as a sailor *before* landing in Haiti as its evasion of dark and difficult activities. With evidence from other Faulkner short stories, Matthew's posits Sutpen as engaged in lucrative, illegal slave trading, a profession he continues to rely on to fund his frenzied building of the house on Sutpen's Hundred.[43] Whatever the source of the chronology problem, then, the Caribbean subtext of the novel is sordid and dangerous, its historical, cultural, and moral transgressions the basis of Sutpen's ultimate fall.

Once we begin to read *Absalom! Absalom!* with a transnational optic we also see the extent to which the narrative's linguistic texture is riddled with reference to Yoknaptawpha's beyond and the threat of otherness coming in. As mentioned, there is constant talk about Sutpen's "wild negroes" and their "dark and fatal tongue."[44] We hear about the variety of languages surrounding Sutpen, from the uncivilized tongue of his slaves to the New Orleans French spoken by the boy, Charles Etienne Bond, and his mother. Every description of Charles Bon (elder) marks him as foreign, from his habit of kissing Ellen Sutpen's hand or handing her into her carriage[45] to his alien attitude to his first wife (not cast out but not acknowledged) and his potential act of bigamy. That Henry Sutpen apes Bon's every mannerism while Judith also "succumbs to the spell" marks Bon's foreignness as seductive, infiltrating, and corrupt.[46] And Judith is not the only one who succumbs to the spell; so too do Quentin, his grandfather, Shreve, Miss Rosa, and we as readers. By constructing the novel as a tale that demands its own unraveling and that depends on our being drawn in by its multiple narrators, Faulkner creates a narrative that positions this seductive corruption at the center of the South's Civil War history. *Absalom! Absalom!* presents a portrait of the South as already shot through with otherness and the logic of the creole but unable to understand its own transnational language.

There is not room enough in this essay to mark the many other US writers whose work shifts dramatically under the practice of what I have been calling a transnational optic – a critical practice that critiques the discursive primacy of national frames of reference and explores texts in relation to other, transnational horizons of expectations. Nella Larsen's Danish roots and William Carlos Williams's Hispanic heritage nurture new readings; the Spanish connections of Ernest Hemingway and John Dos Passos open to a new understanding of the twentieth-century Spanish-Atlantic world.[47] T. S. Eliot's and Hughes's influence in the Caribbean shows, in Anita Paterson's words, the complex "cross-current[s] of New World influences" and the "dense surprising matrix of transatlantic and hemispheric convergences" that characterize much of US modernism.[48] Simply linking Eliot and Hughes in this hemispheric trajectory asks us to think about their work in bold new ways. Deploying a transnational optic to understand US modernism thus demolishes the old, firm distinction between "international modernism" and the writers of US vernaculars, between the Euro-focused cosmopolitans and those who found their inspiration in US locations. A transnational perspective on US modernism pierces the borders between the cosmopolitan and the local and "disrupts, denaturalizes, rearticulates and makes visible" the national(ist) assumptions beneath our readings of twentieth-century US literature.[49] It clears space for us to recognize US modernism as by turns translocal, translational, and diasporic, characterized by global crosscurrents, and ultimately, dispersed.

NOTES

1 Wai Chee Dimock, *Through Other Continents: U.S. Literature through Deep Time* (Princeton, NJ: Princeton University Press, 2008) 3.

2 Ramón Saldívar, *The Borderlands of Culture: Américo Paredes and the Transnational Imaginary* (Durham, NC: Duke University Press, 2006); Gloria Anzaldúa, *Borderlands/La Frontera* 4th ed. (San Francisco: Aunt Lute Books, 2012); Walter Mignolo, *Local Histories/Global Designs: Coloniality, Subaltern Knowledges, and Border Thinking* (Princeton, NJ: Princeton University Press, 2000).

3 Ifeoma Kiddoe Nwankwo, *Black Cosmopolitanism: Racial Consciousness and Transnational Identity in the Nineteenth-Century Americas* (Philadelphia: University of Pennsylvania Press, 2005), 8.

4 David Palumbo-Liu, quoted in Shelley Fisher Fishkin, "Crossroads of Cultures: The Transnational Turn in U.S. Studies – Presidential Address to the U.S. Studies Association, November 12, 2004," *American Quarterly* 57.1 (2005): 21.

5 Paul Lauter, quoted in Fishkin, "Crossroads," 21.

6 Arjun Appadurai, "Disjuncture and Difference in the Global Cultural Economy," *Theory Culture Society* 7 (1990): 296, 303–04.

7 Jenny Sharpe, "Postcolonial Studies in the House of U.S. Multiculturalism," in Henry Schwarz and Sangeeta Ray, eds., *A Companion to Postcolonial Studies* (New York: Wiley, 2008): 112–26.

8 Bill Ashcroft, "Beyond the Nation: Post-Colonial Hope," *The Journal of the European Association of Studies on Australia* 1 (2009): 13.

9 Jahan Ramazani, "A Transnational Poetics," *U.S. Literary History* 18.2 (2006): 333.

10 Anthony Appiah, "Is the Post- in Postmodernism the Post- in Postcolonial?" *Critical Inquiry*, 17.2 (1991): 342.

11 "trans-, prefix," OED Online. December 2015. Oxford University Press.

12 See Jessica Berman, "Is the Trans in Transnationalism the Trans in Transgender?" in *Modernism/Modernity*, forthcoming 2017.

13 Susan Stryker, Paisley Currah, and Lisa Jean Moore, eds. "Introduction: Trans-, Trans, or Transgender?" *Women's Studies Quarterly* 36.3/4 (Fall/Winter 2008): 11.

14 Gayatri Chakravorty Spivak, "Poststructuralism, Marginality, Postcoloniality and Value," in Peter Collier and Helga Geyer-Ryan, eds., *Literary Theory Today* (Ithaca, NY: Cornell University Press, 1990), 228.

15 See Berman, *Modernist Fiction, Cosmopolitanism, and the Politics of Community* (Cambridge: Cambridge University Press, 2001).

16 Edward Said, *Culture and Imperialism* (New York: Knopf, 1993), 188–89.

17 Henry James, "Occasional Paris" in *Collected Travel Writing* v. 2, (New York: Library of America, 1993), 721; *The Portrait of a Lady* in *Collected Novels* v. 2 (New York: Library of America, 1985), 392.

18 G. W. Hunt, "McDermott's War Song." Web, <www.cyberussr.com/hcunn/q-jingo.html>. Accessed 5 June 2008.

19 John Carlos Rowe, "Henry James and Globalization" in Peter Rawlings, ed., *Palgrave Advances in Henry James Studies* (New York: Palgrave, 2007): 296.

20 See Berman, *Modernist Fiction*, 157–77.

21 Gertrude Stein, *The Making of Americans: Being the History of a Family's Progress* (New York: Something Else Press, 1966).

22 Gertrude Stein, *Geographical History of America or the Relation of Human Nature to the Human Mind* (Baltimore: Johns Hopkins University Press, 1995), 93.

23 Gertrude Stein, *Ida: A Novel*, (New York: Vintage, 1941), 34.

24 Ibid., 51.

25 Paul Gilroy, *The Black Atlantic* (Cambridge, MA: Harvard University Press, 1993), 111.

26 Brent Hayes Edwards, *The Practice of Diaspora* (Cambridge, MA: Harvard University Press, 2003), 5, 13.

27 Jahan Ramazani, *A Transnational Poetics* (Chicago: University of Chicago Press, 2009), 29.
28 Claude McKay, "A Midnight Woman to the Bobby," in Allison Donnell and Sarah Dawson Welsh, eds., *The Routledge Reader in Caribbean Literature*, (New York: Routledge, 1996), 65–66; lines 1–4.
29 Ramazani, *A Transnational Poetics*, 29.
30 Donnell and Welsh, *Caribbean Literature*, 67–8, lines 5–8.
31 Wayne F. Cooper, "Introduction," *Home to Harlem* (Lebanon, NH: Northeastern University Press, 1987), xx.
32 Claude McKay, *Home to Harlem*, (Boston: Northeastern University Press, 1987), 131, 129.
33 Claude McKay, *Banjo: A Story Without a Plot*, (New York: Houghton Mifflin Harcourt, 1970), 64.
34 Ibid., 68.
35 Stryker et al., "Introduction."
36 In Doreen Fowler and Ann J. Abadie, eds. *Faulkner and Race* (Jackson: University Press of Mississippi, 1987), 1–34.
37 Edouard Glissant, *Faulkner, Mississippi*, trans. Barbara B. Lewis and Thomas C. Spears (Chicago: University of Chicago Press, 2000).
38 Glissant quoted in Timothy P. Caron, "'He Doth Bestride the Narrow World Like a Colossus': Faulkner's Critical Reception," in Richard C. Moreland, ed., *A Companion to William Faulkner*, (Malden, MA: Blackwell), 494.
39 Edouard Glissant, *The Poetics of Relation*, trans. Betsy Wing (Ann Arbor: University of Michigan Press, 1997), 34.
40 William Faulkner, *Absalom! Absalom! The Corrected Text* (New York: Vintage, 1986).
41 Richard Godden, "*Absalom! Absalom!* Haiti, and Labor History: Reading Unreadable Revolutions," in Fred Hobson, ed., *William Faulkner's Absalom! Absalom!: A Casebook* (Oxford: Oxford University Press, 2003), 251.
42 Barbara Ladd, "'The Direction of the Howling': Nationalism and the Color Line in *Absalom! Absalom!*" in Hobson, *William Faulkner's Absalom! Absalom!*, 219–50.
43 John T. Matthews, "Recalling the West Indies: From Yoknapatawpha to Haiti and Back," *U.S. Literary History* 16.2 (2004): 238–62.
44 Faulkner, *Absalom! Absalom!*, 27.
45 Ibid., 74.
46 Ibid., 85.
47 See George B. Hutchinson, *In Search of Nella Larsen: A Biography of the Color Line* (Boston: Belknap Press, 2006); Julio Marzán, *The Spanish U.S. Roots of William Carlos Williams* (Austin: University of Texas Press, 1994); and Gayle Rogers, "Restaging the Disaster: Dos Passos and National Literature after the Spanish-U.S. War," *Journal of Modern Literature* 36.2 (Winter 2013): 61–79, as well as his forthcoming work on Hemingway.
48 Anita Patterson, *Race, U.S. Literature, and Transnational Modernisms*, (Cambridge: Cambridge University Press, 2008), 95.
49 Stryker et al., "Introduction," 11.

7

DAVID JAMES

Transnational Postmodern and Contemporary Literature

"No novelist can bear the burden of representing a continent and no one novel should have to."[1] So insists Taiye Selasi, author of the acclaimed *Ghana Must Go* (2013). Born in London to parents from Ghana and Nigeria, raised in Massachusetts, Selasi occupies as good a position as any novelist today from which to question what she calls "the prioritization of perceived cultural allegiance over creative output." Among the "literary establishment" at present, critics increasingly have "trouble with writers who belong to diasporas."[2] Selasi's concern is that African writers, regardless of whether or not they address specifically "African" subjects, attract "a particular kind of scrutiny," whereby their fiction either falls prey to "the media's fondness for … little ethnic trends" or else "is forced to play the role of anthropology."[3] The commercial promotion and appeal of narratives of cultural difference or displacement are not always fitting rewards, she implies; still less can such trends do justice to the formal distinctiveness of the works they encompass. Selasi's reservations about the dissonance between prescribed allegiance and writers' individual aesthetic aims strikes at the heart of some of the challenges posed by transnational approaches to contemporary writing.

In what follows, I consider fictions that invite us to embrace head-on these "tensions," as Paul Giles describes them, "between competing conceptions of local affiliation and global dislocation that a transnational remapping of American studies should help to elucidate."[4] Of course, such tensions are not exclusive to teaching and research focused on *contemporary* literature. As Paul Jay has noted, "the discipline of English is in many ways a latecomer to the field of transnational literary studies," and as such we should be alert to presentist assumptions resulting from the recent nature of this "turn," assumptions that might lead us to "see globalization as a strictly contemporary or postmodern phenomenon."[5] Jay's proposal that we explore instead "the long history of globalization on the construction of personal, cultural, and national identities" has been echoed by comparatists working in hemispheric studies and also by contemporary fiction scholars, who identify late twentieth- and twenty-first-century historical novels that reconstruct the emergence of early globalism.[6]

New fictions of transnationalism motivate us to rethink the genealogies of postmodernism, particularly when the postmodern itself remains so thoroughly embroiled in unfinished arguments about how we define and periodize "the contemporary." While some would argue that postmodernity has now "been replaced by the contemporary or superseded by the global," at the same time Jason Gladstone and Daniel Worden suggest that "[h]owever the question of the postmodern is posed, it is clear that it remains central to any adequate conception of both the present moment and its immediate past."[7] For some, then, postmodernism is most viable when viewed historically: observed in retrospect, it's a phase of audacious, often vibrantly self-referential activity, spanning various art forms and occurring through aesthetically diverse mutations from the 1950s to the 1990s. For others, postmodernity denotes a culturally heterogeneous spell of socioeconomic transformation, whose material effects continue to reverberate through our postmillennial present. Either way, postmodernism was inherently "transnational" from the start, especially if we understand its postwar manifestations – as David Harvey and Fredric Jameson have famously done – in relation to the conditions of advanced capitalist production and competition, as the tentacles of commercial expansion reach inexorably across the globe. Harvey's seminal account suggests that postmodernism registers the still-unfolding consequences of early twentieth-century modernization, reflecting in its own "schizophrenic circumstances" the aftermath of "new conditions of production (the machine, the factory, urbanization) and consumption (the rise of markets and advertising)."[8] For his part, though, Jameson could not "stress too greatly the radical distinction between a view for which the postmodern is one (optional) style among many others available and one which seeks to grasp it as the cultural dominant of the logic of late capitalism."[9] And it's precisely this distinction that to some extent troubles postmodernity's viability as a phenomenon in tune with current times, once we embrace the formidable challenge of grasping artistic contemporaneity in planetary terms.[10] For on this scale, postmodernism tends to become, on the one hand, aesthetically all-inclusive, compromising efforts to discern multifarious trajectories of experimentation across late twentieth- and twenty-first-century arts; and, on the other, sociologically amorphous, ample enough in theory yet perhaps ill-equipped in practice for pinpointing how different regional populations are affected by uneven development and financial exploitation.

Postmodernism's critical fortunes also have an institutional context. Its waning appeal and uncertain analytical purchase in recent years is inversely

correlated with the increasing disciplinary strength of contemporary literature studies, a diversifying field that has come to question the limits of
abstract, all-encompassing paradigms for articulating the cultural present.
Alongside a steady "revaluation of the contemporary against the postmodern," remark Gladstone and Worden, recent scholarship on postwar literary
culture has thus "emphasized the ways in which postmodernism was never,
in fact, the dominant cultural logic or literary rubric of the late twentieth
century."[11] In addition to seeing it as a transnationally variegated constellation of artistic innovations, many critics now address postmodernism
primarily as one among many artistic junctures and transitions since the
1960s, a matrix of tendencies from which the particular features and commitments of twenty-first-century writing can be fruitfully distinguished.[12]
But that doesn't mean the term is no longer pertinent, providing we entertain postmodernism as something of "a manufactured artefact," as Brian
McHale has suggested. An umbrella category for "multiple, overlapping,
and intersecting inventories and multiple corpora," the postmodern continues to yield "a plurality of constructions."[13] Moreover, given that a good
deal of foundational postmodern criticism focused on canonical epics from
(white) North American figures such as Thomas Pynchon and Don DeLillo,
McHale points out that the "unexamined assumption that postmodernist
fiction was really one and the same thing everywhere, even when it emerged
far from its Euro-American 'homeland,' seems indefensible today."[14]

As we recognize postmodernism's own global provenances while relat-
ing its traits to some of the latest modes of transnational fiction, we also
need to reconsider how postmodernism formally worked and how, in turn,
more contemporary writers seek to reconfigure its signal forms. As McHale
claimed, "epistemologically-oriented fiction (modernism, detective fiction)
is preoccupied with questions such as: what is there to be known about
the world"; or, how and where "is knowledge transmitted, to whom, and
how reliably?" By contrast, "ontologically-oriented fiction (postmodernism,
SF) is," for McHale, "preoccupied with questions such as: what is a world?
How is a world constituted?"[15] In the critical shift from postmodern writing
to more recent world fiction, this schematic division comes to seem rather
more untenable. Whatever their relation, as artistic legatees, to modernism's
fascination with the epistemic facets and disorientations of memory and
perception, contemporary writers pose questions *both* about how ways of
knowing can be tracked between cultures, customs, or beliefs, and how that
process of thinking across national borders – imagined and real, intellectual and geographical – affects ways of being. To be sure, writers engaged
with transnational concerns today inherit much that is dynamic and enabling from postmodern fiction: collagist arrangements of voices, genres,

and settings; self-reflexive, metafictional references to the composition and reception of the written word across national frontiers; stylized alternations in perspective and idiom that foreground the processes of fiction-making, often to interrogate the veracity of historiography itself; and interactive or collusive forms of narrative address that allow novelists, in Toni Morrison's words, "to have the reader work *with* the author in the construction of the book."[16] All of these strategies help fiction working on a global scale to resist being reduced to "the role of anthropology," as Selasi put it, when expressing the discrete conditions of different cultures. To do so, novelists as distinct in theme and technique as Karen Tei Yamashita, Junot Díaz, or Dave Eggers – in addition to the writers I discuss shortly (Ruth Ozeki, Jessica Hagedorn, Rachel Kushner, and Jhumpa Lahiri) – negotiate local particularism alongside the social and ethical consequences of interethnic encounter. Yet as we embark on this "extensive engagement with differences in narrative forms through time and across space,"[17] as Susan Stanford Friedman has recommended, we soon see that they present a vigorous challenge to the way postmodern literature has itself been theorized, when the so-called epistemological and ontological tendencies of modern and contemporary fiction productively collide.

Within the broader rubric of transnational writing today, then, the specificity of contemporary writing can often be blurred when subsumed under theoretically large-scale generic or cultural-historical categories. If anything, one of postmodernism's most useful bequests is the invitation precisely to formulate other ways of describing literature from recent years that can be conceptually nimble, aesthetically precise, yet capacious enough to bring seemingly unrelated writers into conversation. Among these alternative frames we could include Rebecca L. Walkowitz's recent notion of "world-shaped" fictions. Such narratives not only "feature traveling characters who speak different languages, sometimes within the same national space"; they can also be "world-themed," argues Walkowitz, dramatizing "collaborative projects and private undertakings that operate between or across sovereign states."[18] Few novels are more world-shaped or indeed vivaciously world-building than Ruth Ozeki's *A Tale for the Time Being* (2013). With more than 160 footnotes, numerous appendices, and a bibliography to boot, this compositionally flamboyant and thematically encyclopedic novel certainly chimes with the hallmark self-display of postmodern writing. Ozeki interlocks stories of ecological and personal vulnerability to offer a parable of transcultural displacement and endurance. Ruth, a writer living in an isolated part of the Vancouver Island region, discovers washed up on her local beach a lunchbox containing the diary of Nao Yasutani, a teenage schoolgirl who once felt provisionally at home in Silicon Valley. The zanily energetic tempo and tone of Nao's diary does not quite conceal or compensate for the fact that she is forlorn. Uprooted with her parents amid tech-industry turbulences, she now lives back in Tokyo. Without "any savings," the family's new situation is "a complete bust," leaving Nao's father "sulking around like a jilted lover" while her mother remained "grim and tight and righteous."[19] Nao, meanwhile, appears immediately alienated, culturally and linguistically, feeling "totally fucked, because I identified as American, and even though we always spoke Japanese at home, my conversational skills were limited to basic, daily-life stuff like where's my allowance, and pass the jam, and Oh please please please don't make me leave Sunnyvale" (43). Depression sets in for her father and he repeatedly attempts suicide; in response, Nao too contemplates stepping out of time altogether. For her part, Ruth is unsure whether Nao might be a victim of the tsunami triggered by the 2011 Tohoku earthquake, or whether she can intervene and come to Nao's aid, providing the diary is sufficiently recent. Connecting opposite sides of the Pacific, Ozeki alternates between Nao's family upheaval and Ruth's rather more uneventful but in some senses equally dejected domestic life with her naturalist husband, Oliver, whose preoccupation with wild-life often disregards the extent to which "[t]here were so many other more pressing things she would have preferred to discuss" (54). Ruth becomes utterly absorbed in Nao's journey to stay with her 104-year-old anarchist-Buddhist great-grandmother, Jiko, whose son served as a kamikaze pilot in the final days of World War II, leaving in his wake an eloquent series of hidden letters code-written in French attesting to fact that "he didn't even want to fight in the war," though of course "they made him" (68). Like those letters, Nao implicitly longs to reach a reader, one who might appreciate how increasingly her "life was unreal" (79). As such her diary assumes a manner of direct, often urgent address, voicing an appeal regardless of cultural difference and geographic separation to a compassionate audience who can be attentive to her tale of familial disintegration and gradual self-recovery. This prospect of unforeseeable connection offers its own solace: "not-knowing keeps all the possibilities open. It keeps all the worlds alive" (402). And as Ruth realizes that she "couldn't help but feel a strong sense of almost karmic connection with the girl and her father" (311), she too finds some consolation in realizing her act of reading cultivates an inexorable kinship with Nao – if only for the time being, for as long as it evanescently lasts.

Ruth serves to cipher Ozeki's indictments of American aggression as well as testaments to transnational dispossession. "Canada had never felt safer" to Ruth after "going down south" and witnessing militant republicanism firsthand. "From their fog-enshrouded outpost on the mossy margin of the world, she watched the United States invade Afghanistan and then turn its sights on Iraq," with "troops ... quietly being deployed to the Middle East" (272–73). Watching in an era of virtual connectivity – particularly the extent to which we might be ethically implicated by viewing harms suffered by cultures apparently distinct from one's own – becomes dramatically import-ant to the novel. Through Ruth, Ozeki spotlights issues about the kind of responsiveness, even responsibility, we might claim to exercise when situ-ated as removed viewers other nations' catastrophes. Following the tsunami, the "images pouring in" to Ruth's computer "mesmerized her":

> Every few hours, another horrifying piece of footage would break, and she would play it over and over, studying the wave as it surged over the tops of the seawalls, carrying ships down city streets, picking up cars and trucks and depositing them on roofs of buildings. She watched whole towns get crushed and swept away in a matter of moments, and she was aware that while these moments were captured online, so many other moments simply vanished. (112–13)

The descriptively spare, matter-of-fact catalog of destruction replicates in diction and rhythm some of the horrified yet everyday stance of detach-ment that Ruth is compelled to occupy as a virtual eyewitness of this cata-clysm. Documented and framed in ways that are endlessly replayable, the magnitude of these images is inevitably compromised by their mediation. Ozeki suggests in turn that our capacity to feel affected, to be viscerally moved, has to compete with the knowledge that however immediate our spectatorship feels, the "moments" that happen to be "captured" give only the impression of comprehensiveness. Infinite "other moments," with all their inestimable particularities, are lost to the reportorial selection process of global transmission. Twenty-four-hour Internet news facilitates this tem-poral illusion of participating in the impact of events across hemispheric space, provoking ethical considerations about how we interpret our own responses to the devastation of others.

Even more polyphonic and politically searing than *A Tale for the Time Being*, Jessica Hagedorn's ambitious 2003 novel, *Dream Jungle*, is in some ways a stark reminder that "transnationalism is not to be equated with cosmopolitanism," as Alexa Weik von Mossner notes, "since transnational-ism can exist without cosmopolitanism" and often in the interests of exploit-ative ends.[20] Set in the 1970s, *Dream Jungle* connects the alleged discovery by "playboy explorer" and Manila millionaire Zamora de Legazpi of the Taobo tribe in Mindanao – who he claims are untouched since the Stone Age – with a satirical account of the chaotic filming of *Napalm Sunset*, a Vietnam War movie with distinct echoes of Francis Ford Coppola's 1979 *Apocalypse Now*.[21] Situated against "the rise of the U.S.-backed Marcos dictatorship, the novel suggests important parallels," as Vernadette Vicuña Gonzalez points out, "between U. S. interventions in Vietnam and the Philippines, as well as the imperial fictions and formations of knowledge that legitimate and sustain structures and relations of dominance." As an "indictment of American neocolonialism," *Dream Jungle* posits the "American post-colony as a site where shared hallucinations of imperial violence and dreams of tropical desire are located."[22] For neither was that desire born out of US exoticism alone. The romantic and chauvinistic Zamora is based on the actual figure of Manuel Elizalde, who became the center of a sensational – and still-debated – hoax in 1971, when he claimed to have discovered the "Tasaday," a secluded tribe from the Mindanao rain forest. Hagedorn recalls the occasion she herself tried to get a brief interview with Elizalde in 1974, for which the talk of "proving or disproving the Tasaday myth was not my main concern." Instead, Elizalde's "lost tribe of forest-dwellers were merely catalysts for my explorations into the myths of history, cultural identity and the secrets buried within my own mongrel family" – one "[r]ight at home in the mixed-up, fatalistic, anything-is-possible Philippines."[23]

All is possible at the level of form in this novel, too, as Hagedorn constantly shifts narrative viewpoints, from the iconoclastic Zamora to the precarious perspective of Rizalina, Zamora's beautiful servant and survivor of a ferry accident that killed her father and brothers. Resilient, determined, Rizalina navigates a patriarchal world often by her guile alone, knowing that the "one thing she could count on were her spindly gazelle legs, leaping over the humble graves and crude wooden crosses, over the names of the dead and buried, the tenant farmers, fisherman, and market vendors – their wives, daughters, and sons" (256). Following this panorama of impoverishment and corruption, the novel's second half turns to the figure of Vincent Moody, a sometime child movie star who now in his late twenties sees an opportunity to rescue his acting career by taking a supporting role in *Napalm Sunset*. When he arrives, "Manila astonished Moody," the narrator observes, "The cabbie drove past swamplands and crumbling colonial ruins, past jazzy discotheques, grand hotels, and haunted cathedrals. Past squatters' shacks on vacant lots, past brand new skyscrapers made of smoky glass and steel. Billboards advertised kung-fu movies, Camay soap, and Kikkoman soy sauce. Less familiar products and names fascinated him" (134). Employing one of Hagedorn's favorite rhetorical devices, the taxonomy here of climate and topography itemizes – and thereby vividly juxtaposes – the realities of stark inequality, conspicuous commercialism, and uneven development.

At the set of *Napalm Sunset*, Moody and his fellow cast remain at the mercy of Tony Pierce, an egotistical director whose volatility is documented by Paz Marlowe. Paz is a freelance American journalist who tries to pursue, as Hagedorn herself did, the question of the Taobo's existence with Zamora. Having "played cat and mouse games" with him in arranging the interview (151), Zamora turns out to be unyielding. Realizing that "Zamora had made a fool of her" (155), Paz leaves for the set of *Napalm* where filming is thoroughly, if erratically, under way. As a nomadic observer abroad, Paz exemplifies the way *Dream Jungle* resembles other transnational fictions in which "the representative status of the foreign traveller remains in place," as Caren Irr points out. Along with Moody – who serves to focalize topographies of depredation (as we saw above) – Paz operates as "an outsider rather than a so-called native informant," thus "allow[ing] explanatory narratorial digressions" on domestic divisions of labor, "neo-colonial spoilage," and systemic injustice.[24] In Hagedorn's uncompromising vision, the film's whole production is itself exploitative, as "[w]orkers hired from nearby towns stood behind counters, ready to ladle out whatever was on today's menu" (178). Indigenous people serving as "extras – locals mostly – were left to fend for themselves, while the foreigners were driven to their rented houses in nearby towns" (193). Yet this is a transnational novel that does more than simply critique neo-imperialism; it also offers resistance at the level of form too. Hagedorn's postmodern strategies enact an aesthetic opposition to what Hsiu-chuan Lee calls the "nationalist project of the Philippines": with her innovative "mixture of real-life and fictitious elements, disoriented narrating voices, and gossip-driven fragmentary style," Hagedorn seeks to "distinguish her work from the realist appeal and epic scope of nationalist writings."[25]

For both Hagedorn and Ozeki, then, form itself enables and enacts a kind of critical work. Their aesthetic strategies demonstrate how in transnational fiction "style is fundamentally important," in Jarad Zimbler's phrase, "to the ways a novel mediates and knows the world."[26] Such strategies also have specific geopolitical valences, as Caren Irr has explored. Irr groups Hagedorn alongside Chris Abani, Gish Jen, Rosa Shand, Dave Eggers, and Rachel Kushner, as writers who conceive the world as "overlapping nations and cultures." These "moderate globalists," as she calls them, sometimes "tend to avoid explicit descriptions of political processes, placing faith instead in aesthetic mechanisms for moving from local to more interconnected global scenes."[27] This movement is traceable in Kushner's linguistically and scenically vivid *The Flamethrowers* (2013). The novel centers on the twenty-three-year-old Reno, "wide-eyed and dangerously porous," who enters the New York art milieu of the late 1970s.[28] She falls in love with Sandro, the younger son of the aristocratic Valera family, who made their wealth in Italy from a motor parts and tires company that treated Brazilian

Indian rubber producers like virtual slaves. The company's founder, T. P. Valera, fought with Arditi storm troopers in World War I, and aligned himself with emerging Italian Futurists. After visiting Sandro's family estate in Italy, only then to be betrayed by Sandro himself, Reno becomes embroiled with a volatile group of political activists taking a stand in Rome against the kind of aggressive capitalism promoted by Sandro's older brother, Roberto, who is later kidnapped and killed by the militant Red Brigades. Kushner's critics admired this scope, but noted that while she has "feisty thematic ambitions" in crossing continents and conflicts, her "elevated ideas," in Talitha Stevenson's phrase, "required more than embroidery of description to suture them to story."[29]

The implication here is that stylistic agility alone cannot always resolve the hurdles presented by a novel's transnational plot. This relation between enlargement in scale and integrity in form, between geographical ambition and generic innovation, is one that I will return to later in this chapter. But here, in Kushner's case, it was precisely her novel's transnational reach that, for some, threatened her achievement of dramatic coherence and credibility. Indeed, certain critics tacitly tried to re-nationalize *The Flamethrowers* as a way of praising its central heroine. In Geoff Mak's view, for example, "Kushner has created one of the strongest contenders to stand with Ahab and Gatsby in the great hall of heroes in American Literature." The novel's depiction of "the self as immutable, unknowable, and helplessly agonistic is a uniquely American tradition, paved by writers in the last century like Faulkner and Flanery O'Connor."[30] Some of the warmest – and rather less culturally essentializing – applause came from James Wood, who remarked that as Kushner "constantly entwines the invented and the real" in prototypically postmodern fashion, she also utilizes this "power of invention to give her fiction the authenticity of the reportorial, the solidity of the historical." As such, when she shifts social and material environments to Italy, "the Valera story emerges as worked narrative, not as labored data."[31] These two plot strands invite us to include *The Flamethrowers* among a growing body of texts described by Rebecca Walkowitz as *comparison literature*, "a genre of contemporary fiction that uses narrative structures of comparison to generate new paradigms of transnational collectivity."[32] For Kushner sets out to draw "wildly smart parallels," in one reviewer's estimation, "between the cultural-political chaos of New York and Italy in the '70s, with Little Italy serving as a distorted mirror of defunct Old World values," ultimately "pitting the aesthetics of wealth against the pragmatics of value."[33]

Reno's own values eventually come to the fore abroad, when she is drawn to the reserved yet protective Gianni. A former groundsman for the Valeras, he's now for her "a kind of guardian" in Rome, who facilitates her "acceptance among the group" of protesters there.[34] She notes how his "silence had pulled me in" precisely because it contrasted the garrulous bravado of men she met in New York: "when one finally came along who didn't say much, I listened" (379). Reno understands and empathizes with "the fog of his distance, the burden of secrets, the isolation" (296). While moving evocatively across nations and social milieu, then, *The Flamethrowers* follows also, in essence, an intimate arc from innocence to experience. Reno even feels implicated in events surrounding the demise of Roberto, "whose death I felt connected to in a way I would never be able to disclose" (326). Returning to New York, she feels displaced once again. But in a gesture of self-reassertion after seeing how Sandro was "capable of harm, greatly capable of it" (296), Reno picks up her clothes from his apartment and takes a restored Moto Valera bike "through the streets of New York," experiencing the "sense of being in, but not of, the city, moving through it with real velocity, wind in my face." Reno enjoys the spectacle of her own itinerancy after a precarious transnational adventure that brought her to those crossroads of political unrest and the Veleras's embedded historic privilege, concluding that "maybe women were meant to speed past, just a blur. Like China girls. Flash, and then gone. It was only a motorcycle but it felt like a mode of being" (297).

Intimating other modes of being through the convergence of transnational relocation and domestic acclimation is also a focal point of Jhumpa Lahiri's fiction. Lahiri's work has been included by novelist Patrick Flanery among his examples of the way "more and more of what we call American literature looks outward."[35] A London-born daughter of Bengali immigrants who now lives in Rome, Lahiri has been celebrated for what Urmila Seshagiri – writing in this case on *The Lowland* (2013) – terms her fiction's "New England regionalism": a seemingly localized circle of attention that offers "a portrait of an entire nation through its evocation of a single region."[36] Situating Lahiri as part of a watershed in the development of recent North American writing, Flanery sees that her work is "a natural response to the present moment in the evolution of the American literary canon," where there's a "feeling not that American subjects have been exhausted," but rather that writers are now embracing both the "challenge and possibility" of "turning to other countries as setting and subject of 'American' novels."[37] Formally speaking, Lahiri's crystalline prose complements what some critics have called the "new social realism," as a mode that "transcends" the political and stylistic legacy of "early twentieth-century progressive writing" as well as the later twentieth-century "self-conscious aesthetics of a Rushdean postmodernism."[38] In her 2008 collection of short stories, *Unaccustomed Earth*, Lahiri navigates between the local and the global by tracing the cross-cultural experiences of characters who are seemingly "living antipodal lives" (as we learn in "Once in a Lifetime"), often "under the same roof."[39] The widowed father of the opening story, "Unaccustomed Earth," finds himself after retirement embarking on a somewhat unanticipated transnational life. By contrast, his daughter Ruma has felt compelled to accept her detachment and seclusion in suburban Seattle, where although "she was growing familiar with the roads, with the exits and the mountains and the quality of the light, she felt no connection to any of it, or to anyone" (34). She concedes that this was her "life now," even as she knows that "her mother's example – moving to a foreign place for the sake of marriage, caring exclusively for children and a household – has served as a warning, a path to avoid" (11). On his visit to her home, Ruma's father seems unsettled, and the traditional demands and expectations of the nuclear-family unit won't in themselves guarantee his permanence. Had she stayed "in India, there would have been no question of his not moving in with her" (6). Against not only this social expectation but also defying sexual convention, her father makes travel plans to Europe in order to spend time with a new companion, certain in the knowledge that he does "not want to live in the margins of his daughter's life, in the shadow of her marriage" (53). Generations meet with and depart from one another in uncustomary ways in Lahiri's vision of transnational resettlement and familial detachment, a vision concerned less with the overt "clash of culture, religion, or race," as Seshagiri describes it, than with the paradoxical sense in which a "nation founded on the notion of hospitable soil can only enrich that soil through a transient, uprooted citizenry."[40]

Many of the themes, settings, generic configurations of transnational fiction considered here seem prescient of a set of critical debates about *scale*, intervening in conversations regarding what we expect contemporary literature to incorporate. Mark McGurl is right to point out that there is of course "no one proper scale of literary analysis."[41] Nonetheless, contentions about the regional vs. global ambit of contemporary writing have highlighted thorny questions about the values that transnational criticism seeks, implicitly or purposefully, to attach to the scope of those texts it applauds. Neither are these matters confined to academic discussion, as journalistic reviews reveal. Consider Lydia Millet's 2006 evaluation in *The Globe and Mail* of Alice Munro's collection, *The View from Castle Rock*. Millet spends a good deal of time praising Munro's propensity "to linger, like a local historian, on details of place." But then she becomes rather more impatient with the very localism she initially commends. Although Munro does what "she does with immaculate precision," Millet then asks "why always, with such a richness of skill, this insistent choice on the personal, the proximate world of the self and its near relations? In the cosmology of this world, the personal, social world, the individual is seen delicately negotiating a balance with friends and family." Millet worries that "[s]urely the vast universe beyond the minutely personal is also of some interest." In Munro's work, regional landscapes constitute "a setting primarily for a specific subset of us, for the foibles and discoveries and preoccupations of the social self." Hardly ever "starvation or war," Munro's concerns "tend to be adultery or career disappointment," contributing to "a literary culture whose preoccupation is not meaning or beauty, not right or wrong, not our philosophies or propensity for atrocities or corrupt churches or governments, but rather our sex lives, our social mistakes, our neighbourhood failures and sibling rivalries." Millet concludes that we ought to be "asking simply whether, in a culture where mainstream society is already wholly consecrated to the worship of self, literary culture should be consecrated to the same fate."[42]

It may also be worth asking, of course, whether contemporary writers *need* to take on war or corrupt churches or foreign atrocities in order to address worldly issues about right, wrong, meaning, and beauty. Unambiguously for Millet, that appears to be an obligation. But her generalized notion of the narcissism of "mainstream society" homogenizes contemporary literary culture by seeing it as simply mimetic of insular, privatized, and ultimately "provincial" desires. Clearly, if a consistently global orientation is your primary litmus test for literary-critical and aesthetic success, then your chosen corpus is unlikely to include Alice Munro or, for that matter, other equally "localist" writers, rural and metropolitan alike: think of Carol Shields, Marilynne Robinson, Kent Haruf, or Ben Lerner – more on whom in a moment. What Millet assumes, then, is that a writer cannot reconcile "the foibles and discoveries and preoccupations of the social self" with the job of looking beyond that self, let alone beyond the nation. Obviously that "vast universe beyond the minutely personal," as she calls it, should be "of interest." Yet there is surely something ethically dubious about imposing this planetary "cosmology" as *the* most valuable benchmark against which contemporary fiction's political, emotional, or philosophical impact is measured.

Size also matters to the New York–based Irish writer, Colm Tóibín, author of – among many other novels – the acclaimed chronicle of transatlantic migration, *Brooklyn* (2009). However, Tóibín's sense of what the imperatives of scale might mean to novelists is rather more nuanced than Millet's, as was evident in his review of Javier Marías and Antonio Muñoz Molina. For one thing, Tóibín seems quite willing to play devil's advocate with the assumption that being environmentally bigger is always better for writers who want their work to make some sort of ideological, historical, or affective difference:

How strange it must seem to historians, sociologists, and philosophers that, after all that has happened in the world, the small matter of love, in all its miniscule twists and turns, continues to preoccupy novelists more than, say, the breaking of nations or the fate of the earth. Some novelists have tried to rectify this; they have attempted to make the art of the novel seem more important somehow by treating, say, terrorism or large political questions with great seriousness. But then other novelists return, like scavengers or renegades or deserters or prophets, to the old dramas of fidelity, treachery, and passion among people who are ordinary ... Compared to investigative journalism, history-writing, biography, or self-help books, the novel is a strange, humble, hybrid form; it is perhaps in its very humility, in its pure uselessness, in its instability, in its connection to the merely human that its grandeur lies.[43]

Spending critical energy on the humble and the miniscule in fiction might seem thoroughly unfashionable, or at least out of step with making bold claims about why the novel socially matters across cultures. But it is telling that writers from an even younger generation than Tóibín and Munro seem more alert than ever to the pragmatic and creative requirements for satisfying the task of writing beyond the nation. Take Ben Lerner, for instance, whose latest novel to date, *10:04* (2014), zeroes in on what its narrator calls the localized textural variations of New York, keen to show how even the city's "bad form of collectivity ... can stand as a figure of its possibility," telling a story bracketed by storms: Irene in late August 2011, then hurricane Sandy in October 2012.[44] Lerner displays a deeply self-conscious – one might say, neo-postmodern – attitude toward his own reflexive venture, remarking in one interview that "I think a lot of the time [this] book is talked about, like, 'Oh, here's another Brooklyn novel by a guy with glasses.'" But he's also self-conscious about his raw material, given *10:04*'s apparent withdraw from the global to the local. Lerner makes no apology for the political ramifications of such a geographically confined focus. In fact, he attaches a certain responsibility to this scaled-down mode of attention:

I can see why, if I, the historical person, choose to write a book that's set in Brooklyn and talks about advances and eating bluefin tuna or whatever, that it's just automatically in the category of the self-absorbed. [*10:04*] wants to acknowledge all of that as an attempt to see what spaces for healing can exist, as opposed to the model of fiction that's like "The way I deal with the political is that I pretend to have access to the mind of a nine-year-old boy in Sudan" – instead of evading the material conditions of the book.[45]

Despite his jaunty self-scrutiny here, Lerner actually makes a rather scorching sideswipe at Dave Eggers's 2006 biographical "novel" *What Is the What*, with its first-hand account of atrocity and exile based on Valentino

Deng, a real-life refugee from the second Sudanese Civil War. It's quite a surprising jibe. Because one would think that Lerner might have more in common with Eggers, not least as he aims – in the words of *10:04*'s protagonist – to "work my way from irony to sincerity in the sinking city, a would-be Whitman of the vulnerable grid" (4), in order to show that "Art has to offer something other than stylized despair" (93). For Eggers, after all, has become something of a canonical figure in the paradigm shift that scholars of American fiction are variously describing as the "New Sincerity" or "Post-Irony."[46] Furthermore, Eggers is no stranger to the earnestness with which *10:04* endorses local, quotidian events as valuable optics through which to magnify the worldly consequences of technological transformation: his *A Hologram for the King* (2012) poignantly demonstrated the personal alienations and disaffections of digital dependency against a beguiling Jeddah backdrop.[47]

In the end, Lerner's antagonism is really directed toward his implied audience, disclosing a frustration with what (he thinks) the contemporary reading public expects contemporary fiction to do and how widely throughout the world it should move. And in this complaint he is not alone. Zadie Smith – herself a transnational figure, now based between New York and London's Queens Park; author of the east-coast campus-novel, *On Beauty* (2005), with a British American family at its core and described by one critic as a "transatlantic comic saga" – also suspects that localist solidarity by no means guarantees an actually existing community of multiethnic feeling and joint action.[48] Not only is this suspicion apparent in Smith's experimental depiction of multicultural civic life in *NW* (2012), whose characters identify with the same district in London yet who remain strangely out of sync, either with each other or with their own vision of familial achievements and social opportunities. It's also clear from one of Smith's essays in the *New York Review of Books*, on cosmopolitan life in west London. There she recalls a trip to see her mother that made her reflect on how Britain's high streets have evolved to keep people moving, and thereby to forestall forms of social communion:

> Everybody knows that if people hang around for any length of time in an urban area without purpose they are likely to become "anti-social." And indeed there were four homeless drunks sitting on one of the library's strange architectural protrusions, drinking Special Brew. Perhaps in a village they would be sitting under a tree, or have already been driven from the area by a farmer with a pitchfork. I do not claim to know what happens in villages. But here in Willesden they were sat on their ledge and the rest of us were congregating for no useful purpose in the unlovely concrete space, simply standing around in the sunshine, like some kind of community.[49]

There is something at once utopian and unsentimental about this fleeting moment of collectivity. As in novels like *On Beauty* and *NW*, so in her critical writing, Smith is drawn to these unremarkable scenes, where glimmers of cooperation and mutual acknowledgment are spotted in the weave of an otherwise individuated urban tapestry. If she sounds romantic about the prospect of coming together in an "unlovely concrete space," Smith is nonetheless resigned to what this temporary congregation amounts to or even implies. If there *is* a cosmopolitics of the local simmering here for Smith, then it's a thoroughly protean one. As such, it still appears some way from representing a tangible common cause.

But perhaps that *is* the point. For when writers like Smith, Lahiri, Eggers, and Kushner localize our attentions even within the thematic context of transnational narratives, they also invite us to question our own critical procedures: to resist, that is, the temptation to instrumentalize their work as convenient illustrations of what Bruce Robbins calls "the structuring force of the world capitalist system." Staging moments of recognition or interaction that are no less important for being so inconspicuous or inconclusive, these writers also direct certain provocations at our own interpretive motives. In so doing, they complement Robbins's suggestion that to "some readers, true worldliness might require an honest confession of the novel's inability to tell meaningful stories of identity and relationship at the global scale."[50] Yet the confession should also apply to how criticism regards its own agency as well. This seems especially timely at a moment when leading theorists are arguing that ideologically driven ways of reading do not always engage with literature *as* literature, seeking instead to extrapolate from it political information by "specify[ing] in advance," as Derek Attridge puts it, "the kind of experience the work of art should produce" – only to end up "programming what is inherently and constitutively unprogrammable."[51]

Rather pertinently, Smith herself has talked in similar respects about "the essential hubris of criticism": "When I write criticism I'm in such a protected position: here are my arguments, here are my blessed opinions, here is my textual evidence, here my rhetorical flourish. One feels very pleased with oneself. Fiction has none of these defences."[52] Such is the fraught relation – indeed, friction – between the grandeur of interpretations that promote writers' global implications and the tenor of humility (to recall Tóibín) in the very fiction upon which those critical acts are performed. For this discrepancy suggests that humility is something applicable to criticism's own values too, not least if we are to take a hard, honest look at those aesthetic and institutional merits writers acquire only when they become amenable to the latest agendas of transnational readings. This is not to imply that transnational approaches manifest that tendency, as Taiye Selasi rather acerbically puts it, to endorse diasporic writers merely for "producing explanatory ethnographic texts dolled up as literary fiction."[53] But it does mean we need to recognize that if "[o]ne crucial challenge" transnational thought, as Caroline Levine advises, "comes from the field's insistence that we think responsibly about local experience" so as to "avoid the danger of folding all cultures into an image of the same," then something of fiction's stubborn yet singular humility might continue to resonate with our adjusting priorities.[54] The novel today – at once a plural archive of social experience and a form with perpetually evolving commitments – still undoubtedly has the potential to intervene in how we imagine global ways of thinking to a degree that politically edifies us. Yet at the same time our considered refusal to overstate the effect of this intervention, as students of contemporary writing, may be one step toward fully acknowledging the opportunities and responsibilities yielded by the transnational turn.

NOTES

1 Taiye Selasi, "We Need More Names," *The Guardian Review* (4 July 2015), 19.
2 Ibid. 18.
3 Ibid. 18.
4 Paul Giles, *Transnationalism in Practice: Essays on American Studies, Literature, and Religion* (Edinburgh: Edinburgh University Press, 2010), 13.
5 Paul Jay, *Global Matters: The Transnational Turn in Literary Studies* (Ithaca, NY: Cornell University Press, 2010), 5.
6 See Anna Brickhouse, *Transamerican Literary Relations and the Nineteenth-Century Public Sphere* (Cambridge: Cambridge University Press, 2004); María del Pilar Blanco, *Ghost-Watching American Modernity: Haunting, Landscape, and the Hemispheric Imagination* (New York: Fordham University Press, 2012); and Matthew Hart, "Globalism and Historical Romance," in *The Cambridge Companion to British Fiction since 1945*, ed. David James (New York: Cambridge University Press, 2015), 207–23. Hart draws attention to "novels that impute a long history to globalization, rather than seeing it as the mark of the present," highlighting figures such as Amitav Ghosh, Timothy Mo, and Eleanor Catton, before focusing on Salman Rushdie and David Mitchell (207).
7 Jason Gladstone and Daniel Worden, "Introduction: Postmodernism, Then," *Twentieth-Century Literature*, Special Issue: *Postmodernism, Then*, 57.3–4 (Fall/Winter 2011): 302.
8 David Harvey, *The Condition of Postmodernity: An Inquiry into the Origins of Cultural Change* (Oxford: Blackwell, 1990), 54, 23.
9 Fredric Jameson, *Postmodernism, Or, The Cultural Logic of Late Capitalism* (London: Verso, 1991), 45–46.
10 I have addressed elsewhere some of the methodological and conceptual problems surrounding "modernity" and "postmodernity" in relation to how we engage with contemporary arts: see "Modern/Altermodern," in *Time: A Vocabulary of*

the Present, Joel Burges and Amy J. Elias, eds. (New York: New York University Press, 2016), 66–81.

11 Gladstone and Worden, "Introduction: Postmodernism, Then," 294.

12 See Peter Boxall, *Twenty-First Century Fiction: A Critical Introduction* (Cambridge: Cambridge University Press, 2013), especially chapters 1 and 2; Jeremy Green, *Late Postmodernism: American Fiction at the Millennium* (New York: Palgrave, 2005); and the essay collection edited by Jason Gladstone, Andrew Hoberek, and Daniel Worden, *Postmodern/Postwar–and After* (Iowa City: University of Iowa Press, 2016).

13 Brian McHale, *Constructing Postmodernism* (London: Routledge, 1992), 3.

14 Brian McHale, "Afterword: Reconstructing Postmodernism," *Narrative*, 21.3 (2013): 360.

15 McHale, *Constructing Postmodernism*, 247.

16 Toni Morrison, "Rootedness: The Ancestor as Foundation" (1984), in *What Moves at the Margin: Selected Nonfiction*, ed. Carolyn C. Denard (Jackson: University Press of Mississippi, 2008), 59.

17 Susan Stanford Friedman, "Towards a Transnational Turn in Narrative Theory: Literary Narratives, Traveling Tropes, and the Case of Virginia Woolf and the Tagores," *Narrative*, 19.1 (January 2011): 3.

18 Rebecca L. Walkowitz, *Born Translated: The Contemporary Novel in an Age of World Literature* (New York: Columbia University Press, 2015), 122.

19 Ruth Ozeki, *A Tale for the Time Being* (Edinburgh: Canongate, 2013), 43. Hereafter cited parenthetically.

20 Alexa Weik von Mossner, *Cosmopolitan Minds: Literature, Emotion, and the Transnational Imagination* (Austin: University of Texas Press, 2014), 8.

21 Jessica Hagedorn, *Dream Jungle* (New York: Viking, 2003), 290. Hereafter cited parenthetically.

22 Vernadette Vicuña Gonzalez, "Headhunter Itineraries: The Philippines as America's Dream Jungle," *The Global South*, 3.2 (Fall 2009): 145, 144–45.

23 Jessica Hagedorn, "Jungle In Search of a Dream," *Review: Literature and Arts of the Americas*, Issue 72, 39.1 (2006): 130.

24 Caren Irr, *Toward the Geopolitical Novel: U. S. Fiction in the Twenty-First Century* (New York: Columbia University Press, 2014), 116.

25 Hsiu-chuan Lee, "The Remains of Empire and the 'Purloined' Philippines: Jessica Hagedorn's *Dream Jungle*," *Mosaic*, 45.3 (September 2012): 50.

26 Jarad Zimbler, *J. M. Coetzee and the Politics of Style* (Cambridge: Cambridge University Press, 2014), 6.

27 Irr, *Toward the Geopolitical Novel*, 18.

28 James Wood, "Youth in Revolt," review of *The Flamethrowers*, by Rachel Kushner, *The New Yorker* (8 April 2013), n.p. Web.

29 Talitha Stevenson, review of *The Flamethrowers*, by Rachel Kushner, *The Observer* (23 June 2013), n.p. Web.

30 Geoff Mak, review of a review of *The Flamethrowers*, by Rachel Kushner and *Necessary Errors*, by Caleb Crain, *LA Review of Books* (25 December 2013), n. p. Web.

31 Wood, "Youth in Revolt."

32 Rebecca L. Walkowitz, "For Translation: Virginia Woolf, J. M. Coetzee, and Transnational Comparison," in *The Legacies of Modernism: Historicising Postwar and Contemporary Fiction*, ed. David James (Cambridge: Cambridge University Press, 2012), 245.

33 Cristina García, "Revolutions Per Minute," review of *The Flamethrowers*, by Rachel Kushner, *The New York Times* (26 April 2013), n. p. Web.

34 Rachel Kushner, *The Flamethrowers* (London: Harvill Secker, 2013), 379, 378. Hereafter cited parenthetically.

35 Christopher Holmes, "An Interview with Patrick Flanery," *Contemporary Literature*, 54.3 (Winter 2013): 454.

36 Urmila Seshagiri, "Jhumpa Lahiri's Real America: On *The Lowland*," *L. A. Review of Books* (9 October 2013), n. p. Web.

37 Holmes, "An Interview with Patrick Flanery," 454.

38 Ulka Anjara, "Realist Hieroglyphics: Aravind Adiga and the New Social Novel," *Modern Fiction Studies*, 61.1 (Spring 2015): 114.

39 Jhumpa Lahiri, "Once in a Lifetime," in *Unaccustomed Earth* (London: Random House, 2008), 236. This and other stories from the volume hereafter cited parenthetically.

40 Seshagiri, "Jhumpa Lahiri's Real America: On *The Lowland*."

41 Mark McGurl, *The Program Era: Postwar Fiction and the Rise of Creative Writing* (Cambridge, MA: Harvard University Press, 2009), 401.

42 Lydia Millet, "Alice in Familyland," review of *The View from Castle Rock*, by Alice Munro, *The Globe and Mail* (23 September 2006), n. p. Web.

43 Colm Tóibín, "Lust and Loss in Madrid," *The New York Review of Books* (July/August 2014), 66.

44 Ben Lerner, *10:04* (London: Granta, 2014), 239. Hereafter cited parenthetically.

45 Ben Lerner, interview by Emily Witt, *The Guardian, Review* (3 January 2015), n. p. Web.

46 See Lee Konstantinou, "No Bull: David Foster Wallace and Postironic Belief," in *The Legacy of David Foster Wallace*, Samuel Cohen and Lee Konstantinou, eds. (Iowa City: University of Iowa Press, 2012); and Adam Kelly's "Dialectic of Sincerity: Lionel Trilling and David Foster Wallace," *Post45 Journal* (October 2014). Web, <http://post45.research.yale.edu/2014/10/dialectic-of-sincerity-lionel-trilling-and-david-foster-wallace/>. Accessed 1 February 2016.

47 I consider Eggers's novel at greater length, in relation to alternative paradigms of irony and sincerity, in "How Postmodernism Became Earnest," in *Postmodern/Postwar–and After: Rethinking American Literature*, Jason Gladstone, Andrew Hoberek, and Daniel Worden, eds. (Iowa City: University of Iowa Press, 2016), 81–91.

48 Stephanie Merrit, "Turn Over a New Leaf," *The Observer* (Sunday 2 January 2005), n.p. Web.

49 Zadie Smith, "The North West London Blues," *New York Review of Books* (June 2012), n.p. Web.

50 Bruce Robbins, "The Worlding of the American Novel," in *The Cambridge History of the American Novel*, Leonard Cassuto, Clare Virginia Eby, and Benjamin Reiss, eds. (New York: Cambridge University Press, 2011), 1096, 1097.

51 Derek Attridge, *The Work of Literature* (Oxford: Oxford University Press, 2015), 7.
52 Zadie Smith, Interview by Ted Hodgkinson, *Granta* (6 September 2012), n.p. Web.
53 Selasi, "We Need More Names," 19.
54 Caroline Levine, "Scaled Up, Writ Small: A Response to Carolyn Dever and Herbert F. Tucker," *Victorian Studies* 49.1 (Autumn 2006): 101.

PART III

Critical Geographies

8

DESTINY O. BIRDSONG AND IFEOMA KIDDOE NWANKWO

Black Atlantic and Diaspora Literature

Introduction: Creative and Critical Contexts

Exhausted, she fell against the glass, her feverish face striking the cold one there, crying suddenly because their idea of her was only an illusion, yet so powerful that it would stalk her down the years, confront her in each mirror and from the safe circle of their eyes, surprise her even in the gleaming surface of a table.

Paule Marshall, *Brown Girl, Brownstones* (1959)[1]

In one of the final scenes of *Brown Girl, Brownstones,* Selina Boyce articulates a dilemma that lies at the crux of Black artistic production: the necessary work of speaking back to the "illusions" that have plagued theories about black art for centuries. Selina's realization comes in the wake of a powerful dance sequence, after which the white mother of another dancer congratulates her for her "'natural talent.'"[2] Indeed, Black art – and, by extension, Black literature – have always borne the marks of these kinds of assumptions; writers have often used their texts to recreate and respond to similar moments of disarticulation, wherein the beauty and complexity of the Black experience are boiled down to a few racist assumptions. As such, Black Atlantic and Diasporic literature is necessarily comprehensive in scope, addressing issues of Black humanity as well as gender, sexuality, class, (trans)national origin, acculturation, and cultural trauma, to name a few. And, encompassing everything from autobiography to speculative fiction written by people living in the farthest corners of the world, the field contains a dauntingly immense body of work. However, in this chapter we focus on Black women's migration narratives like the one quoted earlier. Here, writers use various forms of movement to illustrate the international, intercultural, and intergenerational influences that shape Black Diasporic identity. By doing so, they interrogate masculinist, nationalist, and classist notions of identity formation that have often excluded women's voices from the canon.

Before delving into a discussion of specific texts, it is important to point out key theoretical conversations that have given Black Atlantic and Diasporic literature its name. The geographical and genealogical vastness of the field dictates that the theory produced alongside the literature must be both particularizing in its identification of the themes that make such literature "Black" and "Diasporic" but also encompassing enough to include the work of individuals living centuries and oceans apart. As Paul Gilroy writes in *The Black Atlantic: Modernity and Double Consciousness* (1993), the Black Atlantic is "rhizomorphic" and "fractal" in structure, thus the theories by which scholars analyze the art produced within it must be equally so.[3] According to Gilroy, the Black Atlantic is both an antithesis to the nationalistic focus of British and American cultural studies as well as a compact (and, as some would argue, exclusively American, British, and Anglophone) unit that historians and other scholars can use to identify "an explicitly transnational and intercultural perspective" in black art, letters, and music.[4] He also contends that Black Atlantic identity is markedly different from the "particularity" with which he accused many groups (namely African American and British "New Left" intellectuals). For him, it is the product of a "system of cultural exchanges"[5] that operates much like the ships that once moved people of African descent between continents and shores.[6] In fact, for several centuries, black people were transported as both chattel and individuals in search of "emancipation, autonomy, and citizenship"[7] – a phenomenon that engenders and exemplifies the continuously transformative nature of black identity. And, as Gilroy contends, in this constant state of self-reflection and redefinition, Black Atlantic identity is a hallmark of modernism as well as a "counterculture" of modernity that leaves its mark on the art produced by blacks around the world.[8]

The Black Atlantic exploded the field of Diasporic criticism, simultaneously highlighting theoretical issues that plagued the field before the seminal text's publication, and opening the door for contemporary scholars to address lacunae within Gilroy's theories. For several of his contemporaries, including Stuart Hall, truly comprehensive theories of Diasporic subjectivity were not so anti-nationalistic.[9] In "Cultural Identity and Diaspora" (1996), Hall contends that, while the Diasporic subject is a microcosm of dialogic movement, it is also influenced by European, African, and indigenous cultures that are both present and subsumed by a dynamic cultural identity. Similarly, Carole Boyce Davies and 'Molara Ogundipe-Leslie's *Moving Beyond Boundaries* (1995) particularizes definitions of "diaspora" to make space for women of color. The editors contend that "[w]e cannot be comfortable subsuming definitions, when we ourselves have not bothered to discover the rest of these existences outside of our narrow set of identifications."[10] Boyce Davies expands on the notion of black women's diasporas in sentiments that are both similar to and different from Gilroy's anti-nationalist notions of Diasporic identity. She writes that "[s]tudying black women's writing in cross-cultural contexts must begin with the challenge to the assumption of North American/African-American identity as synonymous with Black women's writing in its entirety. This limitation works only to curtail our broader recognition of the many locations of our selves."[11] In each instance, Hall, Ogundipe-Leslie, and Boyce Davies articulate definitions that argue for a more transnational notion of the Black Atlantic Diaspora, and the literature that bears its name.

Other scholars were also hard at work to break long-standing silences in the field, particularly those surrounding women writers and the ways in which migration is read differently in works written by women. In *Routes: Travel & Translation in the Late Twentieth Century* (1997), James Clifford identifies the ways in which gender creates an additional tension for the female Diasporic subject. Although the Diasporic space can often constitute a kind of liberation from nationalist/tribal patriarchies, it can also create new ones when women's and men's experiences are generalized as separate from one another.[12] As Clifford points out, overlapping "articulations" (moments of self-definition that do not assume any essentialist qualities) and "disarticulations" (moments of external identification that reduce the complexities of identity to a few generalizing concepts) abound in the Diasporic space. Belinda Edmondson expounds on this notion, contending that even the terms "exile" and "immigrant" have become gendered in conversations about Black Atlantic literature: male characters are propelled through the space by feelings of outsiderness and general alienation, or for intellectual pursuits (usually to the "metropole," the colonial seat of power).[13] Female characters, on the other hand, are characterized as migrant laborers who suffer from a lack of education and other resources.[14]

Thus, the Black Diasporic literary space, liberating though it may be, is nevertheless potentially problematic – especially for women, who are often operating as the outsiders within, subject to the many disarticulations and silences that either confine them to or exclude them from theoretical conversations. And yet, some of the most dynamic Black Atlantic and Diasporic literature has been penned by women, who are producing complex theories of identity formation that interrogate the approaches most often used to read their texts. Articulating both transnationalist and community-based subjectivities – African American, West Indian, Black British, and native African – these women are writing about the ways in which movement – travel, migration, and other ideological routes of self-discovery – shape the racial, cultural, and ideological formations that have come to define the Black Atlantic as both a theoretical construct and as a body of literature.

Call and Response: Literature as Cultural Work

Perhaps no other genre exemplifies the web of "roots" and "routes" in the formation of Black subjectivity with the same eloquence and sophistication as that of the slave narrative. Often penned at the urging of abolitionist editors, slave narratives were both testimony and historical document, as heavily marked by the moral and socioeconomic confines of their day as they were by the sentimentality of eighteenth- and nineteenth-century literature. Such was certainly the case with narratives like *The History of Mary Prince: A West Indian Slave, Related by Herself* (1831). And yet, as Sandra Pouchet Paquet makes clear, in spite of the fact that this text bears the constraints of the slave narrative (particularly in its coded language about Prince's sexual abuse),[15] it nevertheless chronicles a "journey from slavery to freedom, from childhood to womanhood, from Bermuda to England ... a journey from the private self-consciousness of a child to the politicized, public self-consciousness of an enslaved woman speaking on behalf of all slaves."[16] And, as Ifeoma K. Nwankwo points out, these features make it markedly different from canonized, male-authored narratives like Frederick Douglass's *Narrative of the Life of Frederick Douglass, an American Slave, Written by Himself* (1845), which was much narrower in its geographic scope.[17] In *History*, Prince traces a physical and ideological trajectory wherein she literally writes herself into a space of personhood that bears the marks of a rooted identity that is at once particularly West Indian but also transatlantic.

Originally published as an abolitionist text (and later as a fundraiser for Prince's medical expenses),[18] *The History of Mary Prince* chronicles the life of a West Indian slave whose desires for freedom evolve as her body suffers the ravages of slave labor throughout the Diaspora – first in Bermuda, then in Turks and Caicos, Antigua, and finally Great Britain. Prince herself admits that, as a young girl, she was "too young to understand rightly [her] condition as a slave."[19] However, as her masters grow more and more sadistic in both their expectations of her labor and their forms of punishment, Prince becomes desperate for freedom, running away to her parents after one particularly vicious beating, and finally leaving her masters in England after years of brutal treatment.[20] In her plea for freedom, Prince creates a dual identity on the pages of *History:* She is both human property and a black West Indian woman of Christian sensibilities who argues for her own right to fully benefit from the protection of British law. In fact, her ultimate desire is to procure an emancipation in England that would, in essence, transfer to its colonies in the same way that the rights of British subjects followed them throughout the empire.

As Pouchet Paquet points out, by placing her narrative of abuse alongside a description of the rights of hired help in England, Prince "provides a space for the expression of social dissidence and marginality that is directed at a metropolitan audience in an effort to force a change in the status of the colonial subject and slave."[21] When Prince's masters, the Woods, hire a washerwoman to supplement Prince's labor when she cannot complete tasks on her own, Prince notes that the worker "was not well treated, and would come no more."[22] This juxtaposition of the hired hand's response to the treatment Prince experiences on a daily basis illustrates a contemporary understanding of the expanding rights of all British subjects, and marks a demand for inclusion in these new privileges of subjecthood by calling for the freedom of all slaves. This plea illustrates a deep rootedness in a community of Blacks who, albeit they do not share her quasi-freedom, do share her subjectivity as individuals without rights.[23] In the final words of her narrative, Prince makes a bold declaration, using an all-inclusive "we" that could arguably be read to include "slaves," "Blacks," "women," "West Indians," or all of the above: "We don't mind hard work, if we had proper treatment, and proper wages like English servants, and proper time in the week to keep us from breaking the Sabbath."[24] Again, Prince's sentiments stand at the intersection of a distinctly transatlantic black identity – one that is inextricably linked to an enslaved and socioeconomically disempowered community from which she is separated by an ocean (and conditional emancipation), but on whose behalf she is railing against circumscribed racial roles that prevent them all from achieving equal rights.

Even after the end of slavery, Black Atlantic and Diasporic women writers continued to address issues of migration and its impact on identity formation in both positive and negative ways. For instance, in *Of One Blood* (1903), Pauline Hopkins creates a character who must leave American shores in order to discover his true self. Reuel Briggs, a medical student who is passing for white, reclaims his black identity when he travels to Ethiopia in search of wealth and finds a sophisticated civilization of which he is a long-lost royal descendent. In Nella Larsen's *Quicksand* (1928), however, migration does not produce the same results. Helga Crane wanders from Harlem to Copenhagen in hopes of finding a place where her biraciality is not fetishized, but ultimately finds herself in a small Southern black community, where she lives in quiet despair as the overburdened wife and mother of an impoverished country preacher. In Anne Petry's *The Street* (1946), Lutie Johnson ultimately abandons her own son and boards a bus to Chicago in the hopes of somehow escaping a life plagued by poverty, sexual exploitation, and the impossibility of shielding her son from the negative influences of those around him. Each of these woman-authored texts asks a complicated version of the question Du Bois poses at the turn of the century in *The Souls of Black Folk* (1903): Can black individuals ever reconcile their multiple identities – as blacks (and, in the case of Helga Crane and Lutie Johnson, as black women), and as members of various cultural, ideological, and socioeconomic communities – into "better and truer" versions of themselves?[25]

The answer is probably best answered in Paule Marshall's *Brown Girl, Brownstones* (1959). In it, Selina Boyce develops a black, female, and transnational identity that is formed against and in concert with various forms of Diasporic migration. As she grows into womanhood, she rejects the ideologies of her parents and the Barbadian immigrant community of which they are a part, and instead aligns herself with black and white other mothers who model various identity traits that Selina incorporates into her own. Thus, even though her family history is rooted in a specific narrative of transatlantic movement, her personal identity is shaped by the winding route she takes to womanhood, one that aligns her with West Indian, African American, and Jewish women whose narratives of migration inspire her to set off on her own journey through the Diasporic space.

Brown Girl, Brownstones: Migration, Mimesis, and Rerouting the Self

Brown Girl is a complicated narrative of identity formation, in which influence and antithesis, national and transnational identity, and migration and stasis all come to bear on its main character, Selina, with motherhood as a central concern. In *Becoming Black: Creating Identity in the Black Diaspora* (2004), Michelle Wright offers a staunchly feminist theory of Black Diasporic subjectivity, wherein the maternal figure stands at the helm of identity formation. According to Wright, the Black mother, who connects her children to the past even as she pushes them out into the world and prepares them for the challenges of the future, epitomizes the circular nature of the black experience, which is itself always changing, even as it is always an "undeniable product of the past, shaped by it without being wholly controlled."[26] Daughters too, who ultimately grow into black womanhood embodying and/or challenging their mother's ideologies, are paradigmatic of the black subject, who is always in dialogue with the "complex and contradictory nature of the black experience" both past and present.[27] As such, the mother-daughter dyad often employed in black women's literature is a hallmark illustration of Diasporic identity formation, and illustrates how the "routes" to such identity formation are inextricably connected to the "roots" of ancestry: they are circuitous, reciprocal, and retrospective. Even as a daughter forges an identity that is seemingly in contrast with the mother's, there are still influences and similarities across the divide.

In *Brown Girl*, Marshall introduces a character who is shaped by her mother's migration to the United States as a Barbadian immigrant in search of socioeconomic stability, as well as by her own defiant determination to chart a course to womanhood and independence. Though Silla Boyce once crossed an ocean alone as a young girl of eighteen, her economic struggles in the United States (not to mention her disappointment in her unambitious, philandering husband Deighton) have restricted both her corporeal and ideological mobilities, and have made her anxious to protect her daughters from her own traumas of heartbreak and hardship. When she realizes that her youngest, Selina, is unconcerned with wealth, status, and socially strategic matrimony, Silla attempts to create a mirrored identity for her by physically restricting the young girl's movement and isolating her from every other influence aside from her own. And yet, Selina prevails by subverting her mother's dominance, mapping a route of both improvisation and mimicry. By rejecting Silla's capitalist ideals of wealth, financial stability, and community allegiance, Selina reverses the possibility of suffering her mother's fate of early widowhood, estranged children, and suburban loneliness. But, in her journey toward self-identification, during which she begins a love affair, interacts with non-Barbadian women (much to her mother's dismay), chooses a career as a dancer, and ultimately emigrates from the United States, Selina's defiance allows her to construct a uniquely female Black Diasporic identity that is still heavily influenced by the successes and failures of her mother.

By forming extra-maternal bonds with other mothers, Selina is introduced to alternative representations of womanhood. For example, Suggie Skeete, a Barbadian brownstone tenant who Silla evicts amid allegations of prostitution, models a sensuality and an enjoyment of sexual intercourse that Selina never sees in Silla, and that Selina often reenacts with her lover, Clive Springer. But perhaps one of Selina's most transformative bonds is a nearly life-long friendship with Miss Thompson, a black Southern woman who works in a nearby beauty shop. Through Miss Thompson Selina learns that her skin color creates for her a bilateral positionality in the United States, and this knowledge gives her a new perspective on her own transnational identity, expanding it beyond the confines of the Barbadian American community in which her mother is so staunchly rooted. Miss Thompson is the first woman in the text who offers Selina a glimpse of the ugliness of white-on-black racism when she tells the story of her "life-sore": a putrefying wound on her foot that refuses to heal. As a young woman, Miss Thompson is almost raped by a group of white Southern men, and although she escapes sexual assault, one of them manages to permanently mark her foot by slicing it with a shovel. After hearing this story, Selina feels hatred toward whites for the first time; she imagines taking Miss Thompson's cane and "rush[ing] into some store on Fulton Street" where she would exact revenge by "bringing [the cane] smashing across the white face behind the counter."[28] Later, Selina will feel the same rage after her dance recital, in the wake of her exchange with the white mother who claims that her West Indianness makes her more civilized than other blacks even as she cites Selina's blackness as the seat of her natural talent for dance.[29] After this encounter, Selina remembers Miss Thompson's attack and imagines that the shovel "cutting like a scythe in the sunlight ... was no different from the woman's voice falling brutally in the glare of the lamp."[30] Here, Selina finally realizes that, in the eyes of Margaret's mother, she is no different from the blacks who her mother and other Barbadians ostracize.

In *The Black Atlantic*, Gilroy laments that, although scholars are often reluctant to do so, "[a]cknowledging the intercultural history of the [Jewish] diaspora concept and its transcoding by historians of the black dispersal into the western hemisphere remains politically important" for healing long-standing rifts between the two communities and perhaps building "a better political relationship" between the groups.[31] Interestingly, Marshall alludes to the possibility for such collaboration when Selina learns a powerful form of self-expression from her Jewish classmate and fellow dancer, Rachel Fine. During the watershed performance that precedes Selina's realization of her transnational identity, the two women perform a mimetic dance sequence "as if guided by a single will, as if, indeed, they were simply reflections of each other."[32] Under Rachel's instruction, dance becomes another rerouting of Selina's identity as well as her means of travel when Rachel secures a position for Selina as a dancer on a cruise ship. It also serves as the fulcrum on which Selina cycles back to the influence of – and a resemblance to – her mother. Through dance Selina and Silla share physical and autobiographical resemblances that speak to each other across a temporal divide. In fact, by the end of the novel, Selina's use of dance to fund her sojourn to the Caribbean is a complex reversed, revised, yet reenacted routing of Silla's journey from Barbados to the United States years before. Even though Rachel introduces Selina to the liberative power of dance, it is a talent that, in many ways, runs in the blood. Silla once shared a love for dance when she was Selina's age. According to an old family friend, she once danced until she "'fall out for dead right there on the grass.'"[33] Similarly, Selina's signature performance, the birth-to-death cycle she performs with Rachel, begins with vibrant movement and ends in stillness. Thus, the dance is doubly mimetic: it is performed with Rachel, but the movements of Selina's body actually mimic her mother's.

In a final confrontation in the cloakroom of the Barbadian Association, where Selina has turned down a college scholarship because she plans to leave home for good, the room becomes a microcosmic version of the Black Diasporic space: here, Silla's and Selina's routes cross in one final moment that makes clear how disparate yet mimetic their migrations really are. The cloakroom itself is a fitting metaphor for this. Both literally and figuratively, it is a fluid space – one of comings and goings, perpetual movement. It is here that Silla announces that she has finally "arrived" in the United States, recently putting a down payment on a long-coveted house in Crown Heights. Selina, on the other hand, is departing, and plans to perform as a dancer on a cruise ship that will most likely travel to the Caribbean, her mother's birthplace. And, albeit reluctantly, Silla gives her blessing. "'G'long!'" she tells Selina in a fit of exasperation, "'You was always too much woman for me anyway, soul. And my own mother did say two head-bulls can't reign in a flock. G'long!'"[34] By repeating the same words her own mother once told her, Silla reenacts a moment from the past; however, she is now firmly rooted in American soil while her daughter is preparing for a journey that will most likely preclude the possibilities of mimicking a similar rootedness in the United States via marriage, homeownership, and children. Operating within a cycle of difference and resemblance, and within a complex web of national, filial, and personal allegiances, Selina is leaving her *mother's land* but returning to her motherland, and does so in a literal reversal of her mother's previous transatlantic journey.

Such a reverse route from one homeland to another is proof that Selina's identity, like her departure, is far more nuanced than a simple movement away from her mother. Selina's journey, which began with a deliberate rerouting of her mother's influence, is an interrogation of Silla's notions of black female identity. In the end, however, it also mimics Silla's rejection of the life her own mother wanted her to live. Throughout the novel, Silla has defined personal success and immigrant identity by her ability to "buy house." But in the cloakroom scene, Selina vehemently rejects this, at one point exclaiming: "'I'm not interested in houses!'"[35] And yet, moments later, Selina makes it clear that her desire to leave is, in part, borne out of the stories she once heard her mother tell about expatriation: "Remember how you used to talk about how you left home and came here alone as a girl of eighteen and was your own woman? I used to love hearing that. And that's what I want. I want it!"[36] Indeed, as Selina moves beyond the space of the brownstone, meeting women who teach her survival skills and offer alternative examples of sexual and ethnic identities, she charts a route that is rooted in the movement and the memories of her mother's past.

Brown Girl is both a creative and theoretical text. It narrates a story of identity formation that highlights the complex influences of migration and identity formation, but also offers a theoretical framework for discussing woman-centered texts in Black Atlantic and Diasporic women's literature. Such texts would include Audre Lorde's *Zami: A New Spelling of My Name* (1982), Edwidge Danticat's *Breath, Eyes, Memory* (1994), Loida Maritza Pérez's *Geographies of Home* (1999), and even works of poetry like Natasha Trethewey's *Native Guard* (2006). Each of these texts narrates the journeys of daughters who come to understand their identities as composites of their mothers' as well as of their own self-developed ideas about who they are and how they move throughout the Diasporic space.[37] Like *Brown Girl,* these authors trace their black and female roots to their mothers, but identify routes of identity formation as ones that move through the lives of the mothers to the female characters, who discover themselves by coming to understand their mothers' lives and their sometimes troubled matrofilial relationships.

Redefining Roots: Identity and Diaspora in Contemporary Black Atlantic Literature

Though *Brown Girl* is itself a work of fiction, Marshall has admitted that the mother-daughter narrative within it is based on a lived reality. In an interview with Mary Helen Washington, Marshall's memories of her mother are eerily reminiscent of the contentious relationship between Silla and Selina.[38] Similarly, memoir has become an increasingly important subgenre in Black Atlantic and Diasporic literature in recent decades. From the corpus of Maya Angelou's autobiographies to Lorde's *Zami,* this genre is rich for its writers' ruminations on how racial, class, gender, and identity constructs are influenced by patterns of physical and ideological movement. Recently written texts like Tracy K. Smith's *Ordinary Light* (2015) and Elizabeth Alexander's *The Light of the World* (2015) both chronicle the poets' lives as members of diverse families wherein migration shaped individual identities as well as family dynamics. Smith's memoir focuses on the life and death of her mother, a conservative, religious Southerner whose illness forces her daughter to reconsider everything her mother has taught her to believe about faith, familial history, and her own identity as a black woman raised in the conservative enclaves of Northern California. On the other hand, Alexander's *The Light of the World,* a poignant account of her husband's death from cardiac arrest in 2012, is one such example of memoir's power to encapsulate the trans-linguistic, transnational, and transracial influences that come to bear on a woman in love.

Alexander makes clear the ways in which her husband's transnationality has a profound impact on her own. A native of Eritrea, Ficre Ghebreyesus is East African by birth but cosmopolitan in every sense of the word: a painter influenced by Italian and American art, a political activist, and a world-class chef who speaks eight languages. Alexander describes herself as his "American wife,"[39] but one who admittedly becomes less American as they build a life together, traveling the world and creating a New England house-hold that was awash in their love for books, languages, and exotic cuisine. "'How did my life become so African?' " the poet asks her husband shortly before her marriage.[40] Years later, during a lively Easter celebration that included family from locales as distant as Italy and as near as Harlem, a "play-uncle" exclaims: "'Your life is a foreign film!' "[41] Her mother agrees, telling Alexander that she has fulfilled her father's wish of being "'an African elder with all these children around for him to preside over.' "[42] Alexander's marriage to Ficre creates a global extension of relatives who now make her own identity a truly Afro-Diasporic one.

Alexander also reveals how her husband's knowledge of many languages and cultures has shaped her own, and this is one of her great losses follow-ing his death. After a trip to bookstore, she laments:

> I think of all the books I will never know about because you will not show them to me. I think of the loss of knowledge, all the things I will never know because you are not here to tell me. I cannot ask questions. I cannot be reminded. I can no longer say – though I still do – to the children, "That's a Daddy question," when they ask about the Peloponnesian War, or the Khmer Rouge, or Latin declension, or the quadratic formula, or how sinkholes are formed on limestone beds.[43]

In this moment, the poet understands that her husband's knowledge of a range of histories – from ancient Greek to postcolonial Cambodian – is itself a product of living in Diaspora, one that has shaped her identity as a black woman and artist living in the same space.

We began this chapter by stating that Black Atlantic and Diasporic Literature encompasses an immense body of creative work and criticism. As such, this is in no way an exhaustive analysis; rather, it is entirely heuristic, offering a variety of readings as points of departure for deeper forays into the literature, theoretical approaches, and epistemological concerns of this ever-widening field. Each text stands as an exemplar of scores of others that are performing similar work, and the inclusion of some (which, for the sake of brevity, necessitates the absence of others) should be read as neither oversight nor dismissal. It is, rather, an attempt to provide a concise overview of a body of literature that is as massive as the land- and sea space that the Black Atlantic itself covers. Though the work of Anglophone writers generally garners the bulk of the field's criticism, Francophone, Hispanophone, and Lusophone writers are now adding to the richness of contemporary theoretical conversations. Additionally, texts like NoViolet Bulawayo's *We Need New Names* (2013) and Chimamanda Adichie's *Americanah* (2013) are now placing contemporary African Diasporic literature squarely into conversations about the field. As Yogita Goyal points out in *Romance, Diaspora, and Black Atlantic Literature* (2010), Africa has been markedly absent from discussions about the Black Atlantic; however, these African women writers are interrogating that exclusion by placing African characters alongside their black American counterparts and exploring the nuances of both sets of identities in single texts.[44] As African writers who write about the Black experience in the United States (and sometimes Europe), they not only introduce new narratives of migration, but offer new layers of complexity to the field of African American literature, forcing critics to reevaluate the field's scope and meaning.

Literature of the Black Atlantic is also literally coming off the page, most notably in responses to worldwide protest movements against the violent policing of black individuals from Ferguson to Jerusalem. For example, #BlackPoetsSpeakOut, an online initiative begun by members of the Black poetry collective Cave Canem, features videos of new and established poets reading work by themselves and each other, and is one such moment in Black Atlantic and Diasporic literature that calls for innovative approaches to analysis. In many ways, the videos capture the essence of Black Diasporic subjectivity; they incorporate elements of recitation and spontaneous revision, ekphrasis, pastiche, photography and videography (including footage from protests and violent police encounters), dramatic performances, and music. Such multimodal art, and art created specifically as a form of protest, necessitates multimodal critical approaches that in some cases might need to depart from the confines of the written page. And, as worldwide concerns about the vulnerabilities of black bodies has recently made clear, the term "The Black Atlantic" itself might need to expand its borders to include black subjects who have migrated beyond its admittedly already-fluid geographies. Ethiopian Jews in Israel, who suffer from discrimination that has even begun to encroach on their reproductive rights; the Al-Muhamasheen of Yemen, who are economically disenfranchised and segregated to the most uninhabitable parts of the country's urban areas; and black transgender women in almost every locale on the globe, who are often forgotten in protests for racial and gender equality – all are groups whose members are steadily producing art and beauty in the wake of dehumanizing (and deadly) marginalization. Only time will tell if scholars of Black Atlantic and Diasporic literature will give this work the attention it deserves; however, if the past is any indication of the future, the field is ready – and its writers are willing – to rise to the challenge.

NOTES

1 Paule Marshall, *Brown Girl, Brownstones* (New York: Feminist Press, 2006 [1959]), 291.
2 Ibid., 288.
3 Paul Gilroy, *The Black Atlantic: Modernity and Double Consciousness* (Cambridge, MA: Harvard University Press, 1993), 2.
4 Ibid., 15.
5 Ibid., 14
6 Ibid., 12.
7 Ibid., 16.
8 Ibid., 17.
9 Some reviewers also upbraided Gilroy for the disassociation of contemporary Black identity formation from its African roots. See Louis Chude-Sokei, "The Black Atlantic Paradigm: Paul Gilroy and the Fractured Landscape of 'Race,'" *American Quarterly* 48.4 (1996): 740–45; Alasdair Pettinger, "Enduring Fortresses: A Review of *The Black Atlantic*," *Research in African Literatures* 29.4 (Winter 1998): 142–47; Joan (Colin) Dayan, "Paul Gilroy's Slaves, Ships, and Routes: The Middle Passage as Metaphor," *Research in African Literatures* 27.4 (Winter 1996): 7–14.
10 Carole Boyce Davies and 'Molara Ogundipe-Leslie, preface to *Moving Beyond Boundaries, Volume One: International Dimensions of Black Women's Writing*, Carole Boyce Davies and 'Molara Ogundipe-Leslie, eds. (New York: New York University Press, 1995), xvi.
11 Carole Boyce Davies, "Hearing Black Women's Voices: Transgressing Imposed Boundaries," in *Moving Beyond Boundaries, Volume One: International Dimensions of Black Women's Writing*, Carole Boyce Davies and 'Molara Ogundipe-Leslie, eds. (New York: New York University Press, 1995), 9.
12 James Clifford, *Routes: Travel & Translation in the Late Twentieth Century* (Cambridge, MA: Harvard University Press, 1997), 260.
13 Belinda Edmondson, *Making Men: Gender, Literary Authority, and Women's Writing in Caribbean Narrative* (Durham, NC: Duke University Press, 1999), 153.
14 Ibid., 142.
15 Sandra Pouchet Paquet, *Caribbean Autobiography: Cultural Identity and Self-Representation* (Madison: University of Wisconsin Press, 2002), 33.
16 Ibid., 42.
17 Ifeoma Kiddoe Nwankwo, *Black Cosmopolitanism: Racial Consciousness and Transnational Identity in the Nineteenth Century Americas* (Philadelphia: University of Pennsylvania Press, 2005), 163.

18 Mary Prince, *The History of Mary Prince: A West Indian Slave, Related by Herself,* ed. Sara Salih (1831; repr., New York: Penguin, 2004), Kindle Edition, 3.
19 Ibid., 4.
20 Ibid., 13–14.
21 Pouchet Paquet, *Caribbean Autobiography,* 42.
22 Prince, *The History of Mary Prince,* 27.
23 Pouchet Paquet, *Caribbean Autobiography,* 35.
24 Ibid., 32.
25 W.E.B. Du Bois, *The Souls of Black Folk.* (New York: Dover Publications, 1994 [1903]), 2–3.
26 Michelle Wright, *Becoming Black: Creating Identity in the African Diaspora* (Durham, NC: Duke University Press, 2004), 141, 180.
27 Ibid., 180.
28 Marshall, *Brown Girl,* 216.
29 Ibid., 287, 288.
30 Ibid., 292.
31 Gilroy, *The Black Atlantic,* 211, 206.
32 Marshall, *Brown Girl,* 281
33 Ibid., 144.
34 Ibid., 307.
35 Ibid., 306.
36 Ibid.
37 See Destiny O. Birdsong, "The Mother's Mark: Matrilineal Inscription, Corporeality, and Identity Formation in Mother-Daughter Relationships in Black Women's Literature" (PhD diss., Vanderbilt University, 2012).
38 See Mary Helen Washington, "I Sign My Mother's Name: Alice Walker, Dorothy West, Paule Marshall," *Mothering the Mind: Twelve Writers and Their Silent Partners,* Ruth Perry and Martine Watson Brownley, eds. (New York: Holmes and Meier, 1984), 142–63.
39 Elizabeth Alexander, *The Light of the World: A Memoir* (New York: Grand Central, 2015), 4.
40 Ibid., 58.
41 Ibid., 68.
42 Ibid., 69.
43 Ibid., 148–49.
44 Yogita Goyal, *Romance, Diaspora, and Black Atlantic Literature* (Cambridge: Cambridge University Press, 2010).

9

JOHN ALBA CUTLER

Borders and Borderland Literature

It is ironic that at the moment when borders may have come to seem irrelevant – immaterial to the flows of money, goods, and information that constitute global capitalism – the US-Mexico borderlands have witnessed some of this century's most heated political battles and horrific scenes of violence. Spurred by a combination of economic and political factors, Ciudad Juárez on Mexico's northern frontier suffered through a staggering number of homicides during the 2000s, achieving the dubious distinction of most dangerous city in the world from 2009 to 2011.[1]

Meanwhile, spurred by the military closure of the border at traditional crossing points in Southern California and Texas, hundreds of thousands of Mexican and Central American migrants since the late 1990s have been funneled through the dangerous deserts of southern Arizona. According to the *New York Times*, from 2001 to 2013, more than 2,100 migrants died crossing the Arizona border.[2] Despite this human toll, US politicians have continued to demand stricter immigration controls and a more heavily policed border. In 2006, the US Congress passed the Secure Fence Act, mandating the construction of more than 700 miles of physical barriers along the border. At the same time, US business interests push for freer access to markets and labor in Mexico and throughout Latin America. The North American Free Trade Agreement (NAFTA) in 1994 was followed by free trade agreements with Chile in 2004, Central America in 2005, and Panama and Colombia in 2011, not to mention the numerous free trade agreements signed or proposed with Asian, Middle Eastern, and African nations.

The paradoxical confluence of border retrenchment and neoliberal policy corresponds to the conflicted relationship between borderlands studies and the so-called transnational turn in American studies. Scholars of Chicana and Chicano literature in particular have debated at length whether transnational approaches represent the natural next step in the evolution of the borderlands paradigm pioneered in Gloria Anzaldúa's landmark work *Borderlands / La Frontera* (1987), or whether transnational approaches threaten to eclipse the borderlands at the very moment they seem to have gained significant visibility and urgency. For some critics, notably Ramón Saldívar, literature of the US-Mexico borderlands undergirds the political and aesthetic possibilities of transnationalism.[3] For others, such as José E. Limón, the US-Mexico border is best understood as part of a regional cultural formation, rather than subsumed within an amorphous, sometimes ahistorical transnationalism.[4] These are debates not only about interpretive paradigms but also about institutional power. For some Chicana/o critics, transnationalism appears to threaten hard-won institutional gains for Chicana/o studies by overshadowing the work of local actors.

Yet transnationalism and border studies need not be antagonists. In this essay, I argue that the US-Mexico border continues to be a crucial site of scholarly investigation precisely because some of the most pernicious effects of global capitalism – as well as transnationalism's most promising utopian formations – are located in the borderlands. I begin by defining the borderlands paradigm and surveying the Chicana/o literature and scholarship that gave rise to it, paying special attention to Anzaldúa's *Borderlands*. I then examine three relatively recent literary works that demonstrate the continued urgency of borderlands analysis. Luis Alberto Urrea's nonfiction work *The Devil's Highway* (2005) exposes the dangerous conditions contemporary migrants experience due to border militarization. Mexican writer Rosario Sanmiguel's short story "Moonlit in the Mirror," from her book *Under the Bridge: Stories from the Border* (2008), takes up one of the central themes of borderlands critique – the heightened vulnerability of women under contemporary economic and cultural conditions. Finally, Sesshu Foster's tour-de-force novel *Atomik Aztex* (2005) imagines a radical counterhistory that not only broadens the scope of borderlands analysis but also brings that analysis back to the central conflict between capital and labor.

The Borderlands Paradigm

Borders divide and conjoin at once, marking the separation between nations but also the meeting point. Borders distinguish the boundaries of nations but also facilitate the passage of people, goods, and capital. Borders are historical creations, however naturalized they may have become by cartographic practices or nationalist discourses. As geographers Alexander C. Diener and Joshua Hagen note, borders "exist in the world only to the extent that humans regard them as meaningful."[5] Every border tells a story, often one of violence and displacement. Although borders appear as lines on a map, having no mass or volume, the history of borders often creates border*lands*, zones of ongoing, agonistic contact between cultures, and often the evolution of entirely new cultural forms.

The borderlands paradigm arises out of Chicana/o studies, and as an interpretive framework has taken borderland literature to be synonymous with Chicana and Chicano literature, especially the literature emerging from the activism of the Chicano Movement during the 1960s and 1970s.[6] Chicana/o borderland literature reflects critically on the legacies of US imperialism and westward expansion in the Southwest, a "contact zone," to use Mary Louise Pratt's term, for encounters among US, Mexican, and indigenous peoples.[7] Beginning with the Monroe Doctrine in 1823, the United States began to assert its power in the Western hemisphere, annexing Texas in 1845 and then acquiring more than half of Mexico's territory in the subsequent US-Mexico War. Although the Treaty of Guadalupe Hidalgo that ended the war in 1848 promised to honor the citizenship and property rights of Mexicans who remained in the newly acquired territories, white settlers violently disenfranchised and dispossessed Mexican Americans over the course of the nineteenth century. A history of land grabs, police abuse, illegal deportations, and murder of Mexican Americans extends through the twentieth century.

The idea of the US-Mexico borderlands as a third space between two cultures stems from Gloria Anzaldúa's *Borderlands*, the most important theorization of what I am referring to as the borderlands paradigm. As Mary Pat Brady observes,

> Anzaldúa questioned the production and maintenance of binaries, their exclusionary force, and the maxims that suggest that living with contradiction necessarily entails psychosis. Instead, she mobilized a second spatial metaphor – that of the frontera or borderlands – to insist that one can embrace multiple contradictions and refuse the impossible effort to synthesize them fully, thus turning apparent oppositions into sources of insight and personal strength.[8]

Borders are meant to delimit interior and exterior, to indicate a clear division between what belongs inside the nation and what does not. In the borderlands, the third country that is neither the United States nor Mexico shelters a new culture and a new form of human experience altogether. *Borderlands* thus inaugurates a paradigm not only for thinking about the specific conditions of the US-Mexico border but also for theorizing states of fragmented subjectivity resulting from other sites of conflict. Where Anzaldúa uses *mestizaje* – racial or cultural mixture – as the touchstone for such forms, other theorists have posited similar ideas: hybridity, errancy, and nomadism, among others.[9]

Anzaldúa's theorization of *mestizaje* as a way to understand borderland subjectivity has provided scholars a language to interpret the ambivalence and fragmentation of a range of Chicana/o literary works. For example, Guálinto Gómez, the protagonist of Américo Paredes's novel *George Washington Gómez* (1990), feels split between loyalty to his Mexican heritage and the US patriotism inculcated into him in school, so much so that he imagines his consciousness as a series of "tight little cells independent and almost entirely ignorant of each other, spread out all over his consciousness, mixed with one another like squares on a checkerboard." [10] Lupe Arredondo, the hapless narrator of Sandra Cisneros's short story "*Bien* Pretty," from her book *Woman Hollering Creek* (1991), is similarly conflicted. A middle-class Chicana from northern California, Lupe finds herself attracted to what she perceives as the virile Mexican authenticity of Flavio Munguía, a pest control worker who sprays her new home in San Antonio. When Flavio tells Lupe he doesn't have to put on a performance to feel Mexican, she responds angrily, "I wanted to leap across the table, throw the Oaxacan black pottery pieces across the room, swing from the punched tin chandelier, fire a pistol at his Reeboks, and force him to dance. I wanted to *be* Mexican at that moment, but it was true. I was not Mexican." [11] Yet what Lupe perceives as her own lack of authenticity she eventually comes to embrace as a form of empowerment.

This subjective experience of in-betweenness is perhaps the dominant thematic motif of borderland literature, from Tomás Rivera's *...y no se lo tragó la tierra / And the Earth Did Not Part* (1971) to Norma Cantú's *Canícula* (1997). It also serves as the foundation for much of the scholarly work on borderlands literature for the decade after *Borderlands* first appeared. Héctor Calderón and José David Saldívar's collection *Criticism in the Borderlands: Studies in Chicano Literature, Culture, and Ideology* (1991), for example, includes essays on Paredes, Rivera, Arturo Islas's *The Rain God* (1984), and Chicano poetry and politics. These analyses demonstrate how the conflicted, hybrid discourses of borderlands literature deconstruct myths of national cultural coherence and autonomy. Saldívar sums up this line of thinking in his essay on Chicano border narratives when he asserts, "An invidious, white supremacist rhetoric of performance thus gives way to the possibility of a revitalized Chicano present and future." [12]

Brady praises Anzaldúa for "unveiling the metaphoricity" of the border, but that metaphoricity has led some critics to take issue with *Borderlands*. [13] Most prominent among these critics, Josefina Saldaña-Portillo has argued that Anzaldúa's appropriation of *mestizaje* as the central metaphor for borderlands subjectivity reinscribes the problems of post-revolutionary Mexican nationalism, "recuperating the Indian as an ancestral past rather than recognizing contemporary Indians as coinhabitants not only of this continent abstractly conceived, but of the neighborhoods and streets of hundreds of US cities and towns."[14] Thus, according to Saldaña-Portillo, Anzaldúa's use of *mestizaje* unintentionally replicates some of the very structures of power she sets out to critique. Debra A. Castillo and María Socorro Tabuenca Córdoba assert that precisely the metaphorical thrust of Anzaldúa's work, with its "multiple crossings of cultural and gender borders … tends to essentialize relations between Mexico and the United States…. Anzaldúa's famous analysis does not take into cognizance the many other othernesses related to a border existence; her 'us' is limited to US minorities; her 'them' is US dominant culture."[15] For Castillo and Córdoba, this deficiency is especially felt in the scant attention Anzaldúa pays to Mexican women south of the border.

These critiques are trenchant and persuasive, but it is telling that they work by focusing on the most metaphorically errant passages of *Borderlands*. Indeed, neither critics nor apologists have paid sufficient attention to the way Anzaldúa grounds her work in the economic and social developments of the late 1980s. In the first chapter of *Borderlands,* "The Homeland, Aztlán / *El otro México,*" Anzaldúa adduces economic and cultural changes concomitant with Reagan-era neoliberalism as a framework. This chapter is easily the most cited portion of Anzaldúa's work, but most of those citations come from the opening pages, in which Anzaldúa lyrically describes the US-Mexico border as "*una herida abierta* where the Third World grates against the first and bleeds. And before a scab forms it hemorrhages again, the lifeblood of two worlds merging to form a third country – a border culture."[16] Anzaldúa goes on to review the history of US westward expansion, then ends the chapter with a section titled "*El cruzar del mojado* / Illegal Crossing." This section, which critics rarely attend to, anchors *Borderlands* to a material history that resists the extreme metaphoricity of other parts of the book.

Anzaldúa's account of illegal crossing is notably a transnational history, beginning with *la crisis*, Mexico's debt crisis that in 1982 resulted in the devaluation of the peso. The first illustration Anzaldúa makes of the negative impact of the crisis on Mexico is the explosion of the *maquiladora* industry. Anzaldúa goes on to describe the mass unemployment brought on by Mexico's debt crisis, and the resulting wave of migration north to the United States: "Barefoot and uneducated, Mexicans with hands like boot soles gather at night by the river where two worlds merge creating what Reagan calls a frontline, a war zone. The convergence has created a shock culture, a border culture, a third country, a closed country."[17] The language of this passage echoes the opening metaphors of the chapter, but here we see more clearly how the "third country" results not only from the long history of the border but from the inequality and violence of the Reagan era specifically, manifest in everything from the English-only movement to the escalation of the war on drugs. The "third country" in this passage is on the Mexican side of the border, a consequence of the bottleneck of migrants waiting for a chance to cross.

The chapter ends with Anzaldúa making Mexican women the representative figures of the precarity of illegal crossing, a dramatic departure from the figure of the *bracero* that predominated in representations of Mexican migration beforehand. Here, too, Anzaldúa attends to important economic developments that have had material effects on borderland denizens:

> The Mexican woman is especially at risk. Often the *coyote* (smuggler) doesn't feed her for days or let her got to the bathroom. Often he rapes her or sells her into prostitution.... She may work as a live-in maid for white, Chicano or Latino households for as little as $15 a week. Or work in the garment industry, do hotel work. Isolated and worried about her family back home, afraid of getting caught and deported, living with as many as fifteen people in one room, the *mexicana* suffers serious health problems. *Se enferma de los nervios, de alta presión.*[18]

The threat of sexual violence that accompanies illegal crossing only continues the sexual violence of the *maquiladoras* and of course never dissipates in the workplaces of undocumented laborers. And in Anzaldúa's account, those workplaces have changed dramatically from previous generations. Although agricultural and manufacturing jobs still serve as a draw for many migrants, here Anzaldúa describes women working mainly in the (informal) service industry, as live-in maids and hotel workers, reflecting a large-scale shift in the US economy. This shift even divides Mexican women from Chicanos and Latinos, a prime example of Anzaldúa's attention to "the other othernesses related to a border existence." The entire passage works by zeroing in the individual Mexican woman as a kind of archetype of precarity, with the shift into Spanish vernacular at the end moving us toward a sense of her interiority, as if Anzaldúa were working not only to describe her experience but to allow her to speak for herself.

Although this is only one section of *Borderlands*, the final section of "The Homeland, Aztlán / *El Otro México*" is thematically central to the book, as suggested by the poetic fragment that ends the chapter, once again describing the precarious position of undocumented Mexican women:

> This is her home
> this thin edge of
> barbwire.[19]

The fragment repeats part of the poem that opens the chapter, in which Anzaldúa describes her experience of being divided by the metaphorical violence of borderland subjectivity: *"me raja, me raja,"* she cries ("it slashes me," "it slashes me"), before declaring, "This is my home, / this thin edge of / barbwire."[20] The repeated fragment drops the first-person narrative for the third, but the repetition catalyzes Anzaldúa's identification with the nameless migrant woman. The metaphorical "barbwire" of the opening poem, a figure for the social wounding that the speaker feels from balancing on the thin line between cultures, is replaced at the end of the chapter with the bodily violence of the actual border, increasingly marked by physical barriers. Finally, whereas Anzaldúa's "home" in the first instance is the third space between Mexican and American, in the repeated fragment "home" has become an ironic signifier, since the thin edge of barbwire for the migrant woman represents her literal homelessness. If it appears to us that *Borderlands* is too abstract, too metaphorical, too narrowly concerned with the relatively privileged position of Chicanos in the United States (as opposed to poor Mexicans in Mexico), then we should remember that in the very place where *Borderlands* announces its project, it grounds itself on the material conditions faced by Mexican women during a time when the border was under heavy contestation.

New Borderland Literature

While it is not strictly a work of scholarship, *Borderlands* has exerted enormous influence – direct and indirect – on American literary studies. As Mary Pat Brady observes,

> Where *margin* and *marginality* have disappeared from academic focus, *border* and *borderlands* have appeared, flourishing alongside the proliferation of *post* (postcontemporary, postmodern, posturban, postfeminist). *Post* is always a temporal term, even though it also has a spatial valence (consider its homonym *post*). This preference for its temporal dimension over its spatial in contemporary usage hints as to why *border* has come to appeal so thoroughly to many critics: it is from the vantage point of a (universal) border that theorists of the temporal 'post' may wish to operate.[21]

Not content merely to describe a trend in critical theory, Brady implicitly critiques the widespread turn to a universalized borderlands paradigm as a way of approaching what are essentially temporal arguments.[22] A renewed focus in recent years on the nineteenth-century border marks one intersection of these temporal and spatial paradigms. Committed to "disinterring," as Jesse Alemán puts it, the violence of the US-Mexico border, literary scholars have edited and republished such works as María Amparo Ruiz de Burton's novel *The Squatter and the Don* (1885) and Jovita González and Margaret Eimer's historical romance *Caballero*, which was originally written during the 1940s but not published until 1997.[23] A similar commitment animates historical novels such as Aristeo Brito's *El Diablo en Tejas / The Devil in Texas* (1976) and Cormac McCarthy's *Blood Meridian* (1984), which revisit the nineteenth-century border using so-called postmodern narrative forms.

As Brady's critique suggests, the relationship between the borderlands paradigm and transnational approaches to American literature has sometimes become contentious, with scholars of Chicana/o literature arguing that transnational analyses too often overlook the significance of local histories. Framed by this conflict between the local and the transnational, a work such as Luis Alberto Urrea's *The Devil's Highway* is particularly notable. On the one hand, the book focuses strictly on the US-Mexico border, telling the story of a group of Mexican migrants who were stranded in the Arizona desert in May 2001 while attempting to cross the border illegally. The Wellton 26, as Urrea dubs them, were abandoned by their *coyote* after being lost in the desert, and twelve of the men died before the rest were rescued by Border Patrol agents. This would seem to be borderland literature par excellence. On the other hand, *The Devil's Highway* departs from many of the familiar tropes and concerns of previous borderland literature. It is relatively unconcerned with the long history of Mexican Americans in the borderlands, and rather than dealing with issues of bicultural identity experienced by borderlands subjects, it thinks about how the border acts *on* individuals, usually violently. Some of these differences are a matter of genre; *The Devil's Highway* is a work of nonfiction, though its lyrical, often densely metaphorical language betrays Urrea's literary aspirations. But *The Devil's Highway* also allows us to see the flip side of Brady's critique: if transnational analyses too often use a spatial metaphor (the border) to gain access to temporal theories, then it may be the case that borderlands analyses too often ignore the temporal evolution of the borderlands.

As *The Devil's Highway* makes clear, the border that migrants encounter in the twenty-first century is a very different space from the border migrants encountered in previous generations. Anzaldúa describes the Tijuana–San Diego border disappearing into the ocean and talks about the danger migrants face crossing the Rio Grande into Texas, but border militarization had largely closed off these areas of the border to migrants by the turn of the century. As Urrea notes, "Operation Gatekeeper, the final solution to the border crossings, introduced by California in the late nineties, had ushered in a new era of secure urban borders and trampled wilderness. San Diego, Calexico, Yuma, El Paso, Nogales, Douglas, they were all becoming harder to get through. This looked great for the politicians of the cities. Voila! No more Mexicans!"[24] Operation Gatekeeper was actually a federal initiative, though its initial focus was on California, but Urrea's canny use of the phrase "final solution" – an allusion to the Nazi death camps – emphasizes his point that closing off urban border crossings was not about stopping immigration, but rather about making it invisible by directing it to remote, scarcely populated border regions, particularly the brutal desert-mountain landscape of southern Arizona. In effect, Operation Gatekeeper was a decision to value the *appearance* of border security over the *lives* of migrants that would be lost venturing border crossings in more dangerous locales.

The Devil's Highway evinces the danger of the Arizona landscape by repeated emphasis on the somatic experience of heat death. Urrea refers to the desert throughout the book as "Desolation," alluding to religious traditions telling of "fallen angels bound with chains and buried beneath a desert."[25] Urrea proceeds to personify Desolation in one of the book's most powerful chapters, "Killed by the Light," which describes how human bodies experience the stages of heat exhaustion: "Desolation drinks you first in small sips, then in deep gulps," he warns, then, when describing heat syncope, "Desolation has begun to edit you. Erase you."[26] As Sandra Cox observes, in these passages, "The ravaging of the transient bodies by an aggressive environment becomes a representation of sameness that links readers to the migrants through the mutual terror of death and of bodily destruction."[27] Certainly the second-person pronouns of the passages hail readers the way Cox describes, yet there seems to be more going on here. Even as Urrea's language seems almost excessive in its will to represent the migrants' experience – page after page of detailed description, metaphor after metaphor – the idea of syncope, or contraction, acknowledges the irrefutable silence that sits at the center of the narrative. Abraham Acosta writes that "in seeking to narrate a tragic scene of radical contingency, exception, and abandonment," *The Devil's Highway* "in effect begs its own question. Ultimately, Urrea's narrative constitutes a provisional attempt to glean, from the biopolitical formalization of this particularly crucial stretch of the US/Mexico border, the state of exception that constitutes it, the negative territoriality of its topological ordering, and the negative community abandoned within it."[28] All that remains to add to this astute reading is that Urrea's story take shapes within an evolving transnational system predicated on the devaluation of certain lives. As *The Devil's Highway* follows the migrants from their lives in Veracruz through their journey to and across the border, it replaces the themes of biculturalism that dominated previous borderlands literature with a broad view of the connection between local histories and global designs, the essence of what Walter Mignolo refers to as "border thinking."[29]

Rosario Sanmiguel's collection of short stories *Under the Bridge* (2008) engages in border thinking from Ciudad Juárez, one of the northern Mexican frontier's most conflicted cities. Originally published in Mexico in 1994 as *Callejón sucre y otros relatos*, Sanmiguel's book was republished in a bilingual edition (translations by John Pluecker) by Arte Público Press. The final story in the collection, "Moonlit in the Mirror," centers on Nicole Campillo and Arturo Alcántar, a young couple in El Paso, Texas, whose marriage is tested when Nicole, a lawyer, is called upon to represent a young Mexican woman who accuses the son of one of Arturo's business clients of attempted sexual assault. Nicole is the daughter of migrant farmworkers who self-identifies as Chicana and dedicates her life to providing legal aid to undocumented women. Arturo, by contrast, is the scion of a wealthy Mexican American family; his grandfather fled the outbreak of the Mexican Revolution in 1911 and built a business empire inherited by his son and Arturo each in turn. Whereas the multigenerational matriarchy of the Campillo family has resulted in Nicole possessing absolute confidence in her own abilities and a fierce commitment to protecting the rights of women, the multigenerational Alcántar patriarchy has resulted in resentment and frustration, as Arturo has keenly felt his father's disappointment in his perceived failures of masculinity.

Under the Bridge is attuned to the special dynamics of the Ciudad Juárez-El Paso border region, but as Castillo and Córdoba point out, "The female characters in Sanmiguel's short texts exist in dialogic relation to, and transgressively displace, the image of border women (or least of women from Ciudad Juárez) ... linked almost exclusively in the public mind to the continuing horrors of the unsolved murders of young women in the city."[30] This sensationalist discourse has created the image of Juárez women primarily as victims, a stark contrast, as Castillo and Córdoba assert, to Sanmiguel's depictions of the city as a "vital urban space" with people living their lives there "in an ordinary way."[31] Although "Moonlit in the Mirror" is set primarily in El Paso, Nicole and Arturo's backstories give a sense of the historically interlinked relationship of these sister cities. El Paso was, for example, a prime site of expatriate opposition to the Porfirio Díaz regime before the Mexican Revolution because of its easy access to Juárez's print distribution networks. And throughout the twentieth century, the relatively wealthy Mexican American community has depended on working-class and poor laborers from Ciudad Juárez for a variety of service jobs, including domestic work, Guadalupe Maza's occupation when she is assaulted by Dick Thompson, the son of El Paso's Chamber of Commerce president.

Rather than sensationalizing Guadalupe's assault, "Moonlit in the Mirror" is more interested in the moral dilemmas posed to Guadalupe and Nicole, particularly as those dilemmas are complicated by the social hierarchies dividing them from one another. Guadalupe is a Mazahua Indian, an indigenous group from the state of Mexico that migrated in significant numbers to Ciudad Juárez in the middle of the twentieth century. Spanish is her second language, and she is doubly alienated as a domestic worker in El Paso: not even fully Mexican, let alone Mexican American. Yet she is not merely a victim, and much of the story concerns Nicole's attempts to overcome her reluctance to prosecute Dick Thompson. Having found a religious community as a result of her assault, "Guadalupe felt compensated. Nicole, on the other hand, was willing to make use of all her resources to win the case. Guadalupe was not a helpless indigenous woman, and neither was Nicole a defenseless Chicana. The two were women without privilege, accustomed to daily struggle, children of migrants."[32] The simple declarative sentences here emphasize the autonomy of each woman; yet as they are put in parallel, that autonomy is refracted into a relationship of mutual recognition.

These collisions of acculturation and gendered domination are only possible in a world that assumes transnational movement and belonging as preconditions. "Moonlit in the Mirror" takes transnational movement and identification as a precondition of border life, but amplifies those themes inasmuch as transnationalism also conditions the story's production and distribution. As a Mexican border writer, Sanmiguel has been marginalized within both Mexican and US literary circles, only becoming available in the United States through Pluecker's translation and Arte Público's sponsorship. As if to signal the importance of the transnational community that "Moonlit in the Mirror" attempts to describe, Sanmiguel makes one provocative addition to the version of the story that appears in Arte Público's bilingual edition, adding a dedication to Chicana writer and cultural theorist Emma Pérez beneath the title.[33] Sanmiguel's story bears comparison with Pérez's novel *Gulf Dreams* (1996); both texts center on a case of sexual assault and their protagonists' attempts to navigate the tensions of race, class, and sexuality in Texas. Pérez's theorization of the "decolonial imaginary" is also relevant here as a method of asserting Chicanas' presence into histories from which they have been erased.[34] But beyond these powerful thematic resonances, the dedication performs its own migration, seemingly paying homage to Pérez after the fact of her work, but actually having originally anticipated Pérez's work from the other side of the border.

Both the tragic forced march of the Wellton 26 in *The Devil's Highway* and Guadalupe's sexual assault in "Moonlit in the Mirror" result at least in part from large-scale economic and political developments that have changed the nature of the border. To conclude, I consider one more text, Sesshu Foster's novel *Atomik Aztex* (2005), as another example of how contemporary writers are rethinking the significance of the borderlands. The novel defies easy description. Roughly, it takes place in an alternative universe in which the Aztex (following the novel's idiosyncratic spelling) defeated the Spanish and went on to become an empire. The narrator Zenzontli (his name means "mockingbird" in Nahuatl) is an Aztek warrior who begins to have a recurring dream that he is a Mexican immigrant meatpacker in Los Angeles in our world. Zenzontli speaks at a frenetic pace, and his narration is dense with historical, literary, and pop-cultural allusions, making the temporal setting difficult to pin down; the story appears to begin in the present day, but shifts to 1942 Los Angeles and Stalingrad. All of these features make *Atomik Aztex* a highly self-conscious, demanding postmodern text, reminiscent of Ishmael Reed or Thomas Pynchon.

In relation to the changing nature of the border, perhaps the most important aspect of *Atomik Aztex* is the way it links labor activism to contemporary Mexican immigration. The novel's preoccupation with indigeneity is central to this theme, and corresponds to changes in migrant demographics. The passage of NAFTA in 1994 in particular has had a devastating effect on small farmers in heavily indigenous areas of southern Mexico, leading to large amounts of out-migration.[35] The alternate universe of *Atomik Aztex* takes special notice of these workers in Zenzontli's reflections, which parody North American racism and paternalism:

> Perhaps you are familiar with some worlds, stupider realities amongst alternate universes offered by the ever expanding-omniverse, in which the Aztek civilization was 'destroyed.' That's a possibility. I mean that's what the Europians *thot*. They planned genocide, wipe out our civilization, build cathedrals on TOP of our pyramidz, bah, hump our women, not just our women but the Tlaxkalans, the Mixteks, the Zapoteks, the Chichimeks, the Utes, the Triki, the Kahuilla, the Shoshone, the Maidu, the Klickitat, the Mandan, the Chumash, the Yaqui, the Huicholes, the Meskwaki, the Guarani, Seminoles, endless peoples, decimate 'em with smallpox, measles and shit fits, welfare lines, workaholism, imbecility, enslave 'em in the silver mines of Potosí, the gold mines of El Dorado & Disneylandia, on golf courses and country clubs, *chingados*, all our brothers, you get the picture.[36]

The catalog of indigenous tribes begins with names familiar to those with general knowledge of the Spanish conquest of Mexico: Tlaxcalans, Mixtecs, Zapotecs. But the list soon expands to include tribes indigenous to what is now the United States – Utes, Cahuilla, Shoshone, Maidu, and so on – as well as Mexican and South American natives such as the Huicholes, the

Yaqui, and the Guaraní. This catalog resists dominant Mexican and North American conceptions of what it means to be Indian. Absent from the list are the usual suspects: the Aztecs, obviously, but also the Incas in the south and the Cherokee, Iroquois, and Plains Indians in the north. The catalog thus makes strange again the familiar history of the conquest, showing it to be more far-reaching historically and geographically than popularly understood. Along with that re-estrangement, the passage insists on the violence that marked not only first contact and the early years of the conquest but that also persists into the present through neoliberal labor practices – the Indians providing the labor for Disneyland, golf courses, and country clubs.

While Zenzontli's reflections as Aztek warrior critique the history of the violent colonization of the Americas, his experiences as a meatcutter in the Farmer John pork processing plant demonstrate how contemporary labor practices extend the suppression of Indian culture and identity. The novel is replete with Upton Sinclair-esque descriptions of the meatpacking plant, from the process of slaughtering the pigs on the kill floor, to cleaning up afterward with dangerous industrial cleansers, enduring the freezing temperatures of the chilling room while stamping carcasses with USDA approval, and cleaning out the filter stacks atop the smokehouse roof.[37] The work is grinding and exhausting, and conditions are made even worse by the constant surveillance of the vindictive and petty foreman, Max, who seeks any excuse to dock worker pay. The intense realism in these depictions dramatizes the effects of what Balibar refers to as "class racism," or the way that neoliberal market relations reduce racialized subjects to the status of "*body-men*, men whose body is a machine-body, that is fragmented and dominated, and used to perform one isolable function or gesture."[38] The violence of that process is literalized in the operations of the slaughterhouse, where Zenzontli performs the single motion of slitting pig's throats for hours at a time, pausing only to push a button releasing the next body on the conveyor. Human bodies are thus instrumentalized as animal bodies are rendered for mass consumption:

> Thousands of frosty white carcasses – decapitated torsos – hung on hooks, swaying gently as they proceeded along a vast overhead conveyor, creaking slightly ... I thought these carcasses must be solid and cold as stone, stiff hundreds of pounds each, and I turned to peer up the line, trying to distinguish an end to it, but the shifting, swaying bodies emerged endlessly out of the darkness, swung into sight, blocking my view – I stepped back, looked up and down the line but could see no end.[39]

When Zenzontli tries to distinguish an end to "it," he refers literally to the line of animal carcasses and metaphorically to the violence perpetrated against immigrant workers under the existing labor regime. The slaughterhouse resonates powerfully with the human sacrifices that are the staple of the Aztek empire in the novel. The decapitated animal carcasses are indistinguishable from the human bodies that have also been rendered for mass consumption. Essentially, the novel parallels the familiar savagery of the practice of human sacrifice with the overlooked and untallied human sacrifices made under the banner of Conquest, Manifest Destiny, and global capital. To the extent that US consumers depend on the products of these disposable laboring bodies, we are complicit in the sacrificial system. As Zenzontli puts it, "Where do you think your bologna sandwich comes from?"[40]

Given this class-based critique, we see how Zenzontli's quest to enlist his fellow workers in a labor union is central to the novel's powerful political vision. Indeed, in its attention to the intersections of transnational migration, labor, and the dizzying cultural politics of the contemporary borderlands, *Atomik Aztex* taps into currents animating some of the most dynamic American literary production of the twenty-first century, from Helena María Viramontes's *Their Dogs Came with Them* (2006) to Sandra Cisneros's *Caramelo* (2002) and even Karen Tei Yamashita's *I Hotel* (2010). In these works the question is not so much whether or not the border is a historical reality or merely a metaphor; rather, the question is how the exclusions and limitations of national borders, which materially affect the lives of characters, interact with other aspects of the capitalist world system. Perhaps no better contemporary example of this trend exists than Junot Díaz's celebrated novel *The Brief Wondrous Life of Oscar Wao* (2008), a book in which the racial borders of the United States and the Dominican Republic – products of particular colonial histories – are imbricated with class boundaries and national borders as members of the De León family travel back and forth from the Dominican Republic to New Jersey over the course of three generations. Practically every aspect of *Oscar Wao*, even its dizzying mix of literary genres, meditates on what it means to live in the borderlands between cultures. Urrea's and Sanmiguel's works likewise correspond to important currents in borderland literary production, from Reyna Grande's border-crossing *testimonio* novel *Across a Hundred Mountains* (2006) to Roberto Bolaño's multi-volume epic *2666* (2004), which pivots on a series of murders in a fictional border city that strongly evokes Ciuded Juárez. These works suggest the continued urgency of borderlands analysis as a component of transnational approaches to American literature. The US-Mexico border continues to be ground zero for understanding the failures and fortunes of the nation-state in the twenty-first century.

NOTES

1   The distinction comes from an annual study by the Citizen Council for Public Safety and Criminal Justice in Mexico City, a private think tank. The organization's research is available at www.seguridadjusticiaypaz.org.mx.

2   See Joe Burgess and Haeyoun Park, "Migrant Deaths in Southern Arizona," *New York Times*, May 20, 2013. Web <www.nytimes.com/interactive/2013/05/21/us/migrant-deaths-in-southern-arizona.html>.

3   See Ramón Saldívar, *The Borderlands of Culture: Américo Paredes and the Transnational Imaginary* (Durham, NC: Duke University Press, 2006).

4   Limón uses Américo Paredes's term "Greater Mexico" to name this regional formation. See José E. Limón, "Border Literary Histories, Globalization, and Critical Regionalism," *American Literary History* 20 (2008): 160–82; Ramón Saldívar, "Asian Américo: Paredes in Asia and the Borderlands: A Response to José E. Limón" *American Literary History* 21 (2009): 584–94; Limón, "Imagining the Imaginary: A Reply to Ramón Saldívar," *American Literary History* 21 (2009): 595–603; and Limón, *Américo Paredes: Culture and Critique* (Austin: University of Texas Press, 2011).

5   Alexander C. Diener and Joshua Hagen, *Borders: A Very Short Introduction* (New York: Oxford University Press, 2012), 1.

6   There is also a significant body of border literature by writers of other ethnicities, such as Cormac McCarthy, Philip Caputo, Gail Tremblay, Karen Tei Yamashita, among others. However, what I am calling the borderlands paradigm arose historically out of the Chicana/o literary field.

7   Mary Louise Pratt, *Imperial Eyes: Travel Writing and Transculturation*, 2nd ed. (New York: Routledge: 2008), 8.

8   Mary Pat Brady, "Border," in *Keywords for American Cultural Studies*, Bruce Burgett and Glenn Hendler, eds. (New York: New York University Press, 2014). Web.

9   For theories of hybridity, see Homi Bhabha, *The Location of Culture* (New York: Routledge, 1991) and Nestor García Canclini, trans. Christopher L. Chiappari and Silvia L. Lopez, *Hybrid Cultures: Strategies for Exiting and Entering Modernity* (Minneapolis: University of Minnesota Press, 2005). On errancy, see Edouard Glissant, trans. Betsy Wing, *The Poetics of Relation* (Ann Arbor: University of Michigan Press, 1997). On nomadism, see Rosi Braidotti, *Nomadic Subjects* (New York: Columbia University Press, 1994).

10 Américo Paredes, *George Washington Gómez* (Houston, TX: Arte Público, 1990), 147.

11 Sandra Cisneros, *Woman Hollering Creek* (New York: Vintage, 1991), 151–52.

12 Saldívar, José David, "Chicano Border Narratives as Cultural Critique," in *Criticism in the Borderlands: Studies in Chicano Literature, Culture, and Ideology*, Héctor Calderón and Saldívar, eds. (Durham, NC: Duke University Press, 1991), 178.

13 Brady, "Border," Web.

14 Josefina Saldaña-Portillo, "Who's the Indian in Aztlán?: Re-Writing Mestizaje, Indianism, and Chicanismo from the Lacandón," in *The Latin American Subaltern Studies Reader*, Ileana Rodríguez, ed. (Durham, NC: Duke University Press, 2001): 413. See also Rafael Pérez-Torres's insightful response to Saldaña-Portillo

in *Mestizaje: Critical Uses of Race in Chicano Culture* (Minneapolis: University of Minnesota Press, 2006): 17–22.

15 Debra A. Castillo and María Socorro Tabuenca Córdoba, *Border Women: Writing from La Frontera* (Minneapolis: University of Minnesota Press, 2002), 15.

16 Gloria Anzaldúa, *Borderlands / La Frontera: The New Mestiza*, 3rd ed. (San Francisco: Aunt Lute, 2005), 25.

17 Ibid. 33.

18 Ibid., 34.

19 Ibid., 35.

20 Ibid., 25.

21 Mary Pat Brady, "The Fungibility of Borders," *Nepantla: View from the South* 1.1 (2000): 174.

22 Consider, for example, D. Emily Hicks's description of border writing: "Border writing emphasizes the differences in reference codes between two or more cultures. It depicts, therefore, a kind of realism that approaches the experience of border crossers, those who live in a bilingual, bicultural, biconceptual reality. I am speaking of cultural, not physical, borders: the sensibility that informs border literature can exist among guest workers anywhere, including European countries in which the country of origin does not share a physical border with the host country" (*Border Writing: The Multidimensional Text* [Minneapolis: University of Minnesota Press, 1991]: xxv).

23 Jesse Alemán, "The Other Country: Mexico, the United States, and the Gothic History of Conquest," *American Literary History* 18 (2006): 410.

24 Luis Alberto Urrea, *The Devil's Highway* (New York: Back Bay, 2004), 18–19.

25 Ibid., 4.

26 Ibid., 122–23.

27 Sandra Cox, "Crossing the Divide: Geography, Subjectivity, and Transnationalism in Luis Alberto Urrea's *The Devil's Highway*," *Southwestern American Literature* 38.1 (2012): 21.

28 Abraham Acosta, "Hinging on Exclusion and Exception: Bare Life, the US/ Mexico Border, and *Los que nunca llegarán*," *Social Text* 30.4 (2012): 110–11.

29 Walter Mignolo, *Local Histories / Global Designs: Coloniality, Subaltern Knowledges, and Border Thinking* (Princeton, NJ: Princeton University Press, 2000), 40.

30 Castillo and Córdoba, *Border Women*, 65.

31 Ibid., 65.

32 Rosario Sanmiguel, trans. John Pluecker, *Under the Bridge: Stories from the Border / Bajo el puente: Relatos desde la frontera* (Houston: Arte Público, 2008): 91. For an excellent article on sexual violence in the lives of Mexican migrant women, see Gloria González-López, " 'Nunca he dejado de tener terror': Sexual Violence in the Lives of Mexican Immigrant Women," in *Women and Migration in the US-Mexico Borderlands: A Reader*, Denise A. Segura and Patricia Zavella, eds. (Durham, NC: Duke University Press, 2007): 224–46.

33 The original edition includes no dedication. See Rosario Sanmiguel, *Callejón Sucre y otros relatos* (Tijuana: Ediciones del Azar, 1994), 87.

34 See Emma Pérez, *The Decolonial Imaginary: Writing Chicanas into History* (Bloomington: Indiana University Press, 1998).

35 The final report of the Indigenous Farmworker Study estimates that the percentage of indigenous workers rose from about 7% in 1991 to 29% in 2011. See "Indigenous Farmworker Study Final Report," *Indigenous Mexicans in California Agriculture*, Web <http://indigenousfarmworkers.org/final_report .shtml>.

36 Sesshu Foster, *Atomik Aztex* (San Francisco: City Lights, 2005).

37 Ibid., 5–8, 51–52, 63, 134.

38 Etienne Balibar, "Class Racism," in Balibar and Immanuel Wallerstein, *Race, Nation, Class: Ambiguous Identities* (New York: Verso, 1991), 211.

39 Foster, *Atomik Aztex*, 107.

40 Ibid., 8.

IO

JODI A. BYRD

American Indian Transnationalisms

In "The Real Revolution Is Love," Muskogee poet Joy Harjo describes a political debate across the divides of the Indigenous Americas. On a patio somewhere in the capital of Nicaragua, she presents a scene in which she and other artists from Puerto Rico, the United States, and South America discuss the revolutionary promises of liberation theology, political struggle, and seduction over glasses of yerbabueanas and shots of rum. Struggling with the burdens of being diasporic, displaced, traveling, or just caught between countries and "the land of our dreams," Harjo takes the reader through the "backbone of these tortuous Americas" and asks us to listen with her, "to the splash of the Atlantic and Pacific and see Columbus land once more, over and over again." Though she evokes expansive geopolitical spatialities and temporalities in her poem, she does not concern herself with nation-states and their borders. It is a poem about the failures of states to fully curtail and control how imagination and intimacy might transgress borders to offer new modes of relativity. And in the midst of it all, she articulates the solidarities of Indigenous women who find humor and camaraderie in the face of loss and dispossession: "I argue with Roberto, and laugh across the / continent to Diane, who is on the other side / of the flat, round table whose surface ships / would fall off if they sailed to the other / side. *We are Anishnabe and Muscogee. / We have wars of our own.*"[1]

Originally published in her 1990 collection, *In Mad Love and War*, Harjo's poem is ostensibly about the revolutionary possibilities that love, rather than war, might offer within the long dureé of new world colonization and genocide. Though focused on the dialogic exchanges between individuals, her poem might also be read as emblematic of the pressing awareness that the Americas have a deeper historicity than often acknowledged, and Harjo's romances tangle with desires to decenter the United States as somehow synecdoche for two continents and the islands that make up America as a transhemispheric continuity. Of a particular historical moment and exceeding it, Harjo's poem captures some of the scholarly and cultural transformations of the 1980s and 1990s that sought to find the geopolitical languages, scales, and frameworks to think beyond US exceptionalism, to push against the hegemonic centrality of the nation as superpower, and to stretch the critique of empire through the Atlantic and Pacific worlds of conquest. Harjo, in giving us a "flat, round table whose surface ships would fall off if they sailed to the other side," evokes a history of mapping that compressed the globe into the competitive possessiveness of nations and their conflicting desires for resources as capital and territory as power. She upends it all by reducing the Columbian quincentennial to its absurd smallness as she imagines the ships sailing off the table she and the others have gathered around.

Situated within an expansive continental view of geopolitical and temporal survivals, Harjo's "The Real Revolution Is Love" in many ways anticipates Aníbel Quijano's and Immanuel Wallerstein's 1992 essay, "Americanity as a Concept," that José David Saldívar later discusses as the inspiration for his *Trans-Americanity: Subaltern Modernities, Global Colonality, and the Cultures of Greater Mexico*. Saldívar, calling for an analysis of a trans-Americanity that he describes as a "long colonial encounter within the context of the 'American crucible,'" refigures American studies as a field through which to consider the new world-building systems of dominance that were inaugurated by genocide, slavery, scientific innovation, and capitalism.[2] Americanity reimagined as temporally and geographically fluid becomes, for Saldívar, a way to break down the centrality of Anglo- and Eurocentric modes of nationalisms to prioritize other modes of border crossings, migrancies, and movements across and through the norths and souths of the Americas. With the addition of the trans- he emphasizes the hemispheric and horizontal crossings that speak to a deeper history and movement within the Américas. His work, in other words, seeks to reinforce the "Our America" argument that José Martí and others who sought to reclaim America away from the United States made as a broader transformative political project that included Cuba and other Caribbean islands alongside Central and South America.[3] Redefining America in its entirety as part of the global South beyond the nation-states created and consolidated through colonialism and imperialism, scholars have been innovating methodologies through which to address some of the fugitive histories from below that always resisted and exceeded the statist, masculinist, racist, and heteronormative definitions of national belonging.

This need to expand the transnational scope of American studies was one that arose out of a pressing awareness that the United States, as a global power that exceeded its own boundaries of continental influence, was fundamentally, aggressively, and violently international. This turn, as it is often referenced within the fields of American studies and its allied interdisciplines, responded to critiques from postcolonial and subaltern scholars who demanded a systematic consideration of the lasting effects of European colonialism on the multiple stagings and worldings of nations and societies across the globe. It also addressed the work of ethnic studies scholars who insisted that the United States, as a site of global immigration, was always already transnational in its arrivals and dispersals. As John Carlos Rowe explains, the "transnational turn" of American studies refers to at least three movements and countermovements within academia. The first was the rise of scholarship that "stressed the comparative study of different 'Americas' – Latin America, the Caribbean, the United States – and Canada as the appropriate objects of study for the discipline"; the second was an acknowledgment of a growing body of scholarship undertaken by international scholars outside the United States; and the third aligned the turn to "new theories of cosmopolitanism and postnational conceptions of 'global' or 'planetary' citizenship."[4] Reframed through such vectors of analysis, Kandice Chuh argues, "transnationalism might be seen as a discourse that advances investigations of the technologies of race and U.S. national identity formation, or perhaps more pointedly, the technology of race *as* a technology of U.S. national identity."[5]

As transnational literary studies responded to some of these analyses and insights from other disciplines, and the scope of inquiry both widened and sharpened its focus on how race, space, class, gender, and sexuality were fundamentally altered when placed within a broader, comparative, and global frame, certain absences and elisions became increasingly apparent. In "the alternative geography of the 'worlding' of today's global South," that Gayatri Spivak critiques as unevenly producing the First, Second, and Third Worlds as privileged signifiers, the "Fourth World" of global indigeneity remained largely under theorized, if not invisible.[6] In Saldívar's decentering of the United States as the primary and dominant state-formation, and in his recentering of the border crossings of what he calls "Greater Mexico," the spatial and temporal modes of indigeneity are, at times, subsumed despite the longitudinal and latitudinal vectors of hemispheric sensibilities. The transnational turn in American studies was a necessary step toward reconfiguring the global networks that produce identities, subjectivities, and vested positionalities across the permeability and rigidity of borders. But in collapsing Indigenous Peoples into the racial formations of national belongings, the transnational turns of the past few decades continued to produce the colonial histories of Indigenous dispossession as the condition of possibility for resisting the nation-state in the first place. Underneath the flirtation and play of Harjo's poem there is a sharp sense of loss that exists alongside a fierce sense of the singularities of Indigenous belonging in her testimony that "*We are Anishnabe and Musckogee. / We have wars of our own.*"

Turn, Turn, Turn

Given such elisions, it may be unsurprising that the question of Indigenous transnationalism has been a vexed one for the field of Indigenous literary studies. Partly scale, partly frame, the where, when, and how to (re)draw the boundaries and borders of families, communities, tribes, states, nations, and nation-states provokes and disturbs easy assumptions about the place and location of indigeneity. Often assumed to be outside political being, or perhaps figured as an apolitical formation that exists before and peripheral to other modes of belonging, indigeneity and its concomitant cognates of tribal and native occupy distinct time zones of the pre- and the un-. Precontact and prehistorical often lead to the oral and the traditional, and within our inherited Enlightenment theories of civil societies and political governance, the Indigenous has been construed within colonial and imperial discourses as savage man, without society, language, culture, or civilization. As a result, much of Indigenous literary scholarship and the larger field of Indigenous studies have focused on asserting the cultural, intellectual, and political sovereignty and self-determination of Indigenous communities. Indigeneity, as Daniel Heath Justice defines it, refers to "the constitutive lived relationship and kinship of a people to a particular land, its histories, and its other-than-human inhabitants."[7] Its emphasis on the specificities of origin, place, and belonging often pits it (erroneously, many in the field have and would argue) against movement, dispersal, and diaspora.[8]

For Robert Warrior, the resistance of Native American studies to fully embrace the transnational turn has a number of possible geneses, the first of which, he contends, is the field's "widespread rejection of postcolonial studies" whose emphasis on the post- as the temporal after to or end of colonialism "creates a stumbling block to engagement."[9] Another reason, Warrior suggests, rests in the field's uneasy relationship with American studies more broadly, where Indigenous critiques have often been and have remain marginalized despite the inclusion of a few representative voices.[10] Finally, he indicates that there might be some wariness if not outright refusal on the part of Indigenous scholars to give themselves over to theories that seek to dismantle nationalism more generally. Reflecting on the monograph he wrote with Jace Weaver and Craig Womack in 2006 entitled *American Indian Literary Nationalism,* Warrior points out that "we argue that the discourse on nationalism remains important to Native American literary studies because it remains the domestic and international language in which Native struggle is waged and remains a primary vehicle for fueling Indigenous imaginations."[11] Or, as Joseph Bauerkemper explains, precisely as American studies began its turn to the transnational, "a somewhat parallel and thoroughly divergent scholarly narrative regarding the study of American Indian literatures has been unfolding. This narrative can appropriately be termed the 'nationalist turn' in American Indian literary studies."[12]

With the publication of Warrior's *Tribal Secrets* in 1995 and Womack's *Red on Red: Native American Literary Separatism* in 1999, that nationalist mode of Indigenous literary study became inviolable to the larger theoretical turns that the field has seen over the last two decades. The rise of settler colonial studies and the acknowledgment that the Unites States' relationship with Indigenous Peoples is both imperialist and colonialist placed increasing emphasis on sovereignty and self-determination as the cornerstones to apprehending the political and cultural challenges facing Indigenous Peoples as they strive to assert themselves as nations.[13] Embedded even within the *s* on peoples that signals the Indigenous as separate and distinct polities and not just a singular group of people counted as a racial population captured within the colonizing nation-state, the field insists on unlearning the imperialist knowledges that have collapsed indigeneity into race. Elizabeth Cook-Lynn has recently observed that "Indians are colonial subjects who not only mouth such terms as 'sovereignty' and 'home rule' as though those words have actual power, but who since the beginning have fiercely tried to defend themselves against colonial law."[14] Literary separatism refigures Indigenous literatures as unique and originary to themselves beyond the trajectory of the larger periodizations of American literature; as Craig Womack unambiguously avers, "I say that tribal literatures are not some branch waiting to be grafted onto the main trunk. Tribal literatures are the *tree*, the oldest literatures in the Americas, the most American of American literatures. We *are* the canon."[15]

Still and in substantial ways, one might argue that the emphasis on Indigenous literary nationalism, separatism, and sovereignty has helped facilitate the concurrent inward and outward turns within the field. Joseph Baurkemper, for instance, also recognizes that there is an "emergent mood within American Indian literary studies that is cautiously making its own uses of the transnational turn while continuing to tend to the ethical imperatives elaborated by the nationalist turn holds great promise for the ongoing growth of the field."[16] Allowing a productive tension to emerge between the Indigenous nation and its trans-, scholars in Indigenous studies simultaneously insist on the centrality of nationalist formations as necessary for maintaining the survival and future of Indigenous communities while also recognizing the historical and archeological evidence of the importance of exogamous trade routes and diplomacies that shaped the Americas long before Europeans arrived. For Robert Warrior, this mode of transnationalism is self-evident: "In effect our nationalism is born out of native transnationalism, the flow and exchange of ideas and politics across our respective nations' borders."[17]

In his own theorizations of Cherokee transnationalism, Daniel Heath Justice notes Indigenous Peoples experienced rich, complex, varied, and at times apocalyptic forms of transnationalisms before and after the arrival of Europeans. Emphasizing a scopic range of competitive and/or cooperative interactions between Indigenous Peoples as distinctly transnational in and of themselves well before those between European and Indigenous Peoples began to define the seventeenth, eighteenth, and nineteenth centuries, Justice writes:

[W]hereas Christopher Columbus heralded a dramatic (and catastrophic) level of transnational and intercultural interaction between Indigenous American and European peoples, Native realities in the Americas were, by necessity, transnational, for vast and complex relations of diplomacy, trade, conflict, and kinship connected diverse Native peoples long before European invasion, and they would exercise a profound and direct influence on the lives and political agency of European colonizers well into the nineteenth century.[18]

In taking Indigenous political sovereignty as foundational to understanding Indigenous communities as distinct in and of themselves to other Indigenous communities, the emphasis on Indigenous nationalisms necessitates the transnational as the precondition for any comparative work in the field.

Thus, any scholarship that frames a comparison of, for instance, Chickasaw and Cherokee literary practices would already be transnational, and that is before the additional transnational context that results when those traditions are placed into a broader frame of comparative US ethnic studies, American literature, or global Indigenous studies. In practical terms, this foundational recognition that American Indian and Indigenous studies has always already been transnational is quickly followed by the daunting realization that subject mastery is fundamentally impossible. There are more than 567 federally recognized tribal societies throughout the United States including Alaska, and each in and of themselves is a distinct nation with its own customs, laws, languages, and values that differentiate it from other Indigenous communities as well as the larger colonizing US nation-state. This sense of what Justice refers to as a "localized indigeneity" exists in relation to other localized indigeneities, and it informs the political practices of Indigenous refusal that

Diné scholar Glen Coulthard theorizes as "grounded normativity." It is the basis of Indigenous governing traditions that he defines as "the modalities of Indigenous land-connected practices and long-standing experiential knowledge that inform and structure our ethical engagements with the world and our relationships with human and nonhuman others over time."[19] In rejecting the colonial politics of state recognition that perpetuate colonial dominance, Coulthard's work suggests that resurgence lies within the decolonial possibilities of recognition among indigenous communities that reassert interrelationality as the transformative basis for Indigenous political and cultural life beyond the occupying nation-states of Canada or the United States.

There are, however, other considerations to track within the conflicting terrains shaping how Indigenous literary studies resists, disrupts, contains, and/or refuses the transnational turn within American studies. In trying to develop a theoretical compromise between the need to assert Indigenous sovereignty on the one hand and an awareness that nation-state formations are often critiqued for their enabling modes of biopolitical power and violence on the other, Joseph Bauerkemper gestures in his work toward a dynamic and non-absolutist form of what he theorizes as trans/nationalism within the broader ethics of the theoretical interventions Indigenous literary studies makes to other disciplines. His use of a solidus to break the word apart serves to signal "the cross-pollinating flows of aesthetic, rhetorical, political, cultural, economic, and social knowledges and sensitivities that constitute Indigenous trans/nationalisms" and "have temporal reach to match their spatial range."[20]

Shari Huhndorf makes an even stronger claim for the transnational in contemporary native political cultures in her work when she observes that nation "risks becoming 'its own prison, one created on the terms of colonial ideology.' "[21] Emphasizing how the concept of indigeneity arose in the context of global Indigenous mobilizations leading up to and beyond both the United Nations announcement that 1992 would be the International Year of World Indigenous Peoples and its subsequent adoption of the *Declaration on the Rights of Indigenous Peoples* in 2006, Huhndorf argues that "indigenous transnationalisms in particular extend existing American studies critiques of national identity and imperialism as they radically challenge the histories, geographies, and contemporary social relations that constitute America itself."[22] In drawing out the masculinist traditions that are often embedded within anticolonial nationalist movements, Indigenous or otherwise, Huhndorf's arguments align with the work of other Indigenous feminists including Leanne Simpson, Jennifer Denetdale, Sarah Hunt, Dian

Million, Mishuana Goeman, Cheryl Suzack, Patricia Monture-Angus, Joanne Barker, and Audra Simpson to critique nation-state formations of power that enact heteronormative violences disproportionately on queer, transgendered, disabled, youth, two spirit, and female bodies. The embodied and relational modes of Indigenous belonging, Indigenous feminists assert, require Indigenous decolonization to resist recapitulating to patriarchal, heteronormative, and racist models of nationalism by focusing only on iterations of recognition, sovereignty, and self-determination and instead, according to Sarah Hunt, understand that "our consciousness as legal and political actors must be formed both by looking inward toward the intimate spaces of our homes and communities as well as outward toward our engagement with systems of settler colonial power."[23]

While scholarship in American Indian and Indigenous literary studies continues to consider the role that Indigenous nationalisms and their trans- may or may not play in the resurgent decolonial mobilizations of Indigenous resistances that seek to bring global Indigeneity into conversation, one thing begins to emerge across the many voices engaged in the conversation: the need for culturally grounded and politically aware theories and methods with which to attend to Indigenous intellectual and philosophical traditions on the one hand and to counter to the possessive modes of capitalist and colonialist oppression on the other. Indeed, the opposing movements toward and turns away from nation that continue to inflect the deeper debates within Indigenous studies create an important tension at the site of indigeneity, suggesting that method and approach are fundamental components to Indigenous literary studies. For Daniel Heath Justice, importing the trans/national and cosmopolitan critiques from other disciplines requires us to return to questions of aesthetics in Indigenous studies even as "scholars of Indigenous literatures are reaching out, learning about themselves and one another, looking for points of connection that reflect and respect both specificity and shared concern, localized contexts and broader concerns, rooted perspectives and global viewpoints."[24] Elizabeth Cook-Lynn concurs when she asserts, "[T]he significance of the study of aesthetics and politics cannot be overemphasized."[25] Her interventions into the emergent postcolonial theories of the late 1990s lead her to insist that Third World critiques of cosmopolitanism are fundamental for American Indian literary studies to help us begin to open up and critique how Indigenous authors do and do not place themselves in relationship to land, treaties, nation, and deeper histories of kinship. Whatever the final verdict is on transnationalism's utility for American Indian literary studies, accountability to community, to people, to history, to political autonomy, and to diplomacy remain consistent refrains within the field.

Transnational/Transindigenous Methods

Since the turn of the twenty-first century, American Indian and Indigenous studies has grown rapidly and exponentially in relation to the number of Indigenous studies scholars entering the academy. With the formal incorporation of the Native American and Indigenous Studies Association in 2009, the field has, in substantial and important ways, reached a critical – if all too precarious – mass, especially given that more and more monographs are being published, more and more courses are being offered, and more and more students are finding ways to make Indigenous studies relevant to their own intellectual trajectories. The fundamental interdisciplinarity of the scholarship produced in Native American and Indigenous studies offers a notable challenge to the somewhat arbitrary and artificial divisions that separate fields such as anthropology, biology, geography, genomics, history, literature, linguistics, and political science, to name just a few. That stretching of disciplinary knowledge has frequently been accompanied by an expansive definition of indigeneity that continues to grow and develop. And at times, it has also been met with recalcitrant policing by scholars outside the field who might be and sometimes are threatened by the capaciousness of the field to include Palestinian struggles alongside Māori, Okinawan, Sámi, or Hawaiian resistance mobilizations against militarization and colonial occupation of traditional lands.

One of the many challenges currently facing Indigenous studies, then, is finding commonalities across the diverse regions and histories brought together under the rubric of indigeneity where often it is the shared experiences of dispossession, colonization, and violence that unfortunately link Indigenous Peoples' struggles globally more than some sense of shared aesthetic, cultural, or political ideals or values. Diaspora, forced relocation, and migration have also disturbed the self-evidentiary claims to place and belonging, creating in the process complex, dissonant, and sometimes fractious articulations of authority over a space through time. As Hokulani Aikau observes, "[T]he settler-colonial frame cannot accommodate the diasporic indigene: the natives who have been exiled from their homeland and who carry their own history of dispossession, exploitation, and expropriation with them as they settle in the diaspora."[26] In analyzing how Mormon Hawaiian families situated themselves in Iosepa, Utah as part of a diapsoric community with deep ties and responsibilities to honor ancestors buried in the region, Aikau reminds scholars in Indigenous studies to ask difficult questions: "It was not until I started to contemplated the possibility of digging in the dirt that I asked, how deep do we have to dig before the stories buried there – and the material objects unearthed – stop being about Iosepa, Polynesians, and Mormonism and begin to be about the Goshutes?"[27] The provisional nature of global Indigenous studies requires a generosity and flexibility of thought – and it requires a willingness to listen and learn across temporal, geopolitical, cultural, and increasingly walled borders and boundaries.

Methodology, then, is key to providing the parameters through which ethical and accountable scholarship might be produced within and beyond the academy. Such decolonial research approaches, Linda Tuhiwai Smith argues, requires reorienting one's scholarship toward the communities one serves and recognizing in the process the centrality of Indigenous intellectual, narrative, and philosophical protocols to help direct and guide research questions as well as researchers relationships with individuals, families, communities, agencies, and networks of access and oversight. As she notes, "[L]anguage and the citing of texts are often the clearest markers of the theoretical traditions of a writer."[28] Taking seriously the challenge of generating new methodologies to enable deeply comparative work within Indigenous literary studies, Chadwick Allen emphasizes the need not just for the recovery of texts but the development of a repertoire of tools through which to read and interpret Indigenous literatures, histories, and experiences. His methodology is built from "focused *juxtapositions* of distinct Indigenous texts, performances, and contexts. Where *compare* unites 'together' (*com-*) with 'equal' (*par*), *juxtapose* unites 'close together' (Latin *juxta-*) with 'to place' (French *poser*). Indigenous juxtapositions place diverse texts close together across genre and media, aesthetic systems and worldviews, technologies and practices, tribes and nations, the Indigenous-settler binary, and historical periods and geographical regions."[29] Refusing comparison as the basis for thinking about how discrete and localized grounded Indigenous relationalities might speak to and against one another, Allen's methodology recenters a praxis of proximity rather than close or distant reading in order to acknowledge the wholeness of each Indigenous textual creation in and of itself.

Framing shared Indigenous signifiers such as whales, weavings, carvings, earthworks, and perhaps even canoes as material signs "literally *in transit* between northern and southern hemispheres of an Indigenous Pacific," Allen demonstrates the utility and necessity of thinking through and across Indigenous syntactic, metonymic, and connotative narrative traditions as they shift among and between divergent cultural markers. Concerned with the normative modes of nationalist belonging that can, at times, haunt

Indigenous political resistance, Allen eschews the additive and the comparative to revitalize the prefix trans- as something that alters the Indigenous in ways that are more radical and compelling than the transnational, imported from American studies or political studies, itself might allow. "The point," he says, "is to invite specific studies into different kinds of conversations, and to acknowledge the mobility and multiple interactions of Indigenous peoples, cultures, histories and texts."[30] He continues:

> Similar to terms like *trans*lation, *trans*national, and *trans*form, *trans*-Indigenous may be able to indicate the specific agency and situated momentum carried by the preposition *through*. It may be able to harbor the potential of *change* as both transitive and intransitive verb, and as both noun and adjective.... Turning from *ands* to *comparative* to *trans*- acknowledges that a global Indigenous literary studies (primarily) in English must move beyond scenarios in which Great Book from Tradition A is introduced to Great Book from Tradition B so that they can exchange vital statistics, fashion tips, and recipes under the watchful eye of the Objective Scholar.[31]

Breaking the logics of an ethnographic comparative project that seeks to capture and catalog the similarities and differences informing how the savage mind thinks in different cultures, Allen's trans-Indigenous model suggests approaching interpretation as the juxtaposition of multidirectionally grounded knowledges that speak with and across the culture that produces them and the cultures that encounter them.

Traveling Indigeneity

Whether one approaches American Indian literary traditions as a project that is inherently transnational and/or trans-Indigenous, American Indian authors themselves offer robust languages and creative terrains through which to consider the stakes for thinking about indigeneity as a global, planetary project with rooted and landed implications. From Leslie Marmon Silko's *Almanac of the Dead* published in 1991 to Sherman Alexie's post-9/11 novel *Flight*, many native authors have imagined vectors of Indigenous cross-cultural protocols of encountering differences and negotiating the complexities of identity and positionality created through invasion and its concomitant forced arrival of peoples from around the globe. Indeed, Silko's *Almanac of the Dead* provides a deep historical accounting of the destructive violences inaugurated with Columbus's arrival in 1492 as she also imagines the transnational force of a coming Indigenous uprising that will provide the foundation for a decolonial revolution to sweep the continent south to north and finally fulfill the Ghost Dancers' promise that the land, people, and buffalo will be restored. Alexie's speculative fiction, on the other hand, considers the more intimate modes of violence and temporality as *Flight* charts the struggles of a native adolescent to find family, meaning, and healing within the precarities of nineteenth-century Indian wars that become the twenty-first-century global war on terror.

But perhaps it is Susan Power's recent *Sacred Wilderness* that best captures the multidirectional impulses of Indigenous transnationalisms as the book bridges the intimate relations of kinship and family with the deeper historical movements of conquest, dispossession, and assimilation. Written to respond directly to some of the intellectual debates within contemporary Indigenous studies, *Sacred Wilderness* stages a transnational and trans-Indigenous conversation among Judeo-Christian traditions, the Haudenosaunee Confederacy's Great Law of Peace, and Dakota and Anishinaabe lived experiences in and around Minneapolis, Minnesota. With living Indigenous scholars, artists, and writers making an appearance in its pages alongside historical and religious figures, the novel is an experiment in mixed genre, where fiction and nonfiction, theory and storytelling, the real and the supernatural merge to delve into the entanglements of family history produced by the traumas of colonialism.

Spanning over 400 years of history on the American continent, Power's novel charts the spiritual intervention two ghostly Clan Mothers – Maryam, mother of Yeshua, and Jigonsaseh, mother of Ayowantha – make to Candace's life as she stumbles through the detachment, dissociation, and alienation of modern society and consumerism. Forcing her to confront her own family inheritance as Jewish and Kanien'kehá:ka, Jigonsaseh and Maryam call Candace to understand herself within a broader network of global Indigenous knowledges that have been obscured and overwritten by masculinist, territorial, and oppressive regimes. And it begins with the question Maryam poses to Candace, "How can you mix the mitzvah with the Mohawk?"[32] The rest of the novel demonstrates how the sharing of stories, truth, pain, love, and memory can provide the strands to build relationships across tribal, religious, and cultural divides. "This land," one of the Dakota characters in the novel tells Maryam, "is our closest relative, and we have cherished it, studied it, learned its ways and its stories before any other person walked this ground, hauling their own stories that have no roots beneath the dirt."[33] By the novel's end, we learn that Jigonsaseh and Maryam have together forged the diplomatic protocols and compacts necessary to recognize each other first as mothers of transformative men, then as tribal women, and finally as sisters. In giving Maryam a two-row wampum belt, Jigonsaseh explains how "'We will travel different paths yet find each other again in that place we walk as spirits.'"[34] *Sacred Wilderness* is a novel about how one's origins and roots matter, but it also provides the fictive protocols through which indigeneity might travel through new lands and spaces and still be recognized as Indigenous.

While indigeneity, then, is an identity figured first and foremost as grounded and locatable, much of the literature written by American Indian authors demonstrates just how much indigeneity *moves*. As Scott Richard Lyons explains in *X-Marks*, "[I]f anything can be considered an enduring value for Ojibwe people, it has got to be migration."[35] Understood as a catalyst for change against stagnation, mobility creates the possibility for the production of *difference*. "The old never dies," Lyons continues, "it just gets supplemented by the new."

This sense of Indigenous movement that many scholars in the field attach to the trans- is indebted to Gerald Vizenor's literary and scholarly aesthetics of chance, play, and survivance. As an author who has always pursued the crosscultural in addition to the transnational in his novels including *Heirs of Columbus* (1991) and *Hiroshima Bugi* (2003), Vizenor's work embraces the inherent possibility of language to deconstruct into aleatory meaning and intent. His concept of transmotion, like Indigenous transnationalism, or the trans-Indigenous before it, depends on notions of mobility, unpredictability, and renewal. Rather than insisting on statist modes of nationalism derived through possessive territorality, Vizenor argues that "Native sovereignty is the right of motion, and transmotion is personal, reciprocal, the source of survivance, but not territorial."[36] A few paragraphs later he clarifies, "Sovereignty is transmotion and used here in most senses of the word motion; likewise, the ideas and conditions of motion have a deferred meaning that reach, naturally, to other contexts of action, resistance dissent, and political controversy. The sovereignty of motion means the ability and the vision to move in imagination and the substantive rights of motion in native communities."[37] Claiming sovereignty as a native right to move, act, change, and dissent, Vizenor's transmotion provides useful theoretical modes for thinking through analytic frameworks that embrace the grounded and localized relationalities of kinship networks and knowledges informing distinct Indigenous communities while also insisting on their autonomy to determine when and how they interact with, interpret, or refuse others.

Finally, LeAnne Howe's series of nonfiction essays collected in *Choctalking on Other Realities* presents us with rich examples of the possibilities – and pratfalls – of traveling while Indigenous. From Ada, Oklahoma to Jerusalem and from New Orleans to Romania, Howe's work theorizes indigeneity as an embodied tribalography that, like Vizenor's insistence that native sovereignty is first and foremost transmotion, is always moving across boundaries and borders while retaining a core sense of locatedness with and to place and land. "Native stories are power. They create people. They author tribes," she tells us.[38] Tribalograpahy is the collection of stories, relationships to uncles, mothers, nonhuman relatives, and the earth and dust that mingles the molecules of our bodies with those of the stars. "Here in the telling and retelling," Howe writes, "I've moved across space and time, reflecting on how tribal people embody land and stories. In the process I found my distant ancestors, my mothers, my uncles, myself. At times, my family's pain and my own sense of loss have knocked me to my knees; yet for a writer that's what it means to embody the stories we tell, perform, write, live."[39] Her sense of embodiment begins and ends with the mnemonics of space and movement, and, like Vizenor, insists that native stories, power, and sovereignty do not derive from territorial possession of land but from the land's ability to possess us across time and space, and through love, loss, and grief.

American Indian and Indigenous studies continues to grapple with the national and transnational turns that have conditioned the larger disciplinary conversations that are often assumed to capture and contain indigeneity. And meanwhile, Indigenous writers and scholars continue to innovate the languages, stories, and theories with which to assert the decolonial differences that indigeneity poses to statist forms of possession, territory, nations, boundaries, borders, and regions. Whether through war, family, or love, Indigenous Peoples will continue to travel beyond and exceed the hold we might have over ourselves and others.

NOTES

1 Joy Harjo, "The Real Revolution Is Love," in *How We Became Human: New and Selected Poems: 1975–2001* (New York: W. W. Norton & Company, 2002), 75–77.

2 José David Saldívar, *Trans-Americanity: Subaltern Modernities, Global Coloniality, and the Cultures of Greater Mexico* (Durham, NC: Duke University Press, 2012), xiii.

3 José Martí, trans. Elinor Randall, Juan de Oní, and Roslyn Held Foner, ed. Philip S. Foner, *Our America: Writings on Latin America and the Struggle for Cuban Independence* (New York: Monthly Review Press, 1977).

4 John Carlos Rowe, "Transnationalism and American Studies," in *Encyclopedia of American Studies*, ed. Simon J. Bronner (Baltimore: Johns Hopkins University Press, 2015). Web <http://eas-ref.press.jhu.edu/view?aid=794>. Accessed July 16, 2015.

5 Kandice Chuh, *Imagine Otherwise: On Asian Americanist Critique* (Durham, NC: Duke University Press, 2003), 61.

6 Gayatri Chavravorty Spivak, *The Critique of Post Colonial Reason* (Boston, MA: Harvard University Press, 1999), 200.

7 Daniel Heath Justice, "'To Look upon Thousands': Cherokee Transnationalism, at Home and Abroad," *CR: The New Centennial Review* 10.1 (2010): 171.

8 For instance, in their essay "Decolonizing Resistance, Challenging Colonial States," *Social Justice*, 35.3 (20080–9): 120–38, Nandita Sharma and Cynthia Wright suggest that notions of autochthony, indigenous nationalism, and "native" claims *"can be said to be a neoliberal mode of belonging"* produced by the nation-state and positioned against migrants as an iteration of xeno-phobia (126). Indigenous scholars and authors including Gerald Vizenor, Matt Sakiestewa Gilbert, Vine Deloria, Jack Forbes, Mishuana Goeman, Scott Richard Lyons, LeAnne Howe, Joy Harjo, Susan Power, Vicente Diaz, Noenoe Silva, and many others would argue that indigeneity has never implied static rootedness and has always consisted of exogamous relations and movement across conti-nents and oceans.

9 Robert Warrior, "Native American Scholarship and the Transnational Turn," *Cultural Studies Review* 15.2 (2009): 122.

10 Ibid., 124.

11 Ibid., 126.

12 Joseph Bauerkemper, "Indigenous Trans/Nationalism and the Ethics of Theory in Native Literary Studies," in *The Oxford Handbook of Indigenous American Literature*, ed. James H. Cox and Daniel Heath Justice (Oxford: University of Oxford Press, 2014), 397.

13 I trace the genealogy of settler colonial studies to postcolonial theory. Work including Anne McClintock's *Imperial Leather: Race, Gender, and Sexuality in the Colonial Contest* (New York: Routledge, 1995); Bill Ashcroft, Gareth Griffiths, and Helen Tiffin's *The Empire Writes Back: Theory and Practice in Post-colonial Literatures* (New York: Routledge, 1989); and Nicholas Thomas' *Colonialism's Culture: Anthropology, Travel, and Government* (Princeton, NJ: Princeton University Press, 1994) sits alongside Patrick Wolfe's "Settler Colonialism and the Elimination of the Native," *Journal of Genocide Research* 8:4 (2006): 387–409; Lorenzo Veracini's *Settler Colonialism: A Theoretical Overview* (London: Palgrave MacMillan, 2010); and Lisa Ford's *Settler Sovereignty: Jurisdiction and Indigenous Peoples in America and Australia, 1788–1836* (Cambridge, MA: Havard University Press, 2011).

14 Elizabeth Cook-Lynn, *A Separate Country: Postcoloniality and American Indian Nations* (Lubbock: Texas Tech University Press, 2012), 4.

15 Craig Womack, *Red on Red: Toward Native Literary Nationalism* (Minneapolis: University of Minnesota Press, 1999), 6–7.

16 Bauerkemper, "Indigenous Trans/Nationalism," 400.

17 Warrior, "Native American Scholarship," 125.

18 Justice, "'To Look Upon Thousands,'" 171.

19 Glen Coulthard, *Red Skin, White Masks: Rejecting the Colonial Politics of Recognition* (Minneapolis: University of Minnesota Press, 2014), 13.

20 Bauerkemper, "Indigenous Trans/Nationalism," 398.

21 Shari Huhndorf, *Mapping the Americas: The Transnational Politics of Contemporary Native Cuture* (Ithaca, NY: Cornell University Press, 2009), 12.

22 Ibid., 19.

23 Sarah Hunt, "Violence, Law and the Everyday Politics of Recognition (com-mentary on *Red Skins, White Masks*," presented at the *Native American and Indigenous Studies Conference*, Washington, DC, June 4–6, 2015. Accessible

online at <www.academia.edu/12834803/Violence_Law_and_the_Everyday_
Politics_of_Recognition_commentary_on_Red_Skin_White_Masks>.
24 Daniel Heath Justice, "Currents of Trans/national Criticism in Indigenous
Literary Studies," *The American Indian Quarterly* 35,2 (Summer 2011): 344.
25 Elizabeth Cook-Lynn, *Why I Can't Read Wallace Stegner and Other
Essays: A Tribal Voice* (Madison: University of Wisconsin Press, 1996), 84.
26 Hokulani Aikau, "Indigeneity in the Diaspora: The Case of Native Hawaiians at
Iosepa, Utah," *American Quarterly* 62,3 (2010): 479.
27 Ibid., 478.
28 Linda Tuhiwai Smith, *Decolonizing Methodologies: Research and Indigenous
Peoples*, 2nd ed. (London: Zed Books, 2012 [1999]), 14.
29 Chadwick Allen, *Trans-Indigenous: Methodologies for Global Native Literary
Studies* (Minneapolis: University of Minnesota Press, 2012), xviii.
30 Ibid., xiv.
31 Ibid,. xv.
32 Susan Power, *Sacred Wilderness* (East Lansing: Michigan State University Press,
2014), 33.
33 Ibid., 44.
34 Ibid., 157.
35 Scott Richard Lyons, *X-Marks: Native Signatures of Assent* (Minneapolis:
University of Minnesota Press, 2010), 3.
36 Gerald Vizenor, *Fugitive Poses: Native American Indian Scences of Absence and
Presence* (Lincoln: University of Nebraska Press, 1998), 182.
37 Ibid.
38 LeAnne Howe, *Choctalking on Other Realities* (San Francisco: Aunt Lute,
2013), 13.
39 Ibid., 192.

11

VIET THANH NGUYEN

Pacific Rim and Asian American Literature

Literature, like humanity, yearns to be free. Yet labels and categories persist and serve a function, creating and closing off possibilities. So it is that "Asian American literature" arose in the 1970s, proclaimed by those who began to call themselves Asian Americans in the 1960s. These young radicals saw that their freedom was restricted by a long history of racism and the ramifications of a war in Southeast Asia that was being fought by fellow Americans. These Americans could not distinguish between Asians over there in Southeast Asia and Americans of Asian descent over here in the United States, where some had lived for generations. For Asian Americans to name themselves as such was thus a rebuke to the American perception that they were forever foreigners, or, at best, honorary whites, their status always transitory or ambivalent. Creating an utterly new category thus opened a realm of possibility that Asian Americans are still exploring today, guided by the idea that writer Maxine Hong Kingston helped to pioneer: the necessity, for Asian Americans, of "claiming America."[1]

Besides Kingston, many other authors who can be classified as Asian American have forcefully asserted this claim to America. Sometimes the literature placed its stake in America explicitly through plot and story, but it always did so implicitly through simply existing, written in English. Throughout the 1970s and 1980s, and even into the 1990s, the appearance of a book by an Asian American author writing in English was an occasion for celebration by Asian American readers. The most momentous was, of course, Amy Tan's best-selling *The Joy Luck Club* (1989), which for many readers remains the only Asian American book they have heard of, much less read. Even until the present, the influence of The Joy Luck Club remains felt in publishing circles, where new Asian American writers, particularly women, are often expected by readers and publishers to write mother-daughter stories or tales of woe in Asia. The paucity in numbers of Asian American books and authors meant that the category of Asian American literature itself was emergent and struggling, and hence something to be advocated for and defended by its practitioners, critics, and audience. But by the new millennium, it would be difficult even for the most passionate or professional readers of Asian American literature to keep up with the rate of literary production, as dozens of memoirs, novels, short story collections, and poetry collections poured forth each year. The demographic consequences of the 1965 Immigration Law, which ended racially exclusionary policies directed at Asian immigrants, had been realized. The law created the "children of 1965," as literary critic Min Hyoung Song calls the generation descended from those immigrants who came subsequent to 1965.[2] The effects of the law were immediate and long-term: 135,844 Asian immigrants came in the 1950s; 358,563 came in the 1960s; and in 2013 alone, 389,301 Asian immigrants arrived.[3] The children of these immigrants went to college in large numbers: their percentages in public universities like UC Berkeley (40 percent)[4] and UCLA (33.5 percent),[5] and in private universities like Harvard (21.1 percent),[6] Yale (20 percent),[7] and Princeton (22 percent),[8] far outstrip their portion of the US population (5.6 percent in 2010).[9] Some percentage of these college students became writers. These writers found opportunity in an era born from the new social movements of the 1960s, which pushed American culture toward an embrace of multiculturalism and diversity. By 2001, then, Asian American literature had arrived as an increasingly respectable ethnic subset of American literature, its writers publishing best sellers and gaining wide literary acclaim, including winning the most prestigious prizes in the land. Fiction writer Jhumpa Lahiri and poet Vijay Seshadri, for example, won the Pulitzer Prize in 2000 and 2014, respectively, and Ha Jin won the National Book Award in 1999, as well as two PEN/Faulkner awards.

But while the work of claiming America remains an important one for Asian American writers in a time when racism has hardly dissipated, 9/11 and its consequences would trouble that claim. What exactly were Asian American writers claiming? Belonging and citizenship, yes, but did those come free from those aspects of American culture that troubled some, namely excessive consumption and heedless capitalism, not to mention the desire for global domination and the regular use of American military force? The latent nationalism that underlay the claim to America would become harder to deny after 9/11, when what it meant to be American was thrown into relief against America's Mideast wars. But these wars only made much more visible, and visceral, what had been evident since the very first Asians came to American shores with the Spanish galleons, which was that the plight of Asian Americans could never actually be separated from what happened outside American borders. Perhaps in the future, looking back retrospectively, the period of claiming America for Asian Americans will appear to be a necessary but limited stage in understanding the place of Asian Americans in American and global society. Claiming America, while it does not preclude claiming the world, does discourage it, adopting almost inevitably the American tendency toward national insularity and American exceptionalism, the belief that America was the greatest country of all. Such a belief prevents Asian Americans from seeing how their fates are tied to global currents.

Parallel to the rise of Asian America came the idea of the "Pacific Rim," which began in the 1960s as a way of harnessing some of these global currents for the good of capitalism.[10] Even as Asian Americans were organizing themselves, the engineers of global capital in Japan and the United States – the twin powers of the post–World War II Pacific – were thinking of how the Pacific Rim might serve as a more capacious concept than the nation-state for understanding and promoting the flow of capital. The Pacific Rim included more than just those two countries, but also the emerging capitalist states of Asia, the redoubts of Australia and New Zealand, as well as all of North America and much of Latin America. Of course, capital, as well as its goods and agents, were not the only things moving along the Pacific Rim or through the Pacific Ocean. There were also the people who worked for capital or who were exploited by it, and the militaries deployed to secure the Pacific or struggle over it. Those who celebrated the Pacific Rim tended to overlook problematic figures like laborers or soldiers whose presence implied that the flow of capital across the Pacific was maintained by cheap labor or armed force. Still, the very notion of a Pacific Rim that transcended nations allowed for the possibility of imagining movements, affiliations, and imaginations that crossed borders. So far as we believe the category of a Pacific Rim literature is useful, it is because it allows us to address how people and culture are not easily contained in national categories like American or its subsidiary, Asian American.

Even turning to Kingston, it is easy to see that "Asian American literature" is a useful lens that only focuses on the American dimension of her work. The opening page of *The Woman Warrior* (1976) acknowledges how Chinese men were leaving China destined not only for the United States, but elsewhere:

In 1924, just a few days after our village celebrated seventeen hurry-up weddings – to make sure that every young man who went "out on the road" would responsibly come home – your father and his brothers and your grandfather and his brothers and your aunt's new husband sailed for America, the Gold Mountain. It was your grandfather's last trip. Those lucky enough to get contracts waved goodbye from the decks. They fed and guarded the stowaways and helped them off in Cuba, New York, Bali, Hawaii. "We'll meet in California next year," they said. All of them sent money home.[11]

Kingston's *China Men* (1980) makes even more explicit how the Chinese American experience in the United States needs to be understood in the context of how Chinese migrants traveled all over the Americas, and sometimes ended up in the United States after stops elsewhere. Once a concept like the Pacific Rim is used to pry open the Asian American category, it becomes easier to see how even the American dimension of the Asian American experience is obfuscated. When the term "Asian American" is used in the United States, for example, it means the experiences of Asians in the United States. It does not mean the experiences of Asians in Canada, or Mexico, or any points further south in the Americas, despite the significant numbers of Asian migrants to many countries in the Americas. "Claiming America" for Asian Americans in the United States is thus even more so a claim to the American empire of the United States, and a reinforcement of the claim the United States has made on all of the Americas as its sphere of influence. From one vantage point on the Pacific Rim, Asian American literature, for all that it often records the negative dimensions of migration and assimilation into the United States, also participates in the celebration of the United States as the most exceptional country of the Americas, the only country most people outside of the Americas think of when they hear "America." An event like the Japanese American internment becomes remembered only for the suffering inflicted on Japanese residents of the United States, erasing how Japanese in Latin America were deported to internment camps in the United States, and how Japanese Canadians were deported to the interior of Canada to do forced labor. Joy Kogawa's *Obasan* (1981) connects this experience to the bombing of Hiroshima and Nagasaki, a Canadian trauma and a Japanese trauma that are simultaneous effects of a Pacific war. These events all happen on what will be called the Pacific Rim.

The writing of Karen Tei Yamashita might be classified as the kind of Pacific Rim literature that serves to expose the history of the capitalist and militarized exploitation of the Pacific Rim by powerful countries, particularly the United States and Japan. While her novels *Through the Arc of the Rainforest* (1990) and *Brazil-Maru* (1993) looked at Japanese immigrants who came to Brazil seeking work, *Circle K Cycles* (2001) dealt with their Japanese-Brazilian descendants who went to Japan searching for economic opportunity. Japan of the 1990s was in need of cheap, unskilled labor, but was also fearful of the cultural differences that migrant labor would bring. The government turned to the Japanese Brazilians in hopes that they could fulfill the country's labor needs with minimal disturbance to Japanese culture, given their Japanese heritage. As it turned out, however, the Japanese Brazilians were too Brazilian for the Japanese, symbolized, for example, in the ways that they had difficulty absorbing basic Japanese attitudes toward things like waste. "Which days, at what time, where, and how must we dispose of our trash?" one character anxiously wonders. "I listen to the answers conscientiously. I want to be a good neighbor."[12] The Japanese are punctilious about everything, including their waste, which must be sorted into four trash groups, and would never use secondhand goods. But the Japanese Brazilians "hardly have to buy anything upon arriving in Japan," as plenty of hand-me-downs from other sojourners are to be found.[13] These differing attitudes toward waste and commodities represent economic and cultural attitudes toward wealth, commodities, and lifestyles across the Pacific – a staple of Yamashita's writing.

From a pan-American perspective, though, her work is also Asian American literature, except that it concerns the relationship between Japan, or Asia, and Latin America. Still, her work pushes well beyond the American borders of Asian American literature, whether those borders are in the north or the south. Yamashita is most concerned with the circulation of people who are forced to move by the demands of capitalism, and ultimately with capitalism itself. One of her best-known works, *Tropic of Orange* (1997), takes as one of its subjects the impact of the North American Free Trade Agreement. The novel's political vision reaches its climax in a surreal wrestling match between El Gran Mojado (The Gigantic Wetback) and SUPERNAFTA, characters modeled on lucha libre wrestlers. El Gran Mojado triumphs, and *"everyone gasped as the great SUPERNAFTA imploded."*[14] The novel itself straddles the United States and Mexico, examining an ensemble cast who represent different races, genders, nationalities and economic strata, caught up in not only NAFTA but also the Japanese American internment, undocumented immigration, racial tensions, and natural disasters. The novel is pan-American but also a cultural product of the Pacific Rim, with NAFTA as one manifestation of the efforts of nation-states to build trade agreements that cross borders, even as they also attempt to block people from moving freely across borders.

Yamashita's writing, while always taking into account the Asian presence in the Americas, often overflows these racial and geographic boundaries. This is evident in her most ambitious novel, *I Hotel* (2010). During the 1970s, the I Hotel, inhabited by aging Filipino and Chinese workers, became the site of an important civil rights struggle as community activists sought to defend the workers from eviction. The construction of an Asian American movement depended partially on the idea that Filipinos and Chinese were both Asian, which, at the time, was not necessarily a given for Filipinos. Yamashita connects this fight to defend workers and build a panethnic coalition to the history of the Vietnam War, the antiwar movement that had preceded it, and the journey some of these activists undertook to revolutionary China. The novel affirms how the Asian American movement was always what critics would now call transnational, or would then, in the 1960s, call international. The I of I-Hotel itself stood for International, and becomes a sign of how the hotel's poor workers were emblematic of the global pressures and currents that had brought so many to the United States.

A novel like Ruth Ozeki's *A Tale for the Time Being* (2013) makes literal this idea that currents connect continents. In the novel, a writer named Ruth finds the diary of a Japanese girl washed up on the shore near her Vancouver home, drifting along with the flotsam and jetsam from a Japan recently devastated by a tsunami. The impetus for the novel is thus the ecological and environmental, of which the Pacific Ocean is the most massive embodiment. But the term "Pacific Rim," at least in its most common deployment, avoids the ecological and the environmental by foregrounding instead economic potential. Cultural possibilities come second, and the ecological and environmental are barely mentioned at all by advocates for a capitalist Pacific Rim. For Pacific Rim advocates, whose most contemporary manifestation is embodied in the supporters of the Trans-Pacific Partnership, there is the sense that the possibilities of economic and cultural transformation in the Pacific Rim are contemporary, a part of something called globalization.[15] But Ozeki's novel and its gesture toward the forces of the ocean imply that the Pacific part of the Pacific Rim has been a global force for much longer than the fashionable term "globalization." Furthermore, the impact of globalization on the Pacific's ecosystem will continue far into the future. Even in the short period of human history, the Pacific has long been the site for ships, boats, and people to cross through and over, not to mention live in. Commerce and trade, war and exploration, conducted by Asians, Europeans, and Pacific Islanders, flourished for centuries before the contemporary moment, even before the age of European imperialism. The Pacific Rim is then a belated term, one of several, that arise to help scholars and others make sense of the movements of people, goods, cultures, and ideas across man-made boundaries.[16]

What terms such as "Pacific Rim" allow scholars to do is figure out new ways of classification. A person, a culture, or a text looks different when being called Asian American versus Pacific Rim, or transnational, international, diasporic, or cosmopolitan, which are all influential terms in contemporary academic scholarship. A person, a culture, or a text can be grouped with others in novel ways, depending on the term being used. The utility of

Asian American literature is that it allowed for a grouping of people and texts that had heretofore not been grouped, and as a result had suffered in isolation as being anomalous in the landscape of American culture. Authors such as Sui Sin Far (*Mrs. Spring Fragrance*, 1912) at the turn of the nineteenth century, or Younghill Kang (*East Goes West*, 1937) in the 1920s, or Carlos Bulosan (*America Is in the Heart*, 1946) in the 1940s, or John Okada (*No-No Boy*, 1957) in the 1950s, who when looked at alone were exceptional figures from small ethnic populations, could then, in retrospect, be part of a larger literary and political movement that had greater force in numbers. But every system of classification also excludes and limits, and the drawback of Asian American literature is that it discourages the possibility of seeing Asian American authors as having other alignments, while encouraging Asian Americans to see themselves as Americans. But seeing themselves as international might provoke Asian Americans into adopting the radical vision of Yamashita, where international stands for border-crossing movements of resistance and revolution.

The place of Asian Americans on the Pacific Rim, and the Pacific Rim itself, has unpredictable political possibilities. In the case of Pacific Rim literature, for example, its existence is tied to the idea of the Pacific Rim as part of a "United States Global Imaginary," as Christopher Connery puts it. Likewise, scholar Rob Wilson made the case for doing cultural studies within APEC at the time when APEC, an economic alliance of Asian Pacific countries, was at the forefront of the news. Now, with the Transpacific Partnership being debated by many countries as they ponder signing on to the vast trade agreement, the term "transpacific" is appearing in more and more articles and books dealing with literature and culture. Much as the theorist Slavoj Žižek describes "multiculturalism" as the cultural logic of multinational capitalism, these terms are also the cultural logic of phases in the global organization of the economy. They are made possible by changes in the global economy and the concomitant movements of people, culture, and ideas, and they potentially become sites of critique and resistance to those changes. Asian American as a term serves similar functions.

For Asian American studies, "Asian American" is not simply a demographic category, but the name for a population that is premised on resistance to oppression and injustice.[17] But another way to understand Asian American as a category is in regards to how markers of cultural diversity also facilitate the growth of capital (a point also made in related ways by Inderpal Grewal about feminism's vulnerability to neoliberal exploitation and Rey Chow in regards to ethnic difference as commodity in the academy). Just as one is encouraged by financial advisers to diversify one's investments, all forms of human diversity are vulnerable to investment and exploitation in capitalism. After all, corporations and the military are also interested in diversity, not just civil rights groups and universities. So it is that "Asian American" can also name a population that is another marketing category or a lifestyle, while Asian American people can be as interested in participating in capitalism as they are in social justice struggles. In that sense, Asian American and Pacific Rim as names could be seen as domestic and international mirrors of each other, describing how capitalism categorizes populations on different scales of the local and global.

Nevertheless, because "Asian American" also did arise from a history of political mobilization and resistance, it has a different valence than does Pacific Rim, which was never a term claimed by people seeking to defend themselves. Asian American retains a politically charged, if unresolved, meaning, whereas Pacific Rim still implies something more capitalist and commercial, a cosmopolitanism of the jet-set class rather than what Paul Gilroy calls the vulgar cosmopolitanism of the classes forced to migrate.[18] A novel like Kevin Kwan's *Crazy Rich Asians* (2014) is about the jet-set class, embodied in the Asians of the title, who traverse the Pacific between Singapore and New York at will. They might be called Asian American, given their ability to live and shop in the United States, but Pacific Rim is better. They are the flexible citizens described by anthropologist Aihwa Ong, swearing loyalty not to country but to capital and cash. They are the elite Asians of many countries who send their children to the United States or other foreign countries of the west to study and to earn degrees that will guarantee their career advancement in Asia. They buy property in the west, speak English in addition to an Asian language, and live lives in multiple countries, the parents sometimes in one while the children are in another. Not surprisingly, while scholarly movements have been built around Asian American literature or transnational or diasporic studies, there has been less interest in Pacific Rim literature. Scholars of these fields tend to adopt a more critical stance toward capitalism, and look for literature that would be similarly critical. A Pacific Rim literature that simply reflects the capitalist bias of the Pacific Rim itself does not lend itself to such critical appropriation.

Another issue undermining the attractiveness of Pacific Rim as an organizing motif for literary studies is what it generally overlooks – the actual Pacific itself, meaning not just the ocean but also the islands in it and the peoples who live on those islands. To the extent that some of those islands are owned, more or less, by the United States, they are also potentially the concern of Asian American literature. A literary movement exists in the Pacific Islands, seeking to prove what the scholar Epeli Hau'ofa argued for in his influential essay, "Our Sea of Islands," which is that the Pacific is not empty.[19] Even when it is recognized by Europeans, Americans, and Asians to have inhabitants, these people are thought to be residents of small, inconsequential places. Hau'ofa argues for an epistemology of the Pacific – what he calls Oceania – that arises from the islands and their inhabitants, who he presents as people with rich, complex histories and cultures. They are not simply local or indigenous, but are the inheritors of navigators and explorers who traveled between islands in their own cosmopolitan adventures. The literature of their descendants fits neither into Pacific Rim nor Asian American literature, even if it is sometimes overshadowed by those literatures. Take, for example, the case of "Hawaiian" literature, which is often not written by native Hawaiians even if it is called such. In the United States, one of the best-known "Hawaiian" writers – not including James Michener – is Lois-Ann Yamanaka, who would be described by the residents of Hawai'i as a "local" rather than a "Hawaiian" because she is of Japanese descent. What Americans call "Hawaiian" literature is often comprised of the writings of settlers, whether they are white or Asian or some other group. But as the native sovereignty movement argues, settlers are settlers, regardless of their racial descent.

Foregrounding the Pacific, rather than the rim around it, is the closest equivalent to the insurgent tradition in Asian American literature. Even examining the literature of Asian settlers, like Yamanaka, throws Asian American literature into question, for Yamanaka and other Asians in Hawai'i do not necessarily see themselves as Asian Americans, but as local. Asian Americans from the continental United States are put in their place as part of an American imperium in relation to locals who occupy an ambivalent place in the American nation. Locals identify with a peripheral state that is a colonized outpost of the United States and a forward military base in the American effort to dominate the Pacific. Locals are both colonized subjects and also participants in settler occupation over indigenous people and the projection of American power throughout Asia and the Pacific. But the writings of indigenous peoples in the Pacific, by their very existence, dispute the idea that the Pacific is simply an empty region whose fate is to be decided by others.

Besides Epeli Hau'ofa, writers such as Albert Wendt and Sia Figiel of Samoa have become notable in Pacific literature and elsewhere. Wendt's *Leaves of the Banyan Tree* (1979) examines three generations of West Samoans grappling with family drama and the impact of being colonized by New Zealand, while Figiel's *Where We Once Belonged* (1996) looks closely at the life of a young girl in her village as she struggles with coming of age. These novels insist on the importance of indigenous life as something not to be passed over, either figuratively or literally in a passenger jet. Like Asian American literature, Pacific literature is "minor" literature. While Asian

Americans are a minority in the United States, Pacific Islanders – a majority in their own lands – are minor on a global scale. But being minor does not mean being inconsequential, as Hau'ofa insists. Being minor instead means being able to critique – even feeling that one is called on to critique – the major, the powerful, the dominant.[20]

Can Pacific Rim literature carry out such a task, or is it consigned to supporting, implicitly or explicitly, the capitalist and militarist energies of the nations bordering the Pacific? The answer lies with the writers who might call themselves Pacific Rim writers, and the activists and critics who would read their work or mobilize movements and identifications along the Pacific Rim. Pacific Rim literature allows those writers who do not fit easily into any national or racial classification to find another kind of home with like-minded anomalies. What would emerge as ways of classifying writers, instead of nation, race, or region, would be thematic, experiential, linguistic, or historical issues.

Take war as one example of how to reorganize literature around theme, experience, and history. The history of the Pacific Rim and its development into its current status as a horizon of economic growth is made possible by war and occupation. In the twentieth century, the United States fought Japan during World War II over control of the Pacific. After the United States defeated Japan, it brought the conquered country into a postwar alliance that allowed the loser to become a rebuilt American ally. Twentieth-century wars and conflicts waged after World War II in the Pacific are a part of this American campaign to establish hegemony in the region, from the Korean War to the Vietnam War, and from the suppression of communism in Indonesia to the similar campaign in the Philippines. Under Pacific Rim literature, writers could be taken out of their national traditions or racial groupings and be put into alliance and conversation with each other around this theme of war. Authors with seemingly no connection to each other could be placed in new relationships. Tim O'Brien (*The Things They Carried*, 1990) writes about the Vietnam War from the American perspective, and could be put in conversation with Vietnamese war writers Bao Ninh (*The Sorrow of War*, 1990) and Duong Thu Huong (*Novel without a Name*, 1996). This is not a surprising configuration, but what if Ha Jin was included for his novel *War Trash* (1990), about Chinese "volunteers" in the Korean War and what happened to them as American prisoners-of-war?

Chinese interests in establishing hegemony have helped drive conflict over the Pacific. China had a hand in the Korean and Vietnam wars, and later supported the Khmer Rouge. The plight of Chinese soldiers in the Korean War could then be read in comparison with the experiences of reluctant or disillusioned American and Vietnamese soldiers in the Vietnam War, all pawns of their respective states. Then there is David Henry Hwang's cross-dressing play *M. Butterfly* (1989). While the primary action of the play is about a cross-dressing Chinese spy and his French diplomat lover, the background action is the Vietnam War and China's interest in it, as well as the Chinese Cultural Revolution. Hwang connects the diplomat's belief that he understands Orientals because he has a Chinese lover to the western belief that Asia will behave like a dominated woman. Instead of only reading the play as an Asian American work, it could also be read as a comic drama that situates interracial gender politics against international power politics.

The connections between different authors who write about war in the Pacific and its corollaries of power, violence, and abuse are manifold. This list could stretch to Yusef Komunyaaka (*Dien Cai Dau,* 1988), Ahn Junghyo (*White Badge,* 1989), Suk-young Kim (*Shadow of Arms,* 1994), Le Ly Hayslip (*When Heaven and Earth Changed Places,* 1989), Maxine Hong Kingston (*The Fifth Book of Peace,* 2003), Vaddey Ratner (*The Shadow of the Banyan,* 2012), Anne Fadiman (*The Spirit Catches You and You Fall Down,* 1997), and many more. These authors talk about black American soldiers, Korean soldiers and contractors, and Vietnamese peasants in the Vietnam War, as well as the consequences of the war with the antiwar and peace movements in the United States, the Khmer Rouge genocide in Cambodia, and the struggles of Hmong refugees in California. Jessica Hagedorn's *Dogeaters* (1990), set in a martial law Philippines supported by an America eager for a staging base in the Pacific that could help with the Vietnam War, could also be included.

These events from the 1960s to the 1990s occur as the corporate and governmental imagination of the Pacific Rim is taking shape, and connect the events of one seemingly isolated war to several countries and populations. This list of authors and connections is far from exhaustive, but they gesture at how a Pacific Rim literature oriented around war and its effects produces a very different constellation, or web, of writers, events, and populations than what might be found under Asian American literature. While Pacific Rim literature may not have the same constituency of readers that Asian American literature has, the potential for critics and writers to self-consciously fashion such a literature exists. Pacific Rim literature does not displace or replace Asian American literature, but exists as a supplement, a complement, a partner in dialogue and contrast. The two literatures mutually show the limitations of the other.

Asian American literature fulfills a needed political and cultural function within the borders of the United States, articulating the cultures of an extremely diverse racial minority. The literature is the outcome of decades of political struggle and organizing, and is important not only because it speaks about the population it is named after. Asian American literature also plays a role in the wider fight for greater justice and equality for all American populations. And it has earned an audience, both from within and outside Asian America. But its once radical political spirit has been domesticated to some extent, blunted by its own success and that of some Asian American populations. It also finds itself on territory that is increasingly defined by not only national consciousness but also transnational sensibility, one where being Asian American – with its implicit investment in an American national identity – may seem too local or parochial.

The concerns that have motivated Asian Americans around race, economy, war, inequality, and injustice seem now to be difficult to separate from global contexts. Here a Pacific Rim framework encourages Asian Americans to make common cause with others outside national borders, although that common cause might be to advance capitalism as much as to contest it. A Pacific Rim framework also allows Asian American literature to signify differently, and to allow Asian American writers to attempt an escape from the ethnic ghetto that most minority writers fear. The typical dilemma for minority writers in the American context is to feel that they are offered a choice between identifying as a minority or siding with whiteness. But rather than seeing this as their only choice, or believing that their work is only about Asian Americans, Asian American writers can find a larger horizon on the Pacific Rim. This horizon is already one that states, corporations, and militaries are seeking to control. Contesting this control is one important reason for Asian American writers – at least those who are committed to the widest possible definition of justice – to see themselves as part of a Pacific Rim.

NOTES

1 In *China Men*, one of the Chinese immigrants is described as "coming to claim the Gold Mountain, his own country" (52). Contextually, the Gold Mountain refers to America. See Peter Grier's interview with Maxine Hong Kingston, "Chinese Roots in America," in *Christian Science Monitor*, 23 September 1980, pp. 14–16.
2 Min Hyoung Song, *The Children of 1965: On Writing, and Not Writing, as an Asian American*. Durham, NC: Duke University Press, 2013.
3 United States. Department of Homeland Security. *Yearbook of Immigration Statistics: 2013*. Washington, DC: DHS, Office of Immigration Statistics, 2014.
4 "Diversity Snapshot." Berkeley Diversity. Fall 2013. <http://diversity.berkeley .edu/sites/default/files/Diversity-Snapshot-web-FINAL.pdf>. Accessed 1 February 2016.
5 "Quick Facts about UCLA." UCLA Undergraduate Admission, Fall 2014. <www .admissions.ucla.edu/campusprofile.htm>. Accessed 1 February 2016.

6   "Harvard Admitted Students Profile." Harvard College Admissions and Financial Aid, 2015. <https://college.harvard.edu/admissions/admissions-statistics>. Accessed 1 February 2016.

7   "Yale Facts and Statistics." Office of Institutional Research, 2015. <http://oir.yale .edu/sites/default/files/factsheet_2014-15_0.pdf>. Accessed 1 February 2016.

8   "Admission Statistics." Princeton University Undergraduate Admission, 2015. <https://admission.princeton.edu/applyingforadmission/admission-statistics>. Accessed 1 February 2016.

9   "The Asian Population: 2010." United States Census Bureau, 2011. <www.census .gov/prod/cen2010/briefs/c2010br-11.pdf>. Accessed 1 February 2016.

10   See Arif Dirlik, ed., *What Is in a Rim? Critical Perspectives on the Pacific Region Idea* (New York: Rowman & Littlefield, 1998), an invaluable collection of essays that historicize the meaning of the Pacific Rim.

11   Maxine Hong Kingston, *The Woman Warrior: Memoirs of a Girlhood Among Ghosts* (New York: Knopf, 1976), 3.

12   Karen Tei Yamashita, *Circle K Cycles* (Minneapolis, MN: Coffee House Press, 2001), 28.

13   Ibid., 30.

14   Ibid., 264.

15   See the essays in *The Trans-Pacific Partnership: A Quest for a Twenty-first-Century Trade Agreement*, Deborah K. Elms, C. L. Lim, and Patrick Low, eds. (New York: Cambridge University Press, 2012).

16   For an overview of those terms, culminating in the transpacific, see *Transpacific Studies: Framing an Emerging Field*, Janet Hoskins and Viet Thanh Nguyen, eds. (Honolulu: University of Hawai'i Press, 2014).

17   I elaborate on this point in *Race and Resistance: Literature and Politics in Asian America* (New York: Oxford University Press, 2002).

18   Paul Gilroy, *Postcolonial Melancholia* (New York: Columbia University Press, 2006), 67.

19   Epeli Hau'ofa, "Our Sea of Islands," *The Contemporary Pacific* 6.1 (1994): 147–61.

20   For more on the theory of minor literature, see Gilles Deleuze and Félix Guattari, "What Is a Minor Literature?" *Mississippi Review* 11.3 (1983): 13–33.

12

MARÍA JOSEFINA SALDAÑA-PORTILLO

Hemispheric Literature

Are We There Yet

It seems as though US scholars of literature and culture have been asking themselves this question, *Have we arrived at the moment of a hemispheric literature?*, in essay after essay since at least Janice Radway's 1998 Presidential Address to the American Studies Association (ASA). In it Radway challenged the ASA to shift its privileged focus on US exceptionalism toward an "Inter-American" study, one that would dislodge US culture and history from the center of the field and finally put it in conversation with the culture and history of other nations of the continent. Carolyn Porter, Amy Kaplan, and José Saldívar asked earlier versions of the same question, challenging scholars to move the field beyond its narrow nationalist boundaries.[1]

Perhaps the question has lingered since Herbert E. Bolton's 1932 Presidential Address to the American Historical Association (AHA), where he pressed for a broader American history to challenge a "nation of chauvinists," presenting a sweeping yet detailed account of the continent's shared "long colonial and international background" upon which "the subsequent development of the Western Hemisphere was founded."[2]

Then again, perhaps we must trace the question back to José Martí's infamous 1891 essay "Our America," too often interpreted as a summoning into being of the object its title names. In this romantic, richly metaphoric manifesto, Martí makes many exhortations and issues many imperatives to the citizenry of "our America," urging the Criollo elite of fledgling Latin America republics to cast off the effeminate shackles of Eurocentrism, to forgo racial animosity and make "common cause" with "the oppressed" of their nations (Indians, Africans, peasants), to embrace the robust, masculine character and culture of "*nuestra América mestiza*" (89).[3] Currently, however, the essay is perhaps most celebrated for Martí's admonishment of the "conceited villager" whose own arrogant provincialism and narrow patriotism blinds him to a larger identity of "our America," an admonishment that resonates with scholars calling for a hemispheric turn in literary studies at the end of the twentieth century and beginning of the twenty-first. Rehearsing the common democratic history of independence movements across the American continent as the essence of what unites these republics against the monarchical tyranny of colonial Europe, Martí's essay also prefigured Bolton's address (84).

Nevertheless, Martí's invocation of "our America" is neither naïve nor utopian. Rather, he invoked this common history and broader unity so that "our [Latin] America" might rally to protect itself against its expansionist neighbor to the north. And so Martí was summoning into being a common America that had yet to be, a future conditional: a democratic, antiracist, thoroughly authentic unity that *will have been* free once Cuba and Puerto Rico were free, once the Latin American elite cast off their fascination with all things foreign, and most critically, once the United States "freed" itself from its own "madness and ambition" (93). Martí's hemispheric America is an aspirational one, contingent on Latin American political elites embracing the continent's cultural specificity, its mixed cultural heritage, and producing new decolonized knowledges thereof; on these elites forgoing their own racial and class privilege to share political power with the subaltern classes.[4] Most importantly, the United States would also have to forgo the power accrued from its military superiority and the ideology of racial superiority. Throughout the essay, Martí advocates for a genuine hemispheric knowledge production, yet this remains a quest, a proposition, a challenge. "Our America" is a horizon of possibility that is penned in by the realities of power; a possible outcome of history, but one that must be struggled over on several fronts. Indeed, it is a hemispheric America that may well never come to pass.

In the ever-receding origins of this quest for a hemispheric America, we witness an arrival deferred. And a caution, for in this ongoing quest we also spot a teleological structure of desire. Bolton, after all, issues his call for an American historiography in the aftermath of the unifying "Great War" (World War I). The willingness of Canada, the United States, and eight out of twenty Latin American countries to join the Allied Forces revealed for Bolton the "essential unity of the Western Hemisphere." American nations performed their union through this joint effort, and compelled his plea for a common history to be written. Having moved beyond their narrow nationalist concerns for the sake of a global good, in other words, American republics demonstrated their joint destiny, one that could then be cast back, retroactively, as a joint past. Recognizing a teleological impulse behind the call for a hemispheric future does not refute the entangled histories of empires and nations on the American continent, but it does enable us to evaluate the critical investments in the move toward a hemispheric literature more clearly.

Hemispheric Literature as a Moment in Time

Indeed, the most recent calls for a hemispheric literature are cast in just such teleological terms. The narrative goes something like this. The 1989 fall of the Berlin Wall and the end of the Cold War brought an end to the ideological struggle that had so bitterly divided the American continent. For more than forty years the United States had funded right-wing dictatorships and counterinsurgency movements throughout Latin America, with deadly consequences for its population, in the effort to prevent communism from spreading to the United States' "backyard." Indeed, hemispheric initiatives during the Cold War period, like the Alliance for Progress and the US Army School of the Americas, were US-led impositions to counteract *any* revolutionary efforts that championed economic equality or political independence. Thus, for the Latin American and Caribbean citizenries that suffered the bloody military coups, the scores of disappearances and assassinations, and the repeated suppression of democratic expression at the ballot box as a consequence of these initiatives, the term "hemispheric" is toxically contaminated and perceived as a threat to national sovereignty. Nonetheless, for the proponents of hemispheric studies, the end of the Cold War brought with it the possibility of resignifying the term, and making of hemispheric studies precisely the site for the critique of this imperial history. Moreover, while the United States appeared to have come out of the Cold War as the sole remaining world superpower, globalization quickly put an end to this premature triumphalism. Globalization of culture, neoliberal free trade, and worldwide migration seemed to put the final nail in the coffin of the nation-state. As a consequence of this demise, the hemisphere emerged as an important new unit of analysis for American Studies.

The turn to hemispheric literature, then, is something that must come after the nation, as the unit of analysis that can only properly fulfill its weighty expectations in its aftermath. For an anti-imperialist scholar like Donald Pease, hemispheric literature is a natural outcome of the postnational and postcolonial scholarly movements that coincided with (and to a large degree brought about) the decline of the nation.[5] Hemispheric literary and cultural studies are the outcome of the "post" condition in which we live.[6] The nationalist mythology of United States as exceptionally democratic, assimilationist, egalitarian, and fair-minded succumbed to prescient critique lodged from both inside and outside its borders. Fields like ethnic studies, African American/diaspora studies, early American studies, and migration studies dislodged these myths by clarifying the basis of the US nation as that of genocide, indigenous dispossession, racial slavery, class exploitation, imperialist expansion, and heteronormativity (269, 272).

These fields not only illuminate the undemocratic relations of power within the nation but also demonstrate the enduring transnational cultural affinities of US populations who have either refused assimilation or been denied its possibility (274).

As the mythologies of US exceptionalism crumbled from within, postcolonial scholarship took aim from without, critiquing the nation-state as an ideological construct of a Eurocentric capitalist modernity, one that was deeply indebted to and entangled with the rise of colonialism and modern racism.[7] Far from the natural outgrowth of continuous cultural tradition and contiguous belonging, nation-states were no more than the colonial imposition of arbitrary boundaries, even within Europe and the Americas, where nation-states had presumably evolved organically. As if this critique were not enough to bury the nation-state, the rise of globalization reinforced the artificiality of the national form and its limited historical duration, further ushering in the need for a new unit of analysis.

Earl E. Fitz formulated the hemispheric-studies-by-globalization narrative in his lead article for the 2004 the inaugural volume of the *Vanderbilt e-Journal of Luso-Hispanic Studies*:

> Interest in Inter-American relations suddenly looms larger and more urgent than it ever has before. Concerned with a wide range of issues and agencies, such as NAFTA [North American Free Trade Agreement], popular music, literature, and law, the Americas have become, in the early years of the twenty-first century, a deeply interconnected site of tremendous energy and potential. And of conflict. (13)[8]

Scholarly assessments of hemispheric studies, such as Fitz's, be they literary, cultural, or historical, repeatedly express this urgency of the present.[9] The neoliberal assault on national sovereignty, the time-space compression of global technological advances, the viral dispersal of would-be local cultural expression, the massive displacement of populations across national border as a consequence of these processes: all require a new unit of spatial analysis, one no longer tied to the now static form of the nation-state. For Claire F. Fox as well, "the new spatial lexicon of hubs, borders, Americas and hemispheres retains a familiar spatial progression, even as it displays a preference for the terms that connote transit, commerce, and dynamism."[10] Fox questions the ability of a new generation of "hemispheric" scholars to perform a truly *hemispheric* analysis, given the rigor such a task would entail, and questions whether these scholars are even genuinely interested in this level of analysis. Nevertheless, what remains unquestioned in her assessment of the state of the field is the dynamism of this scalar progression, as well as the familiarity of this progression itself. Bigger, faster, better: hemispheric literature emerged as the vigorous new site of enunciation for now global cultural formations in the Americas, an enunciation that was capable of expressing all that exceeded or internally contradicted the moribund nation-state and particularly the United States with its mythological and provincial "national" culture.

I linger over this "familiar scalar progression" toward hemispheric studies because its teleological expression necessarily contains and remains tied to that which it seeks to surpass. This scholarly account of the rise of hemispheric studies is so tied to a progressive ideology (pun intended) that it reiterates the nation at every turn. Thus, for example, hemispheric literary studies often takes the form of the comparison of genre, of aesthetic style, or of narrative content between US literature and that of another American nation in order to discern the ties that bind across national divides. Or hemispheric literature – literature whose plot and characters may traverse the geography of the United States and that of one or more other American nations – is celebrated for making evident the transnational connections across the hemisphere in counter-distinction to the artificially bounded literary expression of US mythologies. Even hemispheric studies of colonial literatures that predate the rise of American nation-states are interested in the comparative study of northern (British) and southern (Spanish, Portuguese, French) colonialism in a way that prefigures the advent of the United States and Latin American, Brazilian, and Caribbean nations.

Let me be clear: I am not contesting the urgency of the present nor its unique historical conjuncture. Indeed, there are multiple urgent presents as a result of the cataclysmic effects of globalization, which include the rise of fascistic neo-nationalisms and religious cosmologies in reaction to it. Nor am I interested in debating whether or not the nation-state is truly in decline, though the news of its death has been greatly exaggerated, to misquote Mark Twain.[11] All of this hemispheric literary scholarship is laudatory, and the best of it quite rigorous. This is especially true of the hemispheric literary scholarship of the colonial period, where scholars demonstrate formidable training in multiple languages and in multiple historical archives.[12] Generally, hemispheric literary studies expounds progressive principles as well, intent as the field is on unveiling and unraveling the expansionist history of the United States in the American hemisphere as expressed in the literary record. However, and perhaps as a consequence of this progressive impetus, hemispheric literature, in its very refutation of the nation, continues to usher the nation back into the discussion. More specifically, even as hemispheric literary studies decenter the United States, they recenter it as *the* object of critique. Hemispheric literary and cultural studies are primarily, indeed almost exclusively, concerned with examining the relationality of US literature and culture to that of the rest of the continent.

This interest in the United States is sustained precisely due to the political investment in establishing a "postnationalist" literature and in critiquing empire. However, the effect of this postnationalist, postcolonial hemispheric approach to *American* studies is to leave the project of a hemispheric American studies open to accusations of a new scholarly expansionism, as most eloquently articulated by the Latin American cultural critics Sophia McClennen and Diana Taylor.[13] Hemispheric literary study continues to be expansionist not because US scholars venture beyond the borders of the United States, but because it continues to put the literary and cultural production of Latin America, Brazil and the Caribbean, at the service of the study of the United States. This is the structural dilemma at the heart of hemispheric literary and cultural studies, a dilemma that should not be avoided or elided, but addressed directly. And so the question remains: Hemispheric literature – are we there yet?

Hemispheric Literature from Below

On the one hand, "hemispheric" is infused with the sense of that which comes after the nation, freeing the literary from the confines of the nation-state. On the other, the term retains its sense of US paternalism toward Latin America, functioning metonymically as the United States' un-ironic assumption of the mantle of instructing the Latin America in the workings of democracy and freedom. Hemispheric literary studies reiterates this tutelary role, as an intellectual endeavor initiated in the core (American [US] Studies) that spreads outward to the peripheries (Latin American and Caribbean studies), bringing with it the latest, most dynamic models for knowledge production. This is the inherent contradiction within hemispheric studies, due to the freighted history of the term and the teleological structure of its paradigm. There is no way around this problem except to recognize it, and to insist that "hemispheric" is not a descriptive term, not an adjective, not a becoming, but a doing. Hemispheric studies does something in the world, it worlds it as a knowledge structure steeped in power.[14] If hemispheric literature is acknowledged as doing something in the world, rather than simply being something in the world, we can begin to ask a different set of questions. How might every iteration of hemispheric literature be a performative, one that enacts relations of power, but also attempts to change them? Deeply related to this question, we may ask: Who still needs the nation-state and why? What can a hemispheric literary study do for those populations? What can it do for Latin America? The question that should preoccupy us is not what hemispheric literature is – how we might define it – but who hemispheric literature is for?

The question of who is hemispheric literature *for* moves us toward an acknowledged ethical stance in knowledge production. Indeed, several scholars have already called for an *ethics* of hemispheric studies, one I suggest that is best expressed as a hemispheric studies from below.[15] For the remainder of this essay I consider some examples of insurrectional hemispheric literature from below that fruitfully trouble both the temporality and the geography we associate with the American hemisphere.

Bartolomé de Las Casas's *In Defense of the Indians* ([*Defense*] circa 1552) is the written account of his *apologia* before the *Junta de Valladolid* in 1550.[16] The Junta was a specially appointed panel of fourteen learned jurists convened by the Holy Roman Emperor Carlos V to adjudicate the validity of war and *encomienda* as modes of conquest.[17] They were to come to a decision after hearing arguments for both sides: first from Juan Ginés de Sepúlveda, renowned Dominican Renaissance scholar and royal historian, in favor of the practices and on behalf of the conquistadors who benefited from them; and then from Las Casas, Dominican Bishop of Chiapa, against these practices and in defense of the indigenous peoples who suffered their imposition.[18] The Indians of Oaxaca and Chiapa had granted Las Casas the legal authority to represent them before the Council of the Indies, of which the Junta was an extension, while the Indians of Peru authorized Las Casas to offer Spanish monarch, King Philip II, as much money as necessary to end the encomienda. Ginés de Sepúlveda summarized his apologia in two hours before the Junta, but Las Casas famously read his entire *apologia* over the course of five days.

Las Casas's refuted Ginés's Aristotelian arguments on the "natural slavery" of the indigenous peoples point by point, but he also challenged accepted Christian doctrine, refuting biblically based arguments for just war with his own interpretation of various Christian philosophers. Moreover, Las Casas refuted John Major's arguments for the enslavement of American Indians across the continent by recourse to Aquinas, but also by showing Major's ignorance of the indigenous customs he so blithely condemned. Las Casas cited exemplary indigenous practices, gleaned from his first-hand experience in the Caribbean, New Spain, and Central America, as evidence of Ginés's (and Major's) repeated misrepresentation of indigenous peoples. As just one example, he praised their superior urbanization to Europe's, as indigenous peoples in the New World "lived in populous cities in which they wisely administered the affairs of both peace and war justly and equitably, truly governed by the laws that at very many points surpass ours, and could have won the admiration of the sages of Athens" (42–43). However, it is not simply Las Casas descriptive passages of admirable indigenous life ways in the New World that makes *Defense* an example of hemispheric literature from below. After all, only sixty years after initial contact, there were several published descriptions of indigenous peoples in Spanish, Portuguese, and English, some critical, some laudatory. Rather, *Defense* is hemispheric literature from below because Las Casas was attempting to transform European theories of human nature and international law on the basis of his encounter with indigenous peoples.

The most extraordinary chapters of *Defense* are those in which he argued that human sacrifice and cannibalism, where practiced, were not just cause for war against Indians, nor reason for their enslavement (chapters 31–37). Using Aristotle, Las Casas argued that human sacrifice and cannibalism, though sins against God, were nevertheless defensible beliefs because these were in line with a religious cosmology shared by the majority of indigenous nations, including their "kings and great lords:"[19]

> Also, since they rejoice in holding that blasphemous notion that in worshiping their idols they worship the true God, or that these are God, and despite the supposition that they have an erroneous conscience, even if the true [Christian] God is being preached to them by better and more credible as well as more convincing arguments, together with the good example of Christians, they [the Indians] are bound, without doubt, to defend the worship of their gods and their religion by going forth with their armies against all who attempt to take those things from them or injure them or prevent their sacrifices. (244)

Las Casas was not defending these practices and hoped to eradicate them through persuasion, through "better … more credible" arguments. However, these practices were in accord with beliefs held by the majority of Indians, and thereby defensible according to Aristotle. Indians had the right to defend these beliefs against Christians who challenged them in war. Because the costs to life wrought by these wars would be greater than those caused by the sacrifices themselves, Las Casas argued Spaniards should not persecute wars against the Indians in defense of the innocents killed in sacrifice. What was momentous in Las Casas's argument, however, and what makes his book hemispheric literature from below, was his defense of indigenous *reason*. Indigenous peoples, no matter how extreme their practices, were not outside the bounds of human reason, but to the contrary, proved fully equal to Europeans in this capacity. They reasonably held misguided beliefs, and according to natural and Christian law, these reasonably held beliefs could only be dislodged through Christian persuasion, which indigenous peoples were available for, precisely because of their capacity for reason. *In Defense of the Indians* was not just defending indigenous peoples against the cruel practices and unjust incursions of Spanish conquistadores. Rather, Las Casas was defending indigenous reason against Eurocentric reason.

Las Casas was practicing Said's insurrectionary traveling theory, revising European philosophy (by way of Aristotle, Aquinas, Agustin) to write the American continent into the script in an agentful way, disrupting the Enlightenment at its very origin on the basis of the American indigenous experience in order to free indigenous peoples from the tyranny of conquest.[20] His articulation of human reason and rights is not mimetic of European philosophy, but in fact co-constitutive of it. Moreover, his arguments are not his singular contemplative achievement, but rather document the full impact of indigenous humanity on the Catholic Enlightenment. Las Casas's *Defense* is not merely a defense of the Indians of New Spain and of Peru, or of those under the empire of Spain; his is a defense of *all* Indians in the American hemisphere, as the subtitle of his book makes clear: *The Defense of the Most Reverend Lord, Don Fray Bartolomé de Las Casas, of the Order of Preachers, Late Bishop of Chiapa, Against the Persecutors and Slanderers of the Peoples of the New World Discovered Across the Seas.* All persecutors, all slanderers, all indigenous peoples.

Defense stretches the temporal and geographic bounds of hemispheric literature, emerging as it does out of a continental experience that does not exist as yet, as the majority of the continent at this time is still free of European invasion. *Defense* is not prescient, though it is often interpreted as such. Rather, it emerges out of real historical conditions, out of the European encounter with radically different human life ways that historiography has misnamed the "discovery." Thus, this continent can only take shape as a "hemisphere" before and in distinction to Europe, in triangulated relationship to Spain, to Roman law, to colonial mission. In other words, the American content requires triangulation with Europe to emerge *as a hemisphere*, as a unity. It emerges in a historical condition of law and might, as it continues to exist today.

When hemispheric literature is read in this way, from below, it does not even need to emerge out of comparison in order to be hemispheric in its scope. Indeed, reading hemispheric literature from this perspective allows us to revisit texts that have been construed as early expressions of national consciousness. Jesuit cleric and scholar Francisco Clavijero's *Historia Antigua de México*,[21] originally published in 1780 and 1781 as two volumes, is characterized as an early expression of Mexican nationalism in literary form.[22] *Historia* does provide a written and visual account of the flora and fauna of New Spain, as well as "an exhaustive account of its Amerindian past leading up to the Spanish conquest" (Ramos, 5). While Clavijero helped "establish an emerging Spanish American geographic imaginary that increasingly associates cultural autonomy and territorial sovereignty as inextricably linked aims," colonial Latin Americanist scholar Luis Ramos demonstrates that Clavijero's larger project is not narrowly geographic or nationalist, but "offers a sustained critique of influential theories about the physical and moral degeneracy of the New World as expressed in the emerging [European] field of natural history" (1, 4). In this vein, Clavijero's *Historia* was an insurrectionary text seeking to counteract racist Enlightenment climate theory about the degenerate character of the American Indians. Thus, he extolls the virtues of New Spain's climate, flora, fauna, but also of its original peoples as an advocate, seeking to transform the place of the Americas in Enlightenment humanism. Clavijero's approach is less to elevate the Indian as a human specimen, Ramos explains, then to celebrate their averageness. In his line drawings of indigenous peoples, Clavijero references Greco-Roman antiquity to represent them as ideal forms, precisely in their ordinariness (Ramos, 11). Accordingly, indigenous peoples, like Europeans, have ordinary souls:

> By describing the souls of native Mexicans as similar to those of all other children of Adam, Clavijero situates them in a greater human family bound by a shared ancestral origin, thus affirming their shared humanity as equally rational beings ... By characterizing European doubts over the intelligence of Mexican natives as an erroneous use of reason, he reveals the limits and contradictions of Enlightenment discourse. Moreover, by shifting the terms of his defense from one of *Megicanos* to one of *Americanos* more generally, Clavijero extends his critique of European naturalist theory *to all New World inhabitants more generally*.[23]

While New Spain and its descriptive detail may have provided Clavijero the geographic occasion for his *Historia Antigua de México*, it was hemispheric in its ambition. Deciding whether or not Clavijero's *Historia* was a precursor of Mexican independence or its literary expression becomes less important than analyzing whom this literature was written for and about.

It is significant that Clavijero wrote his *Historia* while in exile in Italy. Born and raised in New Spain, Clavijero was one of the hundreds of Jesuits expelled from the Americas by order of the Spanish Crown (Carlos III) in 1767. Thus, his *Historia* once again provided a necessarily refracted vision of the hemisphere, one that must initially emerge from the distance of Europe, in comparison with the alien world he found *there*, and consequently entailed by his exilic longing. Las Casas and Clavijero were colonial elites, both belonging to prestigious and wealthy Catholic orders, highly educated in European philosophy and letters, as their literary references clearly show. Nevertheless, they offer us an American hemispheric literature from below in terms of whom they were writing for. This perspective allows literary critics to reclaim indigenous authors of the period as well – like Inca Garcilaso de la Vega and Felipe Guamán Poma de Ayala (elites in their own right) – as hemispheric literature from below. Why not reconsider their extensive historical writings not only as proto-anthropological accounts of their folkloric Inca past and current culture, as chronicles of the destructive consequences of Spanish conquest on their indigenous communities, or as precursors to Peruvian national literature and consciousness, but as also providing a broader hemispheric critique of and counter-discourse to European modernity, in defense of indigenous rationality across the Americas?[24] After all, Garcilaso's first published work in 1605 was *La Florida del Inca*, an account of Hernando de Soto's expedition through Florida.[25] This reconsideration of colonial literature by (and about) indigenous peoples has the added benefit of placing indigenous populations at the heart of the performance of hemispheric literary studies, where they should be, providing one vital answer to the question, hemispheric literature for whom?

Hemispheric Literature for Today

I would like to close by suggesting *narco* culture, or *narcocultura* as it is known in Spanish, as a rich and important avenue of scholarship for hemispheric literary and cultural studies from below. The very name we have attached to this international phenomenon is geographically deceptive and a function of power. The use of word "narco" in this context comes from the Spanish term *narco traficante*, or drug trafficker, suggesting that narco culture is the sole product of Latin America. Linguistically, the crossover use of the term attempts to contain drug trafficking to Latin America as well, reinscribing it as the source of the problem of drug use. However, drug culture and our fascination with it, like the illegal narcotics the term ultimately references, respects neither national nor linguistic boundaries. This is affirmed by the outsized popularity of such US television shows as *Weeds, The Wire, Breaking Bad,* and *The Bridge*, and by such box-office hits as Robert Rodriguez's *El Machete,* Oliver Stone's *Savages,* or Steven Soderbergh's critically acclaimed *Traffic.* Importantly, the action in these televisions shows and movies inevitably crisscrosses the physical border of the United States and Latin American (usually, though not exclusively, the US-Mexico border) to show the inextricably conjoined nature of the illegal drug trade, its culture, and its consequences across the continent.

More often than not, however, the US characters in these shows and films are portrayed as the victims of Latin American organized crime, even when they themselves may be drug dealers or users. The plot will hinge on the need to rescue the US citizen from the clutches of heinous torturers and rapists, replicating the racial script that the United States must protect its citizens from bestial foreigners from the South, rescuing them from their own worst impulses. Nevertheless, these shows and films cross the border in another way as well, as they are avidly consumed by Latin American audiences, who access them through the thriving market in pirated DVDs. The traffic in *narcocultura* runs in both directions, however, as Latin American soap operas like *La Reina del Sur* (Mexico) and *Sin Tetas No Hay Paraíso* (Colombia) enjoy huge ratings in the United States, while *narcocorridos* (Mexican ballads composed for and about Latin American drug bosses) are favorites in dance halls across the country as well. These telenovelas often transgress and replicate gender roles at once, as women are represented as capable of becoming drug bosses in their own right, but never at the cost of their hyper-femininity or sexuality, even while jumping across building tops, shooting their enemies, or shooting up.

Drug culture, or the cultural apparatus that arises around the production, consumption, and distribution of intoxicants, is ancient, and the ritual and sacred use of drugs has deep roots across indigenous American, as it does globally.[26] Nevertheless, the recent rise of the narco-novel, corrido, *telenovela* and television show, film, and religious practice signals a significant transformation of the hemispheric drug trade since the passage of NAFTA. NAFTA and the hemispheric drug trade are symbiotic, with the success of one directly linked to the success of the other. NAFTA has quadrupled the flow of goods, services, and foreign investment across the borders of Canada, the United States, and Mexico, which has in turn facilitated the increased smuggling of drugs and of laundering of money across the continent, as the billions of dollars in profits produced by this "illegal" industry are reinvested in "legal" modes of production that augment the record profits of transnational corporations. Indeed, it would be difficult to separate clean global capital from the capital generated by this hemispheric drug trade.

It is not the novelty of *narco* culture that should draw our critical attention to it, however, but the transformations to the social relations of production across the hemisphere that it documents and helps us elucidate as critics, because these changes in the social relations of production have devastating consequences on subaltern populations across the Americas. Narco culture records the violent conditions of everyday life to which much of the population in the Americas is subjected as a consequence of the freest trade of all, the drug trade. These violent conditions are not the outward expression of an inner, incomprehensible Latin American racial character, as it is most often represented in the media, in policy statements, and by politicians. Rather, the spread of drug violence is historically specific, and it is relatively easy to trace its recent development. It is the direct result of neoliberal restructuring in agriculture and industry across the continent, of the US military's eradication and interdiction policies that are part of its war on drugs in Latin America (Plan Colombia, Plan Merida), of Latin American governments willingness to go along with these economic and military policies, of the US deportation policy beginning in 1996 that has turned Central America into a bastion of drug gang activity, and of the avid consumer demand for marijuana, cocaine, and heroin in the United States, Canada, and Europe.[27]

Hundreds of thousands of people have died at the hands of drug cartels in the last twenty years, but also as a consequence of the US military and police aid to Latin America, because just as it is impossible to differentiate clean capital from dirty money, it is difficult to disentangle the deaths caused by the intra-cartel wars from those executed by military and police trained and aided by the United States in its war on drugs. What is quite clear, however, is that the vast majority of those killed in the war on drugs are innocent civilians – farmers, students, organizers, workers, young, old, male and female – and not the foot soldiers of the cartels. Moreover, it is US citizens' consumption of drugs that becomes the alibi for this perpetual war against the citizenry of Latin America. A hemispheric study from below of narco literature and culture would not only trace the continental networks of drug production, distribution, and consumption, but also demonstrate the complicity of the entire continent in these murders. Such an approach would also place the burgeoning field of US prison studies in perspective, in an effort to once again decenter the ever-present center of American studies. Incarcerated black and brown bodies in the United States would no longer be the exceptional victims of US state violence, but just one part of much larger hemispheric story of the trillion-dollar industry that is the war on drugs. These daily murders in Latin America, by the hand of cartels or of the corrupted Latin American military and police who receive US aid and training, are a *hemispheric* event documented in narco culture, an urgency of the present that demands the critical attention of a hemispheric studies from below.

NOTES

1 Janice Radway, "What's in a Name? Presidential Address to the American Studies Association, 20 November 1998," *American Quarterly* 51.1 (1999): 1–32; Carolyn Porter, "What We Know That We Do Not Know, Remapping American Literary Studies," *American Literary History* 6 (Fall 1994): 467–526; Amy Kaplan, "'Left Alone in America': The Absence of Empire in the Study of America Culture," in *Cultures of United States Imperialism,* Kaplan and Donald Pease, eds. (Durham,

NC: Duke University Press 1993), 3–21; José David Saldívar, *Dialectics of Our America: Genealogy, Cultural Critique, and Literary History* (Durham, NC: Duke University Press, 1991).

2   Herbert Bolton, "The Epic of Greater America." Hosted by the American Historical Association. Web. <www.historians.org/about-aha-and-membership/aha-history-and-archives/presidential-addresses/herbert-e-bolton>.

3   From Martí, *Our America by José Martí: Writings on Latin America and the Struggle for Cuban Independence,* Phillip S. Foner, ed. (New York: Monthly Review Press, 1977), 84–94. In this English translation *nuestra America mestizaje* is translated as "our half-breed America" (89). While this is not necessarily a mistranslation, I use the original Spanish in this instance because of the imperial history and racist connotation of "half-breed," a connotation that the term *mestizaje* does not carry. The gendering of the European and indigenous Americans (which included mestizos, blacks, and indigenous peoples for Martí), is from the original.

4   That we are still waiting for Latin American political elite to rethink their colonially-derived knowledge/power is underscored by the Latin American theories of Anibal Quijano, Walter Mignolo, and Enrique Dussel, who, with their respective theories of the "coloniality of power," of "decoloniality," and of "transmodernity," struggle to deconstruct and dislodge this racial reasoning of colonialism, the Enlightenment, and modernity. See Quijano, "Coloniality of Power, Eurocentrism and Social Classification," and Enrique Dussel "Philosophy of Liberation, The Postmodern Debate and Latin American Studies, both in Mabel Morana, Enrique Dussel and Carlos A. Jauregui, eds, *Coloniality at Large* (Durham, NC: Duke University Press, 2008), 181–224 and 335–49, respectively; and Walter Mignolo, *The Darker Side of Western Modernity: Global Futures, Decolonial Options* (Durham, NC: Duke University Press, 2011).

5   Donald Pease, "Postnational and Postcolonial Reconfigurations of American Studies in the Post Modern Condition," in *Concise Companion to American Studies,* John Carlos Rowe, ed., 267–283 (Malden, MA: Blackwell, 2010). Quotes on 267, 268.

6   See Wallerstein, "The Rise and Future Demise of the World Capitalist System: Concepts for Comparative Analysis," for a useful complication of Pease's Anglocentric understanding of the national-global binary (*Comparative Studies in Society and History* 16.4 [1974]: 387–415).

7   Pease, "Postnational," 269–71.

8   Earl E. Fitz, "Inter-American Studies as an Emerging Field: The Future of a Discipline," *Vanderbilt e-Journal of Luso-Hispanic Studies* 1 (2004): 13–28.

9   See Michael Hames-García, "Which America Is Ours?: Martí's 'Truth' and the Foundations of 'American Literature,' " *Modern Fiction Studies* 49.1 (2003): 19–53; John Muthyala, "Reworlding America: The Globalization of American Studies," *Cultural Critique* 47 (2001): 91–119; and George Lipsitz, *American Studies in a Moment of Danger* (Minneapolis: University of Minnesota Press, 2001).

10   Claire F. Fox, "Commentary: The Transnational Turn and the Hemispheric Return," *American Literary History* 18.3 (Fall 2006): 638–47, 643.

11   As the Brazilian sociologist Renato Ortiz convincingly argued in his 1998 essay "Espacio y Territorialidad," the local is always comprised of and contains the

national and the global, just as the global is always comprised of and contains the national and the local, and the national of both the global and the local. The global needs the national and the local in order to materialize in space, and vice versa, and thus is not looking to displace the national or local, but rather is always in dialectical relation to them (Renato Ortiz, *Otro Territorio: Ensayos sobre el mundo contemporáneo* [Bogota: Convenio Andrés Bello, 1998], 21–42). See Mark Twain, *New York Journal*, June 6, 1897.

12 Anna Brickhouse, *Transamerican Literary Relations and the Nineteenth Century Public Sphere* (Cambridge: Cambridge University Press, 2004); Jonathan Goldberg, *Sodometries: Renaissance Texts, Modern Sexualities* (Stanford, CA: Stanford University Press, 1992); Kirsten Silva Gruesz, *Ambassadors of Culture: The Transamerican Origins of Latino Writing* (Princeton, NJ: Princeton University Press, 2002); Matthew Guterl, *American Mediterranean: Southern Slaveholders in the Age of Emancipation* (Cambridge, MA: Harvard University Press, 2013); Amy Kaplan, *The Anarchy of Empire in the Making of U.S. Culture* (Cambridge, MA: Harvard University Press, 2002); David Kazanjian, *The Colonizing Trick: National Culture and Imperial Citizenship in Early America* (Minneapolis: University of Minnesota Press, 2003).

13 Diana Taylor, "Remapping Genre through Performance: From 'American' Studies to 'Hemispheric' Studies," *PMLA* 122.5 (2007): 1416–30; Sophia McClennen, *The Dialectics of Exile: Nation, Time, Language, and Space in Hispanic Literatures.* West Lafayette, IN: Purdue University Press, 2004.

14 Diana Taylor's reflections on why the Hemispheric Institute of Performance and Politics had arrived at this name over others inspires my own reflections. I am similarly proposing a hemispheric studies that at once enunciates its troubled origins and politicized futures.

15 See Juan Flores, "Thinking Diaspora from Below: Lines of Definition" in *The Diaspora Strikes Back: Caribeño Tales of Learning and Turning* (New York: Routledge, 2009), 15–32; Ralph Bauer, "Hemispheric Studies," *PMLA* 124.1 (2009): 234–50; and Rodrigo Lazo, "The Place of Hemispheric American Studies," *American Literature* 86.1 (2014): 171–81.

16 Bartolomé De Las Casas, *In Defense of the Indians,* trans. Stafford Poole (DeKalb: Northern Illinois University Press, 1992).

17 Encomiendas were granted to conquistadores by the Spanish Crown for their service to the empire in conquering the Americas through war. It was a form of indentured servitude that often entailed the resettlement of entire indigenous communities onto the *haciendas* of the conquistadors. Though technically maintaining their freedom and their own lands, indigenous communities were required to work on these haciendas in perpetuity without monetary compensation. The borders of colonial-era Chiapa and contemporary Chiapas do not correspond, as previously what now comprises the state was divided administratively between the inland regions (Chiapa) and the lowland coastal zone, Soconusco. The Indians of Chiapa would have been of varying ethnicities and language groups, but were gathered administratively under the term "Chiapa Indians."

18 For a complete historical analysis, see Lewis Hanke, *All Mankind Is One: A Study of the Disputation between Bartolomé de las Casas and Juan Ginés de Sepúlveda in 1550 on the Intellectual and Religious Capacity of the American*

Indians (Dekalb: Northern Illinois University Press, 1974); Rolena Adorno, *The Polemics of Possession In Spanish American Narrative* (New Haven, CT: Yale University Press, 2007); and Luis N. Rivera, *A Violent Evangelism: The Political and Religious Conquest of the Americas* (Louisville, KY: Westminster/John Knox Press, 1992).

19 As Las Casas was debating an Aristotelian, it was very important to him to refute Ginés by following Aristotelian logic. Thus, this question of majority loomed large for Las Casas as it justified misguided indigenous beliefs: "Even though the Indians cannot be excused in the sight of God for worshiping idols, they can be completely excused in the sight of men, for two reasons. First they are following a 'probable' error, for as the Philosopher [Aristotle] notes, that is said to be probable which is approved by all men, either by the majority of wise men or by those whose wisdom has the greatest following" (Las Casas, *In Defense*, 221–22).

20 For Said's revised version, see Edward Said, "Traveling Theory" in *The World, the Text, and the Critic* (Cambridge, MA: Harvard University Press, 1983), 226–47.

21 Francisco Javier Clavijero, *Historia Antigua de México* (Mexico City: Editorial Purroa, 2003).

22 See David Brading, *The Origins of Mexican Nationalism* (Cambridge: Cambridge University Press, 1985).

23 Luis Ramos, "Geographies of Exile and Enlightenment: Creole Patriotism and Bourbon Imperial Ideology in Franscico Clavijero and Juan Luis Maneiro." Paper presented at the 2015 "Migrations and Diasporas" Conference of the Tepoztlán Institue for Transnational History of the Americas, p. 14 (emphasis added).

24 Inca Garcilaso de la Vega, *Comentarios Reales*. Mercedes Serna, ed. (Madrid: Editorial Castalia, 2000); Felipe Guamán Poma de Ayala, *Nueva crónica y buen gobierno*. John V. Murra, Rolena Adorno and Jorge L. Urioste, eds. (Madrid: *Historia* 16, 1987).

25 Inca Garcilaso de la Vega, *La Florida del Inca*. Sylvia-Lyn Hilton, ed. (Madrid: Fundación Universitaria Española, 1982).

26 See the *Cultural Critique* special issue, "Drugs in Motion: Mind- and Body-Altering Substances in the World's Cultural Economy," Brett Neilson and Mohammed Bamyeh, eds., v. 71 (Winter 2009), for an analysis of drug use and its cultures through time, especially Paul Gootenberg's "Talking about the Flow: Drugs, Borders, and the Discourse of Drug Control" therein (13–46).

27 See Adam Isacson, "The U.S. Military in the War on Drugs," in Coletta A. Youngers and Eileen Rosin, eds., *Drugs and Democracy in Latin America* (London: Lynne Rienner Publishers, 2005), 15–60; Peter Andreas, *Border Games: Policing the U.S.-Mexico Divide* (Ithaca, NY: Cornell University Press, 2000); David R. Mares, *Drug Wars and Coffeehouses: The Political Economy of International Drug Trade* (Washington, DC: CQ Press, 2006).

PART IV

Literature and Geopolitics

13

CRYSTAL PARIKH

Transnational Feminism

Global Sisterhood and Other Women

In her landmark memoir, *Loving in the War Years* (1983), Chicana lesbian feminist Cherríe Moraga includes a poem, "It's the Poverty," in which the speaker's lover expresses a wish to drive down the coast with a typewriter. From her lover's perspective, the romantic journey is meant implicitly to play out as a scene of their sexual freedom, meshed with the physical mobility and freedom of expression that American literature often employs as symbols of one another. But for Moraga, this desire inspires anxiety and ambivalence; her economic insecurity ("I can't afford/a new ribbon") and cultural marginalization as the daughter of a Mexican American mother make such a journey less a proclamation of freedom than a marker of confusion, loss, and betrayal.[1] When her lover accuses her of lacking "imagination," she responds:

> *No.* I lack language.
>
> The language to clarify
> my resistance to the literate.
> Words are a war to me.
> They threaten my family.
>
> To gain the word to describe the loss,
> I risk losing everything.
> I may create a monster,
> the word's length and body
> swelling up colorful and thrilling
> looming over my *mother*, characterized.
> Her voice in the distance
> *unintelligible*   *illiterate.*
>
> These are the monster's words.[2]

Adopting the idiom of war prevalent throughout *Loving in the War Years*, Moraga refuses to take the terms of women's agency that are presented to her at face value. Instead, she worries over the harm to other women, first and foremost her mother, that she might enact. Even trying to describe that loss, "characterizing" it, seems to make the speaker over into a "monster," who risks "losing everything." Does the "unintelligible illiterate" voice belong to her mother, made inaudible by the war of words, or does the voice belong to Moraga herself, made alien to the other woman? In either case, the poem insists that "monster's words" interpose themselves, belying any easy notion of community and communicability between women.

Moraga cleaves to the Chicano family and community that distance her from full national belonging in the United States. But it is also a family and community that abjects her queer femininity. Thus, as she wrestles with the implications for her own commitment to herself and to other women, Moraga's memoir takes the form of dispatches from a war front, because her very being seems to be at stake in its being penned. In this regard, Moraga was one of a number of women of color, including Gloria Anzaldúa, Angela Davis, Maxine Hong Kingston, Toni Morrison, Barbara Smith, Alice Walker, and the Combahee River Collective, to name some of the most best-known writers, who refused to relinquish their commitments to antiracist, anticolonial, and nationalist struggles, even as they steadfastly countered the sexist, misogynist, and homophobic sentiments and norms that often pervaded the latter.[3]

These women-of-color feminists (sometimes called "third wave" feminists) wrote with passion about their simultaneous experience of patriarchal, heteronormative, and white supremacist systems of power and the need for social and cultural analytics that were "intersectional" in order to account for the way in which racial and national identities have always been gendered and sexual constructions, and vice versa. In a diverse array of genres, these women further articulated their own political affiliations with those of women in the global south, seeing themselves in solidarity with Third World or postcolonial feminists elsewhere.[4] While "transnational feminism" came into circulation somewhat later and initially as a critical concept in academic contexts, it had its roots in and shares with such US women-of-color activism a keen focus on the differences between women that subtend the political project of feminism.

This is no small point when one recalls that in the heyday of the US second-wave feminist movement the notion that "sisterhood is global" had come to be something of a commonplace. As Robin Morgan wrote in the Introduction of the 1984 anthology with that title, the ambition for a global feminist movement was inspired by the belief in *"a common condition,* which, despite variations in degree, is experienced by all human beings who are born female," one of patriarchal oppression by "male" political systems of family, government, and other social institutions.[5] A host of other international feminist activists, intellectuals, and organizations share the supposition that a unified and singular feminism is necessary to address the many ills to which women are subject. These schools of feminist thought, whether liberal or radical in character, ironically managed to produce hierarchies between women, namely between those they considered to be enlightened by feminist consciousness and those who suffered ongoing "false consciousness" about the truth of their own lives.[6]

Transnational feminism instead arose as a theoretical challenge rooted in different scholarly and activist experiences to dispute presumptions of a shared state of patriarchal oppression and, indeed, the category of "woman" as itself a readily distinguishable identity or social position across space and time. Because such an approach underscores "the multiplicity of community histories and perspectives, as well as the hybrid culture of *all* communities," it also repudiated those brands of feminist politics meant to unify women as political agents in order to emancipate them from subjugation without addressing the specific histories and social worlds in which individuals are located.[7] Instead, beginning in the late 1980s and 1990s – speaking back to liberal and radical feminisms that, while largely Western in character and orientation, nevertheless nominate themselves as "global" in scope – transnational feminists argued that all women and men are subject to, in the influential terms of Inderpal Grewal and Caren Kaplan, "scattered hegemonies."[8]

Transnational scholars and critics of gender and sexuality began to "develop a multinational and multilocational approach" that has the effect of pluralizing feminist politics.[9] Although, as Ella Shohat writes, such political projects "share the critique of masculinist ideologies and the desire to undo patriarchal power regimes," transnational feminist approaches multiply the subjects and sites from which such critique and desires issue forth.[10] Transnational feminist thought and politics is part and parcel of globalization, the types of travel and exchange that increasingly inform all aspects of human life, including, but not limited to, people, capital, culture, identities, commodities, desire, and governance. But many of the discourses surrounding globalization can have a flattening effect, as if all encounters between the local and the global, or the West and its others, have resulted in identical outcomes, not unlike the homogenizing character that a "global sisterhood" takes on. Thus, well into the twenty-first century, media discourses and cultural texts (such as Eve Ensler's *The Vagina Monologues* or Nicholas D. Kristof and Sheryl WeDunn's *Half the Sky*, to name two prominent instances) continue to reproduce a map of the world divided between women who are represented as wholly oppressed and feminists who enjoy the privileges of emancipation. Indeed, such discourses of globalization assume that binaries such as the local/global, West/non-West, and tradition/ progress precede the modern (or postmodern) moment of contact. They accordingly posit the local, the non-West, and the traditional as isolated and static entities, putting under erasure much longer and varied histories of contact, crossings, and exchange that have constituted the "modern" world as such.[11] The "transnational" can instead, as Grewal and Kaplan write in a later essay, bring into relief "the asymmetries of the globalization process," without maintaining an atavistic perception of non-Western societies.[12]

Transnational feminist analyses hence focus on heterogeneous structures of power that constitute "the conditions of possibility" for newly emergent and diversely gendered subjects.[13] Moreover, they presume these subjects to be neither simply oppressed victims nor heroic agents of resistance, but as complexly embedded in and expressive of the histories and modes of knowledge that such contact and exchange involve. These methodologies emphasize grassroots struggles, subaltern knowledge production, and collaborative methods of research, even as these all take place within a globalized frame. Transnational feminist studies has been especially generative for exploring political solidarity movements, examining the political circulation of media images of women's suffering and resistance, and illuminating women's cultural, religious and economic practices.[14] With regards to American Studies, transnational feminism has significant implications for how we approach literature authored by both men *and* women (although I limit myself to a discussion of the latter in what follows). Transnational feminism profoundly challenges our received notions about *what* constitutes American literature and authorship, how and why a national canon is thought to cohere as a somehow transparent reflection of a distinct and valorized national culture. Especially by regarding national ideals and culture from the position of diasporic, regional, and/or local subjects, this methodology can make visible ways of life, the production of value, and social relations that take form at scales other than the nation-state.

Transnational Feminism and American Literature

Transnational literary practice puts distinct pressure on and imagines alternatives to the ideals of linear development and progressive mobility that have so often been postulated as central to both American national culture and second-wave feminist politics. It instead creates alternative imaginaries by adopting *and* adapting the experiential forms of subaltern knowledge that liberal and radical feminisms dismiss as traditional, backward, and oppressive. For this reason, women of color and transnational feminists have always taken expressive culture seriously as a critical site for imagining social transformation. As the writer-activist Audre Lorde eloquently declared, "For women ... poetry is not a luxury. It is a vital necessity for our existence. It forms the quality of the light within which we predicate our hopes and dreams toward survival and change, first made into language, then into idea, then into more tangible action."[15] Lorde – whose family hailed from Grenada, who traveled to Mexico, Germany, Cuba, the Soviet Union, and throughout Africa and the Caribbean in the name of socialist and anticolonial solidarities, and who along with Moraga and Barbara Smith cofounded the Kitchen Table women-of-color press – fathomed how essential literary and artistic work was for the creation of new kinds of lives and for imagining women's desires and communities that remained "until the poem – nameless and formless, about to be birthed, but already felt."[16]

As I have been suggesting, transnational feminism insists that we genuinely grapple with the historical structures, ethical grammars, and material relations that comprise, and cannot be disentangled from, women's identities and daily lives. As a genre, transnational feminist literature can be said to have taken shape only very recently. Possibly only few American writers would directly claim the category for themselves, even as they share sensibilities with a longer genealogy of postcolonial, diasporic, and cosmopolitan women's authorship. As a critical practice, it allows us to reassess not only the women of color that I discussed previously but "worldly" writers from earlier periods, as they pursued their subjects beyond and against the social and political constraints of national culture. For example, as she writes in the eighteenth century about her arrival in New England from Africa as an enslaved child and her later travels to England where abolition had very recently been instituted, how did Phillis Wheatley's poetic accounts of religious conversion reveal the profound moral, political, and economic contradictions in the nation's foundational construction of personhood? Or how did the gendered "questions of travel," through which Elizabeth Bishop wrote of the colonial history and twentieth-century tourists' experience of other nations such as Brazil, also come to inflect her more regional portraits of domestic life in New England and Florida? Likewise, how did the poet Adrienne Rich's growing commitment to what she called a "politics of location" (a concept that has much influenced later transnational feminist practice) shape and transform the literary maps of feminist and national belonging that she produced over her long career in the twentieth and twenty-first centuries?

Further, the contemporary period has seen the germination of literary production that reflects on the social lives, reproductive labor, erotic practices, emotional attachments, and kinship formations of women across national, racial, and ethnic borders. This literature self-consciously negotiates the personal and the political, the local and the global, and the individual and the structural, without resorting to culturalist presumptions, caricatures, and stereotypes about what those conditions and worlds actually are and how they come into contact with others. Transnational feminism instead calls for aesthetic strategies alert to the national, racial, and ethnic borders between women, as well as disciplinary, occupational, and representational ones, and writing that queries other deeply entrenched boundaries, such as those between the public and the private, theory and praxis, individualism and collaboration, the institutional and activist spheres of knowledge production, and the processes of research and the knowledge objects in which these processes result.[17]

Two popular recent novels to which I turn here, Karen Russell's *Swamplandia!* (2011) and *A Tale for the Time Being* (2013) by Ruth Ozeki, provide powerful case studies in transnational feminist practice in contemporary American literature. In Ozeki's and Russell's novels, we might discern a particular concern with what cultural critic Rob Nixon has called a "transnational ethics of place," in which memories of colonial, postcolonial, and racialized "degradation," violence, and labor are brought to bear on landscapes (and seascapes) that are elsewhere routinely rendered romantic and pristine reflections of national culture.[18] With our concern especially trained on the gendered contours of place, we might grapple with how the teenage girl protagonists of both novels serve all at once as keepers of familial and regional histories and local knowledge, the objects of social and sexual violence, *and* the ethical subjects of rapidly changing political, economic, cultural, and natural environments.

A Tale for the Time Being is structured by way of a lively *mise-en-abyme*, with a novelist named Ruth discovering the diary of a sixteen-year-old Japanese girl named Naoko (Nao) Yasutani inside a Hello Kitty lunchbox. Ruth, a transplanted Manhattanite, and her environmental-artist husband Oliver speculate that the lunchbox has been swept across the Pacific Ocean to the remote Canadian Pacific Northwest island where they live. In the concurrent narration of Ruth and Nao's stories alongside one another, Ozeki follows a transnational feminist project of "juxtaposing multiple 'voices'" across the many differences that separate them, as Ruth finds herself completely engrossed in Nao's tale.[19] But transnational feminists also insist that scholars, critics, and artists must remain self-reflexive about their social relation to and distance from their subjects, in order to enact accountability toward those whom they study and represent.[20] Likewise, Ruth's absorption into Nao's story, as I elaborate here, entails her in a relationship of responsibility toward other women that calls into question the very certitude of her own being.

Ruth reads about how Nao has returned to Tokyo with her parents after living for a number of years in California's Silicon Valley where her father worked as a computer programmer before losing his job. In Japan, Nao writes of the virulent bullying she suffers at the hands of her fellow students and the summer vacation she spends with her great-grandmother, a 104-year-old Buddhist nun named Jiko Yasutani, living just north, as Ruth discovers in researching Nao's diary, of the seaside Fukushima prefecture, the site of the nuclear power station meltdown that followed the 2011 earthquake and tsunami.[21] Jiko encourages Nao to cultivate a "superpower" to help her bear the abuse she suffers and instructs her in the method of zazen meditation, which provides her with a sense of home and consolation that has eluded her since returning to Japan (183). Nonetheless, Nao announces in the first pages of the diary (which also serve as the first pages of the novel) her decision to kill herself, but only after she writes the story of "my Jiko." Upon returning to Tokyo in the fall, more and more desperate after her father's second suicide attempt and her fellow students' sexual assault of her, Nao drops out of school and is groomed by an acquaintance to become a sex worker for men seeking underage prostitutes.

In trying to tell her great-grandmother's story and following Jiko's advice that "You should start where you are," Nao opens with the scene of her own writing, which in turn leads into a long and winding narrative that concludes not with "the fascinating life of Yasutani Jiko, the famous anarchist-feminist-novelist-turned-Buddhist-nun of the Taisho era," but with Jiko's death and funeral, during which Nao is reunited and comes to an understanding with her father that they will both desist from trying to end their own lives (19). In the process, however, Nao also unfolds the story of her great-uncle, "Haruki #1" (after whom Nao's own father, "Haruki #2" is named), a student of philosophy conscripted as a kamikaze pilot during World War II, whose letters and antique wristwatch also accompany the diary Ruth finds in the lunchbox. As he writes in French in his own secret diary to his mother about his decision to fly his bomber into the ocean rather than attack a "so-called enemy, whom I have never met and whom I cannot hate," Haruki #1 becomes an inspirational source of conscientious strength for Nao and her father (325).

Nao addresses an imaginary reader, one she cannot locate in the world – "Are you in a New York subway car hanging from a strap, or soaking in your hot tub in Sunnyvale? Are you sunbathing on a sandy beach in Phuket, or having your toenails buffed in Abu Dhabi?" – but whom she surmises to be nevertheless empathetic and committed to the tale by his or her decision to continue reading (3). And indeed, while Ruth (whose mother was Japanese and who has studied Japanese language and literature) becomes the primary translator and reader of Nao's diary, she assembles a community of readers, including Oliver and numerous local residents and farther-flung informants, for insights that help her decode all of the found materials. With the aid of this collective readership, Ruth learns of Nao's father's own ethical struggles, which have led to the family's return to Japan and his death wish. Meanwhile, Ruth pursues clues about Nao's existence online with an urgent sense of her responsibility to prevent Nao's suicide, at least until Oliver points out to her that, given the diary's provenance, such an effort would be useless: "[I]f [Nao] was going to kill herself, she's probably already done it, don't you think? And if she didn't kill herself, then she'd be in her late twenties by now" (313).

Ozeki has been widely recognized as a transnational feminist author, and *A Tale for the Time Being* readily confirms that reputation, given the trans-Pacific interchange she portrays between Ruth and Nao. Karen Russell might, on the other hand, pose a less obvious candidate for this title, since she has instead drawn much praise for her ability as a *regional* writer, capturing the way in which the tourist economy and industrialized agriculture challenge diverse natural ecosystems and local folkways in southern Florida. Russell's scale would thus seem to be "below" or "within" the nation that contains her. Yet, I suggest, approaching *Swamplandia!* as a work of transnational feminist literature yields substantial insights about how women live global change from the ground up.

The novel's title refers to the alligator-themed amusement park, built on an island in the Florida Everglades, run by the Bigtree clan, who have crafted an entire mythology modeled on Indian lore – despite being a family of transplanted white coalminers from Ohio with "not a drop of Seminole or Miccosukee blood in us" – that is also sold as part of the allure of the "Number One Gator-Themed Park and Swamp Café" in the area."[22] Narrated by thirteen-year-old Ava Bigtree, the novel intertwines the fiscal demise of the theme park with Ava's memories of her mother, an alligator-wrestler whose death from cancer occasions the "Beginning of the End" for the Bigtrees' idiosyncratic way of life (8). Having spent their lives working in Swamplandia! and being homeschooled by their family, Ava and her two siblings' contact with the mainland comes mostly through the tourists ferried to their island, the television, and books from a marooned schooner, the old "Library Boat," that still holds most of its collection (70).

With the loss of their mother, who had been the park's star attraction, and the increased competition posed by the nearby corporate theme park World of Darkness, the three Bigtree children are left mostly to fend for themselves as their father, the "Chief," departs in search of financing to pay off the many debts of the now shuttered park. Ava's seventeen-year-old brother Kiwi also leaves to take a job at World of Darkness in hopes of contributing to their upkeep. Her sixteen-year-old sister Osceola (Ossie), who harbors a growing interest in the occult, begins slipping away at night to meet phantom boyfriends. And Ava secretly hatches various schemes she hopes will draw tourists back to their park. The displacement of the Bigtrees to the fictional city of Loomis at the novel's end suggests the antagonism, rupture, upheaval, and even violence that accompany the incorporation of regional lifeworlds into the political and cultural economies of the nation. Thus, for example, Ava spells out quite straightforwardly how the "sly encroachment of the suburbs and Big Sugar in the south" attacks their very livelihood (8). She also relates how even decades before that the US Corps of Army Engineers, beginning in the 1940s, endeavored to drain the swamps and convert the peat beneath "into a pleated yellowland of crops" by introducing the invasive melaleuca tree species, an effort that ultimately leads to rampant wildfires, turns the "last virgin mahogany stands into dust bowls," and chokes off the Everglades' natural diversity (96). As with much of the damage that local communities incur as part of modern "development," the nation forgets the wreckage it has wrought in the name of progress, what Ava's father describes as a "funny amnesia" about these crises that "had each originated as a Corps blueprint" (97).

Ava's irregular education also includes the local social history, in danger of being generally forgotten, to which her family accords a different kind of pedagogical value:

> Grandpa Sawtooth, to his credit, taught us the names of whole townships that had been forgotten underwater. Black pioneers, Creek Indians, moonshiners, women, 'disappeared' boy soldiers who deserted their army camps. From Grandpa we learned how to peer beneath the sea-glare of the 'official, historical' Florida records we found in books. "Prejudice," as defined by Sawtooth Bigtree, was a kind of prehistoric arithmetic – a "damn fool math" – in which some people counted and others did not. It meant white names on white headstones in the big cemetery on Cypress Point, and black and brown bodies buried in swamp water. (250)

Russell thus offers what Nixon calls a "vernacular landscape."[23] Like such "affective, historically textured maps that communities have devised over generations, maps replete with names and routes, maps alive to significant ecological and surface geological features," Ava's account drills deep to unearth the layered histories of indigenous and other marginalized peoples whose past presence she has learned to read in her surroundings and, furthermore, whom Russell recovers to archive in Ava's narrative.

In fact, in recounting how Osceola was named for a Seminole chief and, in turn, the history of the brutal Seminole Wars of the nineteenth century, Ava ultimately re-charts Florida's very place in an Atlantic world:

> [I]t turned out that every human in the Ten Thousand Islands was a recent arrival. The Calusa, the shell builders – they were Paleo-Indians, the closest thing our swamp had to an indigenous people. But the Calusa vanished from all maps hundreds of years ago, and it was not until the late 1800s that our swamp was recolonized by freed slaves and by fugitive Indians, and, decades later, by the shocked, drenched white pioneers shaking out wet deeds ... Florida itself was a newcomer to these parts ... the "suture" between Africa and North America three hundred million years ago, when all the continents were fused. According to the geologic clock, our state was an infant. Our soils contained the fossils of endemic African species – my brother said these feathery stencils of the past in our bedrock sort of gave the lie to the Chief's ideas about the purity of our isolation. (239)

In the transnational ethics of place that underwrites Ava's family history, then, *Swamplandia!* also evokes a spatial and temporal imaginary wildly divergent from that of the nation, the geological time of the planet to which, as I discuss further here, Ozeki's novel is also responsive.

By articulating the lives of Nao and Ava according to a planetary time, as well as in the animated rhythms of local communities, Ozeki and Russell endeavor to meet women where they are, on their own grounds and on their own terms. As works of transnational feminist literature, both *Swamplandia!* and *A Tale for the Time Being* worry less with recovering what Saba Mahmood calls "latent liberatory potentials" than with elucidating "the multiple ways in which one *inhabits* norms."[24] While it would be easy enough to understand Ava and Nao's subjectivities in the strictly binary terms of gendered victimization and resistance, especially given that both their plots turn on scenes of sexual exploitation and assault, the novels in fact situate those pivotal moments as the culmination of historical forces that are variously local, corporate, national, and international in scale. Rendering those contexts not only requires adopting flexible and creative aesthetic strategies but necessitates an imaginative openness to that which modern national culture tends to write off as insignificant, peripheral, outmoded, or just simply "crazy."

Worlds' Ends and Time Beings

To meet women where they are, on their own terms, means coming to terms with all the beings that constitute their worlds and give their lives meaning. To do so, on the one hand, as I have already suggested earlier, both Ozeki and Russell pay close attention to the natural world, so that, for example, in each novel, setting never comprises mere backdrop, but rather constitutes a vital feature of the narratives. At the same time, they also depict spirits and ghosts who inhabit the same spaces as their characters, whether in Tokyo, Sendai, or the Everglades. In fact, both authors blur the boundaries between the animal, human, and spirit beings encountered by their characters to engage in what M. Jacqui Alexander calls "pedagogies of the Sacred."[25] Alexander urges cultural critics to approach the sacred and the spiritual "as an ever-changing yet permanent condition of the universe, and not as an embarrassingly unfortunate by-product of tradition in which women are disproportionately caught."[26]

Thus, unlike the typically secular perspectives of global feminism and liberal nationalism, transnational feminist literatures concede that "the majority of people in the world – that, is the majority of women in the world – cannot make sense of themselves" without religion, the spiritual, or some other concept of the sacred.[27] Other animated presences – natural and supernatural, animal, plant, and divine – indicate "all the seemingly nonmodern, rural, nonsecular relationships and life practices" that the modern nation-state and global capitalism are unable to incorporate as part of national history and neoliberal culture.[28] Both Russell and Ozeki conjure the natural and supernatural as objects of manipulation, the artifacts of past damage, and the incontrovertible limits of human knowledge and agency, but also as essential narrative elements that *enable* the different women at the heart of both novels.

For her part, by subtly but pointedly comparing the melaleuca infestation in the Everglades to cancer ("We kept cutting them down, and the earth kept raising them. It was a haywire fertility, like a body making cancer"), Russell affiliates the surrounding environmental damage with the Bigtrees' loss of Hilola. Every aspect of the family's vulnerability manifests the "slow violence" that the nation enacts on the region, but it is also saturated with fantastic possibilities. When Ava and Ossie discover a dredge barge from the 1930s that has washed up at the edge of the park, they methodically search its contents, even as Ossie makes contact through her Ouija board with the spirit of Louis Thanksgiving, one of the multiracial Civilian Conservation Corps crew who worked on the barge decades before and who becomes her final ghost boyfriend. When Ossie sets out for the "Eye of the Needle," the channel running between two shell islands built by the Calusa Indians, where Louis tells her she can find the "door to the underworld," Ava entrusts herself to a stranger, the Bird Man, one of the seasonal "avian pied pipers" who chases problem birds off local properties and who promises to aid her search in the swamps for Ossie in his skiff (150–51, 163). And while he does help her navigate the uncharted waterways and keeps native bobcats and water moccasins at bay, their journey together ultimately culminates in the Bird Man's rape of her.

As canny as Ava is about the social and political history in which she is situated, then, she remains by design a naïve narrator because of the multiple vectors of power beyond her grasp to which she is nonetheless subject. The secluded topography of the swamp contributes to the singular forms of care and pleasures that Ava's family members provide one another, which stubbornly resist being absorbed into the commercial culture and profit logic of the "mainland." Ava's openness to the other world that preoccupies Ossie actually makes it possible for the two young women to imagine intimacy, pleasure, and care beyond the limited and shallow versions that consumer culture offers (and which are depicted in Kiwi's experience as a low-wage employee at World of Darkness). But her isolation and openness also generate the singular kinds of danger in which Ava finds herself; her remove from the mainland renders her and Ossie's abandonment invisible to others and leaves her especially vulnerable to the Bird Man's assault.

However, rather than simply romanticizing the Bigtrees' quirky existence, on the one hand, or portraying Ava as prey in the Bird Man's sinister scheme, on the other, *Swamplandia!* constructs her emergent feminist consciousness as a kind of capillary action of survival through sensitive adaptation to her given circumstances. The rape is portrayed with little spectacular detail, told instead from Ava's perspective as steeped in pain and confusion, but also as eye-opening rather than world-shattering. Ava hears her mother's voice warning her that, "The Bird Man is just a man ... more lost out here than you are ... I would run, honey, personally," which transmutes Ava from a dependent to the capable subject of a hard-earned knowledge that saves her (332).

Fleeing the Bird Man, dehydrated and disoriented in the swamp, Ava comes upon a seemingly abandoned house that conjures for her the legend of Mama Weeds, a "light-skinned black seamstress descended from freed slaves who lived in the Ten Thousand Islands," rumored to haunt the swamp after having been murdered by local men infuriated by her sense of independence. Confronted by the woman living there, Ava becomes convinced that she has come across this apparition:

> Our eyes met ... What I saw inside them was all landscape: no pupil or colored
> hoop of iris but the great swamp ... Inside each oval I saw a world of saw grass

and no people ... I saw a nothing that rolled forward forcefully forever ...
When she blinked again, her eyes looked black and oily, ordinary. For years
I've wondered if this person I met was only a woman. (364)

This vision of "what would happen at the world's end" recalls the layered
natural and social history that the novel records, which precedes and contests national narratives of modernization and integration. The scene immediately precedes Ava's final escape, not only from the Bird Man but from
an alligator that attacks her as she swims through an underwater tunnel
toward the bay.

Saving herself with a wrestling maneuver that Hilola taught her daughter
before her death, Ava is reunited with Kiwi and Ossie and eventually the
Chief on the mainland. For Ava, her survival is impelled by her mother's
presence, whose disembodied being at once engulfs and gives new meaning
to an existence that Mama Weeds' eyes otherwise evacuates:

> I believe I met my mother there, in the final instant. Not her ghost but some
> vaster portion of her, her self boundlessly recharged beneath the water. Her cour-
> age. In the cave I think she must have lent me some of it, because the strength
> I felt then was as huge as the sun. The yellow inside you that makes you want
> to live. I believe that she was the pulse and bloom that forced me towards the
> surface. She was the water that eased the clothes from my fingers. She was the
> muscular current that rode me through the water away from the den, and she
> was the victory howl that at last opened my mouth and filled my lungs. (389)

Ava's encounters knits both Mama Weeds and her mother into the material, social, and spiritual fiber of her body and life. As spirits who are at the
same time "only" women, they figuratively demarcate the bounds of the
world that Ava inhabits, but also prove essential to her endurance against
the harsh circumstances, immediate and personal, as well as more general
and structural, which threaten her life.

Likewise, Ozeki provides extensive depictions of Pacific marine life,
as well as more terrestrial animals, which serve as both literal and metaphorical indicators of changing planetary conditions. In Ozeki's novel, as
in *Swamplandia!*, all sorts of material, spiritual, and ideological elements
refuse spatial containment. They bleed across the borders meant to separate
the domestic and the foreign, the natural and supernatural, the human and
the animal, and the fictional and the real, composing both threat and possibility for her characters. Moreover, the traversal of temporal boundaries
is essential in *A Tale for the Time Being*, which, as its title suggests, ponders
deeply the character and construction of time through a transnational lens.
As Nao reflects, "It's hard to write about things that happened a long time
ago in the past ... The past is weird. I mean, does it really exist? It feels like

it exists, but where is it? And if it did exist but doesn't now, then where did it go?" (97). To gain access to the past in ways that do justice to other "time beings" – Ozeki's designation for "someone who lives in time," which "means you, and me, and every one of us who is, or was, or ever will be" – is no simple task (3). As Nao muses about her great-grandmother, "When old Jiko talks about the past, her eyes get all inward-turning, like she's staring at something buried deep inside her body in the marrow of her bones ... it's like she's moving into another world that's frozen deep inside ice" (97).

Forcing a world "deeply frozen in ice" to share our present enacts precisely the kind of violence against which transnational feminism warns. Entering the time and space of another therefore requires departing, even if only temporarily, from our own. To do so can feel "crazy," as Ruth constantly worries about herself, first as a writer, and then as a reader of Nao's story: "[L]iving deep inside a fictional world, the days got jumbled together, and entire weeks or months or even years would yield to the ebb and flow of the dream" (313–14). Of course, all of these reflections take place in a novel in which her fictional counterpart shares any number of biographical details with the novelist Ozeki herself, continually blurring the line between invention and reality. Thus, as the narrative takes a surreal turn, its seeming "craziness" is the risk demanded of Ruth the reader, Ozeki the writer, and us as Ozeki's readers. When Nao's words mysteriously begin disappearing from the end of her diary, Ruth searches for Haruki #2 in a dream, where she informs him that Jiko is on the verge of death and urges him to return to and care for his daughter. As Oliver tells Ruth, "Crazy is the price you pay for having an imagination. It's your superpower," and this ardent commitment to the other woman ultimately sustains Nao's life and returns her writing to Ruth (315).

As a kind of parable for how women might speak to one another across difference, A Tale for the Time Being insists that solidarity can "only ensue within the uncertain, at times opaque, conditions of intimate and uncomfortable encounters in all their eventuality."[29] Ozeki's novel closes out with a final gesture of openness to the other woman, as Ruth begins writing to Nao, although it is uncertain that the latter will ever receive her words. If both Swamplandia! and A Tale for the Time Being depict feminist affiliations that materialize between women, it is only because the protagonists forego idealized resistance in exchange for the possibility of transactional knowledge, forged through the embodied attachments to others. Such a feminist cultural politics proves less "a matter of transforming 'consciousness' or effecting change in the significatory system of gender," than "the retraining of sensibilities, affect, desire, and sentiments," by which to keep, in Ruth's words to Nao, "all the worlds alive" (402).[30]

As in "It's the Poverty," where Moraga equivocates about joining her lover on the road trip, transnational feminist approaches to American literature refuse to simply take other women along for the ride, with the route and meanings of that journey already pre-scripted for all involved. Rather than proposing a global sisterhood out of a shared universal female condition or tracking the development and inclusion of these different subjects as members of a national community, transnational feminism plumbs the disjunctures and fissures of women's narratives, contextualizing the specificity of their experiences while also putting them into relation with other women across the various borders that race, nation, empire, capital, and class construct. Transnational feminist literature thus stands witness to women's bodies as the sites of diverse and often contradictory modes of disciplinary power. But it is also a testament to the resilient creativity that women summon in order to "imagine themselves ... as agents of their own lives," and tell their tales in their own time, on their own terms.[31]

NOTES

1 Cherríe Moraga, *Loving in the War Years: Lo Que Nunca Pasó Por Sus Labios* (Boston, MA: South End Press, 1983), 63.

2 Ibid., 62–63.

3 M. Jacqui Alexander, *Pedagogies of Crossing: Meditations on Feminism, Sexual Politics, Memory, and the Sacred* (Durham, NC: Duke University Press, 2005), 257–86, and M. Jacqui Alexander and Chandra Talpade Mohanty, "Introduction: Genealogies, Legacies, Movements" in *Feminist Genealogies, Colonial Legacies, Democratic Futures* (New York: Routledge, 1997), xiii–xx.

4 Perhaps no theorist of postcolonial feminism has been more influential on the shape of transnational feminism than Gayatri Chakravorty Spivak.

5 Robin Morgan, ed. *Sisterhood Is Global: The International Women's Movement Anthology* (New York: The Feminist Press at the City University of New York, 1996 [1984]), 4.

6 For examples in the US context, see Catherine A. MacKinnon, "Feminism, Marxism, Method, and the State: An Agenda for Theory," *Feminist Theory* 7.3 (Spring 1982), 515–44, and *Are Women Human?: And Other International Dialogues* (Cambridge, MA: Belknap Press, 2006); Kate Millett, *Sexual Politics* (New York: Doubleday, 1970); Susan Moller Okin, *Is Multiculturalism Bad for Women*, eds. Joshua Cohen et al. (Princeton, NJ: Princeton University Press, 1999); and organizations such as the Feminist Majority Foundation and the National Organization for Women.

7 Ella Shohat, "Introduction" in *Talking Visions: Multicultural Feminism in a Transnational Age* (Cambridge, MA: MIT Press, 1998), 1.

8 Inderpal Grewal and Caren Kaplan, *Scattered Hegemonies: Postmodernity and Transnational Feminist Practices* (Minneapolis: University of Minnesota Press, 1994), 1.

9 Shohat, "Introduction," 3. See also Alexander, *Pedagogies of Crossing*, 4.

10 Shohat, "Introduction," 2.
11 Inderpal Grewal and Caren Kaplan, "Global Identities: Theorizing Transnational Studies of Sexuality," *GLQ: A Journal of Lesbian and Gay Studies* 7.4 (2001), 671.
12 Ibid., 664.
13 Ibid., 671.
14 See, for examples, Rebecca Dingo, *Networking Arguments: Rhetoric, Transnational Feminism, and Public Policy Writing* (Pittsburgh, PA: University of Pittsburgh Press, 2012); Wendy Hesford, *Spectacular Rhetorics: Human Rights Visions, Recognitions, Feminisms* (Durham, NC: Duke University Press, 2011); Aihwa Ong, *Neoliberalism as Exception: Mutations in Citizenship and Sovereignty* (Durham, NC: Duke University Press, 2006); and Rhacel Salazar Parreñas, *Servants of Globalization: Women, Migration, and Domestic Work* (Palo Alto, CA: Stanford University Press, 2001). *Feminist Genealogies, Colonial Legacies, Democratic Futures*, edited by M. Jacqui Alexander and Chandra Talpade Mohanty, includes exemplary studies from a transnational feminist perspective of a range of local and regional feminist movements and organizations, such as Stree Shakti Sanghatana in Hyderabad, India, the Caribbean Sistren Collective, and indigenous women's organizations in the United States. For a comprehensive overview of different transnational feminist movements, see Rawwida Baksh and Wendy Harcourt, eds., *The Oxford Handbook of Transnational Feminist Movements* (Oxford: Oxford University Press, 2015).
15 Audre Lorde, *Sister Outsider* (Berkeley, CA: Crossing Press, 2007 [1984]), 37.
16 Ibid.
17 Richa Nagar and Amanda Lock Swarr, "Introduction: Theorizing Transnational Feminist Praxis," *Critical Transnational Feminist Praxis* (Albany: SUNY Press, 2010), 6–7.
18 Rob Nixon, *Slow Violence and the Environmentalism of the Poor* (Cambridge, MA: Harvard University Press, 2011), 243–45.
19 Nagar and Swarr, "Introduction," 7.
20 Ibid.
21 Ruth Ozeki, *A Tale for the Time Being* (New York: Penguin Books, 2013), 44. All subsequent citations appear in parentheses.
22 Karen Russell, *Swamplandia!* (New York: Vintage Books, 2011), 6. All subsequent citations appear in parentheses.
23 Nixon, *Slow Violence*, 17.
24 Saba Mahmood, *Politics of Piety: The Islamic Revival and the Feminist Subject* (Princeton, NJ: Princeton University, 2004) 5, 14.
25 Alexander, *Pedagogies of Crossing*, 15.
26 Ibid., 15.
27 Ibid., 15.
28 Chakrabarty, *Provincializing Europe: Postcolonial Thought and Historical Difference* (Princeton, NJ: Princeton University Press, 2007), 11, 65–66.
29 Mahmood, *Politics of Piety,* 199.
30 Ibid., 188.
31 Alexander and Mohanty, "Introduction: Genealogies, Legacies, Movements," xxviii.

14

PETRUS LIU

Queer Transnationalism

In Chris Nealon's poem "White Meadows," queerness embodies a particular form of transnational consciousness.[1] Delectable, thought-provoking, and written with a touch of political anger, "White Meadows" is at once a critical examination of what it means to have a queer voice in North America and a powerful analysis of the racial violence, geopolitical hierarchies, and material inequalities that underlie such voices. Addressed to the Mexican poet Heriberto Yépez who once asked, "What is up with white poets and meadows?" the poem begins with a meta-reflection on the occasion of its own genesis, which is circumscribed by two kinds of missives: Yépez's question from the other side of the US-Mexico border, and the conjured memory of certain "sweet emails" the poetic speaker received from people who praised "the pop culture and gay sex references" in his early "poems about cities/poems about meadows/poems about let's call it the global north" through the 1980s and 1990s. The implications of this juxtaposition are clear: Yépez's question is a sobering critique of white privilege, a reminder that while (white) poets sing about clouds, birds, brooks, meadows, pop culture, and gay sex, they unwittingly erase from view the socioeconomic conditions that allow them to consume and appreciate such images in the first place, privileges that are, as "White Meadows" goes on to suggest, made possible by the fruits of the laboring bodies who know "no meadows/ ... only slums, factories, forced-labor fields, border detention facilities, Guantanamos, Abu Ghraibs, cops, devastated streets and jails." From this ethical perspective, it is impossible to have a disembodied queer voice that can reference "pop culture and gay sex" without at the same time referencing the "white meadows" that signify the geopolitical position of one's enunciation. To have a voice, queer or not, is to have a location, to inhabit a space and a citizenship on a hierarchically divided and racially inscribed planet, a fact that the queer poets of white meadows are likely to forget.

But the poem also presents an important view of the organic linkages between the "North American dream" of the global north and the exploitation of the global south. "In the North American suburbs we used to ride our bikes around when school was out ... /Heriberto I would have liked to ride bikes with you/But you were busy having the childhood that afforded mine./Maybe they made you waste your intellect on building some toy I played with mindlessly/Maybe you assembled my bicycle chain/Up here we were slowly becoming the rust belt." "Every time North-Americans feel 'unsafe,' others get killed abroad." By the middle section of the poem, the poetic speaker realizes, painfully, "The childhood history of bumping into the dream's backdoor – the rejected awareness your whole life was built, as your parents' lives were, on the backs of others elsewhere." By suggesting that the world is an indivisible totality marked by combined and uneven developments, "White Meadows" highlights the political urgency for queer writers to engage and reflect on the problems of transnationalism. In the final section of the poem, "white meadow" metamorphoses once again to refer to the site where the ashes of Patrick Baroch were scattered. Reflecting on Baroch's passing, the poet writes, "I wouldn't call Patty's a political death though the Bush years ground him down/I couldn't tell you exactly how his whiteness was different from mine, just as his queerness was/And I don't know what it sounds like to the rest of the world when one white man remembers another." To this sentiment the poetic speaker then adds a comment on Federico García Lorca's "Ode to Walt Whitman": "For Lorca Whitman is the right kind of faggot – manly, national/In this he resembles nothing so much as half the gay men I know, but that's another poem." If neither whiteness nor queerness can be said to be a unitary identity, it is because the world is not one in a material sense. The recognition that we live in a transnational, divided world rather than a territorially bounded nation-state brings about nothing less than an existential crisis in the speaker, a recognition that it is impossible to speak of the queer without taking stock of, no matter how provisionally, our transnational relationship to others whose lives and labors make possible our love, rage, and modes of embodiment in America.

"White Meadows" is only an example of a larger trend in contemporary North American poetry that can only be described as a transnational turn in queer thinking – a turn toward comparative, diasporic, or cosmopolitan issues, an exploration of the changes technology and globalization created for queer lives in the United States, a sense that thinking about sexuality can never be fully separated from thinking about the nature of the social or linguistic community one inhabits and what polices its boundaries, and a recognition that the political efficacy and semantic clout of "queer" depends on an alterity not just in the sexual sense but a cultural one as well. Academic theory of queer sexuality and identification, as well, responded to the study of such issues in a transnational frame. It is easy to understand why. The small-town lesbian girl whose sole source of information about people like herself came from that dusty copy of *The Well of Loneliness* in the local library could be seen today flying to participate, topless, in Toronto's dykes-on-bikes march. The same boy whose highlight of the week was browsing men's underwear ad at the grocery store might be juggling hookups found on OkCupid, Grindr, Hornet, u2nite, Blued, Zank, and Jack'd while traveling from city to city. Because the social experience of being gay and the academic theorization thereof are both inextricably linked to questions of identity, community, anonymity, survival, and self-expression, sexual minority cultures seem to be dramatically susceptible to the "time-space compression" of globalization, which has fundamentally transformed the nature of queer organizing, community-building, information-sharing, social networking, and modes of embodiment in the last twenty-five years.

The recognition of the importance of transnational analysis has led to new works on the diversity and co-agency of global sexual cultures. It has also resulted in a general disenchantment with a once conventional narrative that locates Stonewall as the mythical origin of modern gay identity and liberation on a global scale. There are many versions of this "Americanist" explanation of the invention of homosexuality as a social identity. Before the transnational turn, queer critics typically used the internal logic of American postwar politics to explain forces that might have brought about the modern, self-affirmative gay community and its subsequent "spread" to other parts of the world. In the 1990s, many critics accepted a theory that located the origins of gay communities in the segregation of men and women during World War II, mass migration to urban centers, or the disruption of traditional patterns of gender relations and procreative sexuality due to developments of free labor capitalism.[2] Over the years, the transnational turn in queer studies has made critics much more aware of "other modernities" and sexual histories in the world that unfolded earlier than, independently of, or in contradiction to the "blueprint" of Stonewall-based American history.[3] While the purchase of Stonewall- or World War II–centered Americanist theories has waned in the face of transnational studies, even within Americanist circles critics are now much more aware of the interpenetration of global and local forces in the making of "American" sexual communities. Several important studies have demonstrated, for example, that the influx of southern and eastern European Catholics, Jews, Southeast Asians, Arab, Latinos, and South Asians into New York City has each time reshaped its sexual culture in distinctive ways.[4] Conversely, the experience of each subcommunity may be radically different, calling for more critical analysis of the intersections of race and sexuality in the form of queer diasporic studies and the queer of color critique.[5] At the same time, the ease of travel, new technologies, and accelerated flows of migrants, commodities, and information across national borders have produced neither a viable strategy for legislating gay rights on a global scale nor a universal consensus on what these should be. As Josephine Ho has demonstrated, the emergence of a global civil society composed of NGOs, human rights watchers, LGBT cultural events, and Internet communities can also assimilate local movements into a moralistic surveillance network with oppressive and sex-negative effects.[6]

If globalization produces ambivalent effects on local queer struggles, it may be because the distinction between global and local is difficult to maintain to begin with. Jon Symons and Dennis Altman point out the irony that, while opposition to gay rights is often justified in the name of culture and tradition and "framed as a defense of sovereignty that resists imposition of western cultural values and identity categories," such anticolonial efforts are often in reality defending laws that were introduced under colonial rule.[7] The complexities of these situations indicate that no satisfactory answer has been given to the analysis of the concrete operations of transnationalism in concrete local situations. These difficulties are not cause for despair. Instead, the need for greater transnational research programs is precisely what continues to animate queer theory and what underlies its political timeliness.

Despite its obvious political promise and efficacy, however, the development of transnational queer studies has been neither uniform nor unilinear. To the contrary, it is much more accurate to say that transnational queer studies has been intellectualized and instituted in contradictory ways. A particular tension arises when international scholars object that US-based transnational queer studies is not only a falsely universalizing cultural imperialism but a self-aggrandizing colonial anthropology in search of differences. For those critics, transnational queer studies reifies and fetishizes the differences between locations, casting non-Western subjects as pre-queer or proto-homosexuals living in societies where cable networks "provide gay pornography to browsers where there are *hjira*, *travesti*, and *kathoeys* but no gay men."[8] Conversely, other critics object that the postulation of a universal gay identity assimilates the experiences and expressions of other cultures into belated copies of US-style sexual identities, a move that replicates rather than challenges the violent colonial history that eroded indigenous social relations with Western medico-scientific knowledge and taxonomies.[9]

In a certain sense, the conundrum in the current transnational queer studies may seem to be merely a replay of an earlier debate between social constructionism and essentialism, which similarly hinges on the question of whether sexuality is an immutable, innate essence of a person or a discursively produced effect. The crucial difference is that whereas the constructionist-essentialist debate begins with a *historical* question – the difference between premodern "acts" and modern "identities" provoked by Michel Foucault's claim that "the sodomite had been a temporary aberration; the homosexual was now a species" – the transnational debate is, in fact, much more complicated because it involves *coeval locations* and competing systems of knowledge.[10] Unlike the acts vs. identities question, the transnational debate cannot be resolved through recourse to philosophical meditations. What is needed instead is a collective effort, a sustained and difficult dialogue between researchers working in different languages and archives. The two debates also differ in their ethical priorities. Before the transnational turn, social constructionism served a clear political purpose: to call in question the perceived self-evidence and naturalness of heterosexuality. If the homo/hetero binary can be shown to be an invention rather than a perennial truth, sexual minorities are in a powerful position to contest the requirements of compulsory heterosexuality. When the question is compounded by transnational differences, suddenly it becomes an invidious choice between the universalizing pretensions of queer theory and an ethnocentrism that characterizes certain human populations as irrelevant or impervious to queer theory. Certainly, an effective strategy to denaturalize heterosexuality is to historicize its invention, but narratives of invented sexual identities inevitably deny the coevalness of human cultures and fall victim to the problem of *allochronism*. In the case of queer transnationalism, a queer critique of heteronormativity comes into conflict with a postcolonial critique of allochronism.

Rather than adjudicating between these positions, I would suggest that the current interest in transnationalism is actually anticipated and shaped by classic queer theory of the early 1990s. It would be a mistake, therefore, to attribute the transnational turn in queer theory purely to globalization. Rather, I would argue that transnationalism has always been at the heart of queer theory, and we may even say that transnationalism was what founded queer theory as such. There has always been a productive tension between transnationalism and theorizations of gender and sexuality. This unresolved tension does not mean that queer theory is intellectually incoherent or politically self-defeating. Rather, queer theory's productive failure – to borrow an idiom from deconstruction – is precisely what keeps the dialogue vital and, indeed, queer in our current political climate where the term seems to have lost its edge and become a bland synonym for gay. Making a critical return to early queer theory's problematic engagement with transnational and transcultural thinking thus can remind us of the incomplete character of queer knowledge and theorization, of its intellectual and political need to be reanimated by transnational dialogues and research programs.

From the beginning, the transnational question was inextricably bound up with the fortunes of queer theory. In retrospect, it is surprising to see how many of the founding texts of queer theory were derived from a theoretical argument for a nonidentity between Eastern and Western cultures. Take, for example, Judith Butler's 1990 *Gender Trouble*, a text primarily known today for its theory of performativity and for its critique of the category of women as the universal basis of feminism. In *Gender Trouble* and later elaborations, Butler argues that gender is not an immutable essence of a person, but rather a reiterative series of acts and a citational practice of norms that are, significantly, culturally variable.[11] The theory of cultural variability underlies *Gender Trouble*'s central claim that a representational politics based on an idealized and dualistic conception of gender forecloses transgressive possibilities and agency. But Butler means several things by the phrase "culturally variable." The immediate context for Butler's intervention is a structuralist legacy in French feminist theory that she understands to be a dyadic heterosexism. In *The Elementary Structures of Kinship*, Claude Lévi-Strauss maintains that the prohibition against incest is not only a universal law present in every culture but also, quite specifically, what founds culture as such. Lévi-Strauss's understanding of the prohibition against incest as a culturally invariable "elementary structure" of human civilization provides the basis of the Symbolic in Lacanian psychoanalysis, which elevates the incest taboo into a heterosexist theory of the Oedipus complex.[12] Later, Butler wonders what would happen if Western philosophy (and gender theory) began with Antigone instead of Oedipus, and formulates an alternative to the Oedipus complex in *Antigone's Claim*.

In *Gender Trouble*, Butler identifies the important links (and discontinuities) between the structuralist legacy (represented by Lévi-Strauss, Ferdinand de Saussure, and Jacques Lacan) and French feminist theory (represented by Julia Kristeva, Hélène Cixous, and Luce Irigaray). While French feminist critics have made numerous contributions, Butler is particularly influenced by their theory of sexual difference, which claims that the fundamental difference between masculine and feminine is a precondition of human signification and communicability.[13] While troubled by the dyadic heterosexism of French theory of sexual difference, Butler acknowledges that the postulation of a universal structure of masculine and feminine signification was indispensable in elevating feminist and gender theory to the center of social analysis: "The speaking subject was, accordingly, one who emerged in relation to the duality of the sexes, and that culture, as outlined by Lévi-Strauss, was defined through the exchange of women, and that the difference between men and women was instituted at the level of elementary exchange, an exchange which forms the possibility of communication itself ...

Suddenly, [women] were fundamental. Suddenly, no human science could proceed without us."[14]

Why was *Gender Trouble*, the foundational text of US queer theory, so preoccupied with the cultural variability debate in structuralist anthropology? In the 1966 preface to the second edition of *The Elementary Structures of Kinship*, Lévi-Strauss openly acknowledges that his theory of kinship was based on insufficient and secondary sources about China and India.[15] Butler returns to Lévi-Strauss's writings on China in *Undoing Gender*, citing the 2001 anthropological findings of Cai Hua to dismiss the structuralist myth of universal kinship.[16] Here, China occupies a strategic place in Butler's quarrels with the structuralists, many of whom (such as Kristeva and Žižek) have also produced famous statements of their own on China.[17] Butler's goal is not only to reveal the heteronormative and cisnormative assumptions in structuralist and psychoanalytic understandings of kinship, but to demonstrate that these laws, norms, and structures are products of human culture and hence subject to social change and democratic contestations.[18] For Butler, cultural variability also indicates social transformability. The thesis of social transformability then requires Butler to demonstrate that such laws must vary from culture to culture. If cultures like China can be discovered to operate outside or, better yet, against Lévi-Strauss's and Lacan's systematic descriptions of universally valid laws and conventions of the human, the structuralist project can be finally overcome.[19] The inassimilable, irreducibly "queer" element of Butler's early theory, as it turns out, is not the socially unintelligible existence of lesbian and transgender individuals in the category of women, but the transnational alterity of non-Western cultures. In the early 1990s, queer battles against the heterosexism of the Symbolic, observations about the culturally constructed nature of social categories become an argument about cultural differences in the anthropological sense, and the critique of gender norms becomes entangled with theories of Oriental exceptionalism.

In *Gender Trouble*, Butler argues that the category of women is an oppressively restrictive notion that is dependent on an equally restrictive imagination of a singular patriarchy.[20] To make this argument, Butler points out that there must be other cultures that do not share Western ideas about what a woman is or what constitutes oppression and patriarchy. In order to deconstruct the fixity of women as a category, Butler has to first caution her reader against the search for a universal patriarchy in non-Western cultures:

> The effort to *include* "Other" cultures as variegated amplifications of a global phallogocentrism constitutes an appropriative act that risks a repetition of the self-aggrandizing gesture of phallogocentrism, colonizing under the sign of the same those differences that might otherwise call that totalizing concept into

question … The political assumption that there must be a universal basis for feminism, one which must be found in an identity assumed to exist cross-culturally, often accompanies the notion that the oppression of women has some singular form discernible in the universal or hegemonic structure of patriarchy or masculine domination … That form of feminism has come under criticism for its efforts to colonize and appropriate non-Western cultures to support highly Western notions of oppression.[21]

What exactly are these "highly Western notions of oppression" and how do non-Western cultures stand in as their conceptual and ethical limits? More specifically, how does an argument that defines non-Western cultures as the unrepresentable and the unspeakable serve as a corrective to the cultural imperialism of Western philosophy? In this critique of the foundational ethnocentrism of the West, paradoxically, the non-West becomes excluded from thought, standing in for the epistemological limits of Western reason. This particular postcolonial critique certainly has its political promises and uses, but the more pressing question is why the ethical call to realign what is possible in human gender and sexual relations in queer theory has to rely on an anthropological hypothesis of the incongruity of Western and non-Western cultures.

Gender Trouble is not the only queer text from the 1990s that is logically and ethically predicated on this transnational imagination of inassimilable cultural Others as the lacunae of Western reason. Another pioneering text of early US queer theory, Eve Sedgwick's *Epistemology of the Closet*, makes a different argument about sexuality via the distinction between the totalizability of the West and the nontotalizable nature of the non-West. Sedgwick's work is generally acknowledged as a paradigm shift that establishes the study of sexuality as the foundation of all social analysis rather than as its footnote. She makes this argument by showing that the definitional crisis of homosexuality/heterosexuality is "epidemic" and central to all organizations of knowledge, even non-sex-specific kinds. In many scenarios that do not appear to be primarily concerned with homosexuality – for example, romantic English poetry – the text's structure of address belies a preoccupation with what Sedgwick calls the triangulation of desire that involves the deflection and disavowal of homosocial desires. In order to show that sexuality is central to *every* node of knowledge, however, Sedgwick has to qualify her argument with the phrase "in Western culture." The West then becomes a totalizable entity, while the non-West is definitionally excluded from this theory of sexuality.

Taking Henry James, Herman Melville, and Marcel Proust as examples of "the West," *Epistemology of the Closet* argues that the (crisis of the) homo/heterosexual definition is constitutive of "twentieth-century Western culture as a whole."[22] Sedgwick's argument builds on her analysis in *Between Men* (1985) that the disavowal or deflection of same-sex desire, often found in English poetry whose manifest theme is the celebration of heterosexual union, constitutes a culturally policed boundary between homosociality and homosexuality that structures the entire social terrain "in the modern West."[23] Sedgwick argues that although the figure of the closet may appear to be a merely sexual or even trivial question, it is actually the paradigm of knowledge/ignorance that organizes the entire domain of modern social thought. Later, Sedgwick elaborates this argument in the discussion of the "privilege of unknowing" in *Tendencies* (1993). Sedgwick shows that social domination depends on a strategic separation of mutually implied forms of knowledge of which the closet is a paradigmatic case.[24] This point is the basis of Sedgwick's claim that the interpretation of sexuality should be taken as the starting point of social analysis rather than as its afterthought. The future of queer studies depends on the promise that rethinking the sexual can lead to the rethinking of the social as well.[25] The power of Sedgwick's work comes from her ability to show that sexuality is revelatory of the ways in which an entire culture organizes itself, and therefore is central to any type of social analysis. Sedgwick, however, cautions that sexuality studies can become the foundation of social analysis only if we do not apply such generalizations, "however sweeping," outside the West:

> It is very difficult for [this book's choice of the Euro-American male as its subject matter] to be interpreted in any other light than that of the categorical imperative: the fact that they are made in a certain way here seems a priori to assert that they would be best made *in the same way everywhere*. I would ask that, *however sweeping* the claims made by this book may seem to be, it not be read as making that particular claim [of applying the analysis to non–Euro-American cultures].[26]

In this formula, the mutually constitutive and dialectical relationship between homosexuality and heterosexuality within Western culture "as a whole" is analytically predicated on the categorical rejection of the commensurability between Western and non-Western cultures. Sedgwick maintains this argument in reference to both sexuality and the cultural tools for understanding it. In a different work, for example, she writes: "Psychoanalytic thought, damaged at its origin, remains virtually the only heuristic available to Western interpreters for unfolding sexual meanings."[27]

Sedgwick suggests that sexuality can maintain its illustrative power as a paradigmatic instance of the ways discourse organizes the entire social field *only* if we accept that it makes sense to speak of "twentieth-century Western culture as a whole" in the first place, but what are the implications of the insistence on the links between these two arguments? What are the historical and theoretical contexts in which Sedgwick's argument for the centrality of sexuality studies comes to be analytically dependent on the totalizability of the West, on our ability to view "twentieth-century West as a whole" as a coherent unit of analysis? If transnationalism questions if the nation is an appropriate unit of analysis, we might extend this insight to ask if "twentieth-century West as a whole" can function as an unproblematic unit of analysis for queer theory.[28] It is unclear whether Sedgwick would consider Spain, Greece, or Serbia part of a West whose definitional axis extends from Marcel Proust to Henry James, Jane Austen, and Herman Melville. But it is clear that the hypothesis of the totality of the West requires the incommensurability between East and West, since it is only in relation to the non-West that the phrase "Western culture as a whole" acquires any meaning and coherence.

While 1990s US queer theory relied on a transnational imagination that reified the incongruity between cultures – and for the founding critics, it is not the differences between French and American cultures that matter – this transnational imagination served a number of important functions in the development of queer theory. The argument that homosexuality was a modern invention (in contrast to, for example, Greek pederasty) is among the most important claims of queer theory.[29] Some queer theorists have argued that the modern period is defined by a newly available conception of homosexuality as the identity of a small and relatively fixed group of people, in distinction from an earlier view of same-sex desire as a continuum of acts, experiences, identities, and pleasures spanning the entire human spectrum. This claim, sometimes known as the "before sexuality thesis," is commonly associated with the work of Michel Foucault, who is quite specific in his dating: Foucault writes that homosexuality as such was invented in 1870 in the West.[30] But in making that claim about the constructedness of homosexuality, Foucault also argues that two different histories, one Western and one Eastern, must be carefully distinguished from each other. Foucault maintains that sexuality is not a timeless, immutable given because sexuality as we know it is absent in the East. The first history, which began somewhere in Greece and migrated to France to produce "the homosexual" as a species in 1870, is called *scientia sexualis*. Foucault's definition of scientia sexualis does not include modern Greece, but draws a line of continuity between modern French culture and ancient Greek culture. The second history, of which Foucault cites China as a primary example, encompasses all non-Western societies without distinguishing their ancient and modern forms. The name Foucault proposes for this second history is *ars erotica* (a term that emphasizes its lack of scientific and logical basis in comparison to scientia sexualis).

Whereas Western civilization (from Greece to France) enjoyed a science of sexuality that discursively produced "the homosexual" as a species in 1870 (in a manner similar to the production of the criminal, the vagabond, the prostitute, the blasphemer, and the insane Foucault analyzes in *Madness and Civilization*), China remains mired in the stage of ars erotica that has blocked the invention of homosexuality: "On the one hand, ... China, Japan, India, Rome, the Arabo-Moslem societies ... endowed themselves with an *ars erotica* ... [On the other hand,] our civilization possesses no *ars erotica*. In return, it is undoubtedly the only civilization to practice a *scientia sexualis*."[31] Foucault further insists that the ars erotica of Asian, Middle Eastern, and ancient Mediterranean societies is precisely what "we" have had to shed in order to achieve modernity: "Breaking with the traditions of the *ars erotica*, our society has equipped itself with a *scientia sexualis*."[32] Here the so-called ars erotica socieites function as the constitutive outside of the modern European homosexual's self-definition, as the negative space against which it becomes possible for individuals who are, presumably, genetically unrelated to the Greeks to speak of a "we" and "our society." While the cultural differences between ancient Greece and France of the 1870s are construed as a historical advance, the distinction between ancient China and modern China, for example, does not interest Foucault much. In fact, the grouping of ancient Rome and unspecified periods of non-Western history as interchangeable examples of ars erotica is justified precisely by the claim that non-Western societies, due to the lack of scientia sexualis, display a developmental stasis through the millennia. Asian and middle-Eastern societies' ars erotica signifies an ossified cultural essence bearing a collective resemblance to the ancient Mediterranean world. In fact, what Foucault means by the ars erotica of "China, Japan, India, Rome, [and] the Arabo-Moslem societies" is a code name for *non-Christian* societies, whereas Europe is defined by "the development of confessional techniques" and "pastoral care" – namely Christianity.

If we learned anything from transnationalism in the twenty-five years since the publication of *Gender Trouble* and *Epistemology of the Closet*, it might be that we can no longer assume that homosexuality has a single origin in Greece or France, or that queer theory should begin with a description of how a certain "we" evolved from a Greek cultural organization of gender and sexuality to the making of the modern French homosexual as a species and, finally, to the twentieth-century homo-/heterosexual definitional crisis in the United States. Queer theory is, after all, a discourse that mobilizes a definitional indeterminacy in the service of politically progressive ends. For some, the transnational turn seems to shift queer theory out of the comfort zone of American postwar history in a way that entails a loss of definition, epistemological certainty, and conceptual anchorage. For most of us, I would hope, the transnational turn means that we would revive the radically anticipatory nature of early queer theory, a willingness to surrender the prerogative to define the terms of the conversation in advance, and an unabashed imagination of a more egalitarian future.

NOTES

1 Chris Nealon, "White Meadows," forthcoming in *The Volta*, Spring 2017.
2 Martin Duberman's *Stonewall* (New York: Dutton, 1993) is arguably the most important work that cemented the event's reputation as the birth of the gay liberation movement. Influential Americanist explanations of the making of the modern homosexual include John D'Emilio, *Sexual Politics, Sexual Communities* (Chicago: University of Chicago Press, 1983) and Barry Adam, *The Rise of a Gay and Lesbian Movement* (Boston, MA: G. K. Hall, 1987).
3 Lisa Rofel, *Other Modernities: Gendered Yearning in China After Socialism* (Berkeley: University of California Press, 1999); Gayatri Gopinath, *Impossible Desires: Queer Diasporas and South Asian Public Cultures* (Durham, NC: Duke University Press, 2005); Joseph Massad, *Desiring Arabs* (Chicago: University of Chicago Press, 2008); Jasbir Puar, *Terrorist Assemblages: Homonationalism in Queer Times* (Durham, NC: Duke University Press, 2007); Elizabeth Povinelli, *The Empire of Love: Toward a Theory of Intimacy, Genealogy, and Carnality* (Durham, NC: Duke University Press, 2006).
4 George Chauncey, *Gay New York: Gender, Urban Culture, and the Making of the Gay Male World, 1890–1940* (New York: Basic Books, 1995); Martin Manalansan IV, *Global Divas: Filipino Gay Men in the Diaspora* (Durham, NC: Duke University Press, 2003); José Esteban Muñoz, *Disidentifications: Queer of Color and the Performance of Politics* (Minneapolis: University of Minnesota Press, 1999).
5 See, among others, Roderick Ferguson, *Aberrations in Black: Toward a Queer of Color Critique* (Minneapolis: University of Minnesota Press, 2003); Juana Rodriguez, *Sexual Futures, Queer Gestures, and Other Latina Longings* (New York: NYU Press, 2014); Darieck Scott, *Extravagant Abjection: Blackness, Power, and Sexuality in the African American Literary Imagination* (New York: NYU Press, 2010); Hoang Nguyen, *A View from the Bottom: Asian American Masculinity and Sexual Representation* (Durham, NC: Duke University Press, 2014); Eng-Beng Lim, *Brown Boys and Rice Queens: Spellbinding Performance in the Asias* (New York: NYU Press, 2014); Natasha Tinsley, *Theifing Sugar: Eroticism Between Women in Caribbean Literature* (Durham, NC: Duke University Press, 2010); and David Eng, *Racial Castration: Managing Masculinity in Asian America* (Durham, NC: Duke University Press, 2001).
6 Josephine Ho, "Is Global Governance Bad for East Asian Queers?" *GLQ: A Journal of Lesbian and Gay Studies* 14.4 (Fall 2008): 457–79.

7 Jonathan Symons and Dennis Altman, "International Norm Polarization: Sexuality as a Subject of Human Rights Protection," *International Theory* 7.1 (March 2015): 65.

8 Elizabeth Povinelli and George Chauncey, "Thinking Sexuality Transnationally: An Introduction," *GLQ: A Journal of Lesbian and Gay Studies* 5.4 (1999): 442.

9 See Altman, "Global Gays/Global Gaze," GLQ: *A Journal of Lesbian and Gay Studies* 3.4 (1997): 417–37.

10 Michel Foucault, *History of Sexuality* v. 1 (New York: Pantheon Books, 1978), 43.

11 Partially derived from Derrida's essay "Signature, Event, Context," Judith Butler's notion of "citationality" is a reformulation of the theory of "performativity" she introduces in *Gender Trouble*. Butler, *Bodies That Matter* (New York: Routledge, 1993), 13. By renaming performativity as citationality, Butler hopes to clarify a misunderstanding that her work suggests that gender is a singular act performed by a humanist subject. Rather, Butler suggests, performativity or citationality is the "iterative power of discourse to produce the phenomena that it regulates and constrains" (Butler, *Bodies That Matter*, 2).

12 For Butler's critique of the psychoanalytic reformulation as the symbolic in Lacan, see Butler, *Gender Trouble* (New York: Routledge, 1990), 49–52; *Bodies That Matter*, 198–207; *Undoing Gender* (New York: Routledge, 2004), 121–26; and Butler, Laclau, and Žižek, *Contingency, Hegemony, and Universality* (London: Verso, 2000), 11–14.

13 See also Butler and Rubin's interview for contrasting definitions of "sexual difference." Judith Butler and Gayle Rubin, "Sexual Traffic," in *differences* 6.2–3 (1994): 62–99.

14 Butler, *Undoing Gender*, 208.

15 Claude Lévi-Strauss, *The Elementary Structures of Kinship* (Boston, MA: Beacon Press, 1969), xxviii.

16 Butler, *Undoing Gender*, 103.

17 See Julia Kristeva, *About Chinese Women* (New York: Urizen Books, 1997). For a collection of Žižek's perspectives on China and Chinese responses to his work, see Tonglin Lu, ed., "The Chinese Perspective on Žižek and Žižek's Perspective on China," *positions: east asia cultures critique* 19.3 (2011).

18 On the difference between her position and the Lacanian psychoanalysis of Žižek, Butler writes, "I agree with the notion that every subject emerges on the condition of foreclosure, but do not share the conviction that these foreclosures are prior to the social, or explicable through recourse to anachronistic structuralist accounts of kinship" (*Contingency, Hegemony, Universality*, 140).

19 Many studies have criticized the construction of China (and Chinese gender and sexuality) as the outside of Western theory. See, for example, Wang Lingzhen, ed., *Other Genders, Other Sexualities? Chinese Differences* (Durham, NC: Duke University Press, 2013).

20 Butler no longer holds these views. She discusses how her views on these points have changed in the 1999 new Preface to *Gender Trouble*, vi–xi, and in *Undoing Gender*, 207–19.

21 Butler, *Gender Trouble*, 3.

22 Eve Sedgwick, *Epistemology of the Closet* (Berkeley: University of California Press, 1990), 1.

23 Eve Segwick, *Between Men* (New York: Columbia Press, 1985), 21.

24 Eve Sedgwick, *Tendencies* (Durham, NC: Duke University Press, 1993), 23–26.

25 Michael Warner also makes this point in his *Fear of a Queer Planet* (Minneapolis: University of Minnesota Press, 1993), x.

26 Sedgwick, *Epistemology of the Closet*, 13–14, emphasis added.

27 Sedgwick, *Tendencies*, 74.

28 For a critique of the internally contradictory definitions of the "West," see Naoki Sakai, "The Dislocation of the West and the Status of the Humanities," in *Traces I: Specters of the West and the Politics of Translation*, Naoki Sakai and Yukiko Hanawa, eds. (Hong Kong: Hong Kong University Press, 2002): 71–91.

29 Significant efforts to elaborate or revise the argument include Jonathan Katz, *The Invention of Heterosexuality* (New York: Dutton, 1995); David M. Halperin, *One Hundred Years of Homosexuality* (New York: Routledge, 1990); and Thomas Laqueur, *Making Sex* (Cambridge, MA: Harvard University Press, 1990).

30 Foucault, *History of Sexuality*, 43.

31 Ibid., 57, 58.

32 Ibid., 67.

15

TIMOTHY MARR

Islam and Transnationalism

> We have created you male and female, and we have made you from
> nations and tribes, so that you may come to know one another.
> (Qur'an, *Surah al-Hujurat*, 49:13)

Muslims, who are born into or convert to a post-Christian faith, have been
difficult for Europeans and Americans to comprehend since the time of the
Crusades. Edward Said has explained that what non-Muslims discursively
call "Islam" is "part fiction, part ideological label, part minimal designation
of a religion called Islam."[1] For centuries Muslim cultures have embraced
the full span of the hemisphere that is not American: from the Moors from
North Africa to the Moros of Maritime Southeast Asia. The fact that both
names are derived from the Greek word *mávros* for "black" dramatizes how
Islam has long been racialized during its career as what Geoffrey Nash has
called "the western world's Other."[2] The European "discoveries" of America
resulted in a modern sense of global consciousness that emerged from
attempts to bypass adherents of Islam who inhabited lands between Europe
and East Asia. Today's forty-nine nations in which Muslims are a majority
comprise the core of the Islamic *umma*: an intercultural *ur*-nation of believers ordinated together toward the *Ka'bah* in Mecca that imbues Muslims
with a transnational consciousness that long preceded the rise of the modern nation-state. Traditional Islamic commentary divided the planet into
Houses or Abodes (*Dar*). Opposing the *umma* was *Dar al-Harb*, or House
of War, whose inhabitants were either subordinated or imagined as infidels
who could be resisted through *jihad* if they encroached on *Dar al-Islam*.
Bipolar "imaginative" and "moral geographies" have mutually demonized
America and Islam as "architectures of enmity" whose clashes are ideologically informed by the countervailing practices of colonialism/postcolonial-
ism and orientalism/occidentalism.[3]

Transnationalism encompasses a revisionary paradigm of twenty-first-
century scholarship with the potential to critically expose the insufficiencies

of exclusive geographies. The difference of Islam, frequently seen as an incommensurate sociopolitical space asserting opposing ethical standards, is often ignored, excluded, maligned, or translated into the internal dynamics of orientalism. National imaginaries of allegiance are necessarily localized in place and provincial in practice even when imperial or universal in aspiration. The notion of a nation is etymologically premised on place of birth and shares the same root with the adjectives native and naïve. Transnational approaches aim to register the overlapping processes of intercultural engagement that have always permeated the boundaries of any nation by uncovering the presence of diversities previously occluded as outside its pale. Advances in transportation and new communication technologies have speeded up globalizing exchanges through integrated trading markets, broader diplomatic alliances, and massive cross-border migrations. These circulations have brought in their wake dynamic processes of transculturation that can multiply the awareness of the international influences that comprise and constitute any localized "homeland." Transnational methodologies attempt to grasp these worldly intersections through a practice that Peter Mandaville has called "the study of encounters and exchanges *within* a particular cultural space as they are experienced in translocality."[4]

The selected literary texts explored in this essay form "cultural spaces" that embody and dramatize translocal engagements of both Muslims with America and Americans with Islam across the chronological expanse of American expression. The scope begins with early encounters between African Muslims and American Christians during the establishment and abolition of American slavery and then expands to examine how Islam became a critical transnational resource of black protest against American racism in the twentieth century. Changes in immigration policy in the 1960s brought large numbers of Muslims to the United States from many nations whose families have since become permanent citizens. Literary works, such as the novels by Laila Halaby, Mohsin Hamid, and Mohja Kahf examined in this essay, address the ongoing challenge – amplified in the age of terrorism – of how Islam is ambivalently excluded as alien to America while also included as a critical element dramatizing its diversity. The transitional status of Muslims as both outsiders and insiders has worked to generate new expressive forms of transnational Islam in America. These voices have also provided critical latitudes from which to challenge the racism, materialism, and inequalities that characterize the US national project.

The double semantics of discrimination make it a useful tool for understanding the complex transnational circuits of Islamic difference in American literary expression. Originally a positive mental capacity denoting the refined discernment of meaningful distinctions, discrimination became ironically inverted to signify a prejudice that bluntly divides peoples based on general type. The challenge of how to discriminate Islam intelligently is complicated both by the ethnic diversities of Muslims and different patterns of practicing and dissimulating their religious adherence, complicated further by the opacity of what that faith signifies to nonbelievers. Literature is a powerful nexus for examining transcultural processes, because authors moderate its own forms of imaginative dissimulation to intimate a deeper discernment of the injustices of prejudice in their readers. These transcultural mixings dramatize how unassimilated variances brought by Islam to America open up emergent possibilities for evolving a fuller planetary ethos of interdependence that can embody fuller fruits of transnational consciousness. How transnational sensibilities are fostered and how much they translate into social actions is a measure of both the potential of literature and its limits as a force that can alter a deep heritage of animosity whose traditions have worked to close off the fertile contaminations of intercultural connections.

The fullest overseas engagement between Americans and Islamic cultures during the early years of the United States constellated around the twenty-year crisis that began in 1785 when American seamen were held captive in the Barbary States of Algiers, Tunis, and Tripoli, setting off debates about the need for a stronger national government to establish a navy for defense. Early transnational literary genres of autobiographical and fictional narratives dramatized these reversals by imagining Muslim spies in the United States and by portraying the "white slavery" of free Americans held in North Africa, the space Muslims call the Maghreb ("the west") because of its ordination to Mecca. In these writings, Muslim cultural practices were often figured as a cruel, infidel, and despotic foil to the rising promise of American republicanism. However, for some writers, global exposure to Muslim alterity placed the provincialism of partisan imaginations in relief to reveal new transatlantic coordinates from which to witness American ideological excesses, racial exclusions, and religious superstitions.[5]

Perhaps the most renowned of these transnational texts was a 1797 novel titled *The Algerine Captive*, one of the earliest American works of fiction to be published in England (in 1802 and 1804). Its author Royall Tyler dramatizes the intercultural transformation of his naïve narrator, Updike Underhill, from serving as a surgeon on a slaving ship to a captive subject to suffering the cruelty of Muslim overseers. Tyler was never directly exposed to North African society, but he used the renegade occasion of his fiction to symbolically "turn Turk" and challenge American impressions of Islam as a "detestably ridiculous … imposture."[6] To escape hard labor, Underhill elects to be taken to a *madrassah* ("college") to meet with the Mollah, a Greek who had converted to Islam. Tyler condenses the five-day conversation into a Socratic dialogue on the relative merits of the Crescent and the Cross during which the Mollah contests, among other arguments, that Christianity had been spread more by the sword than Islam. He silences Underhill by proclaiming that, in contrast to the emancipation of the slave upon conversion to Islam, "We leave it to the Christians of the West Indies, and Christians of your southern plantations, to baptize the unfortunate African into your faith, and then use your brother Christians as brutes of the desert" (62). The insidious renegade proves to be a rational and sincere believer who behaves with gentleness and charity, refusing to take advantage of Underhill's weaknesses, arguing that "A wise man ... will examine the creeds of other nations, compare them with his own, and hold fast that which is right" (54).

The confounding Mollah assists Updike Underhill to gain liberty of movement as well as to practice his medical profession. Underhill performs his ironic role as a "learned slave" (91, 189) by attaining fluency in Arabic and inhabiting Maghrebi dress, displaying how cultural forms themselves can be both captivating or liberating. The sum of Underhill's experience undermines his "natal prejudice" (205) about Muslim bigotry, ferocity, and mercilessness. For example, he is astounded by the regularity of devotion of supposedly "blasphemous" "infidels" (61, 82). One day through the window of a mosque he hears the preaching of an *imam* on the "one God" who is "IMMORTAL, OMNISCIENT ... most MERCIFUL and JUST." The energetic "eloquence" of the "dignified" *khutbah*, and the corresponding reverence of the audience, impresses him so fully that it is related verbatim with no other commentary. The sermon ends with the recitation of the *shahada*: "Lift your hands to the eternal, and pronounce the ineffable, adorable creed: THERE IS ONE GOD, AND MAHOMET IS HIS PROPHET" (172–77). Here, at the conclusion of twelve chapters appraising Algerine life, Tyler narratively testifies the truth of Islam through the impress of Underhill's memorized witness. He avers that the Qur'an's "language ... is so ineffably pure, it can never be rendered into any other tongue," that its ethics "ever exhibited the purest morality and the sublimest conception of the Deity" (154–55), and that it "expressly recommends charity, justice, and mercy towards their fellow men" (157). Underhill ultimately judges Islam as having established a unifying "common faith" in accordance with "reason's law" (159, 150). Tyler does lash out against the cruelty and travesties of many of the cultural practices he witnesses in North Africa, but he uses Underhill's encounters with the Mollah and the *imam* to refashion Islam as a transnational resource for levying a critique of the comparative weaknesses of Christian cultures such as greed, alcoholism, sectarianism, and international divisiveness.

If dozens of American citizens were held in temporary captivity in North Africa, millions of sub-Saharan Africans were forcibly migrated in the other direction across the Atlantic. Scholars have argued that between two and three million Muslims from different areas of West Africa were enslaved in the Americas, comprising the first population of Muslim Americans. Although what Jon Butler called the "spiritual holocaust" of slavery impeded the intergenerational transmission of Islamic belief, nevertheless, Arabic linguistic expressions and Muslim cultural practices have left discernable traces, including a literary genre recording this intercultural encounter.[7]

Transnational approaches, including multilingual analysis, have been able to recover the persistent faith in Islam that some enslaved Africans were forced to hide. For example, Omar ibn Said left many Arabic manuscripts including an autobiography that tells of a Muslim who dissimulated his faith in Islam (in part through the inscrutibility of the Arabic language) to retain his dignity while affirming the Qur'anic teaching that all were slaves (*'abd*) to Allah.[8] The story of Mohammad Ali ben Said is the longest and among the least known of these narratives and is a particularly revealing record of how one author successfully negotiated animosities toward both Africans and Muslims in the English language. Said was a remarkable African who journeyed to the antebellum United States yet was never enslaved in the Americas. He traveled broadly not only in Africa and the Americas but also throughout Europe and into Western Asia, learning at least seven languages. Early in 1860, after having acquired English in London, he agreed to serve as valet to a Dutch couple touring America. While in Canada, his employer absconded with Said's money and he was abandoned to earn his own fortune. After teaching in Detroit, he joined the Union Army in the summer of 1863. After the war, Said traveled throughout the Reconstruction South as a teacher, lecturing on African history, and eventually settled in Bladen, Alabama, where he opened a private school, which he hoped might educate recently emancipated African Americans to resist the imperial encroachment of their African homelands. Said's story dramatizes the translocal experiences of a cosmopolitan African Muslim who, to attract support to publish his narrative in Memphis in 1873, was forced to conceal both his Islamic heritage and his years taking up arms against slavery in the South.[9]

Mohammad Ali ben Said was born into a large and wealthy Muslim family in Bornou in Sudan and was taught Arabic; however, he was sold as a slave to a series of Arab merchants and Turkish officials who took him to Tripoli and then Istanbul, including a journey to Mecca where his unfree status prevented his fulfilment of the *hajj* (491). Said's narrative corroborates Olaudah Equiano's attestations that Turkey was a racially inclusive society that Africans preferred because they were more accepted.[10] While a servant to an Ottoman minister, Said attracted the attention of a Russian diplomat who secretly arranged to purchase him. Later in St. Petersburg, he became the valet of Prince Nicholas Troubetzkoy with whom he traveled throughout many cities of Europe dressed in opulent Turkish dress and a fez, even after he was inveigled in 1855 into being baptized into the Russian Orthodox church and changing his name from Muhammad to Nicholas.

Said's survival is premised on a pragmatic politics of *taqiyya* or dissimulation, which makes it permissible for a Muslim to conceal faith or display non-belief to preserve the believer from injury. Said progressively converts to different denominations (Orthodox, Protestant, Swedenborgian) to invert the gaze of his readers from his own transgressive otherness as an African Muslim. His multilingual intelligence enables him to exert a Muslim critique of coercive western power while defusing such a threat through creative intercultural adaptation. For example, Said states that he prayed regularly as a Muslim in Russia, mentions being beaten for pantomiming Christian prayer, and jests that when forced to kneel in prayer with a priest, "I am not sure but that a few ungainly Mohammedan asperities of language bubbled up to my lips" (144–46). He calls his baptism a "job" (145) not "done right" ("A Native" 495), and comments sardonically that as a "confirmed Christian" he "began to consider myself quite a superior being" (146). Said expresses this critical inversion by mimicking the "strained sanctimoniousness" of Christians, when "they all combine to rail at and revile those who adhere to Mohammed rather than Christ, and roll their eyes in holy horror at the idea of such open infidelity and profanity" (70–71), To survive in the South, Said adopts at times a pose of "intrinsic unworthiness" (v) not unlike the strategy of Senegalese Muslim mutineer Babo in Herman Melville's "Benito Cereno," calling himself "a poor man, a stranger, and a colored man" (223). His adeptness in adapting to the cultural codes expected by those he encountered across many continents enabled his mobility and empowered him to publicize a voice of committed cosmopolitanism that was able to "show the world the possibilities that may be accomplished by the African" (v).

Said's autobiography was not rediscovered until 2000, dramatizing both the long submergence of what Moustafa Bayoumi calls Black Atlantic Islam and African Diasporic Islam as well as the revisionary impetus of contemporary transcultural scholarship.[11] When African Americans rediscovered Islam in the twentieth century as a transnational force of resistance to Christian racism in the United States, they were forced to invent the genealogies that had been destroyed by slavery. This is the case with "The Lost-Found Nation of Islam in the Wilderness of America" that celebrated an influential creation story that the Original Man was a black African whose progeny was killed off by a "rebellious scientist" named Mr. Yakub, dramatized in Amiri Baraka's 1965 play *A Black Mass*. Yakub genetically grafted a "wicked" race of pale white devils who for six thousand years had employed "tricknology" to gain a dominion over remaining black people. A mixedraced Syrian migrant known as W. D. Fard began teaching in 1930 that he would "restore the original nation, or ancient nation, into power to rule forever" launching a movement of Black Islam led by Elijah Muhammad, known as "Messenger of Allah to the Blackman in America."[12] James Baldwin argued in *The Fire Next Time* that "Allah, out of power, and on the dark side of Heaven, had become – for all practical purposes, anyway – black."[13] Black Islam also empowered a dissent from liberal capitalism by pitting "almighty Allah" against "the mighty dollar."[14] By turning east and "flying to Allah," the "so-called American Negro" could revert to an "original" Muslim identity as "Asiatic Black Man," and, according to poet Marvin X, kill both "uncle tom and uncle sam."[15]

It was this visionary narrative that initially "hypnotized" the author of one the most influential American works calling for a "reversion" to Islam, *The Autobiography of Malcolm X*.[16] Published after his *hajj* to Mecca and shortly after his assassination in 1965, this book became renowned for dramatizing the global expansion of Malcolm X's faith in Islam. As a Muslim outside the United States, Malcolm felt he was seen as a human being and not as an American Negro; yet in Mecca, Malcolm confronted his own alienation from Arabic ritual when he encountered Muslims of diverse complexions from many nations who did not speak English. Yet the hospitality and "*brotherhood*" (345) of diverse races and classes left him "utterly speechless and spellbound" (346) and transformed his way of thinking. Whereas whiteness had previously been signified by skin complexion, Malcolm X now associated it primarily with "specific attitudes and actions toward the black man" (340). He feels "blessed with a new insight into the true religion of Islam" (345) and its dedication to a radical Oneness of God and humanity through which "the 'white' attitude was removed from their minds" (347). He grew a beard during the *hajj* and changed his name to El-Hajj Malik El-Shabazz, Shabazz being an allusion to an ancient nation of Asian blacks who settled in Africa. Malcolm's transnational insights made him even more aware of how the "psychological castration" (345) of racism in the United States had "brainwashed" blacks from "thinking *internationally*" (353). The broadened scope of "global black thinking" (358) expressed so powerfully in his posthumous *Autobiography* has been considered perhaps his most important legacy. Sohail Daulatzai writes of how Islam provided Black Americans with the "alternative racial compass" of "Muslim

Internationalism" that radically re-spatialized a new geography of anticolonial resistance to white supremacy that went beyond pan-Africanism to include all nonwhite peoples.[17] For Malcolm X, a homegrown believer in the Nation of Islam, being part of the global *umma* internationalized his spiritual and political horizons. "I'm not an American," Malcolm X argued, claiming instead to be a Muslim human proud to be black experiencing an "American nightmare" as "a victim of the American system."[18]

Malcolm X's realignment with global Sunni Islam enabled an outsider critique of the exploitations of capitalism and imperialism of the purported "free world" upheld by the United States in the Cold War. A persistent anti-American criticism of some Muslims focused on the ways that materialism promotes an immodest sensuality lacking in dignity and depth. The influential Egyptian theologian of conservative Islamic thought, Sayyid Qutb, studied in the United States after World War II and found Americans to be a "strange, but amusing" enigma. Qutb juxtaposed America's "zenith of civilization" with its "nadir of primitiveness." Qutb presented the American Dream as materializing a genie's technological vision of prosperity; yet he found that Americans lacked a sensibility of elegance or a sense of the sacred because their vitality "acknowledges no limit or moral restraint" and was premised on the "temptation of the body alone."[19] Qutb's allegiance to Muslim Brotherhood rejected western excesses as an expression of *jahiliyyih* (ignorant worldliness or unbelief) and he became an influential martyr after he was hanged in 1966 for protesting Egypt's refusal to base its government on the Islamic law of *shariah*. Osama bin Laden, extending such protest, argued that because hatred toward enemies who refuse Islam is "the foundation of our religion," to extinguish this animosity was apostasy and to express it was "a justice and kindness," an oppositional *jihad* violently taken up by other islamists such as those in the ruthless ISIS/ISIL movement.[20]

The year 1965, when Malcolm X was assassinated and his autobiography was published, proved to be the beginning of a larger transformation as the Immigration and Naturalization Act for the first time allowed large numbers of Muslims to migrate to the United States to pursue permanent citizenship. The Islamic religion is a transnational phenomenon marked by what Anouar Malik has called "indispensable polycentricity" because its adherents profess different traditions, practice varied behaviors, and reside in and move through a variety of different ethnic cultures and political constituencies.[21] Over fifty years of continuing settlement has made American Muslims into "the most diverse religious community" within the United States.[22] Some Americans have sought to absorb Islam along with Judaism into an expanded Abrahamic heritage whose pluralized monotheism anachronistically buries the Qur'an within an original Biblical patriarchy.

Nevertheless, the trials that Muslims face in fully finding a home within US pluralism are demonstrated by the backlash after the Iranian revolution of 1979 and especially since the attacks of 9/11. The language of the Patriot Act itself attests that "Arab Americans, Muslim Americans, and Americans from South Asia play a vital role in our Nation and are entitled to nothing less than the full rights of every American," even as its passage ironically authorized the surveillance of supposed Muslim terrorists.[23] Naïve nativists in the United States, forgetful of their own genealogies of migration, are suspicious of the allegiance of Islamic immigrants and can doubt the racial loyalty of indigenous converts, in part because the majority is predominately African Americans. The alien obscurity of Islam is an effect of such attitudes, which are culturally enhanced by covert operations claiming secret intelligence, that the state does not reveal for reasons of security, used to justify the incarceration of Muslims abroad into black sites and prisons such as Guantanamo, and to subject Muslim citizens in the United States to systematic profiling. This disposition to malign Muslims, regardless of their social position, as "forever foreign" and "not quite white" is fostered by fear-mongers who mobilize anti-Muslim sentiment to rally political support.

Such discrimination adds to the many difficulties that Muslim immigrants face as a result of their diasporic displacement from their traditional home cultures. Today Muslim Americans together comprise over 1 percent of Americans – so diverse as to have no national or regional majority – and Americans make up only .15 percent of the world's Muslims.[24] American Muslimness is multiversal, involving a wide diversity of lifestyles – including indigenous, immigrant, and the so-called foreign-born – that are conditioned by a changing calculus of response that brings to each interaction a repertoire of translocal factors. Muslims are allied with intersecting affiliations: with their national culture (e.g., Iranian, Lebanese); with larger ethnic, racial, or regional groupings (e.g., Arab, African, Southeast Asian); by Muslim belief (e.g., Sunni, Shiite, Sufi); and by level of religiosity (e.g., practicing, cultural, secular). The migrations of Muslims to the United States and their growing numbers in the population have created new dynamics of transcultural encounter at a historical moment when American attitudes toward Islam are particularly fraught.

The presence of diverse Muslim citizens serves as a transnational challenge to the provincialities of nativism, a key theme expressed through the emergent field that can be called Muslimerican literature. Muslim American literary works, written by Muslims from across the diversity described earlier, dramatize tensions between adapting to American life and maintaining Muslim traditions and cultural allegiances to other nations. These are represented on a transcultural spectrum ranging between assimilation to rejection that reflects the transnational experience of being a part of a global *umma* while living as a religious minority in the United States. The final section of this chapter contrasts three novels that present diverse ways that Americans from Muslim backgrounds, and migrants and immigrants from Islamic countries, have dealt with the pressures of being Muslim in post 9/11 United States.

The criticisms that Qutb voiced about the empty seductions of American materialism are examined in Laila Halaby's *Once in a Promised Land* (2007), a novel that dramatizes the unsettling discovery that "wishes don't come true for Arabs in America."[25] Halaby, an Arab Arizonian born in Beirut to a Jordanian father and an American mother, poetically describes her transnationalism as being "homeless / with two homes," claiming that one "can't be an immigrant/ if you haven't left somewhere/ can't be a native/ if you're from somewhere else."[26] Her novel anatomizes the marriage of Jassim and Salwa Haddad who lose their moral groundings as the "comfort of routine" (217) of American professional life dries up any regenerative connection with each other and their Arab backgrounds. The crisis of 9/11 exacerbates this process of estrangement by unmooring them from the complacency of assimilation. Despite their secular lives, Jassim and Salwa are profiled as suspicious "Mahzslims" (56, 109), which makes them vulnerable to unmet desires that foster empathy but also leave each lurching into adultery as the dangerous culmination of American liberty. Halaby abandons her anguished Arab couple with no sustaining dream other than an unhomely desire that calls out distantly from the lost source of what Salman Rushdie called "Imaginary Homelands."[27]

Mohsin Hamid's broadly read novel *The Reluctant Fundamentalist* (2007) also disavows the promise of America while confronting readers with a test of how to interpret its Muslim Pakistani protagonist. Hamid was born in California, returned to Pakistan for his education, then attended Princeton before rejecting a life in the United States for London, and later a family life in his home city of Lahore. Hamid acknowledges he has always felt partly "foreign" and "a half outsider," yet his own transnational migrations have made him acutely aware of how "notional" claims of a superior civilization deny the hybridity of individual human experience. Hamid interrogates the "great strain on the hyphen bridging that identity called Muslim-American" to help him "understand my split self and my split world," critically exposing a fundamental paradox that the greatness of the United States "is in part built upon the denial of the equality of others outside its borders."[28] *The Reluctant Fundamentalist* fictively relates how discrimination against the transnational migrant eclipses American professions of democratic pluralism.

Hamid's story is confidently delivered as a streaming first-person mono-
logue by his protagonist Changez during one evening at a café Anarkali
bazaar in Lahore, Pakistan. The narration is delivered to a speechless
American interlocutor he has detained, who may be an undercover CIA
assassin on a corresponding mission to silence him. Changez relates how
he had achieved the undergraduate's dream of being hired as an analyst at
a New York investment firm, and Hamid plays on the irony that his job is
to evaluate the "fundamentals" of corporate worth. The tenacity that produces Changez's success, however, also blinds him to the outside status he
embodies as a result of his "foreignness." His composure crumbles after 9/
11 as his ethnic difference is transmuted from a cosmopolitan "advantage"
into a liability that he cannot evade. Changez's invisible Muslimness suddenly shifts to conspicuous overexposure. New York's subways, where he
"had always had the feeling of seamlessly blending in," become dangerous
spaces where he is "subjected to verbal abuse by complete strangers," and,
at work, he becomes "the subject of whispers and stares" (130). Ultimately
the shame of having sold out his home culture for the supposed success of
western materialism produces an anti-American conversion narrative doc-
umenting what Mucahit Bilici has called "homeland insecurity."[29] Hamid's
novel presents many behaviors that suggest that Changez is neither an
Islamic fundamentalist nor even a practicing Muslim, yet his ethnic difference, his criticism of American imperialism, and the beard he grows all
unfairly incriminate him in the eyes of his associates and tests the discrimination of his readers.

Hamid's observant unfolding of Changez's reluctant resentment educates
the reader about the naiveté of American nativism. Rather than being sym-
pathetic to "shared pain," Americans duplicitously couple equality with
empire, "knowing them to be contradictory and [yet] believing in both of
them." Hamid's analysis of American discriminations, told in a Pakistani
bazaar, dramatizes the "broadening arc of vision" (145) that comprises
the dynamism of transnational critique through which, as Hamid writes
in an essay, "hybrids reveal the boundaries between groups to be false."[30]
Changez's American experience possesses him with an "unwelcome sensibility" perceived though "an ex-Janissary's gaze" of one who had fought for
the empire that had enthralled him. These external eyes provide readers with
the perspective that Mikhail Bakhtin has called "outsidedness," that "our
real exterior can be seen and understood only by other people, because they
are located outside us in space and because they are others."[31] *The Reluctant
Fundamentalist* tests which spectrum of discrimination the reader will bring
to the fiction: a view that affirms that Changez is an anti-American enemy
or one that sees a young migrant who happens to be Muslim declaring

independence by trying to hold America to its own values despite the unjust treatment he has experienced. His novel probes the dilemma that Zareena Grewal charts in *Islam is a Foreign Country* that "where you are demanded to perform your citizenship and belonging as the very possibility of real inclusion [that] is denied in the same breath," you are left "nowhere."[32]

Halaby's and Hamid's novels intimate outsider perspectives that document how the indignities experienced by migrants who are cultural Muslims disqualify the American promise of democratic equality. Mohja Kahf's novel *The Girl in the Tangerine Scarf* (2006) begins with that "nowhere" but ultimately exemplifies how American pluralism can deepen Islamic faith in ways that generate a more transnational and utopian *umma*. Kahf's bildungsroman refigures the American archetype of the western pioneer woman to celebrate the fortitude of a Syrian immigrant named Khadra Shamsy in preserving her independence as a *muslimah* in the United States. During Khadra's upbringing in Indiana, the state that saw the rise of the resurgent KKK earlier in the twentieth century, America symbolized to her and her parents, teachers of Islam, the infidel threat of "shallow, wasteful, materialistic lives" (68) assumed by white supremacists since they took land from the Indians for whom the state is named. Khadra experiences a "battle zone" (123) between "the impossible, contradictory hopes the Muslim community had for her, and the infuriating, confining assumptions the Americans put on her" (358) in a way that refigures *jihad* as a nonviolent struggle for spiritual integration.[33] The novel opens with Khadra's pilgrimage back to her former community, seven years after she left in disgrace after an abortion and a divorce, now as photographer on assignment to report on the Muslims of Indianapolis as "a piece of history that no one in America has acknowledged yet" (391). Kahf's novel distills a deeper record of transnational encounters she opens her narrative lens onto a fuller spectrum of the lights and shadows of varied Muslim groups, experiences, and practices represented in the United States.

Part of the cultural work of Kahf's novel is to radically diversify the demographics and practice of Islam (and other religious beliefs) at the same time that she normalizes Muslim practice as an element of everyday American life. The novel is exuberantly rife with a cast of diverse immigrants of varied national homelands, sectarian backgrounds, and skin complexions, as well as domestic converts whose beliefs evolved across several generations within different racial communities. For example, the book ends with Khadra's brother proposing marriage to a Mormon girl, and Khadra resuming an adult relationship with a childhood friend raised as a Black Muslim, now a Harvard-educated *imam* who secretly plays a trombone in nightclubs. Kahf's novel itself practices the dynamics of Muslim daily life in "'Mreeka" (16) by enacting Islamic prayers and rituals, often through untranslated Arabic words, in ways that makes such strangeness feel familiar to readers. Indeed, Kahf describes how she structured the novel's climaxes around the attitudes of the sequential physical prostrations of obligatory *salat*.[34]

The Girl in the Tangerine Scarf exposes readers to a polycentric view of transnational Islam that transcends the conventions of orthodox ritual. Though born in Syria, Kahf herself had not revisited the country before she wrote the novel, yet Khadra's imagined return provides a unique "road to Damascus" experience in which she is instructed in by a worldly-wise aunt, an Arab Jew, and an enchanted poet of love who serve as muses for a more mystical expression of Islam open to the erotic energies of lyricism. The literary rituals of Kahf's transnational circumambulations melt away solid angles of exclusivity opening a Sufic submission to ecstatic interconnectedness symbolized by the tartness of Khadra's tangerine *hijab*. The novel dramatizes what Susan Koshy has called a "minority cosmopolitanism" that scales beyond the constraints of local attachments to orient itself in the flux of a deterritorialized world.[35] Kahf says in one of her poems, "The Mosque is under your feet, wherever you walk each day," and Khadra's father Wajdy testifies in the novel, "All the world is a prayer mat" (104).[36] Khadra's metamorphosis expresses the flowering of a more transnational expression of what it means to live an "Islamic lifestyle" (402). The novel exemplifies Peter Mandaville's "travelling Islam" through which translocal contacts between diverse Muslims dramatize internal disjunctures within Islam that also generate resources for rearticulating more plural possibilities for a transnational "Muslim public sphere."[37]

Kahf's novel thus counters the vision of America dramatized by several other works discussed in this essay by celebrating the ways that the United States becomes what Richard Gray has called an "interstitial space, a locus of interaction between contending national and cultural constituencies."[38] Kahf's novel expresses how American freedom can empower new expressions of Muslim belief open to the exhilaration of the senses, the uniqueness of individuality, and to the intimate experiences of women that have often been left out of traditional orthodox hierarchies. The novel conjoins Khadra's full and feminized conversion to Americanness (as a "heena'ed Hoosier" [325]) with the reader's progressive introduction to the transnational Islamic *umma*.[39] By the end of the Kahf's novel, the United States comes to represent a plural place where a diversity of Muslim experiences mesh with secular popular culture to form dynamic aspects of a convivial community. These are represented by Khadha's vision of "doing cartwheels in the prayer space" (377), and her friend Hanifa's circumambulations while racing the speedway of the Indianapolis 500 (440–41). Kahf's receptivity to transcultural resonances of secular and the sacred, in both critical and celebratory modalities, artistically exemplifies what Edward Said calls "contrapuntal analysis" – a musical term denoting "discrepant" variations, each with their own pace and formation, that cohere within an overall harmony.[40]

Islam has provided a horizon of global engagement for Americans since before the independence of the United States. Migrating Muslim cultural practices have circulated through the United States in different and at times contradictory registers, and these lines of connection have been recently multiplied through social media. Islamist groups muster support for *jihad* through these channels, *imams* from specific ethnic or national situations extend the reach of their teachings, and believers discover new transnational modes of Muslim belonging that transform their traditional practices. Literary expression is an important field of the transcultural process through which notions of Muslimness are negotiated in ways that can broaden readers' understanding of the contributions of Muslims. Since many Muslims come to the United States from different parts of the world, they embody a resource of difference for refiguring a more planetary involvement beyond the conventional boundaries of nations and homelands. This intercultural influence has been expanded through the growing mobilization, popularity, and circulation by Muslims of American cultural forms such as hip-hop and comedy.[41] Ultimately, the power of all these texts and performances ultimately depends on how non-Muslim Americans and American Muslims engage with and learn from them in ways that alters apprehensions about both Islam and the United States. They document a range of encounters such as Halaby's and Hamid's, who demonstrate how for some Muslims there is "nowhere" to belong as full Americans, to utopian expressions such as Kahf's that imagine how American freedoms can empower Islamic practice to be more transculturally diverse. Transnationalism today, marked by the publication of this volume, represents a transitional practice that registers an emergent planetary ethos whose politics are still limited by the impediments that elide a deeper discrimination of the intercultural flows between established nation-states and beyond their nativist imaginaries.

NOTES

1 Edward Said, *Covering Islam: How the Media and the Experts Determine How We See the Rest of the World* (New York: Pantheon, 1981), xv.
2 Geoffrey Nash, *Writing Muslim Identity* (London: Bloomsbury, 2012), 5.

3 Derek Gregory, *The Colonial Present: Afghanistan, Palestine, Iraq* (Malden, MA: Blackwell, 2004), 117, 263; Michael Shapiro, "Moral Geographies and the Ethics of Post-Sovereignty," *Public Culture* 6.3 (1994): 482.

4 Peter Mandaville, *Transnational Muslim Politics: Reimagining the Umma* (New York: Routledge, 2001), 101.

5 See Timothy Marr, *The Cultural Roots of American Islamicism* (Cambridge: Cambridge UP, 2006).

6 Royall Tyler, *The Algerine Captive; or the Life and Adventures of Doctor Updike Underhill*, v. 2 (Walpole, NH: David Carlisle, 1797), 45.

7 Jon Butler, *Awash in a Sea of Faith: Christianizing the American People* (Cambridge, MA: Harvard University Press, 2003), 130. On African Muslims in the Americas, see Allan D. Austin, Sylviane Diouf, Kambiz GhaneaBassiri, and Michael Gomez.

8 Ala Alryyes, trans. *A Muslim American Slave: The Life of Omar ibn Said* (Madison: University of Wisconsin Press, 2011).

9 Nicholas Said, *The Autobiography of Nicholas Said, A Native of Bornou, Eastern Soudan, Central Africa* (Memphis, TN: Shotwell, 1973). Web. <http://docsouth.unc.edu/neh/said/said.html>. A shorter earlier version was published as "A Native of Bornoo," *Atlantic Monthly* (October 1857): 485–95, and republished in Allan D. Austin, "Mohammed Ali Ben Said: Travels on Five Continents," *Contributions in Black Studies* 12 (2004), viewable at <http://scholarworks.umass.edu/cibs/vol12/iss1/15>. See also Safet Dabovic, "Out of Place: The Travels of Nicholas Said," *Criticism* 54 (Winter 2012): 59–83.

10 Olaudah Equiano stated that "I liked the place and the Turks extremely well" (90). During his two trips there he found Muslims to be more honest, moral, and free of prejudice than many Christians (94, 118–19, 195) and twice resolved to return "to end my days" (119) "never more to return" (124). *The Interesting Narrative of the Life of Olaudah Equiano, or Gustavus Vassa, the African*, v. 2 (London: self-published, 1789). Web. <http://docsouth.unc.edu/neh/equiano2/equiano2.html>. Said averred that "of all the nationalities of people I have seen in my life, I like the Turks the best ... The chief desire of my life, next to a visit to my home, is the desire I entertain of living among the *Osmanlis* again" (68–69).

11 Moustafa Bayoumi, "Moving Beliefs: The Panama Manuscript of Sheikh Sana See and African Diasporic Islam," *Interventions* 5 (2003): 58–91.

12 Elijah Muhammad, *Message to the Blackman in America* (Chicago: Muhammad Mosque of Islam No. 2, 1965), 111.

13 James Baldwin, *The Fire Next Time* (New York: Vintage, 1963), 46.

14 Nas, "Ghetto Prisoners," *I Am ...* (Columbia Records, 1999).

15 Marvin X, *Fly to Allah: Poems* (Fresno, CA: Al Kitab Sudan, 1969), 8.

16 *The Autobiography of Malcolm X, As Told to Alex Haley* (New York: Ballantine, 1965).

17 Sohail Daulatzai, *Black Star, Crescent Moon: The Muslim International and Black Freedom Beyond America* (Minneapolis: University of Minnesota Press, 2012), 22, 43.

18 Malcolm X, *Malcolm X Speaks*. George Breitman, ed. (New York: Grove, 1965), 26.

19 Sayyid Qutb, "Amriki allati Raayt" ["The American I Have Seen: In the Scale of Human Values"] (1951) in Kamal Abdel-Malek, *America in an Arab Mirror: Images of America in Arabic Travel Literature: An Anthology, 1895–1995*, trans. Tarek Masoud and Ammar Fakeeh (New York: St. Martin's, 2000), 9–27.

20 Osama Bin Ladin, "Moderate Islam Is a Prostration to the West," in *The Al Qaeda Reader*, ed. and trans. Raymond Ibrahim (New York: Doubleday, 2007), 43.

21 Anouar Malik, *Unveiling Traditions: Postcolonial Islam in a Polycentric World* (Durham, NC: Duke University Press, 2000), 132.

22 Gallup reports that in the US Muslim population, "African American represent the largest racial group (35%), more than a quarter classify themselves as 'white,' and about one in five identify themselves as 'Asian,' with 18% choosing 'other' and 1% 'Hispanic'" (Gallup's Center for Muslim Studies, *Muslim Americans: A National Portrait* [Washington, DC: Gallup, 2009], 10).

23 The USA Patriot Act is an acronym of "Uniting and Strengthening America by Providing Appropriate Tools Required to Intercept and Obstruct Terrorism Act of 2001" (Public Law 107–56), Sec. 102.

24 *The Future of the Global Muslim Population* (Pew Research Center, Forum on Religion & Public Life, 2011). Web. <www.pewforum.org/2011/01/27/the-future-of-the-global-muslim-population>.

25 Laila Halaby, *Once in a Promised Land: A Novel* (Boston, MA: Beacon Press, 2007), 184.

26 Laila Halaby, *My Name on his Tongue: Poems* (Syracuse, NY: Syracuse University Press, 2012), 119, 77.

27 Salman Rushdie, *Imaginary Homelands: Essays and Criticism, 1981–1991* (New York: Viking, 1991).

28 Mohsin Hamid, *Discontent and Its Civilizations: Dispatches from Lahore, New York, and London* (London: Riverhead, 2015), 3–4, 154, 44, 90–91, 141–42.

29 Mohsin Hamid, *The Reluctant Fundamentalist* (New York: Mariner, 2007), 44, 130; Mucahit Bilici, *Finding Mecca in America: How Islam Is Becoming an American Religion* (Chicago: University of Chicago Press, 2012).

30 Hamid, *Discontent*, xx, 16.

31 Hamid, *Reluctant Fundamentalist*, 124, 157; M. M. Bakhtin, *Speech Genres and Other Late Essays*, trans. Vern W. McGee (Austin: University of Texas Press, 1986), 7.

32 Zareena Grewal, *Islam Is a Foreign Country: American Muslims and the Global Crisis of Authority* (New York: NYU Press, 2013), 11.

33 Mohja Kahf, *The Girl in the Tangerine Scarf* (New York: Public Affairs, 2006), 207.

34 Abdur-Rahman Abou Almajd, "Mohja Kahf in a Dialogue around American Muslim Women," *Arab World Books Debate Corner*, March 4, 2011. Web. <www.forum.arabworldbooks.com/viewtopic.php?f=10&t=923>.

35 Susan Koshy, "Minority Cosmopolitanism," *PMLA* 126 (May 2011): 592–609.

36 Mohja Kahf, "Little Mosque Poems," *Journal of Pan African Studies* 4 (December 2010): 113.

37 Peter Mandaville, *Transnational Muslim Politics: Reimagining the Umma* (New York: Routledge, 2001).

38 Richard Gray, *After the Fall: American Literature Since 9/11* (Malden, MA: Wiley-Blackwell, 2011), 18.

39 Danielle Haque writes: "[T]he novel ultimately envisions the secular context as a place in which to foster the *umma* – the global, transnational community to which every Muslim belongs" ("The Postsecular Turn and Muslim American Literature," *American Literature* 86 [2014]: 801).

40 Edward Said, *Culture and Imperialism* (New York: Vintage, 1994), 32.

41 For example, see Hisham Aidi's charting of transnational popular culture in *Race, Empire, and the New Muslim Youth Culture* (New York, NY: Pantheon, 2014).

FURTHER READING

The scope of the subject of transnationalism in American literature precludes any claim to a comprehensive list of additional reading. This list is meant as a guide to further study and does not include texts already cited in essays in the volume. Thanks to the contributors for their suggestions.

Abu-Lughod, Lila. *Do Muslim Women Need Saving?* Cambridge, MA: Harvard University Press, 2013.
  Veiled Sentiments: Honor and Poetry in a Bedouin Society. Berkeley: University of California Press, 1986.
Adams, Rachel. *Continental Divides: Remapping the Cultures of North America.* Chicago: University of Chicago Press, 2009.
Agamben, Giorgio, trans. Daniel Heller Roazen. *Homo Sacer: Sovereign Power and Bare Life.* Palo Alto, CA: Stanford University Press, 1998.
Agamben, Giorgio. *The State of Exception.* Chicago: University of Chicago Press, 2005.
Ahmed, Rehana, Peter Morey, and Amina Yaqin, eds. *Culture, Diaspora, and Modernity in Muslim Writing.* New York and London: Routledge, 2012.
Albrow, M. *The Global Age: State and Society Beyond Modernity.* Stanford, CA: Stanford University Press, 1997.
Aldama, Arturo J. and Naomi H. Quinonez, eds. *Decolonial Voices: Chicana and Chicano Cultural Studies in the 21st Century.* Bloomington: Indiana University Press, 2002.
Allaston, Paul. *Latino Dreams: Transcultural Traffic and the U.S. National Imaginary.* Amsterdam: Rodopi, 2002.
Altman, Dennis. *Global Sex.* Chicago: University of Chicago Press, 2001.
Alsultany, Evelyn and Ella Shohat, eds. *Between The Middle East and the Americas: The Cultural Politics of Diaspora.* Ann Arbor: University of Michigan Press, 2013.
Aminrazavi, Mehdi, ed. *Sufism and American Literary Masters.* Albany: State University of New York Press, 2014.
Anderson, Benedict. *Imagined Communities: Reflections on the Origin and Spread of Nationalism.* Revised Edition. New York: Verso, 2006 (1983).
  The Spectre of Comparisons: Nationalism, Southeast Asia and the World. New York: Verso, 1998.

Appadurai, Arjun. *Modernity at Large: Cultural Dimensions of Globalization*. Minneapolis: University of Minnesota Press, 1996.

Appiah, Kwame Anthony. *Cosmopolitanism: Ethics in a World of Strangers*. New York: W. W. Norton, 2006.

In My Father's House: Africa and the Philosophy of Culture. New York: Oxford University Press, 1993.

Arac, Jonathan. *Impure Worlds: The Institution of Literature in the Age of the Novel*. New York: Fordham University Press, 2011.

Aravamudan, Srinivas. *Tropicopolitans: Colonialism and Agency, 1688–1804*. Durham, NC: Duke University Press, 1999.

Arendt, Hannah. *The Origins of Totalitarianism*. New York: Harcourt, Brace & Co., 1951.

Armstrong, Nancy and Leonard Tennenhouse. *The Imaginary Puritan: Literature, Intellectual Labor, and the Origins of Personal Life*. Berkeley: University of California Press, 1994.

Arondekar, Anjali. "Border/Line Sex: Queer Postcolonialities or How Race Matters Outside the U.S." *Interventions* 7, no. 2 (2005): 236–250.

Asad, Talal. *Formations of the Secular: Christianity, Islam, Modernity*. Stanford, CA: Stanford University Press, 2003.

Austin, Allan D. *African Muslims in Antebellum America: A Sourcebook*. New York: Garland, 1984.

Azam, Kousar J., ed. *Rediscovering America: American Studies in the New Century*. New Delhi: South Asian Publishers, 2001.

Bailyn, Bernard. *Atlantic History: Concepts and Contours*. Cambridge, MA: Harvard University Press, 2005.

Baker, Houston. *Modernism and the Harlem Renaissance*. Chicago: University of Chicago Press, 1987.

Bald, Vivek. *Bengali Harlem and the Lost Histories of South Asian America*. Cambridge, MA: Harvard University Press, 2013.

Baldwin, Kate A. *Beyond the Color Line and the Iron Curtain: Reading Encounters between Black and Red, 1922–1963*. Durham, NC: Duke University Press, 2002.

Banita, Georgiana. *Plotting Justice: Narrative Ethics and Literary Culture after 9/11*. Lincoln: University of Nebraska Press, 2012.

Baptist, Edward. *The Half Has Never Been Told: Slavery and the Making of American Capitalism*. New York: Basic Books, 2014.

Barrett, Lindon. *Racial Blackness and the Discontinuity of Western Modernity*. Urbana: University of Illinois Press, 2014.

Baucom, Ian, ed. *Specters of the Atlantic: Finance Capital, Slavery, and the Philosophy of History*. Durham, NC: Duke University Press, 2005.

Bauer, Ralph. *The Cultural Geography of Colonial American Literatures: Empire, Travel, Modernity*. Cambridge: Cambridge University Press, 2003.

"Hemispheric Studies." *PMLA* 124, no. 1 (2009): 234–50.

Bauer, Ralph and José Antonio Mazzotti, eds. *Creole Subjects: The Ambiguous Coloniality of Early American Literatures*. Chapel Hill: University of North Carolina Press, 2009.

Bayoumi, Mousafa. *This Muslim American Life: Dispatches from the War on Terror*. New York: New York University Press, 2015.

Behdad, Ali. *A Forgetful Nation: On Immigration and Cultural Identity in the United States.* Durham, NC: Duke University Press, 2005.

Belnap, Jeffrey and Raúl Fernández, eds. *José Martí's "Our America": From National to Hemispheric Cultural Studies.* Durham, NC: Duke University Press, 1998.

Benhabib, Seyla. *Another Cosmopolitanism.* New York: Oxford University Press, 2006.

Benitez-Rojo, Antonio. *The Repeating Island: The Caribbean and Postmodern Perspective.* Durham, NC: Duke University Press, 1996.

Bensch, Klaus and Genevieve Fabre. *African Diasporas in the New and Old Worlds: Consciousness and Imagination.* Amsterdam: Rodopi, 2004.

Bentley, Nancy. *Frantic Panoramas: American Literature and Mass Culture, 1870–1920.* Philadelphia: University of Pennsylvania Press, 2009.

Berlant, Lauren. *The Female Complaint: On the Unfinished Business of Sentimentality in American Culture.* Durham, NC: Duke University Press, 2008.

Berman, Jacob Rama. *American Arabesque: Arabs, Islam, and the 19th-Century Imaginary.* New York: New York University Press, 2012.

Berry, Chris, Fran Martin, and Audrey Yue, eds. *Mobile Cultures: New Media in Queer Asia.* Durham, NC: Duke University Press, 2003.

Berube, Michael. "American Studies without Exceptions." *PMLA* 118.1 (2003): 107–30.

Blackwell, Maylei. *Chicana Power: Contested Histories of Feminism in the Chicano Movement.* Austin: University of Texas Press, 2011.

Blair, Sara. *Henry James and the Writing of Race and Nation.* Cambridge: Cambridge University Press, 1996.

Blood, Chad. *Narrative: Indigenous Identity in American Indian and Maori Literary and Activist Texts.* Durham, NC: Duke University Press, 2002.

Boyce Davies, Carole. *Black Women, Writing, and Identity: Migrations of the Subject.* New York: Routledge, 1994.

Brading, David. *The First America: The Spanish Monarchy, Creole Patriots, and the Liberal State, 1492–1867.* New York: Cambridge University Press, 1993.

Mexican Phoenix: Our Lady of Guadalupe, Image and Tradition across Five Centuries. New York: Cambridge University Press, 2001.

Brady, Mary Pat. *Extinct Lands, Temporal Geographies: Chicana Literature and the Urgency of Space.* Durham, NC: Duke University Press, 2002.

"The Fungibility of Borders." *Nepantla: Views from South* 1.1 (2000): 171–90.

Braham, Persephone, ed. *African Diaspora in the Cultures of Latin America, the Caribbean, and the United States.* Lanham, MD: Rowan and Littlefield, 2015.

Brennan, Timothy. *At Home in the World: Cosmopolitanism Now.* Cambridge, MA: Harvard University Press, 1997.

Brickhouse, Anna. *Transamerican Literary Relations and the Nineteenth-Century Public Sphere.* Cambridge: Cambridge University Press, 2004.

Briggs, Laura. *Reproducing Empire: Race, Sex, Science and U.S. Imperialism in Puerto Rico.* Berkeley: University of California Press, 2002.

Briggs, Laura, Gladys McCormick, and J. T. Way. "Transnationalism: A Category of Analysis." *American Quarterly* 60.3 (2008): 625–48.

Brooks, Daphne. *Bodies in Dissent: Spectacular Performances of Race and Freedom 1850–1910.* Durham, NC: Duke University Press, 2006.

Brown, Bill. *A Sense of Things: The Object Matter of American Literature*. Chicago: University of Chicago Press, 2004.

Brown, Gillian. *Domestic Individualism: Imagining Self in Nineteenth-Century America*. Berkeley: University of California Press, 1992.

Brown, Wendy. *Walled States, Waning Sovereignty*. Cambridge, MA: MIT Press, 2010.

   Regulating Aversion: Tolerance in the Age of Identity and Empire. Princeton, NJ: Princeton University Press, 2008.

Buchenau, Barbara and Annette Paatz, eds. *Do the Americas Have a Common Literary History?* New York: Peter Lang, 2001.

Buck-Morss, Susan. *Hegel, Haiti, and Universal History*. Pittsburgh: University of Pittsburgh Press, 2009.

Buell, Lawrence. *The Dream of the Great American Novel*. Cambridge, MA: Belknap Press, 2016.

Buell, Lawrence and Wai Chee Dimock, eds. *Shades of the Planet: American Literature as World Literature*. Princeton, NJ: Princeton University Press, 2007.

Butler, Judith. *Precarious Life: The Powers of Mourning and Violence*. London: Verso, 2006.

Butler, Pamela and Jigna Desai, "Manolos, Marriage, and Mantras: Chick-Lit Criticism and Transnational Feminism." *Meridians: Feminisms, Race, Transnationalism* 8.2 (2008): 1–31.

Byrd, Alexander X. *Captives and Voyagers: Black Migrants across the Eighteenth-Century British Atlantic World*. Baton Rouge: Louisiana State University Press, 2008.

Cadava, Geraldo. *Standing on Common Ground: The Making of a Sunbelt Borderland*. Cambridge, MA: Harvard University Press, 2014.

Calderón, Héctor and José David Saldívar, eds. *Criticism in the Borderlands: Studies in Chicano Literature, Culture, and Ideology*. Durham, NC: Duke University Press, 1991.

Caliz-Montoro, Carmen. *Writing from the Borderlands: A Study of Chicano, Afro-Caribbean and Native Literatures in North America*. Toronto: TSAR, 2000.

Campt, Tina M. "Reading the Black German Experience: An Introduction." *Callaloo* 26, no. 2 (Spring 2003): 288–94.

Carby, Hazel V. *Cultures in Babylon: Black Britain and African America*. New York: Verso, 1999.

Carby, Hazel V.. *Race Men*. Cambridge, MA: Harvard University Press, 1998.

   Reconstructing Womanhood: The Emergence of the Afro-American Woman Novelist. Oxford: Oxford University Press, 1989.

Castillo, Debra and María Soccoro Tabuenca Córdoba. *Border Women: Writing from La Frontera*. Minneapolis: University of Minnesota Press, 2002.

Castillo, Susan. *Performing America: Colonial Encounters in New World Writing, 1500–1786*. London: Routledge, 2005.

Castronovo, Russ. *Necro Citizenship: Death, Eroticism, and the Public Sphere in the Nineteenth-Century United States*. Durham, NC: Duke University Press, 2001.

Castronovo, Russ and Susan Gilman, eds. *States of Emergency: The Object of American Studies*. Chapel Hill: University of North Carolina Press, 2009.

Caughie, Pamela, ed. *Disciplining Modernism*. New York: Palgrave, 2010.

Césaire, Aimé. *Cahier d'un retour au pays natal [Notebook of a Return to the Native Land]*. 1939. Translated by Clayton Eshleman. Middetown, CT: Wesleyan University Press, 2001.

Discourse on Colonialism. Translated by John Pinkham. New York: Monthly Review Press, 2000.

Chancy, Myriam. *Framing Silence: Revolutionary Novels by Haitian Women*. New Brunswick, NJ: Rutgers University Press, 1997.

Chauncey, George and Elizabeth Povinelli. "Thinking Sexuality Transnationally: An Introduction." Special issue, *GLQ: A Journal of Lesbian and Gay Studies* 5, no. 4 (1999): 439–50.

Cheah, Pheng and Bruce Robbins, eds. *Cosmopolitics: Thinking and Feeling about the Nation*. Minneapolis: Minnesota University Press, 2004.

Chevigny, Bell Gale and Gari Laguardia. *Reinventing the Americas: Comparative Studies of Literature in the United States and Spanish America*. Cambridge: Cambridge University Press, 1986.

Cheyfitz, Eric. *The Poetics of Imperialism: Translation and Colonization from the Tempest to Tarzan*. Philadelphia: University of Pennsylvania Press, 1997.

Chomsky, Noam. *Failed States: The Abuse of Power and the Assault on Democracy*. New York: Metropolitan Books, 2006.

Chu, Patricia. *Assimilating Asians: Gendered Strategies of Authorship in Asian America*. Durham, NC: Duke University Press, 2003.

Chuh, Kandace and Karen Shimakawa, eds. *Orientations: Mapping Studies in the Asian Diaspora*. Durham, NC: Duke University Press, 2001.

Clark, Vévé. "Developing Diaspora Literacy and Marasa Consciousness." In *Comparative American Identities: Race, Sex, and Nationality in the Modern Text*, edited by Hortense J. Spillers, 40–61. New York: Routledge, 1991.

Claviez, Thomas and Winfried Fluck, eds. *Theories of American Culture – Theories of American Studies*. Tubingen: Narr, 2003.

Clifford, James. *Routes: Travel & Translation in the Late Twentieth Century*. Cambridge, MA: Harvard University Press, 1997.

Concannon, Kevin, Francisco A. Lomeli, and Marc Preiewe, eds. *Imagined Transnationalism: U.S. Latino/a Literature, Culture, and Identity*. New York: Palgrave Macmillan, 2009.

Cooper, Frederick and Laura Ann Stoler, eds. *Tensions of Empire: Colonial Cultures in a Bourgeois World*. Berkeley: University of California Press, 1997.

Cueva, T. Jackie, Larissa M. Mercado-López, and Sonia Saldívar-Hull, eds. *El Mundo Zurdo 4: Selected Works from the Meetings of the 2012 Society for the Study of Gloria Anzaldúa*. San Francisco: Aunt Lute Books, 2015.

Davis, Angela Y. *Blues Legacies and Black Feminism: Gertrude Ma Rainey, Bessie Smith, and Billie Holiday*. New York: Vintage, 2011 (1999).

Davis, Angela Y. *Women, Race & Class*. New York: Random House, 1983.

Davis, David Brion. *Inhuman Bondage: The Rise and Fall of Slavery in the New World*. Oxford: Oxford University Press, 2008.

Dawson, Ashley and Malini Johar Schueller, eds. *Exceptional State: Contemporary U.S. Culture and the New Imperialism*. Durham, NC: Duke University Press, 2007.

Dayan, Colin (Joan). "Paul Gilroy's Slaves, Ships, and Routes: The Middle Passage as Metaphor." *Research in African Literatures* 27.4 (Winter 1996): 7–14.

Daymond, Douglas M. and Leslie G. Monkman, eds. *Towards a Canadian Literature: Essays, Editorials, and Manifestoes*, v. 1. Ottowa: Tecumseh Press, 1984.

Dear, Michael. *Why Walls Won't Work: Repairing the US-Mexico Divide.* New York: Oxford University Press, 2013.

DeGuzman, Maria. *Spain's Long Shadow: The Black Legend, Off-Whiteness, and Anglo-American Empire.* Minneapolis: University of Minnesota Press, 2005.

Deloria, Philip J. *Playing Indian.* New Haven, CT: Yale University Press, 1998.

Diaz, Vicente M. *Repositioning the Missionary: Rewriting the Histories of Colonialism, Native Catholicism, and Indigeneity in Guam.* Honolulu: University of Hawai'i Press, 2010.

Diener, Alexander C. and Joshua Hagen. *Borders: A Very Short Introduction.* New York: Oxford University Press, 2012.

Dillon, Elizabeth Maddock. *The Gender of Freedom: Fictions of Liberalism and the Literary Public Sphere.* Palo Alto, CA: Stanford University Press, 2004.

Dimock, Wai Chee. *Through Other Continents: American Literature across Deep Time.* Princeton, NJ: Princeton University Press, 2009.

"Scales of Agregation: Prenational, Subnational, Transnation." *ALH* 18.2 (2006).

Dinshaw, Carolyn. "The History of *GLQ*, Volume 1: LGBTQ Studies, Censorship, and Other Transnational Problems." *GLQ: A Journal of Lesbian and Gay Studies* 12.1 (2006): 5–26.

Diouf, Sylviane. *Servants of Allah: African Muslims Enslaved in the Americas.* New York: New York University Press, 1998.

Dirlik, Arif. "American Studies in the Time of Empire." *Comparative American Studies* 2.3 (2004): 287–302.

Dissanayake, Wimal and Rob Wilson, eds. *Global/Local: Cultural Production and the Transnational Imaginary.* Durham, NC: Duke University Press, 1996.

Doerfler, Jill. *Those Who Belong: Identity, Family, Blood, and Citizenship among the White Earth Anishinaabeg.* East Lansing: Michigan State University Press, 2015.

Doyle, Laura. *Freedom's Empire: Race and the Rise of the Novel in Atlantic Modernity, 1640–1940.* Durham, NC: Duke University Press, 2008.

Doyle, Laura and Laura Winkiel, eds. *Geomodernisms: Race, Modernism, Modernity.* Bloomington: Indiana University Press, 2005.

Dubey, Madhu. "Speculative Fictions of Slavery." *American Literature* 82.4 (2010): 779–805.

Dubinsky, Karen and Adele Perry. *Within and Without the Nation: Canadian History as Transnational History.* Toronto: University of Toronto Press, 2015.

Du Bois, W.E.B., *Black Reconstruction in America.* New York: Oxford University Press, 2014 (1935).

The World and Africa: An Inquiry into the Part Which Africa Has Played in World History. New York: Oxford University Press, 2014 (1947).

Darkwater: Voices from Within the Veil. New York: Oxford University Press, 2007 (1920).

Duggan, Lisa. *The Twilight of Equality?: Neoliberalism, Cultural Politics, and the Attack on Democracy.* Boston: Beacon Press, 2003.

Duvall, John N. and Robert P. Marzec, eds. *Narrating 9/11: Fantasies of State, Security, and Terrorism.* Baltimore, MD: Johns Hopkins University Press, 2015.

Edwards, Brent Hayes. *The Practice of Diaspora: Literature, Translation and the Rise of Black Internationalism.* Cambridge, MA: Harvard University Press, 2003.

Edwards, Brian T. *After the American Century: The Ends of U.S. Culture in the Middle East*. New York: Columbia University Press, 2015.

Morocco Bound: Disorienting America's Maghreb, from Casablanca to the Marrakech Express. Durham, NC: Duke University Press, 2005.

Einboden, Jeffrey. *Nineteenth-Century US Literature in Middle Eastern Languages*. Edinburgh: Edinburgh University Press, 2013.

Elliott, Emory. "Diversity in the United States and Abroad: What Does It Mean When American Studies is Transnational?" *American Quarterly* 59.1 (2007): 1–22.

Elliott, Jane and Gillian Harkins. "Introduction: Genres of Neoliberalism." Special issue of *Social Text*, 31.2 (2013).

Ellis, R. J. "Editorial: Transnational American Studies: For What?" *Comparative American Studies* 6.1 (2008): 3–4.

Elmer, Jonathan. *On Lingering and Being Last: Race and Sovereignty in the New World*. New York: Fordham University Press, 2008.

Elteren, Mel van. "U.S. Cultural Imperialism Today: Only a Chimera?" *SAIS Review* 23 (2003): 171.

Eng, David. *The Feeling of Kinship: Queer Liberalism and the Racialization of Intimacy*. Durham, NC: Duke University Press, 2010.

Eng, David and David Kazanjian, eds. *Loss: The Politics of Mourning*. Berkeley: University of California Press, 2002.

Erkkila, Betsy. "Ethnicity, Literary Theory, and the Grounds of Resistance." *American Quarterly* 47.4 (1995): 563–94.

Fabre, Michel. *From Harlem to Paris: Black American Writers in France, 1840–1980*. Urbana: University of Illinois Press, 1991.

Fadda-Conrey, Carol. *Contemporary Arab-American Literature: Transnational Reconfigurations of Citizenship and Belonging*. New York: New York University Press, 2014.

Fanon, Frantz. *Black Skin, White Masks*. Berkeley: Grove Press, 2008 (1952).

A Dying Colonialism. Berkeley: Grove Press, 1994 (1959).

Ferguson, Roderick. *The Reorder of Things: The University and Its Pedagogies of Minority Difference*. Minneapolis: University of Minnesota Press, 2012.

Fernandes, Leela. *Transnational Feminism in the United States: Knowledge, Ethics, Power*. New York: New York University, 2013.

Fischer, Sibylle. *Modernity Disavowed: Haiti and the Cultures of Slavery in the Age of Revolution*. Durham, NC: Duke University Press, 2004.

Fish, Cheryl J. *Black and White Women's Travel Narratives: Antebellum Explorations*. Gainesville: University Press of Florida, 2004.

Fish, Stanley and Walter Benn Michaels. *Our America: Nativism, Modernism, and Pluralism*. Durham, NC: Duke University Press, 1997.

Fishkin, Shelley Fisher. "American Literature in Transnational Perspective: The Case of Mark Twain," in *Blackwell Companion to American Literary Studies*, eds. Caroline F. Levander and Robert S. Levine. Hoboken, NJ: Wiley-Blackwell, 2011.

"American Studies in the 21st Century: A Usable Past." *Journal of British and American Studies* (Korea) 10 (2004): 31–55.

Fluck, Winfried. "Theories of American Culture (and the Transnational Turn in American Studies)." *REAL* 23 (2007): 59–77.

Fluck, Winfried and Werner Sollors. *German? American? Literature?: New Directions in German-American Studies*. New York: Peter Lang, 2002.

Fluck, Winfried and Johannes Voelz. *Romance with America?: Essays on Culture, Literature, and American Studies*. Heidelberg: Universitätsverlag Winter, 2009.

Fox, Claire. *The Fence and the River: Culture and Politics at the US-Mexico Border*. Minneapolis: University of Minnesota Press, 1999.

Friedman, Susan Stanford. *Planetary Modernisms: Provocations on Modernity Across Time*. New York: Columbia University Press, 2015.

Fuchs, Barbara. *Mimesis and Empire: The New World, Islam, and European Identities*. Cambridge: Cambridge University Press, 2001.

Gaines, Kevin K. *American Africans in Ghana: Black Expatriates and the Civil Rights Era*. Chapel Hill: University of North Carolina Press, 2008.

Gates, Jr., Henry Louis. "Tell me, sir ... what is 'Black' literature?" *PMLA* 105.1 (1990): 11–22.

Gates, Jr., Henry Louis, ed. *"Race," Writing, and Difference*. Chicago: University of Chicago Press, 1985.

George, Rosemary Marangoly. *The Politics of Home: Postcolonial Relocations and Twentieth-Century Fiction*. Cambridge: Cambridge University Press, 1996.

Ghanea-Bassiri, Kambiz. *A History of Islam in America: From the New World to the New World Order*. New York: Cambridge University Press, 2010.

Gikandi, Simon. *Slavery and the Culture of Taste*. Princeton, NJ: Princeton University Press, 2014.

  Writing in Limbo: Modernism and Caribbean Literature. Ithaca, NY: Cornell University Press, 1992.

Giles, Paul. *The Global Remapping of American Literature*. Princeton, NJ: Princeton University Press, 2011.

  Transatlantic Insurrections: British Culture and the Formation of American Literature, 1730–1860. Philadelphia: University of Pennsylvania Press, 2001.

  "Transnationalism and Classic American Literature." *PMLA* 118.1 (2003): 62–77.

Gillman, Susan. *Dark Twins: Imposture and Identity in Mark Twain's America*. Chicago: University of Chicago Press, 1989.

Gilmore, Ruth Wilson. *Golden Gulag: Prisons, Surplus, Crisis, and Opposition in Globalizing California*. Berkeley: University of California Press, 2007.

Gilroy, Paul. *Darker than Blue: On the Moral Economies of Black Atlantic Culture*. Cambridge, MA: Harvard University Press, 2011.

  Postcolonial Melancholia. New York: Columbia University Press, 2005.

  Against Race: Imagining Political Culture beyond the Color Line. Cambridge, MA: Belknap, 2001.

Glissant, Edouard. *Caribbean Discourse: Selected Essays*. Translated by J. Michael Dash. Charlottesville: University of Virginia Press, 1989.

Goeman, Mishuana. *Mark My Words: Native Women Mapping Our Nations*. Minneapolis: University of Minnesota Press, 2013.

Goldstein, Alyosha, "Where the Nation Takes Place: Proprietary Regimes, Antistatism, and U.S. Settler Colonialism." *South Atlantic Quarterly* 107.4 (2008): 833–61.

Gomez, Michael A. *Black Crescent: The Experience and Legacy of African Muslims in the Americas*. New York: Cambridge University Press, 2005.

Gopinath, Gayatri. *Impossible Desires: Queer Diasporas and South Asian Public Cultures*. Durham, NC: Duke University Press, 2005.

"Homo-Economics: Queer Sexualities in a Transnational Frame." In Rosemary George, ed., *Burning Down the House: Recycling Domesticity*, 102–24. Boulder, CO: Westview Press, 1998.

Goudie, Sean. *Creole America: The West Indies and the Formation of Literature and Culture in the New Republic*. Philadelphia: University of Pennsylvania Press, 2006.

Gould, Philip. *Barbaric Traffic: Commerce and Antislavery in the Eighteenth-Century Atlantic World*. Cambridge, MA: Harvard University Press, 2003.

Goyal, Yogita. "Black Nationalist Hokum: George Schuyler's Transnational Critique." *African American Review* 47.1 (Spring 2014): 21–36.

Grewal, Inderpal. *Transnational America: Feminisms, Diasporas, Neoliberalisms*. Durham, NC: Duke University Press, 2005.

Grewal, Inderpal and Caren Kaplan, eds. *Scattered Hegemonies: Postmodernity and Transnational Feminist Practices*. Minneapolis: University of Minnesota Press, 1994.

Griffin, Farah Jasmine. '*Who Set You Flowin'?: The African-American Migration Narrative*. New York: Oxford University Press, 1995.

Gross, Robert A. "The Transnational Turn: Rediscovering American Studies in a Wider World." *Journal of American Studies* 34.3 (2000): 373–93.

Gruesz, Kirsten. *Ambassadors of Culture: The Transamerican Origins of Latino Writing*. Princeton, NJ: Princeton University Press, 2002.

Guidotti-Hernández, Nicole M. *Unspeakable Violence: Remapping U.S. and Mexican National Imaginaries*. Durham, NC: Duke University Press, 2011.

Guterl, Matthew Pratt. *Josephine Baker and the Rainbow Tribe*. Cambridge, MA: Harvard University Press, 2014.

Halberstam, Jack. *In a Queer Time and Place: Transgender Bodies, Subcultural Lives*. New York: NYU Press, 2005.

Hall, Stuart. "Cultural Identity and Cinematic Representation." In *Black British Cultural Studies: A Reader*, edited by Houston Baker, Manthia Diawara, and Ruth H. Lindeborg, 210–22. Chicago: University of Chicago Press, 1996.

"Cultural Identity and Diaspora." In *Contemporary Postcolonial Theory: A Reader*, edited by Padmini Mongia, 110–21. London: Arnold, 1996.

The Floating Signifier. Northampton, MA: Media Education Foundation, 2002.

Portrait of the Caribbean. New York: Ambrose Video Pub, 1992.

Representation: Cultural Representations and Signifying Practices. London: Sage, 1997.

Hall, Stuart and Bram Gieben. *Formations of Modernity*. Oxford: Open University, 1992.

Hardt, Michael and Antonio Negri. *Multitude: War and Democracy in the Age of Empire*. New York: Penguin, 2004.

Harney, Stefano and Fred Moten. *The Undercommons: Fugitive Planning and Black Study*. New York: Autonomedia, 2013

Harris, Cheryl. "Whiteness as Property." *Harvard Law Review* 106.8 (1993): 1707–91.

Hart, Matthew. *Nations of Nothing But Poetry: Modernism, Transnationalism, and Synthetic Vernacular Writing*. Oxford: Oxford University Press, 2010.

Hartman, Saidiya V. *Lose Your Mother: A Journey Along the Atlantic Slave Route*. New York: Farrar, Straus and Giroux, 2008.

Scenes of Subjection: Terror, Slavery, and Self-Making in Nineteenth-Century America. New York: Oxford University Press, 1997.

Harvey, David. *The New Imperialism*. Oxford: Oxford University Press, 2003.

Hassan, Waïl S. *Immigrant Narratives: Orientalism and Cultural Translations in Arab American and Arab British Literature*. New York: Oxford University Press, 2011.

Hayot, Eric. *On Literary Worlds*. Oxford: Oxford University Press, 2012.

Heise, Ursula. *Sense of Place and Sense of Planet*. Oxford: Oxford University Press, 2008.

Holland, Sharon Patricia and Tiya Miles, eds. *Crossing Waters, Crossing Worlds: The African Diaspora in Indian Country*. Durham, NC: Duke University Press, 2006.

Hong, Grace Kyungwon and Roderick Ferguson, eds. *Strange Affinities: The Gender and Sexual Politics of Comparative Racialization*. Durham, NC: Duke University Press, 2011.

Huhndorf, Shari. *Mapping the Americas: The Transnational Politics of Contemporary Native Culture*. Ithaca, NY: Cornell University Press, 2009.

Hutchinson, George. *In Search of Nella Larsen: A Biography of the Color Line*. Cambridge, MA: Harvard University Press, 2006.

Hutner, Gordon. *What America Read: Taste, Class, and the Novel, 1920–1960*. Chapel Hill: University of North Carolina Press, 2009.

Ickstadt, Heinz. "American Studies in an Age of Globalization." *American Quarterly* 54.4 (2002): 543–62.

Irele, Abiola. *The African Imagination: Literature in Africa and the Black Diaspora*. Oxford: Oxford University Press, 2001.

Isaac, Allan Punzalan. *American Tropics: Articulating Filipino America*. Minneapolis: University of Minnesota Press, 2006.

Jackson, Richard L. *Black Literature and Humanism in Latin America*. Athens: University of Georgia Press, 2008.

    The Black Image in Latin American Literature. Albuquerque: University of New Mexico Pres, 1976.

Jacobson, Matthew Frye. *Whiteness of a Different Color: European Immigrants and the Alchemy of Race*. Cambridge, MA: Harvard University Press, 1998.

Jamal, Amaney and Nadine Naber, eds. *Race and Arab Americans before and after 9/11: From Invisible Citizens to Visible Subjects*. Syracuse, NY: Syracuse University Press, 2008.

Jameson, Frederic and Masao Miyoshi, eds. *The Cultures of Globalization*. Durham, NC: Duke University Press, 1998.

Jehlen, Myra. *American Incarnation: The Individual, the Nation, and the Continent*. Cambridge, MA: Harvard University Press, 1986.

Jehlen, Myra and Michael Warner, eds. *The English Literatures of America, 1500–1800*. New York: Routledge, 1996.

Jung, Moon-Ho. "*Black Reconstruction* and Empire." *South Atlantic Quarterly* 111.3 (Summer 2013): 465–71.

Kang, Laura. *Compositional Subjects: Enfiguring Asian/American Women*. Durham, NC: Duke University Press, 2002.

Kaplan, Amy. *The Anarchy of Empire in the Making of U.S. Culture*. Cambridge, MA: Harvard University Press, 2002.

    "Violent Belongings and the Question of Empire Today." *American Quarterly* 56.1 (2004): 1–18.

Kaplan, Caren. *Questions of Travel: Postmodern Discourses of Displacement.* Durham, NC: Duke University Press, 1996.

Kaplan, Caren, Norma Alarcon, and Minoo Moallem, eds. *Between Woman and Nation: Nationalisms, Transnational Feminisms, and the State.* Durham, NC: Duke University Press, 1999.

Kauanui, J. Kehaulani. "Colonialism in Equality: Hawaiian Sovereignty and the Question of U.S. Civil Rights." *South Atlantic Quarterly* 107.4 (2008): 635–50.

Kaup, Monika and Debra J. Rosenthal, eds. *Mixing Race, Mixing Culture: Inter-American Literary Dialogues.* Austin: University of Texas Press, 2002.

Kazanjian, David. *The Colonizing Trick: National Culture and Imperial Citizenship in Early America.* Minneapolis: University of Minnesota Press, 2003.

"Race, Nation, and Equality: Olaudah Equiano's *Interesting Narrative* and a Genealogy of U.S. Mercantilism," in *Post-nationalist American Studies*, ed. John Carlos Rowe, 129–65. Berkeley: University of California Press, 2000.

Keizer, Arlene. *Black Subjects: Identity Formation in the Contemporary Narrative of Slavery.* Ithaca, NY: Cornell University Press, 2004.

Kelley, Robin D. G. *Africa Speaks, American Answers!: Modern Jazz in Revolutionary Times.* Cambridge, MA: Harvard University Press, 2012.

"A Poetics of Anticolonialism." *Monthly Review* 51.6 (1999). <http://monthlyreview .org/1999/11/01/a-poetics-of-anticolonialism/>. Accessed January 1, 2016.

Kelley, Robin D. G. and Sidney J. Lemelle, eds. *Imagining Home: Class, Culture, and Nationalism in the African Diaspora.* London: Verso, 1995.

Kelley, Robin D. G. and Franklin Rosemont. *Black, Brown, & Beige: Surrealist Writings from Africa and the Diaspora.* Austin: University of Texas Press, 2009.

Kim, Jodi. *Ends of Empire: Asian American Critique and Cold War Compositions.* Minneapolis: University of Minnesota Press, 2010.

King, Nicole. *C. L. R. James and Creolization: Circles of Influence.* Jackson: University of Mississippi Press, 2001.

Lauter, Paul. "From Multiculturalism to Immigration Shock." *Journal of Transnational American Studies* 1.1 (2009): 1–20.

"Is American Studies Anti-American?" In *(Anti-)Americanisms*, edited by Michael Draxlbauer, Astrid M. Fellner, and Thomas Fröschl, 18–31. Vienna, Austria: LIT, 2004.

"American Studies at Its Borders: Identity and Discipline." In *Negotiations of America's National Identity, II*, edited by Roland Hagenbüchle, Josef Raab, and Marietta Messmer, 387–404. Tübingen, Germany: Stauffenburg, 2000.

Lazo, Rodridgo. *Writing to Cuba: Filibustering and Cuban Exiles in the United States.* Chapel Hill: University of North Carolina Press, 2005

Lee, Erika. *At America's Gates: Chinese Immigration during the Exclusion Era, 1882–1943.* Chapel Hill: University of North Carolina Press, 2003.

Lee, Rachel. *The Americas of Asian American Literature: Gendered Fictions of Nation and Transnation.* Princeton, NJ: Princeton University Press, 1999.

Lemke, Sieglinde. *Primitivist Modernism: Black Culture and the Origins of Transatlantic Modernism.* Oxford: Oxford University Press, 1998.

Lenz, Günter. "Border Cultures, Creolization, and Diasporas: Negotiating Cultures of Difference in America." In *Negotiations of America's National Identity, II*, edited by Roland Hagenbüchle, Josef Raab, and Marietta Messmer, 362–86. Tübingen, Germany: Stauffenburg, 2000.

"Internationalizing American Studies: Predecessors, Paradigms, and Cultural Critique – A View from Germany." In *Predecessors: Intellectual Lineages in American Studies*, edited by Rob Kroes, 236–55. Amsterdam: VU Press, 1999.

Leonard, Irving. *Books of the Brave: Being an Account of Books and Men in the Spanish Conquest and Settlement of the Sixteenth-Century New World*. Berkeley: University of California Press, 1992.

Levander, Caroline F. *Where Is American Literature?* New York: Wiley-Blackwell, 2013.

Levander, Caroline F., and Matthew Pratt Guterl. *Hotel Life: The Story of a Place Where Anything Can Happen*. Chapel Hill: University of North Carolina Press, 2015.

Levander, Caroline F., and Robert S. Levine, eds. *Hemispheric American Studies*. New Brunswick, NJ: Rutgers University Press, 2007.

Levecq, Christine. *Slavery and Sentiment: The Politics of Feeling in Black Atlantic Slavery Writing, 1770–1850*. Lebanon, NH: University Press of New England, 2008.

Levine, Robert. *Dislocating Race and Nation: Episodes in Nineteenth-Century American Literary Nationalism*. Chapel Hill: University of North Carolina Press, 2008.

Levy, Indra. "Comedy Can be Deadly: Or, the Story of How Mark Twain Killed Hara Hoitsuan." *Journal of Japanese Studies* 37.2 (2011): 325–428.

Lewis, Marvin A. *Afro-Argentine Discourse: Another Dimension of the Black Diaspora*. Columbia: University of Missouri Press, 1996.

Afro-Hispanic Poetry, 1940–80: From Slavery to Negritud in South American Verse. Columbia: University of Missouri Press, 1983.

Li, David Leiwei. *Imagining the Nation: Asian American Literature and Cultural Concerns*. Stanford, CA: Stanford University Press, 1998.

Lim, Shirley Geok-lin, John Blair Gamber, Stephen Hong Sohn, and Gina Valentino, eds. *Transnational Asian American Literature: Sites and Transits*. Philadelphia: Temple University Press, 2006.

Linebaugh, Peter and Marcus Rediker. *Many-Headed Hydra: Sailors, Slaves, Commoners, and the Hidden History of the Revolutionary Atlantic*. Boston, MA: Beacon Press, 2000.

Ling, Jinqi. *Narrating Nationalisms: Ideology and Form in Asian American Literature*. New York: Oxford University Press, 1998.

Lionnet, Francoise, and Shu-mei Shih, eds. *The Creolization of Theory*. Durham, NC: Duke University Press, 2011.

Lipsitz, George. *American Studies in a Moment of Danger*. Minneapolis: University of Minnesota Press, 2001.

Liu, Petrus, and Lisa Rofel, eds. "Beyond the Strai(gh)ts: Transnationalism and Queer Chinese Politics." Special issue, *positions: east asia cultures critique* 18.2 (Fall 2010): 281–289.

Lomas, Clara. "Transborder Discourse: The Articulation of Gender in the Borderlands in the Early Twentieth Century." *Frontiers: A Journal of Women Studies* 24.2–3 (2003): 51–74.

López, Marissa K. 2011. *Chicano Nations: The Hemispheric Origins of Mexican American Literature*. New York: New York University Press.

Lott, Eric. *Love and Theft: Blackface Minstrelsy and the American Working Class*. New York: Oxford University Press, 1995.

Lowe, Lisa. *Immigrant Acts: On Asian American Cultural Politics.* Durham, NC: Duke University Press, 1996.

Lowe, Lisa, and David Lloyd, eds. *The Politics of Culture in the Shadow of Capital.* Durham, NC: Duke University Press, 1997.

Lubin, Alex. *Geographies of Liberation: The Making of an Afro-Arab Political Imaginary.* Chapel Hill: University of North Carolina Press, 2014.

Luciano, Dana, and Ivy Wilson. *Unsettled States: Nineteenth-Century American Literary Studies.* New York: NYU Press, 2014.

Luis, William. *Dance between Two Cultures: Latino Caribbean Literature Written in the United States.* Nashville, TN: Vanderbilt University Press, 1997.

Luis-Brown, David. *Waves of Decolonization: Discourses of Race and Hemispheric Citizenship in Cuba, Mexico, and the United States.* Durham, NC: Duke University Press, 2008.

Lye, Colleen. *America's Asia: Racial Form and American Literature, 1893–1945.* Princeton, NJ: Princeton University Press, 2005.

Ma, Sheng-mei. *Immigrant Subjectivities in Asian American and Asian Diaspora Literatures.* Albany: SUNY Press, 1998.

Makdisi, Saree. *Palestine Inside Out: An Everyday Occupation.* New York: Norton, 2008.

Malave, Arnaldo Cruz, and Martin Manalansan, eds. *Queer Globalizations: Citizenship, Sexualities and the Afterlife of Colonialism.* New York: NYU Press, 2002.

Manalansan, Martin F. *Global Divas: Filipino Gay Men in the Diaspora.* Durham, NC: Duke University Press, 2003.

Marez, Curtis. *Farm Worker Futurism and Technologies of Resistance.* Minneapolis: University of Minnesota Press, 2015.

Marino, Elisabetta, and Begona Simal, eds. *Transnational, National, and Personal Voices: New Perspectives on Asian American and Asian Diasporic Women Writers.* Munster: Lit Verlag, 2004.

Marr, Tim. *The Cultural Roots of American Islamicism.* New York: Cambridge University Press, 2006.

Marti, Jose, and Esther Allen, eds. *Selected Writings.* New York: Penguin, 2002.

Martin, Fran. "Transnational Queer Sinophone Cultures." In Vera Mackie and Mark McLelland, eds., *Routledge Handbook of Sexuality Studies in East Asia.* 35–59. New York: Routledge, 2015.

Mbembe, Achille. *On the Postcolony.* Berkeley: University of California Press, 2001. "Necropolitics." *Public Culture* 15.1 (2003): 11–40.

McBride, Dwight. "The Black Atlantic: Modernity and Double Consciousness." *Modern Fiction Studies* 41.2 (Summer 1995): 388–91.

McClennen, Sophia A. "Inter-American Studies or Imperial American Studies?" *Comparative American Studies* 3.4 (2005): 393–413.

McCloud, Aminah Beverly. *Transnational Muslims in American Society.* Gainesville: University Press of Florida, 2006.

McKenna, Teresa. *Migrant Song: Politics and Process in Contemporary Chicano Literature.* Austin: University of Texas Press, 1997.

Mendoza, Victor. *Metroimperial Intimacies: Fantasy, Racial-Sexual Governance, and the Philippines in US Imperialism, 1899–1913.* Durham, NC: Duke University Press, 2015.

Michaels, Walter Benn. *The Trouble with Diversity: How We Learned to Love Identity and Ignore Inequality*. New York: Metropolitan Books, 2006.

Michaelsen, Scott, and David E. Johnson. *Border Theory: The Limits of Cultural Politics*. Minneapolis: University of Minnesota Press, 1997.

Mignolo, Walter. *The Darker Side of Western Modernity: Global Futures, Decolonial Options*. Durham, NC: Duke University Press, 2011.

   Local Histories / Global Designs: Coloniality, Subaltern Knowledges, and Border Thinking. Princeton, NJ: Princeton University Press, 2000.

   The Darker Side of the Renaissance: Literacy, Territoriality, and Colonization. Ann Arbor: University of Michigan Press, 1995.

Miles, Tiya. *Ties That Bind: An Afro-Cherokee Family in Slavery and in Freedom*. University of California Press, 2005.

Mohanty, Chandra Talpade. *Feminisms without Borders: Decolonizing Theory, Practicing Solidarity*. Durham, NC: Duke University Press, 2003.

Montejano, David. *Anglos and Mexicans in the Making of Texas, 1836–1986*. Austin: University of Texas Press, 1987.

Montgomery, Maureen E. "Transculturations: American Studies in a Globalizing World – the Globalizing World in American Studies." *Amerikastudien/American Studies* 47.1 (2002): 115–19.

Moretti, Franco. *Graphs, Maps, Trees: Abstract Models for Literary History*. New York: Verso, 2007.

   "Conjectures on World Literature." *New Left Review* 1 (2000): 54–68.

Morey, Peter, and Amina Yaqin. *Framing Muslims: Stereotyping and Representation after 9/11*. Cambridge, MA: Harvard University Press, 2011.

Moya, Paula. *The Social Imperative: Race, Close Reading, and Contemporary Literary Criticism*. Stanford, CA: Stanford University Press, 2016.

Muñoz, José Esteban. *Disidentifications: Queers of Color and the Performance of Politics*. Minnesota: University of Minnesota Press, 1999.

Muthyala, John. "'America' in Transit: The Heresies of American Studies Abroad" *Comparative American Studies* 1.4 (2003): 395–420.

Mutman, Mahmut. *The Politics of Writing Islam: Voicing Difference*. New York: Bloomsbury Academic, 2014.

Nadkarni, Asha. *Eugenic Feminism: Reproductive Nationalism in the United States and India*. Minneapolis: University of Minnesota Press, 2014.

Nelson, Dana D. *The Word in Black and White: Reading "Race" in American Literature, 1638–1867*. New York: Oxford University Press, 1992.

Ngai, Mae M. *Impossible Subjects: Illegal Aliens and the Making of Modern America*. Princeton, NJ: Princeton University Press, 2005.

Nunes, Zita Cristina. *Resisting Remainders: Race and Democracy in the Literature of the Americas*. Minneapolis: University of Minnesota Press, 2007.

Nussbaum, Felicity A. *The Global Eighteenth Century*. Baltimore: Johns Hopkins University Press, 2003.

   "Between 'Oriental' and 'Blacks So Called,' 1688–1788," in *The Postcolonial Enlightenment: Eighteenth-Century Colonialisms and Postcolonial Theories*, eds. Daniel Carey and Lynn Festa. 137–66. New York: Oxford University Press, 2009.

   "Slavery, Blackness, and Islam: The Arabian Nights in the Eighteenth Century." *Essays and Studies for the English Association*, eds. Brycchan Carey and Peter Kitson. 150–72. Woodbridge, Suffolk: Boydell and Brewer, 2007.

O'Gorman, Daniel. *Fictions of the War on Terror: Difference and the Transnational 9/11 Novel*. New York: Palgrave Macmillan, 2015.

Ong, Aihwa. *Neoliberalism as Exception*. Durham, NC: Duke University Press, 2006.

Flexible Citizenship: The Cultural Logics of Transnationality. Durham, NC: Duke University Press, 1999.

Palumbo-Liu, David. *The Deliverance of Others: Reading Literature in a Global Age*. Durham, NC: Duke University Press, 2005.

Asian/U.S.: Historical Crossings of a Racial Frontier. Stanford, CA: Stanford University Press, 1999.

Pappe, Ilan. "Zionism and Colonialism: A Comparative View of Diluted Colonialism in Asian and Africa." *South Atlantic Quarterly* 107.4 (2008): 611–33.

Paredes, Américo. *"With His Pistol in His Hand": A Border Ballad and Its Hero*. Austin: University of Texas Press, 1959.

Park, Josephine. *Apparitions of Asia: Modernist Form and Asian American Poetics*. New York: Oxford University Press, 2008.

Parker, Andrew, Mary Russo, Doris Sommer, and Patricia Yaeger, eds. *Nationalisms and Sexualities*. New York: Routledge, 1992.

Paquet, Sandra Pouchet. *Caribbean Autobiography: Cultural Identity and Self-Representation*. Madison: University of Wisconsin Press, 2002.

Patterson, Orlando. *Slavery and Social Death: A Comparative Study*. Cambridge, MA: Harvard University Press, 1985.

Pease, Donald E., and Yuan Shu, eds. *American Studies as Transnational Practice: Turning toward the Transpacific*. Hanover, NH: Dartmouth College Press, 2016.

Pendleton, Mark. "Transnational Sexual Politics in East Asia." In Vera Mackie and Mark McLelland, eds., *Routledge Handbook of Sexuality Studies in East Asia*. 21–34. New York: Routledge, 2015.

Peterson, Carla L. *Doers of the Word: African-American Women Speakers and Writers in the North (1830–1880)*. New Brunswick, NJ: Rutgers University Press, 1998.

Pinto, Samantha. *Difficult Diasporas: The Transnational Feminist Aesthetic of the Black Atlantic*. New York: New York University, 2013.

Porter, Carolyn. "What We Know that We Don't Know: Remapping American Literary Studies." *American Literary History* 6.3 (1994): 467–526.

Posnock, Ross. *Color and Culture: Black Writers and the Making of the Modern Intellectual*. Cambridge, MA: Harvard University Press, 2000.

Pratt, Lloyd. *The Strangers Book: The Human of African American Literature*. Philadelphia: University of Pennsylvania Pressm 2016.

Priewe, Marc. *Writing Transit: Refiguring National Imaginaries in Chicana/o Narratives*. Heidelberg: Winter 2007.

Puar, Jasbir. *Terrorist Assemblages: Homonationalism in Queer Times*. Durham, NC: Duke University Press, 2007.

Quijano, Anibal, and Immanuel Wallerstein. "Americanity as a concept, or the Americas in the modern world-system." *International Journal of Social Sciences* 134 (1992): 134–58.

Rafael, Vicente L. *Motherless Tongues: The Insurgency of Language amid Wars of Translation*. Durham, NC: Duke University Press, 2016.

The Promise of the Foreign: Nationalism and the Technics of Translation in the Spanish Philippines. Durham, NC: Duke University Press, 2005.

Ramazani, Jahan. *A Transnational Poetics.* Chicago: University of Chicago Press, 2015.

The Hybrid Muse: Postcolonial Poetry in English. Chicago: University of Chicago Press, 2001.

Randall, Martin. *9/11 and the Literature of Terror.* Edinburgh: Edinburgh University Press, 2011.

Redmond, Shana. *Anthem: Social Movements and the Sound of Solidarity in the African Diaspora.* New York: New York University Press, 2013.

Rich, Adrienne. "Notes Towards a Politics of Location." In *Blood, Bread and Poetry: Selected Prose 1979–1985.* 210–31. London: Little Brown & Co., 1984.

Rifkin, Mark. *Settler Common Sense: Queerness and Everyday Colonialism in the American Renaissance.* Minneapolis: University of Minnesota Press, 2014.

When Did Indians Become Straight?: Kinship, the History of Sexuality, and Native Sovereignty. New York: Oxford University Press, 2011.

Manifesting America: The Imperial Construction of U.S. National Space. New York: Oxford University Press, 2009.

Robbins, Bruce. *Feeling Global: Internationalism in Distress.* New York: New York University Press, 1999.

Roediger, David. *Working Toward Whiteness: How America's Immigrants Became White.* New York: Basic Books, 2005.

Towards the Abolition of Whiteness: Essays on Race, Class, and Politics. New York: Verso, 1994.

Rofel, Lisa. *Desiring China: Experiments in Neoliberalism, Sexuality and Public Culture.* Durham, NC: Duke University Press, 2007.

Rosenberg, Emily S. *Financial Missionaries to the World: The Politics and Culture of Dollar Diplomacy, 1900–1930.* Durham, NC: Duke University Press, 2003.

Rowe, John Carlos, ed. *The New American Studies.* Minneapolis: University of Minnesota Press, 2002.

ed. *Post-Nationalist American Studies.* Berkeley: University of California Press, 2000.

Rowe, John Carlos. *The Cultural Politics of the New American Studies.* Ann Arbor, MI: Open Humanities Press, 2012.

"Nineteenth-Century United States Literary Culture and Transnationality." *PMLA* 118.1 (2003): 78–89.

Literary Culture and U.S. Imperialism: from the Revolution to World War II. Oxford: Oxford University Press, 2000.

Ruiz, Vicki L. *From Out of the Shadows: Mexican Women in Twentieth-Century America.* New York: Oxford University Press, 1998.

Ruiz, Vicki L.. "Nuestra America: Latino History as United States History." *Journal of American History* 93.3 (2006): 655–72.

Sadowski-Smith. *Border Fictions: Globalization, Empire, and Writing at the Boundaries of the United States.* Charlottesville: University of Virginia Press, 2008.

Said, Edward. *Humanism and Democratic Criticism.* New York: Columbia University Press, 2004.

Reflections on Exile and Other Essays. Cambridge, MA: Harvard University Press, 2000.

Salaita, Steven. *Arab American Literary Fictions, Cultures, and Politics.* New York: Palgrave Macmillan, 2007.

Saldívar, Jose David. *Trans-Americanity: Subaltern Modernities, Global Coloniality, and the Cultures of Greater Mexico.* Durham, NC: Duke University Press, 2011.

Border Matters: Remapping American Cultural Studies. Berkeley: University of California Press, 1997.

Saldívar, Ramón. "The American Borderlands Novel," in *The Cambridge History of the American Novel,* ed. Leonard Cassuto et al. 1031–45. Cambridge: Cambridge University Press, 2011.

Chicano Narrative: The Dialectics of Difference. Madison: University of Wisconsin Press, 1990.

Saldívar-Hull, Sonia, Norma Alarcón, and Rita Urquijo-Ruiz, eds. *El Mundo Zurdo 2: Selected Works from the Meetings of the 2010 Society for the Study of Gloria Anzaldúa.* San Francisco: Aunt Lute Books, 2012.

Sanchez, George J. *Becoming Mexican American: Ethnicity, Culture and Identity in Chicano Los Angeles, 1900–1945.* New York: Oxford University Press, 1993.

Sandoval, Chela. *Methodology of the Oppressed.* Minneapolis: University of Minnesota Press, 2000.

Schueller, Malini Johar. "Postcolonial American Studies." *American Literary History* 16.1 (2004): 162–75.

Scott, Rebecca J. "The Atlantic World and the Road to *Plessy v. Ferguson.*" *American Historical Review* 94.3 (2007): 726–33.

Segura, Denise A., and Patricia Zavella, eds. *Women and Migration in the US-Mexico Borderlands: A Reader.* Durham, NC: Duke University Press, 2007.

Sharpe, Jenny. *Allegories of Empire: The Figure of Woman in the Colonial Text.* Minneapolis: University of Minnesota Press, 1993.

Sharpley-Whiting, Tracy Denean. *Négritude Women.* Minneapolis: University of Minnesota Press, 2002.

Simpson, Audra, and Andrea Smith, eds. *Theorizing Native Studies.* Durham, NC: Duke University Press, 2014.

Singh, Nikhil Pal. "The Afterlife of Fascism." *South Atlantic Quarterly* 105.1 (2006): 71–93.

Black Is a Country: Race and the Unfinished Struggle for Democracy. Cambridge, MA: Harvard University Press, 2005.

"Culture/Wars: Recoding Empire in an Age of Democracy." *American Quarterly* 50.3 (1998): 471–522.

Slotkin, Richard. *Lost Battalions: The Great War and the Crisis of American Nationality.* New York: Henry Holt and Company, 2013.

Regeneration Through Violence: The Mythology of the American Frontier, 1600–1860. Norman: University of Oklahoma Press, 2000.

Smith, Andrea. *Conquest: Sexual Violence and American Indian Genocide.* Boston, MA: South End Press, 2005.

Smith, Barbara, ed. *Home Girls: A Black Feminist Anthology.* New York: Kitchen Table Women of Color Press, 1983.

Sollors, Werner, ed. *Multilingual America: Transnationalism, Ethnicity, and the Languages of American Literature.* New York: NYU Press, 1998.

Sommer, Doris. *Bilingual Aesthetics: A New Sentimental Education.* Durham, NC: Duke University Press, 2004.

Foundational Fictions: The National Romances of Latin America. Berkeley: University of California Press, 1993.

Spanos, William V. *Shock and Awe: American Exceptionalism and the Imperatives of the Spectacle in Mark Twain's A Connecticut Yankee in King Arthur's Court.* Hanover, NH: Dartmouth College Press, 2013.

Spanos, William V.. *American Exceptionalism in the Age of Globalization: The Specter of Vietnam.* New York: SUNY Press, 2008.

America's Shadow: An Anatomy of Empire. Minneapolis: University of Minnesota Press, 1999.

Spellberg, Denise A. *Thomas Jefferson's Qur'an: Islam and the Founders.* New York: Alfred A Knopf, 2013.

Spillers, Hortense J. *Black, White, and in Color: Essays on American Literature and Culture.* Chicago: University of Chicago Press, 2003.

Spillers, Hortense J., ed. *Comparative American Identities: Race, Sex, and Nationality in Modern Text.* New York: Routledge, 1991.

Spivak, Gayatri Chakravorty. *In Other Worlds: Essays in Cultural Politics.* 1987. Reprint, London: Routledge, 2006.

A Critique of Postcolonial Reason: Towards a History of the Vanishing Present. Cambridge, MA: Harvard University Press, 1999.

St. John, Rachel. *Line in the Sand: A History of the Western US-Mexico Border.* Princeton, NJ: Princeton University Press, 2011.

Stephens, Michelle. *Black Empire: The Masculine Global Imaginary of Caribbean Intellectuals in the United States, 1914–1962.* Durham, NC: Duke University Press, 2005.

Stoler, Ann Laura, ed. *Haunted by Empire: Geographies of Intimacy in North American History.* Durham, NC: Duke University Press, 2006.

Race and the Education of Desire: Foucault's History of Sexuality and the Colonial Order of Things. Durham, NC: Duke University Press, 1995.

Streetby, Shelley. *American Sensations: Class, Empire, and the Production of Popular Culture.* Berkeley: University of California Press, 2002.

Sundquist, Eric J. *Empire and Slavery in American Literature, 1820–1865.* Jackson: University of Mississippi Press, 2006.

To Wake the Nations: Race in the Making of American Literature. Cambridge, MA: Harvard University Press, 1993.

Taketani, Etsuko. *U.S. Women Writers and the Discourses of Colonialism, 1825–1861.* Knoxville: University of Tennessee Press, 2003.

Tamarkin, Elisa. *Anglophilia: Deference, Devotion, and Antebellum America.* Chicago: University of Chicago Press, 2008.

Tompkins, Kyla. *Racial Indigestion: Eating Bodies in the Nineteenth Century.* New York: NYU Press, 2012.

Truett, Samuel. *Fugitive Landscapes: The Forgotten History of the US-Mexico Borderlands.* New Haven, CT: Yale University Press, 2008.

Turner, Joyce Moore. *Caribbean Crusades and the Harlem Renaissance.* Urbana: University of Illinois Press, 2005.

Ty, Eleanor, and Donald C. Goellnicht. *Asian North American Identities: Beyond the Hyphen.* Bloomington: Indiana University Press, 2004.

Vazquez, Alexandra. *Listening in Detail: Performances of Cuban Music*. Durham, NC: Duke University Press, 2013.

Versluys, Kristiaan. *Out of the Blue: September 11 and the Novel*. New York: Columbia University Press, 2009.

Von Eschen, Penny M. *Race Against Empire: Black Americans and Anticolonialism, 1937–1957*. Ithaca, NY: Cornell University Press, 1997.

Wald, Priscilla. *Constituting Americans: Cultural Anxiety and Narrative Form*. Durham, NC: Duke University Press, 1994.

"Minefields and Meeting Grounds: Transnational Analysis and American Studies." *American Literary History* 10.1 (1998): 199–218.

Walder, Denis. *Post-Colonial Literatures in English: History, Language, Theory*. Oxford: Blackwell, 1998.

Wallerstein, Immanuel. *The Modern World-System*. 4 vols. Berkeley: University of California Press, 2011.

The Capitalist World-Economy. Cambridge: Cambridge University Press, 1979.

Warren, Kenneth W. *What Was African American Literature?* Cambridge, MA: Harvard University Press, 2012.

Warrior, Robert. "Native American Scholarship and the Transnational Turn." *Cultural Studies Review* 15.2 (2009): 119–30.

The People and the Word: Reading Native Nonfiction. Minneapolis: University of Minnesota Press, 2005.

Warrior, Robert, Jace Weaver, and Craig Womack, eds. *American Indian Literary Nationalism*. Albuquerque: University of New Mexico Press, 2006.

Washington, Mary Helen. *The Other Blacklist: The African American Literary and Cultural Left of the 1950s*. New York: Columbia University Press, 2014.

"Disturbing the Peace: What Happens to American Studies If You Put African American Studies at the Center?" *American Quarterly* 50.1 (1998): 1–23.

White, Melissa Autumn. "Ambivalent Homonationalisms: Transnational Queer Intimacies and Territorialized Belongings." *Interventions: International Journal of Postcolonial Studies* 15.1(2013): 37–54.

Wiegman, Robyn. *American Anatomies: Theorizing Race and Gender*. Durham, NC: Duke University Press, 2012.

Wilson, Christopher P. *Cop Knowledge: Police Power and Cultural Narrative in Twentieth-Century America*. Chicago: University of Chicago Press, 2000.

Wilson, Ivy G. *Specters of Democracy: Blackness and the Aesthetics of Politics in the Antebellum U.S*. New York: Oxford University Press, 2011.

Winkiel, Laura. *Modernism, Race and Manifestos*. Cambridge: Cambridge University Press, 2008.

Wright, Michelle M. *Physics of Blackness: Beyond the Middle Passage Epistemology*. Minneapolis: University of Minnesota Press, 2015.

Wynter, Sylvia, and Katherine McKittrick, ed. *Sylvia Wynter: On Being Human as Praxis*. Durham, NC: Duke University Press, 2015.

Zimmerman, Marc. *South to North: Framing Latin and Central American, Caribbean and Latino Literature*. Santiago: Global LA CASA, 2006.

INDEX

#BlackPoetsSpeakOut, 154
10,04 (Lerner), 134–35
abolition and abolitionists, 95–97
Achebe, Chinua, 53
Adichie, Chimamanda, 154
aesthetics, transnational, 4, 72–74, 79–80
    The American (James) and, 78–79
    globalization and, 81–85
    Paine and, 77–78
Africa, 53
    Du Bois on, 56
    label of the African writer, 61
African Americans, 56. *See also* Black
    Atlantic and diasporic literature;
    black nationalism
    internal colony analogy and, 55–60
African Cultural Society, 58
African writers, 107, 122, 154
Ahmad, Aijaz, 62
Aids to Reflection (Coleridge), 92
Aikau, Hokulani, 182
Alexander, Elizabeth, 152–53
Alexander, M. Jacqui, 231
Alexie, Sherman, 184, 185
Algerine Captive (Tyler), 102–03, 253–54
Allen, Chadwick, 183–84
Almanac of the Dead (Marmon Silko), 184
American Indian Literary Nationalism
    (Weaver, Womack, and Warrior), 177
American Indian literature and studies,
    11, 187. *See also* Indigenous
    transnationalism
    aesthetics in, 181
    challenges facing, 182
    growth of field of, 182
    Marmon Silko and Alexie and, 184
    methodology in, 182–84
    mobility and travel and, 186–87

nationalist turn in, 178
    Real Revolution is Love (poem, Harjo)
        and, 174–75
    turn to transnationalism and, 177–82
American Studies Association, Fishkin's
    presidential address to, 19
Americanah (Adichie), 154
Americanity as a Concept (essay, Quijano
    and Wallerstein), 175
Anderson, Jill, 30
Anglophone literature, 61
Anzaldúa, Gloria, 11, 23–24, 157, 159.
    See also Borderlands / La Frontera
    critics of, 160–61
Arredondo, Lupe, 160
Asian American literature and studies, 29, 30
    Asian American as term, 12
    claiming America, 190–93
    Korean and Korean American
        literature, 24–25
    literary acclaim of, 191
    as marketing or lifestyle category,
        196, 197
    1965 Immigration Law and, 191
    9/11 and, 191
    Pacific Rim literature and,
        192–93, 200–01
Atomik Aztex (Foster), 168–70
Autobiography of Malcolm X, 257–58

Baldwin, James, 1, 3, 257
    Nobody Knows My Name, 3
    in Turkey, 28
Bandung Conference, 56
Banjo (McKay), 115–16
Barbary captivity narratives, 102–03
Bauerkemper, Joseph, 178, 180
belonging, 30

Beloved (Morrison), 55
Benito Cereno (Melville), 97
Berman, Jessica, 10
Beyond a Boundary (James), 46
Bhabha, Homi, 55
Bien Pretty (short story, Cisneros), 160
Bishop, Elizabeth, 225
Black Atlantic (Gilroy), 144–45, 150
Black Atlantic and diasporic literature,
   113–16, 143–44, 152, 153–55. *See also*
   diaspora; *Brown Girl, Brownstones*
   (Marshall)
   Black women's migration narratives, 143,
      144–46, 147
   identity formation and, 147
   memoirs and, 152–53
   slave narratives and, 146–47
   worldwide protest movements and, 154
Black Jacobins (James), 44–45
black nationalism, 56–57, 59, 96, 116
Black Power era (U.S.), 56
Blauner, Robert, 56
Bolton, Herbert E., 203, 204
Borderlands / La Frontera (Anzaldúa), 11,
   157, 159
   critics of, 160–61, 163–64
   illegal crossings in, 161–62
   Mexican women and, 162–63
Borderlands of Culture (Saldívar), 28
borderlands paradigm, 11, 158–59, 170
   Atomik Aztex (Foster) and, 168–70
   border thinking, 107
   critique of, 163–64
   Devil's Highway (Urrea) and, 164–66
   mestizaje as the central metaphor for, 160
   subjective experience of
      in-betweenness, 160
   Under the Bridge (Sanmiguel)
      and, 166–68
Boyce Davies, Carole, 144–45
Brady, Mary Pat, 163–64
Brazil-Maru (Yamashita), 193
Brickhouse, Anna, 98
Brief Wondrous Life of Oscar Wao
   (Díaz), 170
Brodhead, Richard, 91
Brooklyn (Tóibín), 133
Brown Girl, Brownstones (Marshall), 11,
   143, 148–52
Buck-Morss, Susan, 73
Buell, Lawrence, 26
Bulawayo, NoViolet, 154
Butler, Judith, 242–44

Calderón, Héctor, 160
Casanova, Pascale, 37–38
Castronovo, Russ, 9
Cave Canem (Black poetry collective), 154
Cherokee transnationalism, 179
Chicana/o literature and studies, 11, 160
   borderlands paradigm and, 159
   Cherríe Moraga and, 221–22
   critique of transnational approach
      to, 157–58
Chih-Ming Wang, 29
China
   Mark Twain and, 25–26
China Men (Kingston), 193
Chinese and Chinese American literature, 29
Choctalking on Other Realities
   (Howe), 186
Chuh, Kandice, 176
Circle K Cycles (Yamashita), 193–94
Cisneros, Sandra, 160
Clavijero, Francisco, 211–12
Clifford, James, 145
Coindreau, Maurice-Edgar, 37
Cold War
   hemispheric literature and, 205
Cole, Teju, 9, 61, 65–68
Coleridge, Samuel Taylor, 92
Colonial Grammar (Figueroa), 21
Common Sense (Paine), 73, 77–78
Communist Manifesto (Marx and
   Engels), 80–81
*Connecticut Yankee in King Arthur's
   Court* (Twain), 101
Contracanto a Walt Whitman
   (poem, Mir), 19–22
Cook-Lynn, Elizabeth, 178, 181
cosmopolitanism, 176
   Gertrude Stein and, 112–13
   Henry James and, 110–12
Coulthard, Glen, 180
Crazy Rich Asians (Kwan), 197
*Criticism in the Borderlands, Studies in
   Chicano Literature, Culture, and
   Ideology* (Calderón and Saldívar), 160
Critique of Judgment (Kant), 74, 78
Crossing the Peninsula (Lim), 30
Cruse, Harold, 56
Cultures of United States Imperialism
   (Kaplan and Pease), 4

Davis, David Brion, 95
*Declaration on the Rights of Indigenous
   Peoples* (2006), 180

decolonization, 8, 55–57, 204.
  See also postcolonialism and
  postcolonial theory
  decolonial imaginary, 167
  Fanon and, 58–59
  indigenous decolonization, 180, 181, 183,
    184, 187
  internal colony analogy in U.S., 55–60
  postcolonial studies and, 62
Delany, Martin, 96
Demir-Atay, Hivren, 22
deportation, 30
Devil's Highway (Urrea), 164–66
Dial (transcendentalist journal), 95
diaspora, 11, 12–13, 56, 60, 61, 63, 65, 68,
    174, 177, 182, 197, 205, 224. *See also*
    Black Atlantic and diasporic literature
  queer diasporic studies, 239
Díaz, Junot, 170
Dimock, Wai Chee, 8, 55, 107
Dogeaters (Hagedorn), 200
Douglass, Frederick, 95–97, 146
Doyle, Laura, 79
Dream Jungle (Hagedorn), 127–29
Dred (Stowe), 96
Dred Scott decision of 1857, 96
Du Bois, W.E.B., 8, 56–57, 58, 148

Eagleton, Terry, 75
Edmondson, Belinda, 145
Eggers, Dave, 134–35
Einboden, Jeffrey, 22, 31
El Clamor Público (19th century
    periodical), 99
El Mundo Nuevo/La América Ilustrada
    (19th century periodical), 99
Elementary Structures of Kinship
    (Lévi-Strauss), 242, 243
Eliot, T.S., 119
Ellis Island, 39
Emerson, Ralph Waldo, 93–94
*Empire of Necessity, Slavery, Freedom,
    and Deception in the New World*
    (Grandin), 27
Engels, Friedrich, 80–81
Epistemology of the Closet
    (Sedgwick), 244–45
Erkkila, Betsy, 101–02

Fanon, Frantz, 58–59
Faulkner, William, 10
  transnational optic on, 116–19
  as world literature, 37

feminism, 6, 13, 242, 244. *See also*
  transnational feminism
  indigenous feminism, 181
  women of color activists and, 222–23
Ferguson, Missouri, 59
Figiel, Sia, 198
Figueroa, Víctor, 21
Fire Next Time (Baldwin), 257
Fishkin, Shelley Fisher, 8, 101
  Mapping American Studies in the
    Twenty-First Century, 29
Fitz, Earl E., 206
Flamethrowers (Kushner), 129–31
Flight (Alexie), 184, 185
Fluck, Winfried, 4
Following the Equator (Twain), 27
Formations of United States Colonialism
    (Goldstein), 4
Foster, Sesshu, 11, 168–70
Foucault, Michel, 246–47
Fourth World of global indigeneity, 176
Fox Girl (Okja Keller), 25
Fox, Claire F., 206
Free Food for Millionaires (Lee), 30
free trade agreements, 157, 194, 206, 214
Fuller, Margaret, 92, 95–96, 97

Gender Trouble (Butler), 242–44
George Washington Gómez (Paredes), 160
Ghana Must Go (Selasi), 122
Ghosh, Amitav, 8, 47–51
Giles, Paul, 29
Gillman, Susan, 23
Gilroy, Paul, 144–45, 150
Girl in the Tangerine Scarf (Kahf), 262–64
Global Mapping of American Literature
    (Giles), 29
globalization, 13, 207
  Asian-American literature and, 12, 192
  Communist Manifesto and, 80–81
  emergence of early globalism, 122
  hemispheric literature and, 205, 206–07
  Henry James and, 110–12
  localist writers and, 131, 132, 133
  Melville and, 27
  moderate globalists, 129
  Pacific Rim literature and, 192, 195, 196
  postmodernism and, 123, 124,
    127, 136–37
  queer theory and lives and, 238, 239,
    240, 241
  transnational aesthetics, 81–85
  transnational feminism and, 223–24

globalization (*cont.*)
  transnational modernism and, 108, 109
  Twain on American imperialism
    and, 27–28
  US-Mexico border and, 158, 170
  vs. transnational frames, 4, 6, 7, 9, 176
Goethe, Johann Wolfgang von, 93
Goldstein, Ayosha, 4
Goppi (*The Bridle*, Yoon), 25
Goyal, Yogita, 154
Grandin, Greg, 27
Grass Roof (Kang), 24–25
Gruesz, Kirsten Silva, 99

Hagedorn, Jessica, 127–29, 200
Halaby, Laila, 260
Halkin, Simon, 22
Hall, Stuart, 62, 145
  Cultural Identity and Diaspora, 144
Hamid, Mohsin, 260–62
Harjo, Joy, 174–75
Hau'ofa, Epeli, 197, 198
Hawaiian literature, 198
hemispheric literature and studies, 12, 13,
    98, 203
  Cold War and, 205
  as expansionist, 207–08
  globalization and, 206–07
  Historia Antigua de México (Clavijero)
    and, 211–12
  In Defense of the Indians (Las Casas)
    and, 209–11
  indigenous communities and, 212–13
  narco culture and, 213–15
  Our America (essay, Martí), 203–04
  postnational and postcolonial scholarly
    movements and, 205–06, 208
  progressive ideology in scholarship of, 207
  reading from below, 208–13
  scholarship of the colonial periods, 207
  transnationalism in 19th century American
    literature, 98–100
Historia Antigua de México
    (Clavijero), 211–12
*History of Mary Prince, A West Indian Slave,
    Related by Herself* (Prince), 11, 146–47
History of Sumatra (Marsden), 76
Hologram for the King (Eggers), 135
Home to Harlem (McKay), 114–15
Hopkins, Pauline, 147
Howe, LeAnne, 186
Hughes, Langston, 23, 119
Huhndorf, Shari, 180

Hunt Jackson, Helen, 23
Hunt, Sarah, 181
Hwang, David Henry, 200

I Hotel (Yamashita), 194–95
In Defense of the Indians (Las
    Casas), 209–11
Indigenous transnationalism, 176–79, 187,
    212–13. *See also* American Indian
    literature and studies
  American Indian studies turn to
    transnationalism and, 177–82
  Cherokee transnationalism, 179
  indigeneity defined, 177
  indigenous feminism, 181
  localized indigeneity and, 179
  mobility and travel and, 186–87
internal colony analogy, 8, 55–60, 61
Iraq, 4
Irr, Caren, 129
Islam and transnationalism, 14
  Algerine Captive (Tyler) and, 253–54
  Autobiography of Malcolm X and, 257–58
  autobiography of Mohammad Ali ben
    Said and, 255–56
  discrimination in U.S. and, 251–53
  Girl in the Tangerine Scarf (Kahf)
    and, 262–64
  Once in a Promised Land (Halaby)
    and, 260
  Reluctant Fundamentalist (Hamid)
    and, 260–62
Islas, Arturo, 160

Jacobson, Matthew Frye, 53
James, C.L.R., 8, 39, 45–46. *See also*
    Black Jacobins; *Mariners, Renegades,
    Castaways*
  Beyond a Boundary, 46
  Ellis Island and, 46
  Every Cook Can Govern essay, 46
James, David, 10
James, Henry, 78–79
  cosmopolitan modernism and, 110–12
Japanese American internment, 193
Jay, Paul, 122–23
Jim Crow, 57
Jong Lee, Kun, 25
Joy Luck Club (Tan), 190
Justice, Daniel Heath, 179, 181

Kahf, Mohja, 262–64
Kang, Younghill, 24–25

Kant, Immanuel, 74–79
 sensus communis of, 74–76
Kaplan, Amy, 4, 53, 54, 58, 101
Keller, Nora Okja, 25
Kingston, Maxine Hong, 190, 192–93
Kogawa, Joy, 193
Korean and Korean American literature,
 24–25, 30. See also Asian American
 literature and studies
Kunow, Rüdiger, 27
Kushner, Rachel, 129–31
Kutzinski, Vera M., 23
Kwan, Kevin, 197

Lahiri, Jhumpa, 131–32
Lai-Henderson, Selina, 25
Larsen, Nella, 147
Las Casas, Bartolomé de, 13, 209–11
Leaves of the Banyan Tree (Wendt), 198
Lee, Kun Jong, 24
Lee, Min Jin, 30
Lee, So-Hee, 25
Lee, Steven S., 28
Lerner, Ben, 134–35
Lévi-Strauss, Claude, 242–43
Lewis, Sinclair, 20–21
Light of the World (Alexander), 152–53
Limón, José E., 158
Linebaugh, Peter, 43–44
Lomas, Laura, 22
Lorde, Audre, 152, 225
Los Otros Dreamers (eds. Anderson
 and Solis), 30
Loving in the War Years (Moraga), 221–22
Lyons, Scott Richard, 186

M. Butterfly (play, Hwang), 200
magic realism, 63
Malaysia, 30
Malcolm X, 257–58
Many-Headed Hydra, Sailors, Slaves,
 Commoners, and the Hidden History of
 the Revolutionary Atlantic (Linebaugh
 and Rediker), 43
Mariners, Renegades, Castaways
 (James), 39. See also James, C.L.R.;
 Melville, Herman
 genre switching in Moby Dick and,
 42–44
 publication history of, 39–40
 work in Moby Dick and, 40–42
Mark Twain in China
 (Lai-Henderson), 25, 28

Mark Twain in Japan, The Cultural
 Reception of an American Icon
 (Ishihara), 25
Marsden, William, 76–77
Marshall, Paule, 11, 148–52
Martí, José, 100, 203–04
 on Twain, 101
Marx, Karl, 80–81
McCann, Colum, 81
McKay, Claude, 28, 113–16
Melville, Herman, 46, 55. See also James,
 C.L.R.; Mariners, Renegades, Castaways
 (James); Moby Dick; Pequod
 Amitav Ghosh and, 47–51
 Benito Cereno (1855), 97
 travels of, 26–27
memoirs, 152–53
mestizaje (racial or cultural mixture), 159
Mexico, 30, 176. See also Borderlands /
 La Frontera (Anzaldúa); borderlands
 paradigm; US-Mexico borderlands
 Ciudad Juárez in, 157
 in Historia Antigua de México
 (Clavijero), 211–12
 trade agreements and, 157
 translation of Poe in, 22
Miller, Perry, 53
Millet, Lydia, 132–33
Mir, Pedro, 19–22
Moby Dick (Melville), 8. See also James,
 C.L.R.; Mariners, Renegades, Castaways
 (James); Melville, Herman
 genre switiching in, 42–44
 work in, 40–42, 45–46
Moonlit in the Mirror (short story,
 Sanmiguel), 166–68
Moraga, Cherríe, 221–22, 235
 It's the Poverty (poem), 221, 235
Morgan, Robin, 222
Morrison, Toni, 55
Munro, Alice, 132–33, 134

narco culture, 13, 213–15
Narrative of the Life of Frederick Douglass,
 an American Slave, Written by Himself
 (Douglass), 97, 146
nations and nationalism
 American Indian literature and studies
 and, 11, 177, 178, 179, 180, 181, 186
 Asian American literature and, 191
 black nationalism, 56–57, 59, 96, 116
 borderlands paradigm and, 170
 Common Sense (Paine) and, 73, 77

nations and nationalism (*cont.*)
  hemispheric literature and, 205
  internal colony analogy in U.S., 55–60
  Mexican in Anzaldúa, 160
  Mexican in *Historia Antigua de México*
    (Clavijero) and, 211–12
  nation-centric categories, 29
  postcolonial theory and, 62, 65
  transnational aesthetics and, 72
  transnational feminism and, 13, 231
  transnationalism as critique of, 7,
    108, 174–77
  in *Uncle Tom's Cabin* (Stowe), 23
  Whitman and, 19–22, 101–02
Nealon, Chris, 237–38
networked world literature, 38
Nigeria, 61, 63, 122
Nineteenth-Century U.S. Literature
  in Middle Eastern Languages
  (Einboden), 22
Nixon, Rob, 13
Norris, Frank, 9, 81–85
North American Free Trade Agreement
  (NAFTA), 157, 194, 206, 214
Nosotros para nosotros (Valerio), 21
Nuestra América (essay, Martí), 100

O'Brien, Tim, 199
Obasan (Kogawa), 193
Octopus (Norris), 81–85
Of One Blood (Hopkins), 147
Ogundipe-Leslie, Molara, 144–45
On Beauty (Smith), 135
Once in a Promised Land (Halaby), 260
Open City (Cole), 9, 61, 65–68
Ordinary Light (Smith), 152
Orientalism (Said), 57
Otra Vez Caliban/Encore Caliban,
  Adaptation, Translation, Americas
  Studies (Gilman), 23
Our America (essay, Martí), 203–04
Our Sea of Islands (essay, Hau'ofa), 197
Ozeki, Ruth, 13, 125–27, 129, 195, 226–28,
  230, 233–34

Pachinko (Lee), 30
Pacific Rim literature, 192–93
  Asian American literature and, 200–01
  cosmopolitanism and, 197
  Hawaiian literature and, 198
  Karen Tei Yamashita and, 193–95
  Pacific Islands literary movement and,
    197, 198, 199

Tale for the Time Being (Ozeki) and, 195
  war and, 199–201
Paine, Tom, 72, 73, 77–78
Paredes, Américo, 28, 160
Passage to India (poem, Whitman), 101–02
Pease, Donald, 4, 57, 80
Pechey, Graham, 62
Pequod (Melville), 39, 41
Petry, Anne, 147
Poe, Edgar Allan, 22
postcolonialism and postcolonial
  theory, 53–55
  comparisons with U.S. writers, 55
  internal colony analogy, 55–60
  as method, 61, 64–65
  Open City (Cole) and, 65–68
  postcolonial literature defined, 61, 63–64
postmodernism, 10. *See also* transnational
  postmodernism and contemporary
  literature
Pouchet Paquet, Sandra, 146–47
Power, Susan, 185–86
practical consciousness, 45

queer transnationalism, 13, 14, 247–48
  allochronism and, 241
  before sexuality thesis of Foucault, 246–47
  constructionist-essentialist debate
    in, 240–41
  development of, 238–40
  Eve Sedgwick and, 244–46
  Gender Trouble (Butler) and, 242–44
  Lévi-Strauss and, 242–43
  queer theory of 1990s and, 241–42
  White Meadows (poem, Nealon)
    and, 237–38
Quicksand (Larsen), 147
Quijano, Aníbel, 175

Radway, Janice, 203
Rain God (Isla), 160
Rainie, Lee, 38
Ramazani, Jahan, 29, 109
Ramona (Hunt Jackson), 23
Real Revolution is Love (poem,
  Harjo), 174–75
*Red on Red, Native American Literary
  Separatism* (Womack), 178
Rediker, Marcus, 43–44
religion, 28, 92, 103, 132, 185, 210,
  231, 251. *See also* Islam and
  transnationalism
Reluctant Fundamentalist (Hamid), 260–62

Robbins, Bruce, 136
Rollason, Christopher, 22
Romance, Diaspora, and Black Atlantic Literature (Goyal), 154
Routes, Travel & Translation in the Late Twentieth Century (Clifford), 145
Rowe, John Carlos, 27, 176
Rushdie, Salman, 63
Ruskin, John, 72
Russell, Karen, 13, 226, 228–30, 231–33

Sacred Wilderness (Power), 185–86
Said, Edward, 57, 110
Said, Mohammad Ali ben, 255–56
Saldívar, José David, 160, 175, 176
Saldívar, Ramón, 28, 158
Salut Au Monde! (poem, Whitman), 101–02
Samoan authors, 198
Sanmiguel, Rosario, 11, 166–68
Secure Fence Act (2006), 157
Sedgwick, Eve, 244–46
Selasi, Taiye, 122, 137
September 11th, 2001, 4, 31, 191
Shirley Geok-lin Lim, 29
Shohat, Ella, 223
Silko, Leslie Marmon, 184
slavery, 23, 27, 54, 56, 66, 75, 80, 96, 101, 102, 146, 147, 175, 205, 209, 252, 253, 255, 256. *See also* abolition and abolitionists; Black Atlantic and diasporic literature; Douglass, Frederick; *History of Mary Prince*
slow violence (Rob Nixon), 13, 231
Smith, Sydney, 72
Smith, Tracy K., 152
Smith, Zadie, 135–36
Solis, Nin, 30
Souls of Black Folk (Du Bois), 148
Spanish-language periodicals (19th century), 99
Spencer, Harry, 45
Spivak, Gayatri, 62
Stein, Gertrude
  cosmopolitanism and, 112–13
Stowe, Harriet Beecher, 23, 96
Street, The (Petry), 147
Swamplandia! (Russell), 226, 228–30, 231–33

Tale for the Time Being (Ozeki), 125–27, 195, 226–28, 230, 233–34
Tan, Amy, 190
Tendencies (Sedgwick), 245

The American (James), 78–79
Thoreau, Henry David, 93–94
Through the Arc of the Rainforest (Yamashita), 193
Tóibín, Colm, 133–34
Trans-Americanity, Subaltern Modernities, Global Colonality, and the Cultures of Greater Mexico (Saldívar), 175
TransAtlantic (McCann), 81
Translated Poe (eds. Esplin and Vale de Gato), 22
Translating Empire, José Martí, Migrant Latino Subjects, and American Modernities (Lomas), 22
transnational aesthetics, 9, 72–74, 79–80
  The American (James) and, 78–79
  economics and, 80–81
  globalization and, 81–85
  Paine and, 77–78
  sensus communis of Kant and, 74–76
  transnational poetics, 109
transnational feminism, 13. *See also* feminism
  approaches to American literature by, 235
  Cherríe Moraga and, 221–22
  globalization and, 223–24
  homogenizing character of global sisterhood in, 222, 223
  methodologies for analysis, 224
  Swamplandia! (Russell) and, 228–30, 231–33
  Tale for the Time Being (Ozeki) and, 226–28, 230, 233–34
  women of color activists and, 222–23
transnational modernism, 107–08, 119, 136–37
  cosmopolitanism and, 110–13
  Faulkner and, 116–19
  transnational as term in, 108
  transnational black modernism, 116
  vagabondage and black diasporic writers, 113–16
transnational optic, 119
  defined, 119
Transnational Poetics (Ramazani), 29
transnational postmodernism and contemporary literature, 10, 136–37
  Alice Munro and, 132–33
  Ben Lerner and, 134–35
  Colm Tóibín and, 133–34
  Dave Eggers and, 134–35
  Jessica Hagedorn and, 127–29
  Jhumpa Lahiri and, 131–32
  localisms and, 132–33

transnational postmodernism and
  contemporary literature (*cont.*)
  Rachel Kushner and, 129–31
  Ruth Ozeki and, 125–27
  Zadie Smith and, 135–36
transnational turn in American studies, 1,
  11, 79, 92, 107, 178
  borderland studies and, 157
  critics of, 2–3
  Fishkin's address to ASA and, 8
  indigenous peoples and, 176, 187
  new approaches and methodologies in, 4–7
  postcolonial studies and, 55
  three movements in, 176
transnationalism. *See also* borderlands
  paradigm; Black Atlantic and diasporic
  literature; hemispheric literature and
  studies; Indigenous transnationalism;
  Islam and transnationalism;
  postcolonialism and postcolonial
  theory; queer transnationalism;
  transnational aesthetics; transnational
  feminism; transnational modernism;
  transnational postmodernism
  genealogy of, 2
transnationalism in 19th century American
  literature, 91–92
  abolition and abolitionists and, 95–97
  hemispheric formations and, 98–100
  international novel and, 97–98
  paradigm of empire criticism and, 100–03
  world literature and, 92–94
*Transpacific Migrations, Student Migration and
  the Remaking of Asian America* (Wang), 29
Tribal Secrets (Warrior), 178
Tropic of Orange (Yamashita), 194
Tsuyoshi Ishihara, 25
Turkey, 29
Twain, Mark
  American imperialism and, 27–28, 101
  anti-imperialism in China of, 25–26
  José Martí on, 101
  travels of, 27–28
Two Faces of Empire (Grandin), 27
Tyler, Royall, 102–03, 253–54

Uncle Tom's Cabin (Stowe), 23
Under the Bridge (Sanmiguel), 166–68
Urrea, Luis Alberto, 11, 164–66
US-Mexico borderlands, 11, 170. *See also*
  borderlands paradigm
  border retrenchment and neoliberal
  policy and, 157

vagabondage, 113–16
Valerio. Miguel Alejandro, 21
*Vanderbilt e-Journal of Luso-Hispanic
  Studies*, 206
View from Castle Rock (Munro),
  132–33
Vizenor, Gerald, 186

Walden (Thoreau), 93
Walkowitz, Rebecca L., 125
Wallerstein, Immanuel, 175
War Trash (Ha Jin), 199
Warrior, Robert, 177–78, 179
We Need New Names (Bulawayo), 154
Wealth of Nations (Smith), 93
Weaver, Jace, 177
Wellman, Barry, 38
Weltliteratur (World Literature), 8. *See also*
  World Literature
Wendt, Albert, 198
What Is the What (Eggers), 134
Wheatley, Philis, 225
Where We Once Belonged (Figiel), 198
White Meadows (poem, Nealon), 237–38
Whitman, Walt, 19–22
  American imperialism and, 101–02
  Contracanto a Walt Whitman (poem, Mir)
    and, 19–22
  Youssef's translation of, 30–32
Williams, Raymond, 45
Womack, Craig, 177, 178
Woman Hollering Creek (Cisneros), 160
Woman Warrior (Kingston), 192
world literature, 61, 92–94
  James and, 39
  networked world literature, 38
Worlds of Langston Hughes
  (Kutzinski), 23
Wretched of the Earth (Fanon), 58

X-Marks (Lyons), 186

Yamanaka, Lois-Ann, 198
Yamashita, Karen Tei, 10, 12, 193–95
Yépez, Heriberto, 237
*Yo también soy América, Langston Hughes
  Translated* (Kutzinski), 23
Yoon, Jung-Mo, 25
Youssef, Saadi, 22, 30–32

Zaborowska, Magdalena, 28
Zami (Lorde), 152
Zygadło, Grażyna, 24

Cambridge Companions to…
Authors

Edward Albee edited by Stephen J. Bottoms

Margaret Atwood edited by Coral Ann Howells

W. H. Auden edited by Stan Smith

Jane Austen edited by Edward Copeland and Juliet McMaster (second edition)

Beckett edited by John Pilling

Bede edited by Scott DeGregorio

Aphra Behn edited by Derek Hughes and Janet Todd

Walter Benjamin edited by David S. Ferris

William Blake edited by Morris Eaves

Boccaccio edited by Guyda Armstrong, Rhiannon Daniels, and Stephen J. Milner

Jorge Luis Borges edited by Edwin Williamson

Brecht edited by Peter Thomson and Glendyr Sacks (second edition)

The Brontës edited by Heather Glen

Bunyan edited by Anne Dunan-Page

Frances Burney edited by Peter Sabor

Byron edited by Drummond Bone

Albert Camus edited by Edward J. Hughes

Willa Cather edited by Marilee Lindemann

Cervantes edited by Anthony J. Cascardi

Chaucer edited by Piero Boitani and Jill Mann (second edition)

Chekhov edited by Vera Gottlieb and Paul Allain

Kate Chopin edited by Janet Beer

Caryl Churchill edited by Elaine Aston and Elin Diamond

Cicero edited by Catherine Steel

Coleridge edited by Lucy Newlyn

Wilkie Collins edited by Jenny Bourne Taylor

Joseph Conrad edited by J. H. Stape

H. D. edited by Nephie J. Christodoulides and Polina Mackay

Dante edited by Rachel Jacoff (second edition)

Daniel Defoe edited by John Richetti

Don DeLillo edited by John N. Duvall

Charles Dickens edited by John O. Jordan

Emily Dickinson edited by Wendy Martin

John Donne edited by Achsah Guibbory

Dostoevskii edited by W. J. Leatherbarrow

Theodore Dreiser edited by Leonard Cassuto and Claire Virginia Eby

John Dryden edited by Steven N. Zwicker

W. E. B. Du Bois edited by Shamoon Zamir

George Eliot edited by George Levine

T. S. Eliot edited by A. David Moody

Ralph Ellison edited by Ross Posnock

Ralph Waldo Emerson edited by Joel Porte and Saundra Morris

William Faulkner edited by Philip M. Weinstein

Henry Fielding edited by Claude Rawson

F. Scott Fitzgerald edited by Ruth Prigozy

Flaubert edited by Timothy Unwin

E. M. Forster edited by David Bradshaw

Benjamin Franklin edited by Carla Mulford

Brian Friel edited by Anthony Roche

Robert Frost edited by Robert Faggen

Gabriel García Márquez edited by Philip Swanson

Elizabeth Gaskell edited by Jill L. Matus

Goethe edited by Lesley Sharpe

Günter Grass edited by Stuart Taberner

Thomas Hardy edited by Dale Kramer

David Hare edited by Richard Boon

Nathaniel Hawthorne edited by Richard Millington

Seamus Heaney edited by Bernard O'Donoghue

Ernest Hemingway edited by Scott Donaldson

Homer edited by Robert Fowler

Horace edited by Stephen Harrison

Ted Hughes edited by Terry Gifford

Ibsen edited by James McFarlane

Henry James edited by Jonathan Freedman

Samuel Johnson edited by Greg Clingham

Ben Jonson edited by Richard Harp and Stanley Stewart

James Joyce edited by Derek Attridge (second edition)

Kafka edited by Julian Preece

Keats edited by Susan J. Wolfson

Rudyard Kipling edited by Howard J. Booth

Lacan edited by Jean-Michel Rabaté

D. H. Lawrence edited by Anne Fernihough

Primo Levi edited by Robert Gordon

Lucretius edited by Stuart Gillespie and Philip Hardie

Machiavelli edited by John M. Najemy

David Mamet edited by Christopher Bigsby

Thomas Mann edited by Ritchie Robertson

Christopher Marlowe edited by Patrick Cheney

Andrew Marvell edited by Derek Hirst and Steven N. Zwicker

Herman Melville edited by Robert S. Levine

Arthur Miller edited by Christopher Bigsby (second edition)

Milton edited by Dennis Danielson (second edition)

Molière edited by David Bradby and Andrew Calder

Toni Morrison edited by Justine Tally

Alice Munro edited by David Staines

Nabokov edited by Julian W. Connolly

Eugene O'Neill edited by Michael Manheim

George Orwell edited by John Rodden

Ovid edited by Philip Hardie

Petrarch edited by Albert Russell Ascoli and Unn Falkeid

Harold Pinter edited by Peter Raby (second edition)

Sylvia Plath edited by Jo Gill

Edgar Allan Poe edited by Kevin J. Hayes

Alexander Pope edited by Pat Rogers

Ezra Pound edited by Ira B. Nadel

Proust edited by Richard Bales

Pushkin edited by Andrew Kahn

Rabelais edited by John O'Brien

Rilke edited by Karen Leeder and Robert Vilain

Philip Roth edited by Timothy Parrish

Salman Rushdie edited by Abdulrazak Gurnah

John Ruskin edited by Francis O'Gorman

Shakespeare edited by Margareta de Grazia and Stanley Wells (second edition)

Shakespearean Comedy edited by Alexander Leggatt

Shakespeare and Contemporary Dramatists edited by Ton Hoenselaars

Shakespeare and Popular Culture edited by Robert Shaughnessy

Shakespearean Tragedy edited by Claire McEachern (second edition)

Shakespeare on Film edited by Russell Jackson (second edition)

Shakespeare on Stage edited by Stanley Wells and Sarah Stanton

Shakespeare's History Plays edited by Michael Hattaway

Shakespeare's Last Plays edited by Catherine M. S. Alexander

Shakespeare's Poetry edited by Patrick Cheney

George Bernard Shaw edited by Christopher Innes

Shelley edited by Timothy Morton

Mary Shelley edited by Esther Schor

Sam Shepard edited by Matthew C. Roudané

Spenser edited by Andrew Hadfield

Laurence Sterne edited by Thomas Keymer

Wallace Stevens edited by John N. Serio

Tom Stoppard edited by Katherine E. Kelly

Harriet Beecher Stowe edited by Cindy Weinstein

August Strindberg edited by Michael Robinson

Jonathan Swift edited by Christopher Fox

J. M. Synge edited by P. J. Mathews

Tacitus edited by A. J. Woodman

Henry David Thoreau edited by Joel Myerson

Tolstoy edited by Donna Tussing Orwin

Anthony Trollope edited by Carolyn Dever and Lisa Niles

Mark Twain edited by Forrest G. Robinson

John Updike edited by Stacey Olster

Mario Vargas Llosa edited by Efrain Kristal and John King

Virgil edited by Charles Martindale

Voltaire edited by Nicholas Cronk

Edith Wharton edited by Millicent Bell

Walt Whitman edited by Ezra Greenspan

Oscar Wilde edited by Peter Raby

Tennessee Williams edited by Matthew C. Roudané

August Wilson edited by Christopher Bigsby

Mary Wollstonecraft edited by Claudia L. Johnson

Virginia Woolf edited by Susan Sellers (second edition)

Wordsworth edited by Stephen Gill

W. B. Yeats edited by Marjorie Howes and John Kelly

Zola edited by Brian Nelson

TOPICS

The Actress edited by Maggie B. Gale and John Stokes

The African American Novel edited by Maryemma Graham

The African American Slave Narrative edited by Audrey A. Fisch

African American Theatre by Harvey Young

Allegory edited by Rita Copeland and Peter Struck

American Crime Fiction edited by Catherine Ross Nickerson

American Modernism edited by Walter Kalaidjian

American Poetry Since 1945 edited by Jennifer Ashton

American Realism and Naturalism edited by Donald Pizer

American Travel Writing edited by Alfred Bendixen and Judith Hamera

American Women Playwrights edited by Brenda Murphy

Ancient Rhetoric edited by Erik Gunderson

Arthurian Legend edited by Elizabeth Archibald and Ad Putter

Australian Literature edited by Elizabeth Webby

British Literature of the French Revolution edited by Pamela Clemit

British Romanticism edited by Stuart Curran (second edition)

British Romantic Poetry edited by James Chandler and Maureen N. McLane

British Theatre, 1730–1830, edited by Jane Moody and Daniel O'Quinn

Canadian Literature edited by Eva-Marie Kröller

Children's Literature edited by M. O. Grenby and Andrea Immel

The Classic Russian Novel edited by Malcolm V. Jones and Robin Feuer Miller

Contemporary Irish Poetry edited by Matthew Campbell

Creative Writing edited by David Morley and Philip Neilsen

Crime Fiction edited by Martin Priestman

Early Modern Women's Writing edited by Laura Lunger Knoppers

The Eighteenth-Century Novel edited by John Richetti

Eighteenth-Century Poetry edited by John Sitter

Emma edited by Peter Sabor

English Literature, 1500–1600 edited by Arthur F. Kinney

English Literature, 1650–1740 edited by Steven N. Zwicker

English Literature, 1740–1830 edited by Thomas Keymer and Jon Mee

English Literature, 1830–1914 edited by Joanne Shattock

English Novelists edited by Adrian Poole

English Poetry, Donne to Marvell edited by Thomas N. Corns

English Poets edited by Claude Rawson

English Renaissance Drama, second edition edited by A. R. Braunmuller and Michael Hattaway

English Renaissance Tragedy edited by Emma Smith and Garrett A. Sullivan Jr.

English Restoration Theatre edited by Deborah C. Payne Fisk

The Epic edited by Catherine Bates

European Modernism edited by Pericles Lewis

European Novelists edited by Michael Bell

Fairy Tales edited by Maria Tatar

Fantasy Literature edited by Edward James and Farah Mendlesohn

Feminist Literary Theory edited by Ellen Rooney

Fiction in the Romantic Period edited by Richard Maxwell and Katie Trumpener

The Fin de Siècle edited by Gail Marshall

The French Enlightenment edited by Daniel Brewer

French Literature edited by John D. Lyons

The French Novel: from 1800 to the Present edited by Timothy Unwin

Gay and Lesbian Writing edited by Hugh Stevens

German Romanticism edited by Nicholas Saul

Gothic Fiction edited by Jerrold E. Hogle

The Greek and Roman Novel edited by Tim Whitmarsh

Greek and Roman Theatre edited by Marianne McDonald and J. Michael Walton

Greek Comedy edited by Martin Revermann

Greek Lyric edited by Felix Budelmann

Greek Mythology edited by Roger D. Woodard

Greek Tragedy edited by P. E. Easterling

The Harlem Renaissance edited by George Hutchinson

The History of the Book edited by Leslie Howsam

The Irish Novel edited by John Wilson Foster

The Italian Novel edited by Peter Bondanella and Andrea Ciccarelli

The Italian Renaissance edited by Michael Wyatt

Jewish American Literature edited by Hana Wirth-Nesher and Michael P. Kramer

The Latin American Novel edited by Efraín Kristal

The Literature of the First World War edited by Vincent Sherry

The Literature of London edited by Lawrence Manley

The Literature of Los Angeles edited by Kevin R. McNamara

The Literature of New York edited by Cyrus Patell and Bryan Waterman

The Literature of Paris edited by Anna-Louise Milne

The Literature of World War II edited by Marina MacKay

Literature on Screen edited by Deborah Cartmell and Imelda Whelehan

Medieval English Culture edited by Andrew Galloway

Medieval English Literature edited by Larry Scanlon

Medieval English Mysticism edited by Samuel Fanous and Vincent Gillespie

Medieval English Theatre edited by Richard Beadle and Alan J. Fletcher (second edition)

Medieval French Literature edited by Simon Gaunt and Sarah Kay

Medieval Romance edited by Roberta L. Krueger

Medieval Women's Writing edited by Carolyn Dinshaw and David Wallace

Modern American Culture edited by Christopher Bigsby

Modern British Women Playwrights edited by Elaine Aston and Janelle Reinelt

Modern French Culture edited by Nicholas Hewitt

Modern German Culture edited by Eva Kolinsky and Wilfried van der Will

The Modern German Novel edited by Graham Bartram

The Modern Gothic edited by Jerrold E. Hogle

Modern Irish Culture edited by Joe Cleary and Claire Connolly

Modern Italian Culture edited by Zygmunt G. Baranski and Rebecca J. West

Modern Latin American Culture edited by John King

Modern Russian Culture edited by Nicholas Rzhevsky

Modern Spanish Culture edited by David T. Gies

Modernism edited by Michael Levenson (second edition)

The Modernist Novel edited by Morag Shiach

Modernist Poetry edited by Alex Davis and Lee M. Jenkins

Modernist Women Writers edited by Maren Tova Linett

Narrative edited by David Herman

Native American Literature edited by Joy Porter and Kenneth M. Roemer

Nineteenth-Century American Women's Writing edited by Dale M. Bauer and Philip Gould

Old English Literature edited by Malcolm Godden and Michael Lapidge (second edition)

Performance Studies edited by Tracy C. Davis

Piers Plowman by Andrew Cole and Andrew Galloway

Popular Fiction edited by David Glover and Scott McCracken

Postcolonial Literary Studies edited by Neil Lazarus

Postmodernism edited by Steven Connor

The Pre-Raphaelites edited by Elizabeth Prettejohn

Pride and Prejudice edited by Janet Todd

Renaissance Humanism edited by Jill Kraye

The Roman Historians edited by Andrew Feldherr

Roman Satire edited by Kirk Freudenburg

Science Fiction edited by Edward James and Farah Mendlesohn

Scottish Literature edited by Gerald Carruthers and Liam McIlvanney

Sensation Fiction edited by Andrew Mangham

The Sonnet edited by A. D. Cousins and Peter Howarth

The Spanish Novel: from 1600 to the Present edited by Harriet Turner and Adelaida López de Martínez

Textual Scholarship edited by Neil Fraistat and Julia Flanders

Theatre History by David Wiles and Christine Dymkowski

Transnational American Literature edited by Yogita Goyal

Travel Writing edited by Peter Hulme and Tim Youngs

Twentieth-Century British and Irish Women's Poetry edited by Jane Dowson

The Twentieth-Century English Novel edited by Robert L. Caserio

Twentieth-Century English Poetry edited by Neil Corcoran

Twentieth-Century Irish Drama edited by Shaun Richards

Twentieth-Century Russian Literature edited by Marina Balina and Evgeny Dobrenko

Utopian Literature edited by Gregory Claeys

Victorian and Edwardian Theatre edited by Kerry Powell

The Victorian Novel edited by Deirdre David (second edition)

Victorian Poetry edited by Joseph Bristow

Victorian Women's Writing edited by Linda H. Peterson

War Writing edited by Kate McLoughlin

Women's Writing in Britain, 1660–1789 edited by Catherine Ingrassia

Women's Writing in the Romantic Period edited by Devoney Looser

Writing of the English Revolution edited by N. H. Keeble